Ethical, Legal, and Professional Issues in the Practice of Marriage and Family Therapy

Third Edition

Samuel T. Gladding
Wake Forest University

Theodore P. Remley, Jr.
University of New Orleans

Charles H. Huber
New Mexico State University

Merrill
Prentice Hall

Upper Saddle River, New Jersey
Columbus, Ohio

Library of Congress Cataloging-in-Publication Data

Gladding, Samuel T.
    Ethical, legal, and professional issues in the practice of marriage and family therapy /
  Samuel T. Gladding, Theodore P. Remley, Jr., Charles H. Huber.—3rd ed.
      p. cm.
    Previous ed. cataloged under: Huber, Charles H.
    Includes bibliographical references and index.
    ISBN 0-13-769233-1
    1. Family psychotherapy—Moral and ethical aspects. 2. Marital psychotherapy—Moral and ethical
aspects. 3. Family therapists—Professional ethics. 4. Family therapists—Legal status, laws, etc. I. Huber,
Charles H. Ethical, legal, and professional issues in the practice of marriage and family therapy.
II. Remley, Theodore Phant III. Title.
  RC488.5 .H8 2001
  174'.2—dc21   00-056119

Vice President and Publisher: Jeffery W. Johnston
Executive Editor: Kevin M. Davis
Editorial Assistant: Christina M. Kalisch
Production Editor: Kimberly J. Lundy
Design Coordinator: Diane C. Lorenzo
Cover Design: Jason Moore
Text Design: Ed Horcharik
Production Manager: Laura Messerly
Director of Marketing: Kevin Flanagan
Marketing Manager: Amy June
Marketing Services Manager: Krista Groshong

This book was set in Century ITC by Carlisle Communications, Ltd. It was printed and bound by R. R.
Donnelley & Sons Company. The cover was printed by Phoenix Color Corp.

10 9 8 7 6 5 4 3 2 1
ISBN: 0-13-769233-1

Preface

Although less than 100 years old, professional psychotherapy has become a major influence in society. Therapists contribute to and considerably affect many aspects of modern life. During this time, psychotherapy has broadened its perspective. No longer is it practiced exclusively on a one-therapist-to-one-client basis. Group therapy efforts have become commonplace in almost every mental health setting. Likewise, the last several decades have seen the advent of another expansion within the psychotherapeutic field, that of marriage and family therapy.

Many therapists have replaced or supplemented their traditional individual and group models of practice with one emphasizing couples and families as the dominant treatment focus. This is not to suggest that contact with marital partners and other family members had been completely ignored. Rather, marital partners and family members had always been considered in light of the individual client's concerns and from an individually oriented therapeutic perspective.

As the practice of marriage and family therapy has evolved, training procedures have become more explicit, replicable, and accessible. Specific theories and techniques have been identified. Broad curricular components for training have been compiled. And specific content, goals, and teaching methods for university coursework and professional workshops have been delineated. These materials and strategies all continue to be researched, evaluated, and enhanced. Noticeably lacking before the publication of the first edition of *Ethical, Legal, and Professional Issues in the Practice of Marriage and Family Therapy*, however, were sources addressing "nontherapy" issues necessary to supplement the therapeutic training of marriage and family therapists (Piercy & Sprenkle, 1983).

The importance of these nontherapy issues was emphasized in an article entitled "Family Therapy May Be Dangerous for Your Health" (Hare-Mustin, 1980), in which the author states:

> In sum, family therapy may not be in the best interests of individual family members. Family therapists and their clients need to be aware of possible risks to the rights of the individual member. By being required to participate, individuals may have to subordinate their own goals and give up limited confidentiality and privacy. In addition, therapists who idealize the traditional family may foster stereotyped roles and expectations in the family that disadvantage individuals and limit their well-being and mental health. (p. 938)

Although offerings in the professional literature and training opportunities at conferences and workshops have increased in both number and quality, nontherapy issues—particularly ethical, legal, and associated professional concerns—are still underrepresented in relation to their potential impact on the practice of many mental health professionals. The simple fact that marriage and family therapy differs from individual and group therapy on both conceptual and pragmatic levels requires that therapists be adequately prepared to handle controversial issues from a marriage and family perspective as well. Questions that are difficult in individual and group therapy can become significantly more complicated when a couple or whole family presents itself for services (Margolin, 1982).

The American Association for Marriage and Family Therapy, the professional organization with which most marriage and family therapists are primarily affiliated, specifies graduate-level coursework in "professional studies" as a requirement within its educational requirements for clinical membership. In response, courses in "ethical, legal, and professional issues" have been developed and constitute a core component of marriage and family training programs. The first and second editions of *Ethical, Legal, and Professional Issues in the Practice of Marriage and Family Therapy* served as a basic text for these courses as well as a primary source for practicing professionals seeking to expand their knowledge of ethical, legal, and professional issues in marriage and family therapy.

ORGANIZATION OF THE TEXT

This third edition has been updated and expanded so that it may continue to serve as a basic resource for both beginning students and practicing professionals. It is divided into three parts. Part 1 addresses ethical issues in marriage and family therapy. Chapter 1 examines major ethical issues confronting all therapists, particularly the beginning marriage and family therapist and the experienced practitioner who is shifting from an individual approach to a marriage and family perspective. Chapter 2 discusses ethical issues inherent in the interactive nature of marriage and family therapy. Chapter 3 presents contemporary ethical issues for which there is little precedent; positions advocated in the professional literature and recommendations made for handling these issues are reviewed. Chapter 4 offers a "casebook" of examples with critiques highlighting the AAMFT Code of Ethics (American Association for Marriage and Family Therapy, 1998). Part 2 considers legal issues in marriage and family therapy. Chapter 5 investigates the roles and relationships of marriage and family therapists within the legal system. Chapter 6 examines relevant family law. Chapter 7, like Chapter 4, is a casebook of examples with critiques discussing the impact of legal issues on marriage and family therapy. Part 3 focuses on professional issues. Chapter 8 discusses "valuing" and the professional practice of marriage and family therapy. Chapter 9 explores the professional identity of a marriage and family therapist. Chapter 10 offers another casebook of examples addressing professional questions.

Special attention should be paid to the three casebook chapters: 4, 7, and 10. We recall our days as clinicians-in-training seeking to fathom those notions we garnered from our readings. Classroom instructors and clinical supervisors, knowledgeable and skilled from years of experience, provided case examples to illustrate the concepts more clearly. Those illustrations made learning a more concrete experience, from which we emerged much better prepared.

Overall, this book seeks to encourage a greater familiarization and expansion of knowledge relevant to ethical, legal, and professional issues necessary to supplement clinical training and practice in marriage and family therapy. We hope that you will gain an introduction to some of the issues you may encounter and that you will be stimulated to think about your own position as a marriage and family therapist, whether as a primary source of professional identity or professional specialization.

ACKNOWLEDGMENTS

So many persons have contributed, both directly and indirectly, to our personal and professional development and to the writing of this book that it is impossible to thank them all. We thank the majority of them as a group by offering this book as a contribution of social interest that will, we hope, enhance the lives of mental health professionals and the clients with whom they interact. A few individuals, however, need to be singled out for special thanks.

Lee Baruth coauthored the first edition of this book. Without his many contributions, this work would not have been possible. For their constructive suggestions during the preparation of the manuscript, we thank reviewers Robert Barrett, University of North Carolina–Charlotte; Sarah G. Gabbay, Colorado State University; Lizbeth Ann Gray, Oregon State University; and Michael Polson, East Carolina University. We are particularly indebted to Kevin Davis, the executive editor for this project at Merrill/Prentice Hall.

Finally, we thank those who have made personal contributions to our lives. From Sam Gladding: "I am indebted to my parents, Russell and Gertrude, for their attention to teaching me the importance of values at a young age. My wife, Claire, and our children, Ben, Nate, and Tim, have been both understanding and supportive during my times of writing for this book. A family's encouragement and company cannot be valued enough." From Ted Remley: "I want to thank my parents, T.P. and Era, for giving me the education necessary to write books. I also appreciate my extended family, close friends, colleagues, and graduate students for tolerating my absences when I write and my crabby disposition when I am trying to make deadlines." And from Charles Huber: "I thank my parents, Charles and Helen, for modeling for me those core ethical qualities I had only to label, not learn, when I began my professional training and later entered clinical practice. My partner, Betsy, and our children, David and Morgan, have been most patient during the writing of the revision."

Samuel T. Gladding, Ph.D.
Theodore P. Remley, Jr., Ph.D.
Charles H. Huber, Ph.D.

REFERENCES

American Association for Marriage and Family Therapy. (1998). *AAMFT code of ethics.* Washington, DC: Author. Available: http://www.aamft.org/about/ethic.htm

Hare-Mustin, R. T. (1980). Family therapy may be dangerous for your health. *Professional Psychology, 11,* 935–938.

Margolin, G. (1982). Ethical and legal considerations in marriage and family therapy. *American Psychologist, 7,* 788–801.

Piercy, F. P., & Sprenkle, D. H. (1983). Ethical, legal and professional issues in family therapy: A graduate level course. *Journal of Marital and Family Therapy, 9,* 393–401.

Discover the Companion Website Accompanying This Book

THE PRENTICE HALL COMPANION WEBSITE: A VIRTUAL LEARNING ENVIRONMENT

Technology is a constantly growing and changing aspect of our field that is creating a need for content and resources. To address this emerging need, Prentice Hall has developed an online learning environment for students and professors alike—Companion Websites—to support our textbooks.

In creating a Companion Website, our goal is to build on and enhance what the textbook already offers. For this reason, the content for each user-friendly website is organized by topic and provides the professor and student with a variety of meaningful resources. Common features of a Companion Website include:

For the Professor—

Every Companion Website integrates **Syllabus Manager**™, an online syllabus creation and management utility.

- **Syllabus Manager**™ provides you, the instructor, with an easy, step-by-step process to create and revise syllabi, with direct links into Companion Website and other online content without having to learn HTML.
- Students may logon to your syllabus during any study session. All they need to know is the web address for the Companion Website and the password you've assigned to your syllabus.
- After you have created a syllabus using **Syllabus Manager**™, students may enter the syllabus for their course section from any point in the Companion Website.
- Clicking on a date, the student is shown the list of activities for the assignment. The activities for each assignment are linked directly to actual content, saving time for students.
- Adding assignments consists of clicking on the desired due date, then filling in the details of the assignment—name of the assignment, instructions, and whether or not it is a one-time or repeating assignment.

- In addition, links to other activities can be created easily. If the activity is online, a URL can be entered in the space provided, and it will be linked automatically in the final syllabus.
- Your completed syllabus is hosted on our servers, allowing convenient updates from any computer on the Internet. Changes you make to your syllabus are immediately available to your students at their next log-on.

For the Student—

- **Topic Overviews**—outline key concepts in topic areas
- **Electronic Bluebook**—send homework or essays directly to your instructor's email with this paperless form
- **Message Board**—serves as a virtual bulletin board to post—or respond to—questions or comments to/from a national audience
- **Chat**—real-time chat with anyone who is using the text anywhere in the country—ideal for discussion and study groups, class projects, etc.
- **Web Destinations**—links to www sites that relate to each topic area
- **Professional Organizations**—links to organizations that relate to topic areas
- **Additional Resources**—access to topic-specific content that enhances material found in the text

To take advantage of these and other resources, please visit the Companion Website for *Ethical, Legal, and Professional Issues in the Practice of Marriage and Family Therapy*, Third Edition, at

www.prenhall.com/gladding

About the Authors

Samuel T. Gladding is a professor in and director of the Counselor Education Program at Wake Forest University. He is a Licensed Professional Counselor in the state of North Carolina, a National Certified Counselor, and a National Certified Mental Health Counselor. Dr. Gladding is a Clinical Member and Approved Supervisor in the American Association for Marriage and Family Therapy (AAMFT).

Dr. Gladding received a B.A. and M.A. Ed. from Wake Forest University, an M.A.R. from Yale University, and his Ph.D. from the University of North Carolina at Greensboro. He is the author of numerous publications including *Family Therapy: History, Theory, and Practice* (3rd ed). He is the former editor of the *Journal for Specialists in Group Work* and a former president of the Alabama Association for Marriage and Family Therapy. Dr. Gladding is married to the former Claire Tillson. They are the parents of three children. As a family they enjoy travel, camping, and attending athletic and artistic events.

Theodore P. Remley, Jr. is a professor and coordinator of the Counseling Graduate Program at the University of New Orleans. His is a member of the bar in Virginia and Florida and is licensed as a Professional Counselor in Louisiana, Mississippi, and Virginia. He is a National Certified Counselor. Dr. Remley holds a B.A. in English, an M.Ed., an Ed.S., and a Ph.D. in Counseling from the University of Florida, and a J.D. from Catholic University in Washington, D.C. Dr. Remley is the co-author with Barbara Herlihy of *Ethical, Legal, and Professional Issues in Counseling*. In addition, he has edited and written books and monographs, book chapters, and numerous articles in professional journals on the topic of legal issues in mental health. He is a former Executive Director of the American Counseling Association and was founding president of the American Association of State Counseling Boards. He has served on the counselor licensure boards in Louisiana, the District of Columbia, Mississippi, and Virginia. Dr. Remley is an officer in the Mardi Gras Krewe of Orpheus and enjoys jogging and sailing with his friends in New Orleans.

Charles H. Huber is on the faculty in the Department of Counseling and Educational Psychology, New Mexico State University. A licensed psychologist in the states of Connecticut, Florida, and New Mexico, he also holds diplomas in family psychology and behavioral psychology with the American Board of Professional Psychology. In addition, Dr. Huber is a clinical member and approved supervisor of the American Association for Marriage and Family Therapy and an approved supervisor and fellow of the Institute for Rational Emotive Behavioral Therapy. He maintains a private practice with Associates for Marriage and Family Therapy in Las Cruces, New Mexico.

Dr. Huber received his B.A. from Upsala College, M.Ed. and Ed.S. from Florida Atlantic University, and Ph.D. from the University of South Carolina. He has authored or co-authored 10 books, served as editor of several professional journals, and written numerous articles and book chapters. He is active in a number of professional organizations, most recently serving as president of the New Mexico Association for Marriage and Family Therapy. Dr. Huber has been married for over two decades to his partner, Betsy. They and their two children raise and train labrador retrievers as their family hobby.

Contents

Ethical Issues in Marriage and Family Therapy

The training of the family therapist requires attention to ethical issues as well as to techniques. Self-awareness and social responsibility are an important part of the professional ethics of therapists. By being demanding of ourselves in our professional role, we may be able to be more reasonable toward our patients.

(Fieldsteel, 1982, p. 267)

1

Promoting Ethical Practice

Ethics is concerned with the conduct of human beings as they make moral decisions. These decisions reflect judgments that lead to action, and they involve the use of words known as *moral predicates:* "ought," "should," "right," "good," and their opposites (Brandt, 1959). Unlike a discipline such as mathematics, ethics is normative rather than factual. "Ethical thinking is not simply a matter of black and white categorization" (Herlihy & Corey, 1996, p. 297). That is, ethics addresses principles that *ought* to govern human conduct rather than *do* govern it (Daubner & Daubner, 1970). Therefore, ethical reasoning, judgment, and decision making involve a "complex interplay of morals, values, and priorities" (Cottone & Tarvydas, 1998, p. 122).

Although morality is frequently considered to be synonymous with ethics, the distinction between the two terms is critical. Barry (1982) defines ethics as "the study of what constitutes good and bad human conduct, including related actions and values" (p. 4). While recognizing the difficulty of maintaining a separation between ethics and morality, he proposes that the terms *moral* and *morality* be restricted to the *conduct* itself and *ethical* and *ethics* be employed for the *study* of moral conduct or a code a person follows. Mowrer (1967) likewise reports finding the two terms being used interchangeably but cautions that *morals* definitively refers to the goodness or badness of behavior, whereas *ethics* represents an objective inquiry.

Ethics addresses questions that have no ultimate answers yet are important in planning, justifying, and carrying out decisions. Consider the following situation:

> A woman initially presented herself for individual therapy, seeking to resolve a number of personal conflicts, only one of which was the state of her marriage resulting from an extramarital affair in which she was engaging. Later, her husband accompanied her to therapy for conjoint efforts. The woman

was still engaged in the affair, and it was obvious to the therapist that this involvement impeded progress with her husband. She demanded, however, that the therapist maintain the confidentiality of what was discussed during the individual sessions.

"Should" the therapist respect the individual confidences of one marital partner when doing so clearly impedes those goals overtly agreed to by both? Ethics offers guidance in answering such a question. Ethics, however, is primarily concerned with helping the therapist decide what is right, not with getting the persons involved to do what is believed to be right (W. T. Jones, Sontag, Beckner, & Fogelin, 1977).

VIRTUE ETHICS AND PRINCIPLE ETHICS

The promotion of ethical practice in the mental health fields has tended to emphasize the application of ethical principles to situations involving a dilemma. Although these dilemmas take a variety of forms, they typically involve the competing rights and responsibilities of therapists, clients, and institutions. In such dilemmas, some therapists are most concerned with following the law and their codes of professional ethics so that they will stay out of trouble. Other therapists, although also concerned with the law and their profession's code of ethics, further take into account what is best for their clients.

A. E. Jordan and Meara (1990) make a distinction between what they term *principle ethics* and *virtue ethics*. As the basis for ethical judgments, *principle ethics* emphasizes the use of objective, rational standards, rules, or universal codes. Principle ethics focuses on acts and choices in an impartial manner and leads a person to answer the question, "What shall I do?" *Virtue ethics*, on the other hand, emphasizes the use of historical "virtues" and the development of individuals' character. Virtue ethics focuses subjectively on the qualities, traits, and habits of the person carrying out the action or making the choice and leads the person to answer the question, "Who shall I be?"

Simply stated, principle ethics looks to established societal and/or professional standards and asks, "Is this choice or action consistent with the norms?" Virtue ethics asks, "Is this the best thing to do?" Where virtue ethics predominates, ethical awareness is a constant, even in the absence of an ethical dilemma (Corey, Corey, & Callanan, 1998).

Therapy is a human endeavor; the therapist cannot help but be involved as a person. Wylie (1989), for example, sees this human factor as critical in the therapist and then raises the crucial question, "Is he or she honest, trustworthy, sensitive, knowledgeable, courageous, open-minded, modest, and rigorously self-reflective?" (p. 33). Likewise, Hundert (1987) asserts that personal experiences "must and should influence our moral experience within our professional life" (p. 843). These authors are asserting the essential importance of virtue ethics.

Virtue ethics and principle ethics, however, are not mutually exclusive. Therapeutic training has traditionally sought to set limits on the influence of personal identity, its goal being to integrate the personal and the professional. So it is with virtue ethics and professional ethics. Both are important elements in promoting ethical practice.

> A 35-year-old male sought therapy to address longtime sexual difficulties with women he dated. He attributed the problems to his experience of being sexually abused as a child. The perpetrator was his now-deceased stepfather. The therapist was aware of a sex therapist in the city who was well known for successful work with victims of abuse but chose not to refer the client.

Although the therapist in this case illustration could legally and ethically justify seeing this client, it might be more "virtuous" to refer him to the expert (Corey et al., 1998).

A. E. Jordan and Meara (1990) conclude, "The ideals . . . must include conscientious decision-making, but they must also include virtuous deciders, who emphasize not so much what is permitted as what is preferred" (p. 112). Although the discussion now moves to professional codes of ethics, which are rooted in principle ethics, therapists must maintain a virtuous character—their own sense of what is right—as they interpret and apply the principles of these codes if they are to achieve the best ethical practice possible.

PROFESSIONAL CODES OF ETHICS

"The establishment of ethical guidelines is relatively new" to the helping professions, with the first code of ethics being established by the American Psychological Association in 1953 (Neukrug, Lovell, & Parker, 1996, p. 98). The first American Association for Marriage and Family Therapy (AAMFT) code of ethics was approved by the membership in 1962 (Brock, 1998). Ethical codes are important because they set the standards of moral conduct for a society or subgroup. A code of ethics for a profession is meant to "enhance, inform, expand, and improve" members of the profession's "ability to serve as effectively as possible those clients seeking their help" (Zibert, Engels, Kern, & Durodoye, 1998, p. 35).

Universal aspects of ethical codes among the professions have been identified by Van Hoose and Kottler (1985). These codes reflect concerns and define basic principles that "ought" to guide professional activities. They provide a position on standards of practice to aid members in deciding how to act when conflicts arise. They assist in clarifying professionals' responsibility to clients and society. They give society some guarantee that professionals will demonstrate a sensible regard for the mores and expectations of the society. Finally, they give professionals themselves a means of safeguarding their freedom and integrity.

With regard to this last point, Van Hoose and Kottler (1985) posited that codes of ethics aid professionals in dealing with potential dangers from three groups: government, the professionals themselves, and the public:

1. Codes of ethics are designed to protect the profession from the government. All professions desire autonomy and seek to avoid undue interference and regulations by lawmakers. Professional codes assert a self-regulatory stance.
2. Codes of ethics offer protection to a profession from potential self-destruction occasioned by internal discord in the absence of such areas of common agreement. For example, it is unethical to entice colleagues' clients to leave them. Such a standard enables professionals to live in harmony.
3. Codes of ethics protect professionals from the public. Professionals who act according to accepted professional codes have some protection if sued for malpractice.

With respect to the mental health professions, the first two statements require little explanation; the last can be clarified in light of recent litigation.

Ethical codes are adopted by professional associations as a means of offering norms relative to the conduct of their members to ensure that the members properly represent the profession. Self-regulation through established ethical codes involves both informal and formal discipline. *Informal discipline* is seen in the subtle or overt pressure colleagues exert on one another in the form of consultations about practices and referrals of clients. *Formal discipline* is seen in the power exercised by professional associations in publicly criticizing or censuring members and, in extreme cases, barring violators from membership. Although this threat of formal discipline does have some influence on professionals who are not members of their representative professional associations, an association's code of ethics is binding only on its actual members. Consequently, sanctions can be imposed only on those violators who are members of the association.

If sued for malpractice, a therapist will be judged in terms of actions appropriate to other therapists with similar qualifications and duties. Ethical standards of the profession will be a probable basis for comparison (Corey et al., 1998). If therapists act in good faith, they are not likely to be found responsible for a client's lack of progress or mistake in judgment on their part if the mistake were the type a "careful and skillful" therapist could make (Anderson & Hopkins, 1996).

The application of the "careful and skillful" test originated in medical ethics, representative portions of which have been made into law. Physicians are expected to display behavior suitable to their profession:

> The law imposes on [physicians who undertake] the care of a patient the obligation of due care, the exercise of an amount of skill common to [their] profession, without which [they] should not have taken the case, and a degree of care commensurate with this position. (61 Am. Jur. 2d)

Corresponding standards from the ethical codes of other professional associations are listed in Table 1–1.

Table 1–1   Ethical Considerations Relating to Due Care/Therapist Competence

American Association for Marriage and Family Therapy (2001)
"Marriage and family therapists do not diagnose, treat, or advise on problems outside the recognized boundaries of their competence."

American Counseling Association (1995)
"Counselors practice only within the boundaries of their competence, based on their education, training, supervised experience, state and national professional credentials, and appropriate experience."

American Psychological Association (1992)
"Psychologists provide services, teach, and conduct research only within the boundaries of their competence, based on their education, training, supervised experience, or appropriate professional experience."

National Association of Social Workers (1996)
"Social workers should accept responsibility or employment only on the basis of existing competence or the intention to acquire the necessary competence."

International Association of Marriage and Family Counselors (1993)
"Members do not attempt to diagnose or treat problems beyond the scope of their abilities and training."

> Physicians also have a duty to act in good faith and advise patients regarding the best possible treatment: [Physicians occupy] a position of trust and confidence as regards [their] patient, and it is [their] duty to act with the utmost good faith; if [they know] that the treatment adopted by [them] will probably be of little or no benefit, and that there is another method of treatment that is more likely to be successful, which [they have] not the training or facilities to give . . . [they] must advise [their] patient. (61 Am. Jur. 2d)

Standards from the codes of ethics of other professional associations are clearly in agreement with this position. Some of these standards are listed in Table 1–2.

Codes of ethics provide the bases from which responsibilities of professionals are articulated. A code of ethics represents the consensus of a large number of reputable members of a profession (Scalise, 2000). As such, it demands primary attention from those seeking to practice in an ethical manner. Consider the circumstances of the following case:

> A male therapist has been working for several months with a couple seeking a divorce. He finds the wife attractive and exciting. He is aware that she has similar feelings toward him and would like to become involved with him socially and sexually. Because of his desire to become intimate with her, he often finds it difficult to concentrate during therapy sessions.

Standards set by the codes of ethics of a number of major professional associations can offer relatively explicit guidance in this regard. Some of these standards are listed in Table 1–3.

Table 1–2 Ethical Considerations Relating to Good Faith/Client Referrals

American Association for Marriage and Family Therapy (2001)
"Marriage and family therapists continue therapeutic relationships only so long as it is reasonably clear that clients are benefiting from the relationship."

"Marriage and family therapists assist persons in obtaining other therapeutic services if the therapist is unable or unwilling, for appropriate reasons, to provide professional help."

American Counseling Association (1995)
"If counselors determine an inability to be of professional assistance to clients, they avoid entering or immediately terminate a counseling relationship. If clients decline the suggested referral, counselors should discontinue the relationship."

American Psychological Association (1992)
"Prior to termination for whatever reason, except where precluded by the patient's or client's conduct, the psychologist discusses the patient's or client's views and needs, provides appropriate pretermination counseling, suggests alternative service providers as appropriate, and takes other reasonable steps to facilitate transfer of responsibility to another provider if the patient or client needs one immediately."

National Association of Social Workers (1996)
"Social workers should terminate services to clients, and professional relationships with them, when such services and relationships are no longer required or no longer serve the clients' needs or interests."
"Social workers who anticipate the termination or interruption of services to clients should notify clients promptly and seek the transfer, referral, or continuation of services in relation to the clients' needs and preferences."

International Association of Marriage and Family Counselors (1993)
"Members have an obligation to withdraw from a counseling relationship if the continuation of services is not in the best interest of the client or would result in a violation of ethical standards. If a client feels that the counseling relationship is no longer productive, the member has an obligation to assist in finding alternative services."

These standards imply that the therapist's considerable influence must be properly used. The creation of this type of dual relationship with a client (both therapeutic and intimately personal/sexual) is clearly unethical (Brock, 1998). Codes of ethics, however, more frequently offer only general philosophical guidance for conceptualizing and responding to conflicts. It is not their purpose to recommend specific behaviors in limited situations. If it were, codes would become voluminous, lack broad-based support, and infringe on the role of the individual professional in ethical decision making (Huston, 1984). Stude and McKelvey (1979) share this belief:

> They [codes of ethics] are statements of principle, which must be interpreted and applied by the individual or group to a particular context. They present a rationale for ethical behavior. Their exact interpretation, however, will depend on the situation to which they are being applied. (p. 453)

Table 1–3 Ethical Considerations Relating to Sexual Relationships With Clients

---

American Association for Marriage and Family Therapy (2001)
"Marriage and family therapists are aware of their influential positions with respect to clients, and they avoid exploiting the trust and dependency of such persons. Therapists, therefore, make every effort to avoid conditions and multiple relationships with clients that could impair professional judgement or increase the risk of exploitation. . . . Sexual intimacy with clients is prohibited."

American Counseling Association (1995)
"Counselors do not have any type of sexual intimacies with clients and do not counsel persons with whom they have had a sexual relationship."

American Psychological Association (1992)
"Psychologists do not engage in sexual intimacies with current patients or clients."

National Association of Social Workers (1996)
"The social worker should under no circumstances engage in sexual activities or sexual contact with current clients whether such contact is consensual or forced."

International Association of Marriage and Family Counselors (1993)
"Members do not harass, exploit, coerce, engage in dual relationships, or have sexual contact with any current or former client or family member to whom they have provided professional services."

ETHICAL DECISION MAKING

Therapists must have a clear process for understanding ethical decision making if they are to act ethically (Stevens, 1999; Van Hoose, 1980). Such an understanding should allow therapists to critically evaluate and interpret their professional code of ethics. Furthermore, it should guide therapists in integrating virtue ethics by helping them analyze feelings as appropriate or inappropriate bases for ethical behavior. There are several models for understanding the processes of ethical decision making. We will mention only two and will elaborate on the second one most because of its specific relevance to marriage and family therapy. The first model of ethical decision making is by Kidder (1995). According to Kidder, ethical decisions are (a) end-based, (b) rule-based, or (c) care-based. "End-based thinking, or utilitarianism, asserts the greatest good for the greatest number drives the ethical decision-making process. In rule-based thinking, one relies on obligations to a set of codes or principles, regardless of outcome. Care-based thinking is committed to the Golden Rule: Do unto others as you would have them do unto you" (Stevens-Smith, 1997a, p. 251).

The second model of ethical decision making is by Kitchener (1986), who synthesized the work of Rest (1983) in identifying four major psychological processes underlying applied ethics in psychotherapy. Ethical decision making according to Kitchener demands proficiency in all four processes.

Process 1: Interpreting a Situation as Requiring an Ethical Decision

This process involves the ability to perceive the effect of one's actions on the welfare of others. Several relevant psychological research findings have important implications here. First, many persons have difficulty interpreting the meaning of even simple situations. Sometimes failure to intervene in a situation calling for ethical action may be attributable to a misunderstanding about what is actually occurring. Second, individuals differ in their ability to be sensitive to the needs and welfare of others (S. H. Schwartz, 1977). Welfel and Lipsitz (1984), for example, estimated from a number of research studies that between 5% and 10% of mental health practitioners are substantially insensitive to the ethical dimensions of their work. Third, the ability to infer the effect of one's actions on others as well as to infer others' needs develops with age and experience. Fourth, a social situation may arouse a strong emotional response before there is time to reflect on it (Zajonc, 1980); thus, to interpret a situation, persons must understand their feelings about it.

Process 1 depends on therapists' developing ethical sensitivity and empathy. This development is essential to effective therapy. Therapists must be continually aware that their actions have real ethical consequences that can help but also potentially harm others. Virtue ethics and principle ethics interact to establish a central framework for professional behavior and responsibility. This framework provides guidance in identifying situations in which an ethical decision is needed (e.g., confidentiality in therapy).

Process 1 furthermore recognizes the fact that feelings may not always be good guides for ethical action. For example, the therapist who breaks confidentiality to prevent serious harm to the client or another person will feel bad. On the other hand, the therapist would feel worse if the client or another person suffered unduly for the sake of maintaining confidentiality. In an ethical dilemma such as this, a lesser harm is balanced against a greater harm. As Nozick (1968) asserts, such situations ought to leave therapists with feelings of dissatisfaction and regret that, to make the most ethical decision, they had to violate other ethical responsibilities. Ethical action does not always feel good, nor does it always lead to choices that are "good" in an absolute sense.

Process 2: Formulating an Ethical Course of Action

It is not enough to be aware that an ethical situation exists. One must also be able to integrate various considerations into an ethically justifiable course of action. Process 2 underscores the need for fundamental ethical guidelines. In proposing a model for ethical reasoning, Kitchener (1984a, 1985) distinguished between the *intuitive level* and the *critical-evaluative level* of ethical justification.

The *intuitive level of ethical justification* addresses immediate feeling responses to situations. It affords a basis for immediate action that is necessary in some situations (e.g., dealing with a suicidal client). In many situations, however, intuitive responses alone are not appropriate (e.g., when intuition leads to sexual relations with clients).

The *critical-evaluative level of ethical justification* is composed of three tiers. At the first tier, an ethical course of action can be judged by formal ethical rules (e.g., one's professional code of ethics). Therapists can, for example, receive ready guidance regarding sexual contact with clients from their code of ethics. If the ethical standards of such a code are insufficient, movement to a second tier is in order. This tier encompasses more general and fundamental ethical principles that serve as a foundation for formal codes of ethics. For example, therapists might justify a particular standard in their ethical code by citing underlying principles (the right to make one's own decisions, the need to respect the rights of others to make free choices). The third tier of critical evaluation is that of ethical theory. Many ethicists (Abelson & Nielson, 1967; Baier, 1958; Toulmin, 1950) have posited that, when principles are in conflict, ethical actions should emanate either from what one would want for oneself or significant others in the same circumstances or from what would produce the least amount of avoidable harm.

Process 3: Integrating Personal and Professional Values

It is possible for persons to know what they "should" do ethically (Process 2) but decide against taking ethical action because of competing values and motives. Process 3 recognizes that how individuals decide to act is heavily influenced by factors such as ambition, money, and self-interest. Research and ordinary observation have consistently shown that persons do not always do what they think they "should" do but rather respond to personal values and practical considerations in determining what they actually "would" do (T. S. Smith, McGuire, Abbott, & Blau, 1991). For example, a therapist who knows that a colleague is acting unethically may, because of friendship or loyalty, decide not to intervene.

One explanation for the degree of congruence between what therapists believe to be correct and their willingness to carry out this action is the concept of *personal consistency* (Blasi, 1980). Blasi proposes that lack of personal consistency "does not simply indicate the situational specificity of traits but suggests expediency and opportunism" (p. 6). Professional ethical conflicts encountered by therapists frequently do involve issues of expediency and opportunism. For example, it is simpler (i.e., more expedient) not to report the inappropriate professional actions of a colleague and thereby to avoid possible confrontation and recriminations (T. S. Smith et al., 1991).

Process 3 recognizes the impact of virtue ethics on ethical decision making. The gap between understanding and implementation of ethical behavior is a function not only of how much a therapist knows about principle ethics (e.g., professional ethical standards, "the letter of the law") but also of the degree to which a therapist possesses or lacks virtue ethics (e.g., honesty and personal integrity, a willingness to follow "the spirit of the law").

Process 4: Implementing an Action Plan

Perseverance, resoluteness, and character are elements of virtue ethics that are also involved in acting on any decision (Rest, 1982). Process 4 addresses therapists' need to develop and maintain their virtue ethics, particularly a sense of ethical responsibility. It is not enough to be aware of and concerned about ethical issues, nor even to think wisely about them. Professional practice requires that therapists take responsibility for their actions and the consequences of those actions.

An important aspect of assuming responsibility is the ability to tolerate the ambiguity that accompanies ethical decision making. Therapists must understand that few absolute answers exist; certainty is frequently impossible. At the same time, ethical reasoning can be precise and can in many cases resolve dilemmas. In more difficult situations, it can at least identify the precise nature of the dilemma.

To make solidly grounded ethical decisions, it is important to refer to one's professed code of ethics (Cottone & Tarvydas, 1998). One must also, however, identify basic ethical concepts that can serve both as a supplement to the code and as additional sources of guidance in ethical decision making. Van Hoose (1980) summarizes a rule of thumb for therapists faced with ethical decisions:

> The counselor or psychotherapist is probably acting in an ethically responsible way concerning a client if (a) he or she has maintained personal and professional honesty, coupled with (b) the best interests of the client, (c) without malice or personal gain, and (d) can justify his or her actions as the best judgment of what should be done based upon the current state of the profession. When these four components are present, ethically responsible behavior is likely to be demonstrated. (p. 11)

Tymchuk et al. (1982) draw a similar conclusion from their survey of psychologists. They found a low consensus of opinion about the ethics of situations that were either not addressed by the *Ethical Standards of Psychologists* (American Psychological Association, 1981) or not of immediate concern to the psychologists. Those authors called for a model of ethical conceptualization as an adjunct to the code.

In 1982, Margolin cautioned that insufficiencies in the *Ethical Standards of Psychologists* (American Psychological Association, 1981) as they applied to practitioners of marriage and family therapy were not being fully appreciated. Almost a decade later, Patten, Barnett, and Houlihan (1991), in a review of the literature on ethics in marriage and family therapy, echoed Margolin's comments in asserting that the same insufficiencies still remain. With the exceptions of the *AAMFT Code of Ethics* (American Association for Marriage and Family Therapy, 2001) and the *Ethical Code for the International Association of Marriage and Family Counselors* (International Association of Marriage and Family Counselors, 1993), similar insufficiencies can be found in the codes of ethics of other professional associations whose members engage in the practice of marriage and family therapy. These codes have been established in and reflect an atmosphere where traditional individual and group therapy models predominate.

The generality inherent in codes of ethics on such topics as client welfare, confidentiality, and informed consent can make ethical decision making difficult when a therapist is dealing with individual clients. The difficulties are compounded when the primary treatment unit consists of a cohabitating couple or multiple family members. The balance of this chapter addresses ethical decision making in relation to these thorny topics, first from a therapist–individual client perspective and then from a therapist–couple/family perspective.

CLIENT WELFARE

The codes of ethics of all major professional associations affirm that a therapist's primary responsibility is to the client. The needs of clients, not therapists, take first priority in the therapeutic relationship. Also implied is that therapeutic relationships should be maintained only as long as clients are benefiting from them. Relevant standards from the codes of ethics of several professional organizations are listed in Table 1–4.

Recognition of the primacy of the clients' welfare is relatively clear. Corey et al. (1998), however, raise several cogent questions that tend to cloud this simple assertion:

- What criteria should be used to determine whether a client is benefiting from the therapeutic relationship?
- What should be done if a client reports that she or he is benefiting from therapy but the therapist is unable to identify any signs of progress?
- What courses of action are available to the therapist who believes that a client is seeking only to purchase friendship and has no intention of pursuing therapeutic change?

These and other questions call for a conceptual framework for ethical decision making as an adjunct to the guidance available from formal ethical standards. Five principles applied by Beauchamp and Childress (1994) to biomedical

Table 1–4   Ethical Considerations Relating to Client Welfare

American Association for Marriage and Family Therapy (2001)
"Marriage and family therapists advance the welfare of families and individuals. They respect the rights of those persons seeking their assistance, and make reasonable efforts to ensure that their services are used appropriately."

American Counseling Association (1995)
"The primary responsibility of counselors is to respect the dignity and promote the welfare of the client(s)."

American Psychological Association (1992)
"This Code is intended to provide the general principles and the decision rules to cover most situations encountered by psychologists. It has as its primary goal the welfare and protection of the individuals and groups with whom psychologists work."

National Association of Social Workers (1996)
"Social workers' primary responsibility is to promote the well-being of clients."

International Association of Marriage and Family Counselors (1993)
"Members demonstrate a caring, empathic, respectful, fair, and active concern for family well-being. They promote client safety, security, and place-of-belonging in family, community, and society."

ethics have been recommended as specifically relevant to issues of client welfare in psychotherapy: autonomy, beneficence, nonmaleficence, justice, and fidelity (Kitchener, 1984a).

Autonomy is the principle that all human beings have the right to make decisions and act on them in an independent fashion. *Beneficence* is the principle that one must actively attempt to benefit another in a positive manner. The principle that one must avoid causing harm to another is *nonmaleficence*. *Justice* is the principle that all individuals should be treated fairly; equals must be treated as equals, and unequals must be treated in a way most beneficial to their specific circumstances. *Fidelity* is the principle of commitment to keep promises, uphold truth, and maintain loyalty.

Treatment recommendations pose many of the more perplexing ethical dilemmas concerning client welfare. A notable illustration that has evolved from studies of the battered woman syndrome is that a battered woman (or any battered partner) should be encouraged by the therapist to leave the abusive relationship (Betancourt, 1997; Roberts, 1996). Ethically, this recommendation creates a dilemma: Should the therapist encourage her to leave the relationship? On one side of the question is respect for her autonomy and an assumption that she possesses sufficient psychological competence to act in her own best interests. On the other side is the conviction that the experience of battered woman syndrome sufficiently justifies compromising the client's autonomous functioning. The five principles of Beauchamp and Childress (1994) can be of guidance in deciding just what would best serve the standard of primacy of the client's welfare.

Beneficence demands that therapists confer benefits and promote clients' well-being. The literature describing the battered woman syndrome often notes that separation from the batterer will maximize a woman's psychological growth, facilitate a more objective assessment of the relationship, and reduce the immediate potential of injury or death.

> Only after women feel protected from another assault, can they begin to deal with the reality of the battering situation. (L. Walker, 1981, p. 88)

> The symbiotic dependency bonds must be broken and each partner taught independence and new communication skills. (McG Mullen & Carroll, 1983, p. 34)

> Marriage counseling cannot proceed while the wife is living in fear. (Wentzel & Ross, 1983, p. 427)

These sentiments suggest that a therapist should actively encourage a battered female client to leave the batterer.

Beneficence also demands that benefits and harms be balanced; that is, positive outcomes must be weighed against the risks (Beauchamp & Childress, 1994; Bograd & Mederos, 1999). Studies have shown that battered women who leave the batterer and go to a shelter where help is available have far greater success in overcoming the emotional and motivational deficits induced by the feelings of helplessness they experience (Walker, 1984). Less success in overcoming these feelings of helplessness has been reported when women remain with battering partners and try to change the relationship to a nonbattering one (Flax, 1977).

Because the benefits outweigh the harms, a therapist should assert the value for a battered client in leaving the batterer.

The principle of nonmaleficence is epitomized by the adage "above all, do no harm." Not encouraging a battered woman to leave circumstances that are certainly dangerous violates this principle. Although a therapist may not personally be inflicting the harm, he or she is allowing the client to return to a setting in which she will most probably be abused in the future (Walker, 1984; Wentzel & Ross, 1983).

The principle of justice demands that clients with equal needs not be discriminated against through either a therapist's incompetence or denial of treatment. However, clients with unique needs requiring special interventions are entitled to unique treatment (Huston, 1984). Battered women, because of the psychological reactions concomitant to living in a violent environment, display unique characteristics and needs. Some authors have likened battered women to hostages who, unable to escape life-threatening or identity-threatening situations characterized by social isolation and dependency, form deep attachments to their captors. Because of this trauma, they are unable to assess their real plight or risk; the batterer's intermittent but persistent abuse has destroyed their subjective realities (Graham, Rawlings, & Rimini, 1988; Painter & Dutton, 1985). Justice, therefore, lends support to the use of a distinct treatment approach for a battered client.

Fidelity emphasizes the importance of therapists' faithfulness and loyalty to clients. L. Walker (1981) reports that battered women generally believe that their batterer's charm will seduce anyone, even professionals: A "battered woman may misinterpret any attempt at developing a therapeutic alliance with the batterer" (p. 85). A battered client must be assured that the therapist will be loyal to her above any connection to the batterer or to the unconditional maintenance of the marriage. Fidelity also demands that therapists be truthful with clients. Herein is suggested the therapist's obligation to inform a battered client of research findings indicating that it is dangerous and not psychologically helpful to her to return to the batterer (Huston, 1984).

The ethical dilemma created by potential infringement of the client's autonomous functioning is less easily resolved. Autonomy proposes that an individual has a right to make her or his own decisions if those decisions do not violate the rights of others. To tell a client to leave her home can be viewed as an infringement of her autonomy. It can also be argued that respect for the autonomous functioning of battered women is vital because of their vulnerable and dependent nature, particularly given the inherent transference aspects of the therapist–client relationship. Transference issues with battered women tend to include withholding anger from and/or being overly compliant with persons of authority (Heppner, 1978; McG Mullen & Carroll, 1983). Therapists must be cautious lest they misuse their position as object of the transference phenomenon by being overly directive with these clients (Huston, 1984).

The right of individuals to autonomy can be affected by their deemed level of psychological competence. An individual whose psychological competence is limited is unable to make consistent rational judgments (Beauchamp & Childress,

1994). Mills (1985) describes battering victims' debilitating use of minimization (e.g., "compared to others, my problems are small") to mistakenly justify their circumstances and to allow them to tolerate violent marriages. Similarly, Ferraro and Johnson (1983) describe how women "rationalized" being abused—by saying such things as "I asked for it," "He's sick," and "He didn't injure me"—and demonstrate how these rationalized accounts prevent the women from seeking help.

Walker (1979) describes battered women as experiencing a form of learned helplessness because of a consistent and well-reinforced message that nothing they can do will change their situation. Because battered women can consequently become immobilized, they may be considered as having limited psychological competence and therefore being in desperate need of someone to assist them to get out of what they see as a "hopeless" situation (Huston, 1984).

Battered women can also be immobilized by a state of extreme fear. Symonds (1979) cites research findings indicating that many victims of violent crimes become reduced to an infantile obedience to and cooperation with their attacker. Symonds suggests that a battered woman who follows this response pattern "experiences terror which traumatically infantilizes her" (p. 169). Heppner (1978) describes battered women reporting that they remain in abusive relationships out of fear of the consequences of leaving. These findings all suggest that battered women are in need of directive assistance.

Thus, it seems ethically justifiable to encourage a battered woman to leave her relationship if she is judged to have limited psychological competence because of the severity of her circumstances. Whether it is ethically justifiable to force her to leave or to deny her treatment should she refuse to leave is questionable. Forcing her to leave can amount to an overt violation of her right to autonomy. If an initial effort is unsuccessful, the therapist might better maintain a position of respect for autonomous decision making. As Wolf-Smith and LaRossa (1992) assert, "Respecting the choices that women make is an integral part of the counseling/therapeutic process. Victims must always know that there are people ready and willing to listen to them and assist them" (p. 329).

Huston (1984) proposes that a therapist should then adopt more of a "maternalistic" treatment stance:

> Maternalism as the recommended treatment approach for battered women can be defined as offering a nurturing, directive stance at early stages of the client's development and an acceptance of more autonomy at later developmental stages. This approach recognizes that battered women as clients move through developmental stages of growth in objectively understanding their battering relationships. The women demonstrate different needs at different stages, and treatment must vary accordingly. . . . This stance is congruent with feminist treatment beliefs, because it acknowledges a deep respect for the autonomous functioning of the individual and yet recognizes the unique needs of specific populations and developmental tasks. (p. 831)

The literature in the women's movement has pointed out that paternalism can be a debilitating mode of interaction with many women, reinforcing predominant societal conditioning of them as passive and dependent. The maternalistic alternative espoused by Huston involves initial assertion but recognizes the potential need to patiently await developmental movement toward increased independence, positive self-worth, and autonomous action.

MULTIPLE-CLIENT CONSIDERATIONS

North American culture is highly individualistic; each person's rights take precedence. Consequently, multiple clients, such as those in marriage and family therapy, can create dilemmas for therapists. In some situations, an intervention that serves one member's best interest may be countertherapeutic to another. Indeed, the very reason why couples and families seek out professional assistance is that they have conflicting goals and interests (Margolin, 1982). Consider the following illustration:

> Two parents come to family therapy with their 17-year-old son. They seek to have their son acquiesce more readily to their directives, invoking a rather rigid "honor thy father and mother" dictum. The son's actions as described during the therapy are not destructive, but he has been actively disobedient.

Achieving the parents' goal of having their son respond more readily to their commands might ease the parents' tension as well as perhaps provide secondary benefits for their marriage. The son, however, is at a developmental life stage wherein he is attempting to launch himself from the family. Achieving the parents' goal would not be necessarily advantageous to the son's overall development.

Marriage and family therapists must strive to see that the status of one partner or family member does not improve at the expense of the other partner or another family member. This objective is not entirely unique to marriage and family therapy (Margolin, 1982). Persons in individual therapy can also make changes that cause discomfort to, or conflict with, the desires of significant others. Individually oriented therapists are always wise to encourage clients to explore the potential consequences of their actions on those around them. What sets marriage and family therapists apart, however, is their commitment to promote the welfare of each family member. Through direct involvement with all members, marriage and family therapists are able to assess how each member's actions affect the others. Thus, marriage and family therapists take on more responsibility for exercising judgment about the welfare of more than one individual.

The marriage and family therapist can respond to this dilemma of conflicting interests by identifying the marital or family system, rather than a single individual, as the "client." Such a stance should be a natural outgrowth of the therapist's theoretical position. The therapist who is an advocate of the system avoids becoming an agent of any one marital partner or family member. Working within a framework that conceptualizes change as affecting and being affected by all family members, marriage and family therapists define problems and consider plans for change in the context of the entire family. Consider the following situation:

> A couple presents themselves for therapy stating opposite goals. She wants divorce counseling; he is seeking to save/improve the marriage.

The system advocate works to define the couple's problem as a relationship concern, seeking to help them establish and pursue relationship goals. Whether marriage enhancement or divorce is the ultimate result, reorganizing their relationship interactions so that they can problem solve more effectively can only be in the best interests of both.

Functioning as a system advocate occasionally has the paradoxical effect of actually creating greater variance between the aims of the therapist and those of marital partners or family members. Functioning as a system advocate suggests a knowledge that often goes beyond the specific and sometimes self-centered goals of the individual members (Margolin, 1982). Most couples and family members enter treatment wanting to change their partner or a specific family member's behavior or attitude. "If only he/she/they would change" is likely the most frequent complaint communicated to marriage and family therapists. The system advocate's problem definition and goal orientation are at odds with those of some couples and families and must be reconciled when they are unacceptable. Marriage and family therapists should clearly communicate the nature of their commitment as system advocate. Informed of the therapist's stance as advocate of the system, most marital partners and family members generally understand and accept this position, although during therapy they may at times seek to solicit the therapist as a personal ally (Margolin, 1982).

Although the stance of system advocate works well in the majority of instances, it does not eliminate the problems of conflicting interests. In certain circumstances, such as treatment of the client with battered woman syndrome, the immediate course of action recommended calls for the overt primacy of individual needs. The system is not set aside, but it is given an apparent secondary focus, as it is when the welfare of an individual member is in jeopardy. It still is, of course, in the best interest of all members of the system that the welfare of a member in jeopardy be prioritized. In addition to clinical considerations, there are also laws requiring that certain actions be taken when the welfare of an individual is in danger. For example, in a case of child neglect or abuse, child abuse reporting laws require therapists to inform authorities if they learn that a child is suffering from neglect or being abused, regardless of the negative consequences likely to be incurred for future family treatment efforts.

Margolin (1982) summarizes the complex responsibilities of therapists seeking to promote optimal client welfare from a system advocate's position:

> Attempting to balance one's therapeutic responsibilities toward individual family members and toward the family as a whole involves intricate judgments. Since neither of these responsibilities cancels out the importance of the other, the family therapist cannot afford blind pursuit of either extreme, that is, always doing what is in each individual's best interest or always maintaining the stance as family advocate. (p. 790)

Framo (1981) offers the commonsense, but perhaps understated, conclusion that "part of the skill of the therapist resides in finding the appropriate balance between the conflict of goals and expectations of all family members as well as those of the therapist" (p. 143).

CONFIDENTIALITY

The single most widely recognized ethical issue in the practice of psychotherapy is confidentiality, which is "often referred to as the cornerstone of ethics" (Kaplan & Culkin, 1995, p. 336). Confidentiality had its genesis in the physician–patient relationship in the 16th century, when physicians began to realize that contagious diseases were being spread by persons who feared that detection of their affliction would condemn them to social isolation (Slovenko, 1973). More recently, confidentiality has become intertwined with legal constraints dictated by state and federal legislation and court decisions regarding *privileged communication* and *privacy*. The terms *confidentiality, privileged communication,* and *privacy,* however, should not be used interchangeably, because they have different meanings.

G. D. Erickson (1998) defines *confidentiality* in this way: "Confidentiality is the ethical responsibility required of all national counseling organizations and some state licensing boards that nothing disclosed within the counseling session will be revealed to another person without the client's expressed consent" (p. 223). Denkowski and Denkowski (1982) identify two reasons for maintaining confidentiality in psychotherapy:

1. Confidentiality protects clients from the social stigma frequently associated with therapy.
2. Confidentiality promotes vital client rights, integral to therapists' professed concern for the welfare of clients.

Confidentiality is maintained as a standard by the ethical codes of all professional therapy organizations. Relevant standards from the codes of ethics of several professional organizations are listed in Table 1–5.

Little else in psychotherapy commands as much agreement as the belief that therapists have a responsibility to safeguard information obtained during the treatment process. Confidentiality is considered to be essential for a satisfactory therapist–client relationship. Therapists' training in this matter has traditionally emphasized a stern but simplistic admonition about the sanctity of psychotherapeutic confidentiality with references to principles stated in professional codes of ethics.

From the perspective of the legal system, confidentiality is generally viewed as a narrowly drawn exception to the principle that all relevant information should be available to judicial decision makers (Gumper & Sprenkle, 1981). Furthermore, state and federal legislation and court decisions have increasingly mandated disclosure of information in certain situations and imposed penalties for noncompliance, most notably in instances of child abuse. Likewise, procedures for disclosure of therapy information in educational settings must be determined in accordance with the Family Educational and Privacy Rights Act of 1976. Maintaining confidentiality in the treatment of minors with alcohol or drug abuse problems may also not be possible after the first interview, as mandated by the Confidentiality of Alcohol and Drug Patient Records Act of 1975 (DePauw, 1986).

Table 1–5 Ethical Considerations Relating to Confidentiality

American Association for Marriage and Family Therapy (2001)
"Marriage and family therapists have unique confidentiality concerns because the client in a therapeutic relationship may be more than one person. Therapists respect and guard confidences of each individual client."

American Counseling Association (1995)
"Clients have the right to expect confidentiality and to be provided with an explanation of its limits."

"Counselors respect their clients' right to privacy and avoid illegal and unwarranted disclosures of confidential information."

American Psychological Association (1992)
"Psychologists have a primary obligation and take reasonable precautions to respect the confidentiality rights of those with whom they work or consult, recognizing that confidentiality may be established by law, institutional rules, or professional or scientific relationships."

National Association of Social Workers (1996)
"Social workers should protect the confidentiality of all information obtained in the course of professional service, except for compelling professional reasons."

International Association of Marriage and Family Counselors (1993)
"Clients have the right to expect that information shared with the counselor will not be disclosed to others and, in the absence of any law to the contrary, the communications between clients and marriage and family counselors should be viewed as privileged."

Hence, a thorough understanding of the concepts of privileged communication and privacy is prerequisite to offering and maintaining client confidentiality.

Privileged Communication

Privileged communication is "a legal right which exists by statute and which protects [clients] from having [their] confidences revealed publicly from the witness stand during legal proceedings without [their] permission" (Shah, 1969, p. 57). Where privileged communication laws apply, therapists are prevented from testifying in court about clients without their consent. If a client waives this privilege, a therapist has no grounds for withholding information. The privilege belongs to the client and is meant for the protection of the client, not the therapist (Corey et al., 1998). It is important to note that privileged communication for the therapist–client relationship is not legally supported in a large number of states (Bray, Shepherd, & Hays, 1985). Furthermore, even when clients have not waived their right, privileged communication can be subject to exceptions such as those listed in Table 1–6.

Table 1–6 Exceptions to the Right of Privileged Communication

---

- When the therapist is acting in a court-appointed capacity—for example, to conduct a psychological examination (DeKraai & Sales, 1982)

- When the therapist makes an assessment of a foreseeable risk of suicide (Schultz, 1982)

- When the client initiates a lawsuit against the therapist, such as for malpractice (Denkowski & Denkowski, 1982)

- In any civil action when the client introduces mental condition as a claim or defense (Denkowski & Denkowski, 1982)

- When a client is under the age of 16 and a therapist believes that the child is the victim of a crime—for example, incest, child molestation, rape, or child abuse (Everstine et al., 1980)

- When the therapist determines that the client is in need of hospitalization for a mental or psychological disorder (DeKraai & Sales, 1982; Shultz, 1982)

- When criminal action is involved (Everstine et al., 1980)

- When information is made an issue in a court action (Everstine et al., 1980)

- When clients reveal their intention to commit a crime or when they can be assessed as "dangerous to society" or dangerous to themselves (DeKraai & Sales, 1982; Shultz, 1982)

Note. From *Issues and Ethics in the Helping Professions* (2nd ed., p. 172) by G. Corey, M. S. Corey, and P. Callanan, 1984, Monterey, CA: Brooks/Cole. Copyright 1984 by Wadsworth, Inc. Reprinted by permission of Brooks/Cole Publishing Company.

Gumper and Sprenkle (1981) have examined the potential repercussions of privileged communication laws for psychotherapy. They report a wide variation in legal statutes, and this variation presents particular problems for marriage and family therapists. Dominant among the problems that arise is the question, "Who owns the right to waive privilege in marriage and family therapy?" Gumper and Sprenkle specifically reemphasized that ownership of this privilege—and therefore the right to waive it—resides with the client, not the therapist.

Margolin (1982) has addressed this question in discussing the case of a New Jersey couple seen in conjoint marital therapy by a psychologist:

> When the couple, who were seen in marital therapy, decided to divorce, the psychotherapist was subpoenaed by the husband's lawyer to testify in court about statements made during the conjoint therapy sessions. Since the wife refused to waive privilege, the therapist refused to testify. On the basis of psychologist–patient privilege in New Jersey, the wife's confidentiality would not have been protected. The judge decided to rule to protect the wife's confidentiality, however, on the basis of laws in that state for marriage counselors. (p. 793)

Margolin notes similar cases involving psychiatrists. She reports cases in which courts in New York and Tennessee upheld privilege but a Virginia court denied the psychiatrist that protection. As reported by Herrington (1979), the Virginia judge ruled that "when a husband and wife are in a counseling session with a psychiatrist . . . there is no confidentiality because statements were made not in private to a doctor, but in the presence of the spouse" (p. 1).

The model for statutory privilege provisions that apply in psychotherapeutic contexts was drawn from and has largely concerned one-to-one (i.e., attorney–client, husband–wife) relationships. Most privileged communication statutes tend to be ill-defined for situations in which two or more clients are seen simultaneously. In some states, for example, the presence of a third party is construed to mean that necessary confidentiality is lacking and the therapist–client privilege is accordingly deemed lost or waived (Gumper & Sprenkle, 1981). Questions also arise as to whether privilege applies to client-to-client communications. Because some states extend privilege to persons who aid in the delivery of personal services and are present during the uttering of confidential information (e.g., nurses, medical technicians), a liberal interpretation of privilege statutes can identify family members as agents of the therapist (Bersoff & Jain, 1980).

Gumper and Sprenkle (1981) argue that in states where statutory protection of communications in multiperson therapies is unclear, marriage and family therapists should take the position that the "client" is the couple or family as a unit. Rather than identifying family members as agents of the therapist, they recommend claiming that third-party limitations on privilege do not apply because only one client (the couple or family) is present. Lacking definitive legislation on these issues, however, marriage and family therapists cannot comfortably assume that existing privilege statutes protect the confidentiality of communications in their work with couples and families.

Legal protection against court-compelled disclosure of therapy communications is thus qualified and particularly flawed with respect to marriage and family therapy. Given this cloudy mixture of protection and compelled disclosure, Gumper and Sprenkle (1981) offer several practical suggestions to therapists for preparing themselves to confront this issue:

1. *Whatever their credentials, therapists should acquaint themselves with the particular privilege provisions of their state.* It is insufficient to simply know that "some kind of privilege statute" exists.

2. *In marriage and family therapy, especially when divorce may be a real possibility, therapists would be wise to obtain a written agreement from all parties not to make or seek court disclosures of therapy communications.* Courts may differ in the enforcement of such agreements, but when they have been entered into, efforts to obtain court disclosures are more likely to be restrained, that is, stopped by restraining order.

3. *If contacted by an attorney, a therapist should advise the attorney that a written release signed by the participating clients is necessary before the therapist can give out information.* The conversation should be one-way (i.e., the therapist can ascertain but not divulge information) until such a release is obtained. Details about the pending proceeding and the attorney's plan for

involving the therapist might be elicited. Such information may be helpful in arriving at a position on the disclosure issue.

4. *A therapist who decides to take a position of nondisclosure with an attorney should do so firmly and persistently, but without the loud indignance of a crusader seeking to protect therapist–client confidentiality.* Most attorneys are conditioned to react to such a militant stance in an adversarial manner. A calm, reasoned approach, emphasizing the therapist's duty as opposed to the attorney's, is less likely to polarize the parties. This calmer approach will allow the attorney not to lose face and potentially conclude that the therapy information is not worth the effort necessary to obtain it.

5. *Subpoenas should be viewed as the formal commencement, not the conclusion, of any disclosure controversy.* A therapist should not testify without a subpoena but, conversely, need not testify simply because a subpoena is present. When subpoenaed, a therapist should have, or can obtain, sufficient time to carefully consider ethical and legal obligations before making any decision regarding disclosure. Unless steps are taken to have a subpoena canceled or limited by the court, the therapist must respond by being present at the hearing in question. The therapist or the therapist's attorney can, however, still make arguments against testifying or providing records or reports. If a subpoena requiring court appearance is presented on short notice, the therapist should simply notify the court representative of when the subpoena was received and request time to consult legal counsel.

6. *Ideally, therapists should maintain their own independent legal counsel.* This policy is especially important when the therapist is subpoenaed and the client is not represented by counsel in the proceeding, when the therapist perceives her or his ethical or legal interests to be at odds with the client's, or when interests conflict between clients who are marital partners or family members.

Privacy

Privacy with regard to psychotherapy has been defined as "the freedom of individuals to choose for themselves the time and the circumstances under which the extent to which their beliefs, behavior, and opinions are to be shared or withheld from others" (Siegel, 1979, p. 251). More simply stated, privacy is the "right of persons to choose what others may know about them and under what circumstances" (Stadler, 1990, p. 102). "Privacy not only deals with communications . . . but also relates to the disposal of records, not being identified in a waiting room, tape recordings, use of credit cards for billing, use of computer services for scoring of tests or billing, and other documentary or business activities" (Cottone & Tarvydas, 1998, p. 66). The concept of privacy is addressed by the Fourth Amendment to the U.S. Constitution, that portion of the Bill of Rights protecting a person's home against illegal search and seizure by the government. A rich tradition of case law concerns the application of the basic principle of this amendment to a wide range of contemporary issues. In effect, persons are protected against invasion of their privacy by their government or by the agents of government. Everstine et al. (1980) raise important questions about preserving privacy:

- To what extent should psychological or emotional states be protected from the scrutiny of others?
- Who may intrude on persons' privacy? Under what circumstances and by what means should this decision be made?

These questions are particularly important when insurance companies and other third-party payers attempt to gain access to therapy information about clients or when therapists are bound by law and/or professional codes of ethics to break confidentiality (e.g., in child abuse cases in which clients pose a serious danger to themselves or others). The questions are somewhat less important in circumstances involving professional consultation, tape recording, and third-party observation/supervision of therapeutic activities. And the issue of privacy involves practitioners who also teach courses, offer workshops, write books and journal articles, and give lectures.

Therapists should maintain a current record of third-party reimbursement requirements (such as insurance) to apprise clients of the kinds of information that will need to be released, particularly diagnostic labels, and who may have access to the information. When they understand the requirements, many clients choose to assume self-responsibility for therapy fees (i.e., they themselves pay), for example, when employers have access to reimbursement requests. Therapists who seek professional consultation and supervision or who utilize case examples from their clinical work in teaching and writing should obtain clients' consent beforehand and/or take adequate measures to ensure that clients' identities are disguised (Corey et al., 1998).

In addressing the question "Whose agent is the therapist?" Shah (1970) notes that in some governmental agencies and institutions the therapist is not primarily the client's agent. In these situations, therapists are faced with conflicts between obligations to clients and obligations to their agency or institution. Shah maintains that potential conflicts should be clarified before beginning diagnostic or therapeutic relationships. Denkowski and Denkowski (1982) support Shah's position in contending that therapists must inform clients of potential breaches of confidentiality. They also urge that therapists go further to assure "that all reasonable steps be taken to restrict the legally sanctioned dissemination [of] confidential client information to its bare minimum" (p. 374).

The Duty to Protect

All the professional organizations in the Western world whose members practice psychotherapy have taken the position that certain information must be revealed when there is clear and imminent danger to an individual or to society: Therapists have a "duty to protect." Consistent with this ethical position are legal mandates from legislation and court decisions (to be discussed in Chapter 5).

Addressing therapists regarding their duty to protect, Knapp and VandeCreek (1982) write: "Psychotherapists need only follow reasonable standards in predicting violence. Psychotherapists are not liable for failure to warn when the propensity toward violence is unknown or would be unknown by other psychotherapists using ordinary skill" (pp. 514–515). These authors caution therapists not to become intimidated by clients' statements of potential hostility; not every impulsive threat is evidence of imminent danger. In their opinion, recent behaviors are the best predictors of future violence. In cases of likely danger, in addition to warning potential victims, Knapp and VandeCreek suggest that therapists also consider alternatives that could defuse the situation and, simultaneously, satisfy their ethical and/or legal obligations. They particularly recommend that therapists consult with professionals having expertise in dealing with potentially violent persons and that they document all steps taken.

Corey, Corey, and Callanan (1984) offer a set of procedures for therapists to follow if they determine that a client poses a serious danger of violence to others:

1. Therapists should inform their clients of the possible action they must take to protect a third party in situations where violence might be inflicted on that party.
2. When a client makes threats against others, everything observed and stated in the session should be documented.
3. The therapist should inform his or her supervisor in writing of any serious threat.
4. The therapist should consult with colleagues qualified to offer opinions on how to proceed. This consultation should be documented.
5. The police and other proper authorities should be alerted.
6. The intended victim must be notified; in the case of a minor, her or his parents should also be notified.

Therapists have an obligation to inform clients that the duty to protect exists (Everstine et al., 1980). Furthermore, clients should be told that therapists also have a "duty to report" suspected instances of child abuse, incest, and other actions that constitute a threat to others as well as to clients themselves. Everstine et al. (1980) aptly summarize therapists' overall obligations in matters of privacy: "Although a therapist, a person is still a citizen and he or she must protect and contribute to the common good. As a private citizen, the person of good conscience will not hesitate to warn an intended victim" (p. 836). Likewise, the person of good conscience would not hesitate to prevent the continuation of child abuse, incest, or other forms of violence.

Confidentiality in Marriage and Family Therapy

Therapists must inform clients in individual therapy of the limits of confidentiality. Marriage and family therapists have the same responsibility; moreover, they have an additional obligation toward marital partners and/or other family members:

They must decide what confidentiality means for the couple or family group and how it is to be maintained.

Margolin (1982) identifies two standard but opposing positions on maintaining confidentiality taken by therapists working with couples and families. One position calls for therapists to treat each marital partner or family member's confidences as though that person were an individual client. Information obtained during a private session, in a telephone call, or from written material is not divulged to a spouse or fellow family member. Therapists adhering to this position often arrange for sessions with individual spouses and family members to actively encourage the sharing of "secrets" to better understand what is occurring within the relationship system. The therapist then works toward a goal of enabling that individual to disclose therapeutically relevant information in the marital or family session. Should the individual fail to do so, however, the therapist still upholds the individual's confidentiality.

A second position adopted by marriage and family therapists is that of nonsecrecy. The therapist discourages the sharing of information that might lead to, or maintain, an alliance between the therapist and one family member or between individual family members. Therapists subscribing to this approach generally avoid receiving individual confidences by conducting only conjoint or family sessions. This safeguard can prove insufficient, however. Unless clients are informed of a nonsecrecy policy when they initiate therapy and are able to adequately consider its consequences, many will seek to influence the therapist.

Some therapists select an intermediate position between these two extremes. These therapists inform clients that information shared in individual sessions, over the phone, through written messages, or by similar means may be divulged as the therapists determine to be in accordance with the greatest benefit for the couple or family. They simply reserve the right to use their professional judgment about whether to maintain individual confidences (Corey et al., 1998). This intermediate approach creates greater responsibility for therapists who select it. Identifying information as ultimately helpful or hurtful places an increased burden on therapists' clinical abilities. The consequences of maintaining or divulging information in an untimely or what might be perceived as an inappropriate manner can cause an abrupt, premature termination of therapy as well as a souring toward future psychotherapeutic assistance of any kind.

Karpel (1980) critiques a number of ethical and practical considerations confronting therapists seeking to select a position with regard to handling marital and family secrets. In this critique, which is especially perceptive concerning this intermediate position, Karpel advocates a distinction between secrecy and privacy in terms of how relevant information is to those unaware of it. For example, a traumatic episode in one's childhood, now reasonably well resolved and not significantly affecting the present relationship, would be considered private. The client might at some time decide to share this history with his or her partner or children but does not *owe* it to them to do so. Similarly, intimate details of a marital partner's previous love relationships having no important implications for her or his current relationship are private, not secret. In contrast, a spouse engaged in an extramarital affair maintains a secret in the sense that it involves deception as well as a violation of reciprocity. Likewise, parents who withhold the fact that a child is adopted violate that child's right to a complete self-definition and identity.

Karpel advocates a policy of "accountability with discretion." A therapist would share or withhold information based on his or her clinical judgment involving (1) a consideration of the relevance of the material for the person who is unaware of it, (2) an attempt to perceive the situation as much as possible from the perspective of the person who is unaware, and (3) a sensitivity to the timing and consequences for the person who is unaware.

> This means, to use an everyday expression, trying to "put yourself in the other person's shoes," trying to understand what they need and what they are owed. It also means that when a decision to share is made, it takes the other's situation and likely reactions into account. For example, one does not reveal a secret that is likely greatly to upset the other in the midst of his/her surprise birthday party or when s/he is already in crisis due to an unrelated situation. This stance clearly reflects . . . a respect for individuation, an effort to maximize trust and trustworthiness in relationships, and an attempt to balance the two fairly. (Karpel, 1980, p. 298)

Karpel supports his stance of "accountability with discretion" by arguing that therapists who agree to keep secrets collude with secretholders and thereby betray the trust of unaware members while enhancing the potentially destructive power of secretholders. Karpel warns that although keeping secrets may be a well-intentioned attempt to protect the unaware members, this stance carries significant risk. The secret information may unexpectedly be revealed, resulting in negative consequences for the individuals, the relationship, and the therapy. Karpel acknowledges that therapists' need to know relevant information for diagnostic and treatment purposes and their obligation to maintain trustworthiness frequently come in conflict. He proposes a solution of discussing with the couple or family in the initial session the dangers posed by special confidences, asking them to agree on the direction the therapy will take:

> The therapist might describe the likely decrease in effectiveness that occurs when something important is known in therapy that can't be discussed. Having explained this, s/he can ask how they would like this to be handled. It can also be made clear, if they sanction such confidences, that this arrangement may become unworkable at some point. If so, the therapist will tell them so and they will have to choose between disclosure and termination. (Karpel, 1980, p. 305)

Another factor that complicates confidentiality obligations is a change in the format of therapy, specifically when individual therapy is replaced by marriage or family therapy. Margolin (1982) raises a number of critical issues to address when considering such a change:

> How does the therapist handle the information that he or she has obtained during individual therapy? One possibility is to obtain the individual client's permission to use such information, when necessary, in the conjoint sessions. If permission is not granted, however, that information must be kept confidential, a resolution far from desirable for the therapist who prefers not maintaining individual confidences in

conjoint therapy. Even if the client permits the information to be shared, this permission has been granted *after* the information was obtained. Does the client remember all that she or he has confided under the previously assumed condition of confidentiality? Would that person have responded differently in individual therapy if it were known from the outset that such information would be available to the spouse? (p. 791)

Karpel (1980) uses two case examples to illustrate what he refers to as "reparative strategies" for therapists to employ in responding to a change in format from individual to marriage and family therapy.

CASE 1

Mrs. T. is a 35-year-old, childless, married woman. She comes self-referred to an outpatient mental health clinic requesting an appointment for herself. She complains of some anxiety and depression, which she attributes to long-standing marital problems. She reveals that she has carried on a secret three-year affair with her husband's married brother. She is inflexible in her request for marital therapy, her insistence that the affair never be revealed to her husband, and her refusal to give it up. There are no indications of suicidal or homicidal ideation or intent. (Karpel, 1980, p. 303)

In this case, it was recommended that the therapist communicate to the woman the extent to which her requests are incompatible. Improving her marital relationship requires building greater trust and reciprocity. She is unwilling to give up a competing relationship that violates both. She is also unwilling to discuss it. The therapist was advised to offer the woman additional individual sessions to explore her feelings about the situation with the hope that this additional counseling would help her decide on a course of action incorporating more realistic goals.

CASE 2

Mr. and Mrs. L. seek psychiatric help for problems involving their 9-year-old son who is described as being withdrawn and depressed, with a poor relationship with his father. Mr. L. is a successful architect who is heavily involved in community affairs. There are two teenage children. As part of a routine family evaluation, the parents are seen together and separately. In her individual meeting with the therapist, Mrs. L. impulsively discloses that in the past her husband has been involved in homosexual extra-marital affairs. He has not done so for several years, although she says she remains somewhat jealous and anxious about this recurring. She immediately regrets having disclosed this and asks the therapist not to reveal his knowledge to her husband. She makes a persuasive argument that her husband might be able to tolerate the therapist's knowing this once he knew and trusted the therapist more but that finding out at this early stage would almost certainly drive him and therefore the family from treatment. (Karpel, 1980, p. 303)[1]

In this second case, it was recommended that the therapist communicate the potential importance of informing the husband of the disclosure. Therapy may eventually reach a point where the therapist must revisit the issue with the wife unless she is able to inform her husband of her disclosure or he spontaneously discloses relevant facts in therapy. The therapist must clearly communicate that treatment efforts can go only so far if significant information is withheld.

The situation in this latter case example allows for a gradual, less rigid approach. The therapist's insistence, for ethical and practical reasons, that the disclosure eventually be shared remains unchanged. The circumstances and timing of this sharing, however, are negotiable.

INFORMED CONSENT

Basic to ethical psychotherapeutic practice is the assurance that clients are adequately informed of their rights and responsibilities. For most clients, the therapeutic setting is new. They present themselves for assistance and unquestioningly accept what the therapist says or does. Little thought is given to the possible discomfort to be endured as well as to the considerable effort necessary to gain therapeutic benefits. Clients need to know what will be expected of them, what they may expect from the therapist and therapy, and generally what their rights as clients are. "This information should be given to clients in a package that includes an acknowledgement sheet that can be signed and returned to you" (Kaplan & Culkin, 1995, p. 335). It is ethically incumbent on therapists to inform and educate clients. Only when clients understand and act on their rights and responsibilities can therapists facilitate positive movement within the therapeutic process.

---

[1]*Note.* From "Family Secrets: I. Conceptual and Ethical Issues in the Relational Context: II. Ethical and Practical Considerations in Therapeutic Management," by M. A. Karpel, 1980, *Family Process, 19*, p. 303. Copyright 1980. Reprinted with permission.

Table 1–7 Ethical Considerations Relating to Informed Consent

American Association for Marriage and Family Therapy (2001)
"Marriage and family therapists respect the rights of clients to make decisions and help them to understand the consequences of these decisions. Therapists clearly advise the clients that they have the responsibility to make decisions regarding relationships such as cohabitation, marriage, divorce, separation, reconciliation, custody, and visitation."

American Counseling Association (1995)
"When counseling is initiated, and throughout the counseling process as necessary, counselors inform clients of the purposes, goals, techniques, procedures, limitations, potential risks and benefits of services to be performed, and other pertinent information."

American Psychological Association (1992)
"Psychologists obtain appropriate informed consent to therapy or related proce-dures, using language that is reasonably understandable to participants. The con-tent of informed consent will vary depending on many circumstances; however, informed consent generally implies that the person: (1) has the capacity to consent, (2) has been informed of significant information concerning the procedure, (3) has freely and without undue influence expressed consent, and (4) consent has been appropriately documented."

National Association of Social Workers (1996)
"Social workers should provide services to clients only in the context of a profes-sional relationship based, when appropriate, on valid informed consent."

International Association of Marriage and Family Counselors (1993)
"Members pursue a just relationship that acknowledges, respects, and informs clients of their rights, obligations, and expectations as a consumer of services, as well as the rights, obligations, and expectations of the provider(s) of service."

The codes of ethics of all the major professional organizations whose mem-bers engage in the practice of psychotherapy require that clients be given ade-quate information to make informed choices about entering and continuing a therapeutic relationship. The responsibility of therapists to educate clients in this regard is referred to as the ethical issue of *informed consent*. Relevant standards from the codes of ethics of several professional organizations are listed in Table 1–7.

Hare-Mustin, Maracek, Kaplan, and Liss-Levenson (1979) outline three types of information clients should have in order to make informed choices about enter-ing into and continuing therapy: (1) the procedures, goals, and possible side effects of therapy; (2) the qualifications, policies, and practices of the therapist; and (3) other available sources of help. Most therapists who recognize the need to educate clients about their rights and responsibilities employ some form of writ-ten document to introduce and record the implied contract that consent for treat-ment represents. Two such types of written communications are the therapeutic contract and the professional disclosure statement.

Therapeutic Contracts

The purpose of a therapeutic contract is to clarify the therapeutic relationship. Providing information and obtaining agreement through the use of a contract defines therapy as a mutual endeavor to which therapists contribute their professional knowledge and skills and clients bring a commitment to work. The development of a contract encourages all concerned parties to specify relevant goals, expectations, and boundaries (Hare-Mustin, Maracek, et. al., 1979).

Most therapeutic contracts consider such issues as the specific therapeutic approach and procedures to be employed, the length and frequency of sessions, the duration of treatment, the cost and the method of payment, provisions for cancellation and renegotiation of the contract, the extent of each party's responsibilities, and the degree of confidentiality. Areas actually covered by any contract may vary according to a therapist's orientation and the inclination of the client. Most important, however, is the fact that concrete, identifiable ground rules are decided on in advance and endorsed with signatures before the hard work of therapy begins.

Everstine et al. (1980) outline a sample document incorporating the basic elements of informed consent in contract form. An adapted version of this document is illustrated in Figure 1–1.

Mary E. Spates, Ph.D.
Licensed Psychologist (Connecticut No. 972)
62 Broadway, Suite 401
Bridgeport, Connecticut 06602
203/268-7899

PART I: *Your Rights as a Client*

1. You have a right to ask questions about any procedures used during therapy; if you wish, I will explain my usual approach and methods to you.
2. You have the right to decide *not* to receive therapeutic assistance from me; if you wish, I will provide you with the names of other qualified professionals whose services you might prefer.
3. You have the right to end therapy at any time without any moral, legal, or financial obligations other than those already accrued.
4. You have a right to review your records in the files at any time.
5. One of your most important rights involves confidentiality: Within certain limits, information revealed by you during therapy will be kept strictly confidential and will not be revealed to any other person or agency without your written permission.

Figure 1–1   A Therapeutic Contract

Note. From "Privacy and Confidentiality in Psychotherapy" by L. Everstine, D. S. Everstine, G. M. Heymann, R. H. True, D. H. Frey, and R. H. Seiden, 1980, *American Psychologist, 35,* pp. 828–840. Copyright 1980 by the American Psychological Association. Adapted by permission of the publisher and authors.

6. If you request it, any part of your record in the files can be released to any person or agency you designate. I will tell you, at the time, whether or not I think releasing the information in question to that person or agency might be harmful in any way to you.

7. You should also know that there are certain situations in which I am required *by law* to reveal information obtained during therapy to other persons or agencies *without your permission*. Also, I am not required to inform you of my actions in this regard. These situations are as follows: (a) if you threaten grave bodily harm or death to another person, I am required by law to inform the intended victim and appropriate law enforcement agencies. (b) If a court of law issues a legitimate subpoena, I am required by law to provide the information specifically described in the subpoena. (c) If you reveal information relative to child abuse and neglect, I am required by law to report this to the appropriate authority; and (d) if you are in therapy or being tested by order of a court of law, the results of the treatment or tests ordered must be revealed to the court.

PART II: *The Therapeutic Process*

One major benefit that may be gained from participating in therapy includes a better ability to handle or cope with marital, family, and other interpersonal relationships. Another possible benefit may be a greater understanding of personal goals and values; this may lead to greater maturity and happiness as an individual. Other benefits relate to the probable outcomes resulting from resolving specific concerns brought to therapy.

In working to achieve these potential benefits, however, therapy will require that firm efforts be made to change and may involve the experiencing of significant discomfort. Remembering and therapeutically resolving unpleasant events can arouse intense feelings of fear, anger, depression, frustration, and the like. Seeking to resolve issues between family members, marital partners, and other persons can similarly lead to discomfort, as well as relationship changes that may not be originally intended.

PART III: *Fees and Length of Therapy*

1. I agree to enter into therapy with Mary E. Spates, Ph.D. for _____ one-hour sessions during the next _____ weeks.
2. I agree to pay _____ for each completed one-hour session. Payment may be made by me or by a third party when billed.
3. I understand that I can leave therapy at any time and that I have no moral, legal, or financial obligation to complete the maximum number of sessions listed in this contract; I am contracting only to pay for completed therapy sessions.

Client(s):_____

_____

_____

_____

Therapist: _____ Date _____

Figure 1–1 *continued*

Hare-Mustin et al. (1979) advocate contracts as an integral part of therapy. They caution, however, that therapists should first resolve certain questions before beginning this practice:

- How much should the contract specify?
- What should be done if the therapist has personal or moral concerns about clients' goals?
- What should be done with clients who are unable to be specific about their goals?
- How should therapists respond to clients refusing to agree to a contract?

It is impossible to specify all that might occur during the course of therapy. Most therapists feel that providing clients with an understanding of the broad outlines is sufficient. They seek to offer only the assurance of a degree of predictability about potential processes and procedures. Hare-Mustin et al. (1979) posit, however, that procedures at odds with clients' values should be specified. Clients should be clearly apprised if any aversive techniques or physical contact is planned or if the use of medication is expected. Therapists who follow up on clients should secure their permission in the contract to do so, even if this follow-up might bias future responses.

Practices such as sexual relations with clients are unethical and remain so even if agreed to by clients. Some have argued that treatments objected to by many therapists, such as primal scream or "tickle" therapy, should be permitted if clients freely agree to their use with full knowledge of potential risks and benefits. It must be remembered, however, that there is initial inequity in the bargaining power between clients and therapists in that many clients' vulnerability opens them to manipulation; thus, such contracts are likely unconscionable (Schwitzgebel, 1975, 1976).

Clients occasionally present goals neither appropriate nor desirable but instead detrimental to the best interests of the clients themselves or others. Halleck (1976) proposes that "therapists try to change behaviors they believe should be changed and be reluctant to change behaviors they view as understandable or socially acceptable" (p. 167). He cites the case example of a woman who wanted to eliminate feelings of possessiveness and jealousy yet whose current life circumstances suggested that these feelings were entirely appropriate and that what she lacked was the ability to better cope with being oppressed.

Where clients' goals are at odds with therapists' professional values, the potential consequences of working toward goals sought by clients should be examined. If therapists feel that they cannot agree with clients' expressed goals, they should not work with those clients. Referral to another therapist or source of assistance should be offered (Hare-Mustin et al., 1979).

Therapists must negotiate with clients who are unable to be specific about their goals. These clients challenge therapists to help them translate vague complaints into concrete concerns. For such clients, an initial therapeutic goal might be to explore what prevents them from being specific about their desires with more definitive behavioral goal setting to follow. Outside-session tasks such as keeping records and diaries can encourage specificity. Time limits on therapy may also provide an incentive to set goals. Therapists who allow clients to stay in therapy without specific goals only increase the ambiguity of treatment efforts and deprive clients of the benefits inherent in pursuing a sought objective.

For some clients, negotiation and establishment of a therapeutic contract may be threatening. Certain clients may reject a contract because they suspiciously see it as benefiting only the therapist. For these clients, considerable orientation to the idea may be necessary. This orientation, however, must be presented in a manner that retains clients' right to refuse (Hare-Mustin et al., 1979). Rosen (1977), using a sample of more than 900 clients in a study investigating reasons why clients relinquish their rights, found that when clients were not informed of their right to refuse, all signed away their rights to privacy; when informed that such an option existed, only 41 percent signed.

Professional Disclosure Statements

A number of authors have advocated a written professional disclosure statement as a means of meeting informed consent provisions of codes of ethics (Gill, 1982; Gross, 1977; J. L. Swanson, 1979; Winborn, 1977). *Professional disclosure statements* take many forms, but essentially they entail a process of introducing prospective clients to a therapist's qualifications, the nature of the therapeutic process, and administrative procedures relating to time and money. An adaptation of Winborn's (1977) professional disclosure statement illustrated in Figure 1–2 provides a model.

Besides contributing to the ethical objective of gaining clients' informed consent, a professional disclosure statement also yields developmental benefits for practitioners. Creating such a statement clarifies professional practices and identity. Personal beliefs, values, strengths and weaknesses, and objectives pertaining to therapeutic relationships must be examined. By concisely stating who they are and what they are trained to do, therapists define a set of competencies and an approach identifying them as unique providers of beneficial human services. As Gill (1982) puts it:

> Are we shrinks, faith healers, or gurus whose mystical understandings of the universe magically transform problems into solutions? Or, are we trained specialists who utilize a set of skills and a body of knowledge to help people cope with normal life problems? If we are the latter, we should be able to describe who we are and what we do. (p. 444)

Gill (1982) suggests that putting into writing one's approach to the therapeutic process is a particularly demanding experience. As a way of facilitating therapists' preparation of this part of the professional disclosure statement, Gill has synthesized a set of questions from the recommendations of a number of professional disclosure advocates (Gross, 1977; J. L. Swanson, 1979; Witmer, 1978):

- What do you believe is the purpose of psychotherapy?
- What do you believe helps persons lead more satisfying lives?
- What should clients expect as a result of engaging in therapy efforts?
- What is your responsibility during therapy?

David Morgan, M.S.
Licensed Marriage and Family Therapist (Florida No. 475)
Child Guidance Clinic
181 Atlantic Avenue
Orlando, Florida 33310
904/342-7658

Some Things You Should Know About Your Therapist and Therapy

Since therapy is conducted in a number of different ways, depending on the therapist and his or her orientation, this description has been prepared to inform you about my qualifications, how I view the therapeutic process, and what you can expect from me as your therapist.

  My Qualifications. I received my graduate degree from the Florida State University with a major in Marriage and Family Therapy. I have been employed as a therapist for more than 8 years, the past 6 years here with the Child Guidance Clinic. I am a licensed Marriage and Family Therapist in Florida. I am also a Clinical Member and Approved Supervisor in the American Association for Marriage and Family Therapy. I have written over 30 articles for professional journals and coauthored 2 books relating to marriage and family therapy.

  The majority of my experience has been working with couples and families. While I do see individuals alone, especially children, I attempt to involve the entire family where appropriate and when possible. I have worked with individuals, couples, and families experiencing a wide range of problems. My training and experience provide me with the ability to assist with concerns that range from children's poor school achievement to marital problems and family hostility, as well as social skills training and alleviating fears, anxiety, and depression.

  I am not a physician and cannot prescribe or provide any medication, nor perform any medical procedures. If medical treatment is indicated, I can recommend a physician and in certain situations, I have worked in concert with and under the supervision of a psychiatrist.

  The Therapeutic Process. Marriage and family therapy is a learning process that seeks for you and your marital partner, parents, and/or other family members or significant persons to better understand yourself and others and the interactions that occur between and among you. Additional goals include achieving better functioning as a couple and/or family so that healthy interactions are established and greater satisfaction is attained. Further, by gaining a more harmonious relationship with significant persons around you, individual concerns can be more effectively and efficiently dealt with.

  There are several steps in the therapeutic process. First, we will need to spend some time exploring the problems that have brought you to therapy. I need to get to know you, how you view yourself, and how you and significant persons in your life interact. You will likely come to understand your situation better as we proceed in this manner. Obviously, we need to discuss things openly and honestly. My responsibility

Figure 1–2 A Professional Disclosure Statement

at this point in the therapeutic process is to listen, to assist you to communicate with me and others who may take part in the therapy, and to provide an environment of trust so that all present can interact freely and speak what is on their mind.

All of our sessions will, of course, be confidential to persons outside of the therapy. Therapy will likely involve the participation of family members and/or other significant persons. I do not guarantee confidentiality among participants in the therapy, although I would use my professional discretion in disclosing communications related to me. My professional code of ethics prevents me from discussing what is said during sessions with anyone other than participants in the therapy or releasing any records without your/their permission. The only exceptions to this are if someone is in danger of being harmed or if the law explicitly states that confidentiality provisions do not apply.

After we have explored and developed sufficient background to proceed, we will decide upon specific goals and objectives. We will then develop a treatment plan outlining how these goals will be achieved. Such a plan will likely require strong efforts, and feelings of discomfort inherent in change will be experienced. We will regularly evaluate progress in terms of whether the plan is effective in attaining the desired objectives, comparing progress with the situation when therapy began. Treatment efforts will conclude when the sought-after goals are sufficiently achieved. This will be determined through mutual agreement among the participants, including myself as therapist.

Fees and Length of Therapy. Therapy sessions are normally for one hour. Depending upon the nature of the presenting problems, sessions are held one or two times per week. It is difficult to initially predict how many sessions will be needed. I will be better able to discuss the probable number of sessions after we have explored and gained some background into the situation—usually after two or three sessions. I will verbally discuss fees with you as the Child Guidance Clinic operates on a *sliding scale* fee structure, meaning the cost of sessions varied according to clients' yearly income.

Please Ask Questions. You may have questions about me, my qualifications, or anything not addressed in the previous paragraphs. *It is your right* to have a complete explanation for any of your questions at any time. Please exercise this right.

Figure 1–2 continued

- What are the responsibilities your clients can be expected to assume during therapy?
- What is your primary therapeutic approach, and what are the general intervention strategies that emanate from that approach?
- What types of presenting problems have you been most effective in assisting clients with in the past?
- Under what circumstances might clients be offered referral to another source of assistance?
- How do you handle the confidential nature of the therapeutic relationship?

INFORMED CONSENT CONCERNS IN MARRIAGE AND FAMILY THERAPY

A primary concern in marriage and family therapy is that procedures for informed consent be conducted with all persons who participate in treatment efforts, including those who may join therapy at a later time (Margolin, 1982). This concern is especially pertinent because risks and benefits for individuals tend to be much different in marriage and family therapy than in individual therapy. Consider the following example:

> A couple sought treatment for marital problems. In the process that ensued, the wife recognized her unwillingness to expend the effort necessary to eventually gain the satisfaction she wanted from the marriage, and so she stated her rational desire to seek a divorce. The husband reacted to his wife's statement with a verbal attack upon the therapist for allowing this outcome to occur: "Therapy was supposed to save our marriage!"

Clients need to be forewarned that marriage and family therapy can lead to outcomes viewed as undesirable by one or another of the participants, for example, the wife's decision to divorce.

Similarly, marriage and family therapy may not always be in the perceived best interests of individual marital partners or family members. Priority placed on the good of the couple or family as a whole calls for individuals at times to subordinate personal desires that are not congruent with the overall goals. The following case example illustrates this point:

> Parents of a 15-year-old son and a 17-year-old daughter complained of the teenagers' unwillingness to follow their directives unquestioningly. Interaction during the initial evaluation session clearly showed the parents as excessively authoritarian and the youths' actions as normal developmental strivings. As therapy progressed, the parents eventually came to realize that their "overparenting" was a major part of the presenting problem; they nevertheless experienced significant anguish in allowing their son and daughter to take on greater self-responsibility.

Different family members can benefit unequally from therapy, at least in terms of the immediate changes resulting from treatment efforts that are aimed at enhancing the overall functioning of the family.

Hare-Mustin (1980) urges that therapists recognize their responsibility for minimizing the risks in marriage and family therapy and share this recognition with therapy participants. She suggests that these objectives are best accomplished by clearly stating goals the therapist wishes to pursue. Marital partners and family members should be encouraged to question these goals so that they can better identify how their individual needs align or contrast with overall goals of the marital or family relationship. Therapists must be explicit about the extent to which individual goals are incompatible with the relationship goals, need to be subordinated to the relationship goals, or are simply unacceptable to the marital partner and/or other family members.

Although general procedures for informed consent in marriage and family therapy appear rather basic, therapists need to carefully consider how well their primary therapeutic orientation matches their informed consent practices. This question is most relevant in determining the degree of specificity in information presented (Margolin, 1982). Most marriage and family therapists offer an overview of objectives (e.g., more satisfactory family functioning, clearer communications) as well as the format that sessions will take (e.g., length and frequency of sessions, approximate duration of treatment efforts). More precise information, however, may be detrimental to some types of treatment efforts, such as strategic therapy, for example, in which the therapist attempts to mobilize oppositional tendencies of participants through paradoxical interventions (Haley, 1976; Stanton, 1981; see also Chapter 2).

Most marriage and family therapists advocate certain "maneuvers" that indirectly limit fully informed consent and free choice about therapy (Margolin, 1982). For example, in relating benefits to be expected from treatment efforts, therapists cannot ethically guarantee positive change. Most therapists, however, do express optimism about the potential outcome of treatment to reduce participants' anxiety, raise their expectations, and increase their persistence in pursuing agreed-to goals (Jacobson & Margolin, 1979).

Another such therapeutic maneuver involves certain explanations and interpretations offered to marital partners and family members. Several major marriage and family therapy approaches advocate reframing or relabeling behaviors and interactions in ways that do not reflect a couple's or family's current reality but rather facilitate their interactions in more efficient and effective ways. Relabeling two marital partners' constant arguments as evidence of "your persistence in seeking to communicate clearly with each other" introduces a positive goal orientation where hostility is present. The likelihood of the couple's pursuing a common course of future action will be greater if they accept the therapist's reframing of their interaction, even if it is seen by an objective observer as an inaccurate description of an actual occurrence.

Bray et al. (1985) propose that marriage and family therapists have a responsibility to inform family members about the nature of the procedures they will use, the more probable consequences of these procedures, alternative treatments, and the risks of therapy. They do not, however, view it as realistic to discuss every possible risk. They recommend that family members be informed of those risks they might find important in deciding whether or not to consent to treatment.

Margolin (1982) summarizes marriage and family therapists' need for balance between informed consent and appropriate therapeutic action:

> Thus, even though clients deserve an accurate portrayal of therapy in informed consent procedures, complete objectivity and openness may not be possible. At the same time that families need factual information to make an informed decision about therapy, they also need the therapist's support, encouragement, and optimism for taking this risky step. An overly enthusiastic discussion of alternatives to therapy or overly detailed explanation of the risks of therapy may convince the client that the therapist does not want him or her in therapy. (p. 795)[2]

SUMMARY AND CONCLUSIONS

Therapists must be well versed in the theory and procedures of the therapeutic approaches they advocate. They must also be able to recognize and respond to ethical issues directly affecting the delivery of services and public acceptance of those services. One way of doing so is to have a clear understanding of ethical decision making. Such an understanding allows therapists to critically evaluate and interpret their professional code of ethics. Furthermore, it guides them in being human as well as professional by enabling them to analyze feelings as appropriate or inappropriate bases for ethical behavior.

This chapter has emphasized the importance to therapists of the interaction of their principle ethics and virtue ethics, not as a means of procuring definitive guidelines for professional conduct but, rather, as a way of becoming aware of options for ethical decision making. Promoting ethical practice frequently involves ambiguity, not simple choices between right and wrong, good and bad. Optimal outcomes more often than not contain elements of both extremes. The challenge is not only to identify an ethical position to take but also to consciously apply that position.

We presented and discussed several major areas of ethical inquiry in this chapter. Ethical questions relating to client welfare, confidentiality, and informed consent in marriage and family therapy require special attention. These three issues, although frequently encountered in all therapists' practices, are only a few of the ethical issues therapists must address. Chapter 2 considers some of these other ethical issues traditionally associated with the practice of marriage and family therapy. Chapter 3 looks at a number of contemporary issues with limited precedent for shaping ethical decision making that are particularly challenging for today's marriage and family therapists. Chapter 4 provides an opportunity to gain greater expertise by offering case examples and critiques emanating from the *AAMFT Code of Ethics* (American Association for Marriage and Family Therapy, 1998a).

---

[2]*Note.* From "Ethical and Legal Considerations in Marriage and Family Therapy," by G. Margolin, 1982, *American Psychologist, 7*, pp. 790, 791, 793, 795. Copyright 1982. Reprinted with permission.

Ethical Considerations in the Interactional Context of Marriage and Family Therapy

Marriage and family therapy is not simply a treatment approach. It is a way of understanding human behavior and conceptualizing problems—how symptoms develop and how they are resolved. Marriage and family therapy has traditionally viewed the *transactions between individuals* rather than the individual characteristics of given persons as the primary therapeutic focus (Sluzki, 1978). Even when attention is zeroed in on a single person, that person's actions are analyzed in terms of how they affect and shape the actions of other members of the relationship system as well as how other members' actions reciprocally affect and shape the individual's original actions.

Marriage and family therapy contrasts with an individually oriented view of psychological functioning in adopting a systemic framework that emphasizes interdependence between and among persons, information exchange, and circular feedback mechanisms (Gladding, 1998b). Individuals' symptomatic behaviors are viewed as actively maintained by the interpersonal context in which they currently function. Further, these symptoms are seen as serving a regulating, stabilizing, and communicating function in that context (O'Shea & Jessee, 1982). When observing marital partners' and family members' interactions, marriage and family therapists consider effects rather than intentions. The effects of behaviors on behaviors and the way interpersonal sequences are organized are the primary focus of observation, not the personal motivation of those parties (Sluzki, 1978).

Marriage and family therapists do not deny the existence of individual motivation or intention. Rather, the inferences that can be drawn from assertions about persons' intentions or inner motivations are simply of secondary importance for purposes of diagnosis and treatment. The use of a systemic perspective for understanding and modifying the way couples and families interact requires focusing on certain clinical considerations at the expense of others. Relevant variables are selectively attended to and acted on while lesser regard is paid to other variables.

The selective clinical attention and actions called for in adopting a systemic perspective cause therapists to confront long-standing social, cultural, and religious assumptions. On a sociocultural level, marriage and family therapists are often at odds with North American ideology and legal tradition, which emphasize individual self-sufficiency, value individual responsibility and accountability, and sanction individual rights over group preferences. On a religious level, Judeo-Christian tradition incorporates strong limits for the behavior of couples and families as well as profound assumptions about how marital and family organizations should proceed. Notable examples include "Honor thy father and thy mother" and "Thou shalt not commit adultery."

In proposing to see the couple or family unit as the focus for therapeutic efforts, therapists must consider the many deep-seated beliefs they may be confronting and the professional ethics involved in doing so. These confrontations create conflicts that are concrete manifestations of the clash among the practice of marriage and family therapy, individually oriented theories of psychological disturbance and treatment, and standards (social, cultural, or religious) that espouse individualism and/or prescribe marital and family mores. Some major ethical dilemmas stemming from a therapeutic focus on the couple or family unit as the "client" include issues of problem definition, participation in therapy, the role of the therapist as a direct and active change agent, the use of paradoxical procedures, and agency triangulation.

DEFINING THE PROBLEM

In the typical interaction occurring in the opening phase of most marriage and family therapy efforts, either one member of a dyad or family is presented as the "identified patient" or an individual coming alone requests assistance. The therapist who defines the problem as one of relationship makes an assumption that immediately raises an ethical issue (Fieldsteel, 1982). The therapist has taken on the obligation of imposing a new set of values and beliefs on the individual and/or members of the relationship system. The couple, family, or individual seeks therapeutic assistance for a specific concern; the therapist implicitly or explicitly informs them that they must put aside their beliefs and adopt those of the therapist.

Most therapists assume the right to define clients' presenting problems in terms of their own therapeutic orientation. They make this assumption with the belief that, as owners of greater psychological knowledge and professional qualifications, they have the prerogative to assert themselves without violating their clients' rights. Because most clients accept the perceived role inequality between patient and professional, they tend to accept therapists' assertions as actual fact. Although this redefinition of clients' problems is not limited to marriage and family therapy, it is more dramatic in this kind of therapy (Fieldsteel, 1982). This point is illustrated by certain therapeutic definitions in the treatment of schizophrenic disorders, particularly the premise that weaning from both institutional and family caregiving will stimulate the "identified patient" to develop skills necessary for independent community living. Dincin, Selleck, and Streicker (1978) take a family therapy tack common in the management of schizophrenia in their work with parents of schizophrenic offspring:

> The consistent message of the agency is that the greatest love parents can show . . . is to allow and encourage the child to separate from the parental home. We believe that living at home is usually counterproductive to long-term growth and that psychological damage occurs when parents are unwilling or unable to "let go." (p. 599)

Madanes (1983) demonstrated a similar stance in her work using a Strategic Family Therapy approach:

> Parents typically avoid defining the family hierarchy as one in which they have power over their offspring. They do so because . . . they are afraid to do the wrong thing and harm the youth, because they are afraid they are to blame and wish to do no more harm. . . . The therapist must respond with various counteracting maneuvers to keep the parents in charge. (p. 216)

Terkelsen (1983), in contrast, questions the degree to which family interaction contributes to the etiology of schizophrenia, a position that has dominated contemporary family therapy even in the absence of solid empirical confirmation. He holds that sociogenic models of schizophrenia and their attendant assumptions may be not only incorrect but even harmful to families. He foresees the potential for similar harm to the relationship between families and clinicians and has indicated a need for more research in this area.

Terkelsen describes his own dilemmas encountered in 10 years of work with families having schizophrenic offspring. He was trained in "a tradition that assumed madness to be an interpersonal affair" (p. 192). In early sessions with families, he had attuned himself to abstract from family members' reports only those interactional phenomena representative of parental pathogenicity that would "explain" the individual pathology. Treatment sessions constituted efforts to cloister the identified patient, to separate her or him from the rest of the family, with the belief that it was the family interaction maintaining the patient's pathology. The usual result was a sense of alienation as he found family members unwilling or unable to conform to his theoretical formulations.

Grunebaum (1984), in commenting on Terkelsen's experience, proposes that therapists' first and foremost task is to understand and share the pain of parents and other family members who find themselves in such a predicament. He identifies this understanding as a precondition necessary for family members to open themselves to alternative explanations of their circumstances. Family members focus on the identified patient because they do not know how to cope with the manifestations of mental illness in any other way. Grunebaum offers a case example involving a 25-year-old woman with mild retardation and her parents:

> Now it would appear to many clinicians that these parents needed to be reassured that their daughter was not suicidal, that she was highly unlikely to commit suicide, and that by responding to her slightest threats, they were responding to a manipulation on her part. In fact, the daughter would leave the community placements, wan-

der around for a few hours and then call home. Her parents would then immediately come and get her. Reassurance about suicide had been given before and fallen on deaf ears. . . . The parents then left the room and the staff continued the discussion. Present were the three nurses who had been on call for such cases. They included the two nurses responsible for community placements and one nurse from the ward from which the patient had been discharged. The latter, who knew the patient well, did not believe the patient was suicidal. She stated that she did not think the patient should have been readmitted. The other two nurses were equally clear that they were responsible for the patient and if she expressed suicidal thoughts or feelings, she had to be hospitalized. They were willing to delegate that responsibility to someone else but not to "take a chance." They turned to the ward nurse and asked, "Can you promise she won't kill herself?" (1984, pp. 422–423)

These three nurses, trained mental health professionals, were unwilling to put their roles in interacting with the woman at risk by allowing her to determine her own well-being. Yet they had just suggested that the woman's parents should take that very risk and assume the responsibility of not letting themselves be manipulated by their daughter's threats.

Grunebaum (1984) proposes that families who appear to interfere with attempts to foster the independence of the identified patient are sometimes making positive moral choices, even though these choices involve capitulating to manipulation or intimidation at the hands of the schizophrenic member. It is his supposition that many of these individuals suffer from disruption of fundamental neurobiological processes. Their insistence on being taken care of by their family is often a "default position." Their experiences in the community have been characterized only by impossible challenges, humiliating failures, and rejection by others. Life with their family comes to be seen as the one respite from the continual agony of constant defeat.

Terkelsen (1983) summarizes his own discussion and Grunebaum's comments:

> If, under these circumstances, the family permits the patient to manipulate his or her way back into a dependent status, perhaps the family has come to feel that enough is enough. . . . If, . . . and I speak as a family therapist to family therapists—we lose sight of this sensibility, we will also have lost contact with the very people whose burden we seek to alleviate. (p. 427)

There is little doubt that couples, families, and individual clients present themselves for therapy because they are experiencing a sense of distress and desire to gain relief. They seek professional assistance because they attribute power to therapists on the basis of their clinical knowledge and skills. It is thus critical that therapists recognize the difference between appropriate professional judgment and biased personal power. By redefining presenting problems as relationship rather than individual issues, therapists ask members of relationship systems to sacrifice, at least temporarily, their autonomy. The therapist who imposes a specific problem definition on a relationship system can do so only with the cooperation of the members of that system. There is often a question, however, as to whether this cooperation is obtained under circumstances that could realistically be construed as involving clients' "informed consent."

Marriage and family therapists have an ethical obligation to help the members of a relationship system seeking treatment understand what is involved in the therapist's definition of their presenting concern. Reasons why such a definition is therapeutically beneficial and what it will demand of them should be provided (Fieldsteel, 1982). Couples, families, and individuals may be labeled "resistant" or "poor therapy risks" for many reasons. Therapists have a further ethical obligation to examine how their expectations and biases may lead to fulfillment of these prophecies (Hines & Hare-Mustin, 1978). This statement is not meant to suggest that empirical evidence and clinical experience should be ignored. Characteristics of certain clients, especially as they interact in relationship systems, are highly suggestive of a poor therapeutic prognosis. Rather, therapists must be cognizant of the long-term significance of the definitions they impose and the extent to which these definitions follow from an inability to deal with beliefs and value systems different from their own.

COMPLICATIONS IN CONVENING THERAPY

Most families do not seek therapeutic assistance by specifically requesting relationship therapy. Although this behavior pattern is changing as public awareness of marriage and family therapy as a treatment option increases, typically, one marital partner or family member seeks an appointment. Marriage and family therapists have as a critical task during this initial "presession" contact to promote the assembling or convening of significant familial or extrafamilial members for the upcoming first session. This convening session is especially important because (1) an adequate relationship assessment requires the presence of all significant members of that relationship, (2) convening as a marital dyad or total family symbolically accents the systemic or relationship nature of the presenting problem and its potential treatment, (3) it becomes increasingly more difficult to bring in absent members as therapy progresses, and (4) convening represents the first test of a therapist's ability and commitment to effectively manage relationship resistance (Teismann, 1980).

This desire by marriage and family therapists to engage all significant members of a relationship system raises the ethical issue of voluntary participation (Margolin, 1982). Obviously, coercion of reluctant members by their marital partner, family members, or the therapist is unethical. However, therapists should encourage reluctant members to participate in at least the initial evaluation session to investigate what therapy may entail. Therapists should also pay attention to what may be contributing to this reluctance, for example, general anxiety, insistence on individual treatment for the identified patient, lack of effort on the part of the initiating members or the therapist, denial of any existing problem, or covert maneuvering by the participating member to exclude the reluctant member.

The most common ethical dilemma raised by the convening process involves the therapeutic policy put forth by many marriage and family therapists of refusing treatment unless all significant members of a relationship system become involved. Should willing members seeking assistance go untreated because one individual refuses to participate? This issue is particularly problematic for therapists employed in public agencies where such withholding of services is not only ethically but legally and politically questionable, given that they are tax-supported, legally mandated to serve those requesting help, and often funded on the basis of how many clients they serve (O'Shea & Jessee, 1982).

Napier and Whitaker (1978) refer to the convening process in marriage and family therapy as the "battle for structure," that is, the overt or covert attempt by a couple or family to control and resist change by dictating the terms of therapy. More often than not, the absent member or members are contributors to the symptom being presented and thus crucial to accurate identification of and intervention in the problem. Napier and Whitaker assert that therapists' ability to convene all significant relationship members is a necessary factor in achieving successful treatment outcomes.

O'Shea and Jessee (1982) argue that withholding treatment in the battle for structure does not constitute a refusal to provide mental health services. They describe it instead as an "insistence on providing services appropriate to the nature of the difficulty, and thus, it is a responsible, competent, professional practice" (p. 6). They liken a therapist who withholds treatment to a physician who orders tests and prescribes medication on the basis of what is appropriate to a patient's illness or injury, not on the basis of what the patient wishes.

Teismann (1980) argues against the withholding of treatment in the battle for structure on the grounds that doing so denies services to motivated marital partners and family members and risks the creation of an implicit alliance between the therapist and the nonparticipant. He identifies two types of strategies, short of refusing or withholding services, for involving reluctant members of a relationship system: *enforcing* and *enabling.*

He labels a strategy as enforcing when therapists mobilize referral agents to exert pressure on relationship systems to convene for therapy as a total system. Rather than directly requesting reluctant members to come to therapy, therapists indirectly do so through the referral source. Enforcing, if it is used in an authoritarian manner, can be tantamount to coercion.

Enforcing done in a proactive manner, however, as opposed to a reactive manner, allows for greater freedom of choice to all involved. Enforcing requires preplanning and a prereferral agreement between therapists and referral agents. For example, a physician may make family therapy a prescribed part of medical treatment. Juvenile court services may offer family therapy as an alternative to prosecution or sentencing, with the stipulation of total family participation. Employee assistance program referral sources can similarly provide options such as marital or family therapy to workers whose personal problems affect their jobs. It is recommended that referral agents be present at the initial evaluation session to explain the reasons for the referral and reconfirm the marital partners' or family members' right to refuse treatment. Although potentially negative consequences may result, the understanding that there is an alternative course of action is critical to therapists' ethical practice.

Teismann (1980) explains enabling from two perspectives. In the first method of enabling, the therapist works to increase the attractiveness of attending. Essentially, therapists who use this enabling strategy seek to decrease the threat a reluctant member perceives from participation in therapy and simultaneously to persuade the member that there is something to be gained personally from participating. The therapist must first make contact with the reluctant member, preferably in a face-to-face meeting. To alleviate reluctant members' anxiety about the unknown that therapy represents, therapists might provide a verbal outline of the process, photocopies of relevant articles from popular magazines, or a referral to former clients willing to make themselves available to share their experience in marriage and/or family therapy. Frequently, a simple description of expectations, potential experiences, and probable effects offered directly by the therapist sufficiently relieves many reluctant members' anxiety. In interacting with the reluctant member, the therapist should also seek to increase the attractiveness of attending by appealing to and confirming the individual's strength and potential and focus on his or her position and special importance in the relationship system. For example, the therapist can point out to a reluctant father that his son needs a strong and able male role model that only he can readily offer. Or a wife can be told that her husband needs someone with the courage and tenacity to temporarily, at least, take charge of the disorganization he is experiencing in his life. Such proposals frequently provide reluctant members with a sense of purpose that leads them to participate in therapy.

The second form of enabling involves decreasing the attractiveness of being absent from therapy. Often, reluctant members offer rationalizations for declining to participate in therapy. Therapists can use the members' own reasoning to emphasize the additional problems they potentially foster by not attending. For example, one man believed that his wife had "serious personal problems" that required individual attention. The therapist agreed and added that the husband may have underestimated the seriousness of the problems and that the help of both the husband and other family members would likely prevent the problem from worsening. In another case, a reluctant parent voiced concern that a family should not "hang out its dirty laundry" for all to see (meaning the therapist). The therapist replied with full agreement and went on to note that therapy appeared to be a last resort to stop the trend, because the dirty laundry was already visible at the child's school (truancy) and to the police (marijuana possession).

Wilcoxon and Fenell (1983) suggest a therapist-initiated letter for engaging a nonattending spouse in marital therapy. Given to the participating member as a homework assignment, the letter not only acts as an enabling strategy for engaging the reluctant member but also offers a structured task for the couple to complete in their home. This task facilitates clarification of their intentions regarding their marriage as well as the marital therapy process. Figure 2–1 represents a sample of such a letter.

When enforcing or enabling efforts at convening all significant relationship members have been unsuccessful, therapists can still choose to treat the marital partner or family members who wish therapy rather than offer the ultimatum of

(Date)

Mr. John Jones
111 Smith Street
Anytown, USA 00000

Dear Mr. Jones:

As you may know, your wife, Jill, has requested therapy services for difficulties related to your marriage. However, she has stated that you do not wish to participate in marital therapy sessions.

As a professional marriage therapist, I have an obligation to inform each of you of the possible outcome of marital therapy services to only one spouse. The available research indicates that one-spouse marital therapy has resulted in reported increases in marital stress and dissatisfaction for both spouses in the marriage. On the other hand, many couples have reported that marital therapy which includes both spouses has been helpful in reducing marital stress and enhancing marital satisfaction.

These findings reflect general tendencies in marital research and are not absolute in nature. However, it is important for you and Jill to be informed of potential consequences which might occur through marital therapy in which only your spouse attends. Knowing this information, you may choose a course of action which best suits your intentions.

After careful consideration of this information, I ask that you and Jill discuss your options regarding future therapy services. In this way, all parties will have a clear understanding of one another's intentions regarding your relationship.

As a homework assignment for Jill, I have asked that each of you read this letter and sign in the spaces provided below to verify your understanding of the potential consequences to your relationship by continuing one-spouse marital therapy. If you are interested in joining Jill for marital therapy, in addition to your signature below, please contact my office to indicate your intentions. If not, simply sign below and have Jill return the letter at our next therapy session. I appreciate your cooperation in this matter.

Sincerely,

Therapist X

_____

We verify by our signatures below that we have discussed and understand the potential implications of continued marital therapy with only one spouse in attendance.

Attending Spouse_____ Date_____

Non-Attending Spouse_____ Date_____

Figure 2–1 Letter to Engage a Non–attending Spouse

Note. From "Engaging the Non-attending Spouse in Marital Therapy Through the Use of Therapist-Initiated Written Communication" by A. Wilcoxon and D. Fenell, 1983, *Journal of Marital and Family Therapy, 9,* 199–203. Copyright 1983 by the American Association for Marriage and Family Therapy. Reprinted by permission.

no therapy. Patten, Barnett, and Houlihan (1991) caution in this regard, however, that the decision to conduct individual therapy for relationship issues may result in less than optimal outcomes. They cite empirical findings in the professional literature supporting systemic intervention as opposed to traditional, single-client intervention for relationship issues (Gurman & Kniskern, 1981; Wohlman & Stricker, 1983):

1. Family therapy is at least as effective as individual therapy for most clients' complaints and leads to significantly greater durability of changes made.
2. Specific forms of family therapy are significantly more effective than individual interventions in addressing certain complaints (e.g., structural family therapy in addressing substance abuse).
3. The presence of both parents (particularly noncompliant fathers) in family therapy significantly improves the chances for successful therapeutic outcomes.
4. With marital complaints, therapy with both spouses present is nearly twice as effective as individual therapy with one spouse.
5. Relationship treatment not conducted within a conjoint or systemic format may promote negative therapeutic effects (e.g., problem exacerbation rather than problem resolution).

These findings indicate that change to a relationship, although less than optimal, is still possible if key relations and dynamics are identified and interventions are planned and executed from a systemic perspective. When a couple or family is resistant to convening together, the therapist can focus on individual change within the static relationship system to bring about change (P. Watzlawick, Weakland, & Fish, 1974).

For example, a very motivated 33-year-old woman, after gaining awareness that her unconditional caretaking perpetuated her husband's substance abuse, agreed to spend the night in a motel whenever he came home drunk. She left him a note explaining that she had been hurting him with her caretaking, that she wanted to stop doing so, and that she would return the next day. This strategy effectively interrupted a basic interaction sequence symbolic of the system's dysfunction. It further redefined the problem as residing in the wife and thus enabled her to initiate change in herself and simultaneously to introduce change into the relationship.

In clarifying whether or not a marital partner or particular family member needs to participate in therapy efforts, therapists must be able to identify the extent to which each member of the relationship will be expected to participate. For example, some members may attend sessions in the role of observer simply to learn enough about the therapeutic process so that they will not impede its progress. Therapists with a strong preference for convening all members of a relationship system should inform persons seeking assistance that other therapists do not necessarily share this view (Margolin, 1982). A list of competent referral sources should then be made available. The ethical issue is not so much a question of whether therapists have a definition of what is conducive to optimal psychological functioning as whether they can acknowledge their professional views and be willing to be flexible in offering options to persons seeking help.

THE THERAPIST AS AGENT FOR CHANGE

All couples and families enter therapy with their own idiosyncratic styles of communicating with implicit patterns of meaning and relationship rules embedded in what can appear to an outsider as unimportant, insignificant, conventional interactions (F. Watzlawick, Beavin, & Jackson, 1967). Therapists beginning therapy with a couple or family are not privy to the special importance many of these interactions have within the relationship system. This lack of familiarity puts therapists at an immediate disadvantage, not unlike that of a new member seeking entrance into a secret organization without benefit of the required password (O'Shea & Jessee, 1982). The therapist must decipher the relationship's communication style and gain access to the meanings and rules employed by the members of the system. Only then can the therapist accurately assess, intervene with, and ultimately facilitate change within the couple or family.

The importance of marriage and family therapists' functioning in an active, directive manner has been clearly stressed by a majority of family therapy approaches (M. P. Nichols & Schwartz, 2001). To be effective, marriage and family therapists need to be influential. Although therapists' influence and power are a recognized part of individually oriented therapies, the means by which marriage and family therapists achieve such a position characteristically stands in ready contrast. Marriage and family therapists recognize the necessity of assuming power. Wachtel (1979), in describing the movement from an individual to a marriage and family therapy perspective in her practice, suggests that the more reflective and insight-oriented stance common in individual therapy is influential only because of the traditional nature of the therapeutic contract and is conferred largely as a result of clients' seeking to alleviate personally felt distress. She found that it was difficult to share more control over the content and direction of sessions with family members because her position with them was of less authority and centrality than with an individual client. The importance of assuming an active position of power to gain influence became readily evident as her experience with couples and families increased.

Most marriage and family therapists are direct about their role as agents of change. For example, family theorist and therapist Salvador Minuchin expressly describes his own Structural Family Therapy as a "therapy of action." Minuchin (1974) writes that families are organized around the specific functions of their members. The power of the therapist is considered to be the primary means of bringing about change: "Change is seen as occurring through the process of the therapist's affiliation with the family and his [or her] restructuring of the family in a carefully planned way, so as to transform dysfunctional transactional patterns"

(p. 91). Other marriage and family theorists and therapists convey similar messages, as is evident from the titles of their major writings (e.g., Virginia Satir's *Peoplemaking*, Jay Haley's *Changing Families*).

Corey, Corey, and Callanan (1998) raise several ethical considerations about the power- and action-oriented approach advocated by most marriage and family therapists:

- Should therapists impose their control on couples and families?
- Should the primary responsibility for defining how change should occur rest with the therapist as opposed to the individual marital partners or family members?

The power of the therapist is a vital component in marriage and family therapy and in itself is not inherently a negative force. It is when that power is misused that ethical misconduct comes into question. The major potential for misuse of a therapist's power is generally evidenced when it encourages a client's dependence. Some therapists establish their power and influence in a marital or family relationship system at the cost of reducing the adaptive autonomy of system members. Fieldsteel (1982) has pinpointed the ethical dilemma confronting therapists who assume an inordinate share of responsibility for change in relationship systems: "There is a danger that the role of the therapist as a more active agent for change may shift the responsibility for the direction of change from the patient to the therapist" (p. 262).

A related issue involves marital partners and family members who attribute to therapists magical qualities to effect changes in their marital or family functioning. This mystification process tends to intensify clients' dependence and reduces clients' ability to assert their rights in the therapy process (Hare-Mustin, Marecek, Kaplan, & Liss-Levinson, 1979). Stensrud and Stensrud (1981) have proposed that some therapists teach persons to be powerless instead of teaching them to trust themselves. They describe this powerlessness as a "learned state of generalized helplessness in which clients (a) believe they are unable to have an impact on their environment, and (b) need some external force to intercede on their behalf" (p. 300). Stensrud and Stensrud caution that clients can develop self-fulfilling prophecies, whereby expectations of powerlessness evolve into regular experiences of powerlessness. They urge therapists to relate to clients in ways that maintain client self-responsibility—by regularly challenging clients to actively participate throughout the entire therapeutic process. Consider the following therapist's actions:

> A marriage and family therapist in a family services agency devoted many more hours to her position than she was expected to and overtaxed herself by taking on an inordinately large caseload. She frequently let sessions run overtime and encouraged clients to call her at home at any time. Couples and families were maintained much longer in therapy with her than her colleagues. Her former clients had a recidivism rate that was significantly higher than that of her colleagues' clients.

This therapist clearly has an obligation to examine the ways she established and misused her power base to keep clients so dependent.

Wachtel (1979) proposes that as the therapist's role is demystified, clients become more active. In discussing therapists' actions in this regard, she suggests that they openly and explicitly communicate their preferences. This explicit communication leaves clients knowing more clearly what is going on and where they stand. They may still feel pressure and anxiety in response to a therapist's expectations, but they are potentially in a much better position to differentiate their own preferences from those of the therapist. Fieldsteel (1982) affirms the power of marriage and family therapists as agents of change. She urges that they not delude themselves into thinking that therapy is an egalitarian, democratic relationship, especially at the outset. Rather, Fieldsteel calls for this egalitarian relationship to be a goal toward which therapists should work, much as this relationship becomes one of the major goals of child rearing.

Another major ethical dilemma confronting marriage and family therapists is occasioned by the priorities they set: Relationship change is primary, and individual change, although possibly equal, is more likely secondary. O'Shea and Jessee (1982) suggest that therapists confront a central, ethical dilemma when they accept the notion that the symptomatic individual serves a homeostatic, protective, stabilizing function in his or her relationship system. They raise the question of how much distress or risk one member should tolerate for the sake of long-term benefit to the greater marital or family relationship system.

It has been repeatedly recognized that many couples and families manifest a rigid scapegoating pattern toward one or more members and select specific members to bear the brunt of systemic discomfort. Therapists attempting to intervene can expect symptoms to escalate accordingly. To counteract this rigid homeostatic balance, it may be necessary to increase individual distress to a crisis level to facilitate a fundamental change in how the relationship system operates (Hoffman, 1981). O'Shea and Jessee (1982) assert, however:

> The therapist who attempts to precipitate a structural shift in the system by tolerating or deliberately intensifying the distress in the system does so in opposition to the medical ethic and cultural expectation that helping professionals should relieve rather than prolong suffering. Clearly, a physician, despite the use of anesthetics, often inflicts immediate pain on the patient in the process of restoring a more global and long-term health. In systems therapy, however, the distress must at times be amplified before the family is motivated to change its dysfunctional avoidance behavior patterns. The therapist must, as it were, overcome the self-anesthetizing effect of the family's dysfunctional interactions by getting the family to experience the full thrust of anxiety and tension. (p. 12)

Several examples can serve to illustrate this ethical dilemma. The common and preferred legal response in cases of child abuse is to protect the victim by removing the abused or abusing member from the home. Marriage and family therapists are likely to view the abusing and/or abused member as actively fulfilling and maintaining a stabilizing, homeostatic function within the family system. From this therapeutic perspective, optimal treatment calls for the inclusion of the whole family, without the removal of the abused and/or abusing member, for the sake of a more important and likely lasting change: a change in the basic family functioning. The potential risks inherent in such a path are obvious (Kemp, 1998).

The presenting of destructive behaviors such as suicidal potential make treatment decisions even more precarious. Therapists who emphasize the importance of having a primary impact on the relationship system face a trade-off between conservatively safeguarding the suicidal client through immediate hospitalization, thus reinforcing the system's scapegoating process, and risking self-harm to the identified patient by denying the necessity of hospitalization in favor of outpatient treatment of the entire relationship system (Langsley & Kaplan, 1968). Marriage and family therapists prepared to accept this risk to the identified patient for the sake of a more meaningful and important relationship change should also be prepared to receive censure by individually oriented colleagues. However, precautions such as including all members of a relationship system in the evaluation and treatment of an identified patient exhibiting suicidal symptomatology may reveal that what appears as a mild suicidal risk when seen in isolation is actually more serious viewed within the context of a lethal relationship system (Richman, 1979).

Less dramatic ethical confrontations in this regard frequently occur within the confines of the therapy hour when marriage and family therapists encourage direct expression of negative feelings and evoke and escalate confrontations among members of relationship systems. Minuchin and Fishman (1981) offer a representative case example in which the therapist purposely uses mocking and inflammatory language to describe the static behavior patterns into which a married couple has fallen and the unspoken attitudes they hold about the relationship, thereby provoking them to articulate their problems:

> **[Wife]:** In the last five years I said to myself the only way not to be hurt is to try to be more like him, and I did. I tried to be like that. I tried to say, "I don't care. I don't need anybody." But I don't want to be like that anymore! I really want to be like I used to be, and then I found that I couldn't, that I have really changed. It's hard when somebody reaches out to you. The normal thing would be to respond. I find that I'm not quite able to do that. It happened before: he touched me and I don't know what to do.

> **Minuchin:** That is saying again that you want to sit on your shit!

> > The therapist's pressure produces a response in the wife. . . . ("That is saying that you want to sit on your shit") is not a challenge to the dynamics of the wife but rather a reiteration of the demand for a transformation of the spouse subsystem.

> **[Wife]:** But then he'll stick a knife in my back. (To husband.) If I drop my defenses when you feel like it, you'll withdraw and you'll start throwing little needles at me, and I don't know when it's going to happen.

> **Minuchin:** Milt, she is throwing you a lot of nonsense. She is saying, "Love me, but don't do it because I will kick you in the balls." She is saying to you, "Hold me," and pushing you away. Don't listen to her.

> **[Wife]:** Is that true? Is that what I have been doing all these years?

> **[Husband]:** Well, I felt that before, too.

[Wife]: Why didn't you tell me that?

[Husband]: I'm not a talker, but you push yourself away. I know in the past I felt you preferred to be unhappy.

[Wife]: I don't know what to say. I don't know what to do next. I don't want to be unhappy like this.

[Husband]: Well, the problem in the past—why I didn't tell you things—was because you get angry when you're criticized. Any kind of criticism on what you are or what you do gets a very strong reaction from you.

> The insistence of the therapist on stressing the system in the direction of changing the family members' perspective vis-à-vis each other produces a transformation of the spouse subsystem. The wife now takes the patient position, not as an isolating technique, but as a request for help. This change in the wife is complemented by the response of the husband.[1]

The degree to which potential risk to an identified patient or to other members should be tolerated for the sake of improved functioning in the total system also raises the problem of deterioration effects in marriage and family therapy. Gurman and Kniskern (1978) identify an important distinction between *deterioration* and *relapse*. They define deterioration as a negative change or escalation of symptoms during treatment. Relapse, in contrast, is a negative change occurring between posttreatment and follow-up in the direction of the pretreatment level of functioning. Thus, the risk of deterioration poses a more serious ethical dilemma for therapists than relapse, because relapse suggests that treatment was ineffective but not necessarily harmful (O'Shea & Jessee, 1982).

Although deterioration effects are a concern for all therapists, individually oriented as well as marriage and family, the latter incur a greater obligation because the scope of their responsibility must be expanded to include multiple members of a relationship system. Furthermore, marriage and family therapists' position as active, directive agents of change increases the likelihood that they could precipitate deterioration. The review by Gurman and Kniskern (1978) of research on deterioration in marriage and family therapy clearly indicates this possibility. They identify a therapist's levels of functioning as dominant among those factors that could contribute to deterioration effects. They state:

> In summary, the available evidence points to a composite picture of deterioration in marital-family therapy being facilitated by a therapist with poor relationship skills who directly attacks "loaded" issues and family members' defenses very early in treatment, fails to intervene in or interpret intra-family confrontation in ongoing treatment, and does little to structure and guide the opening of therapy or to support family members. Such a style is even more likely to be counter-therapeutic with patients who have weak ego-defenses or feel threatened by the nature or very fact of being in treatment. . . . [T]he therapist seems clearly to occupy a central role in most negative treatment outcomes. (p. 14)

---

[1]*Note.* From *Family Therapy Techniques* (pp. 188–189) by S. Minuchin and H. C. Fishman, 1981, Cambridge, MA: Harvard University Press. Reprinted by permission.

Attempting to alter the predominant mode of interaction within a couple or family, promoting change in one member of the system, or seeking change in an area of the total relationship's functioning is likely to evoke new or increased distress or dysfunction in the system, at least temporarily. Therapists who encourage the enhancing of distress and intensification of symptomatology within the therapy hour must be concerned with the continued occurrence of these actions when the session ends. Marital partners or other family members may suffer from embarrassment, anxiety, and loss of respect in the eyes of their mate or other members of the system when they are pressured to make disclosures in session (Hines & Hare-Mustin, 1978). Angry outbursts and strong feelings may be provoked in marital and family sessions; if they are not resolved in the session, they can lead to increased hostility and bitterness.

Therapists who do not address this possibility run the risk of promoting premature termination from therapy, not to mention marital and family dissolution (Mace, 1976). Hines and Hare-Mustin (1978) suggest "inoculation" to guard against potential marital or family disintegration resulting from the direct facilitation of increased stress in the system; that is, therapists should alert members during the initial stage of therapy to the stresses that can likely be expected in resolving their problems. This procedure also alleviates much of the ethical conflict occasioned in therapists' escalating symptomatology and distress in the interest of potential outcome. Therapists, however, must ultimately learn to weigh the safety and immediate well-being of individual members of a relationship system against effective treatment strategies for the overall system. Boszormenyi-Nagy (1974) identify this ultimate goal as "a restoration of balanced reciprocity of fairness" in marriage and family relationships.

PARADOXICAL PROCEDURES

According to Haley (1976), two major types of interventions are possible in marriage and family therapy: (1) interventions in which therapists direct clients with the expectation of compliance and (2) interventions in which therapists direct clients with the expectation of noncompliance. The latter type of intervention specifically suggests the purpose of a paradoxical procedure: The couple or family changes by rebellion or noncompliance. For example, Hoffman (1981) cites the case of a wife whose constant jealous questioning of her husband only reinforced the husband's reticence toward her. This reticence in turn reinforced her jealousy. A paradoxical procedure was employed to disrupt this destructive sequence of behavior. The wife was directed by the therapist to redouble her jealous questioning. The expected result was achieved when the wife rebelled against the task, which led to a resolution of the presenting problem.

The use of paradox has been a central and frequently controversial topic in marriage and family therapy (Keim, 2000). Proposing that a couple or family continue dysfunctional patterns of behavior with the suggestion that these interactional sequences have a benevolent function constitutes a therapeutic intervention that seems contradictory to the couple's or family's expressed desire for problem resolution. Paradoxical procedures are designed to block or change dysfunctional sequences by using indirect and seemingly illogical means. They "encourage" rather than attack symptoms and objectionable behaviors. They are used instead of direct attempts to introduce change when it is assumed that the couple or family cannot or will not comply with the therapist's advice or persuasion (M. P. Nichols & Schwartz, 2001). Paradoxical procedures can thus require selective disclosure to marital partners and family members by the therapist.

Regardless of their therapeutic orientation, all therapists selectively highlight certain facts and ignore, deemphasize, or avoid others. Although such behaviors constitute selective disclosure (or distortion) of information, the ethical issue that arises involves whether or not therapists are actually deceiving or harming clients (O'Shea & Jessee, 1982). Haley (1976) proposes that ethical prescriptions requiring therapists to disclose to clients everything they sense about them are naive and that therapists who are unwilling to draw a boundary between themselves and their clients and insist on sharing all not only risk failure but also risk doing harm. Haley maintains that the marriage and family therapist should function as a trained expert, not an equal partner.

In contrast, others (Fisher, Anderson, & Jones, 1981; O'Shea & Jessee, 1982) have stated that paradoxical procedures are effective precisely because they do represent the actual situation the couple or family is experiencing. These procedures embody each marital partner's or family member's phenomenological experience of being involved in a dysfunctional system. P. Watzlawick et al. (1974) are quite explicit in this respect in defining change that occurs through *reframing*. They identify this process as an attempt to alter "the conceptual and/or emotional setting or viewpoint in relation to which a situation is experienced and to place it in another frame which fits the facts of the same concrete situation equally well or even better, thereby changing its entire meaning" (p. 95). In other words, the meaning attributed to the situation is altered or redefined, and therefore, its consequences change as well. Such a paradoxical directive brings covert patterns of interaction to the surface; the family responds by choosing either to continue or stop the problematic sequences. In either case, the problematic style of interaction now falls within the family's control.

Some paradoxical procedures, however, are directives given to clients without an explicit explanation or rationale. Hoffman (1981), for instance, describes a therapist's telling a depressed wife to become more subservient to her husband. Not surprisingly, the wife rebelled in defiance of the therapist's directive. According to Hoffman, the paradoxical directive unbalanced a dysfunctional complementary balance in the marital relationship, which then became more functionally symmetrical. Previously, the husband and wife had been balanced in a relationship in which he was one-up and she was one-down. By requesting that she put herself even further down (which she had been doing almost daily), the therapist provoked a rebellion, and the couple was able to establish a relationship characterized by greater equality. In discussing this case illustration offered by Hoffman, however, M. P. Nichols and Schwartz (2001) question why this outcome should have resulted as Hoffman presented it. Why did the couple not simply reestablish the same complementary relationship?

This question raises an added ethical concern: Therapists can never be sure how a relationship system will absorb and respond to a given intervention (Selvini-Palazzoli, Boscolo, Cecchin, & Prata, 1978). O'Shea and Jessee (1982) propose that out of the wide range of possible responses, the use of paradoxical procedures in particular "comes close to being based on faith" (p. 11). Gurman (1978) further asserts that paradoxical reframing and interactional tasks used without explanation or education may at times prolong the couple's or family's dependence on the therapist, preventing the relationship system from developing its own coping mechanisms. O'Shea and Jessee (1982) indicate the appropriateness of paradoxical procedures that are factual from the couple's or family's frame of reference and truly systemic—procedures that include and affect all members of the relationship system and that employ language or metaphor in harmony with members' subjective experience of their marital or family life. With such paradoxical procedures, the couple or family will more likely identify with the task, change in a more functional manner, and experience the change under their own direction (Selvini-Palazzoli et al., 1978).

Fraser (1984) makes a strong case for the use of paradox as a primary procedure in marriage and family therapy. In doing so, he states:

> For a therapist to look for "a paradox," and then decide whether to do or not to do the supposed paradoxical action is a contradiction in itself. Seeing an action as paradoxical implies that it is contradictory to an accepted body of beliefs. If these beliefs are the guiding premises of the therapist, then choosing to perform the perceived paradoxical action implies the need to question or alter the very principles which guide the therapist's action. System-based intervention should ideally evolve from consistent employment of system theory and a subsequent description of system patterns. Consequent choice of therapeutic action should thus make "sense" to the therapist from within the theory. (p. 370)

Paradoxical procedures are clearly unethical if they are used as a spur-of-the-moment ploy based on limited data. Ethical, responsible use of a paradox requires a therapist's competency and experience gained from a thorough understanding of the role of the symptom within the relationship system, a theoretical/therapeutic approach conducive to the use of paradox, and sufficient clinical supervision and continuing consultation (Fisher, Anderson, & Jones, 1981). For example, Madanes (1980) has concluded that certain steps are necessary for the use of paradoxical procedures in alleviating relevant psychiatric problems in children. She describes a specific six-step process emanating from a Strategic Family Therapy orientation:

1. The problem should be clearly defined and specific goals set.
2. The therapist should conceptualize the problem (to him- or herself only) as one in which the child is protecting one or both parents or a relative through his or her symptoms. (This conceptualization depends on the therapist's theoretical orientation.)

3. The therapist must plan to intervene in offering the parents a directive that they will give their child; other family members potentially participate in auxiliary ways. The directive must include a prescription:
   a. To have the problem.
   b. To pretend to have the problem.
   c. To pretend to help the parents.
4. The directive should be practiced in the session before being carried out at home.
5. In the session following the one in which the directive is given, the therapist must obtain a report on the performance of the directive and then continue to prescribe the same directive.
6. As change occurs and the presenting problem behavior begins to disappear, the therapist should drop the issue of the symptom and terminate therapy or begin dealing with other problem behaviors in the same or different ways. Credit should always be given to the parents for their child's improvement.

Madanes' six-step process encompasses a clear, conceptual rationale for the choice of, as well as the content of, a paradoxical procedure ethically considered and employed (Rohrbaugh, Tennen, Press, & White, 1981).

AGENCY TRIANGULATION

Triangulation as used in the marriage and family therapy literature has been defined as "the process by which a dyadic emotional system encompasses a third system member for the purpose of maintaining or reestablishing homeostatic balance" (Sauber, L'Abate, & Weeks, 1985, p. 172). Bowen (1978) asserts that two-person emotional systems become unstable in the face of conflict and stabilize by forming three-person systems or triangles. In general, the concept of triangulation has been used to describe interactional problems within the context of a marital or family system or within the therapy setting itself; for example, a therapist may become "triangulated" in a conflict between two marital partners, as in this case illustration:

> A couple with increasing marital difficulties presented themselves for therapy. Immense hostility was clearly evident between the pair almost immediately when the wife voiced her opinion that therapy "was a waste of time." The husband remained after the conclusion of the initial evaluation session to complain about his wife's unwillingness to "try." The therapist, a relative novice, felt good that the husband was open in confiding further information and was reinforced in fantasizing about rescuing the couple—or at least the husband, who was more open and accepting of the therapist's assistance.

The emerging triangulation process will be destructive to all three paired relationships: the therapist and wife, the wife and husband, and the therapist and

Figure 2–2 Triangulation Involving the Therapist

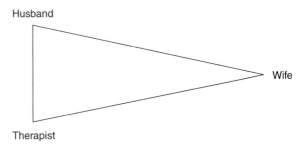

husband as well. Triangulation here represents two close and two distant poles (Figure 2–2). Sympathizing with the husband alienates the wife even further. It also makes it less likely that the husband will do anything to directly work out his complaints with his wife. Although this triangulation process may give the therapist the illusion of being close to the husband, it is at best a false intimacy. Defending the wife offers no better solution. That alternative only moves the therapist from the husband to the wife and widens any gulf between them. As long as the triangulation continues, personal and direct one-to-one interactions cannot develop between the couple.

Even though marriage and family therapy involves individuals who display symptoms in the larger context of their marital or family system, couples and families themselves are part of a larger social-cultural system. The concept of triangulation likewise can extend beyond the boundaries of the couple–therapist or family–therapist relationship system (Gladding, 2001). This is a fact often neglected by marriage and family therapists, even though they regularly address triangulation in the context of the couple or family relationship system. Unwittingly, many therapists become part of dysfunctional triangles created by the very sources that refer couples and families to them for help (Carl & Jurkovic, 1983). The ethical dilemmas presented can be most troublesome. Bowen (1978) addresses one part of this problem:

> In periods of very high tension, a system will triangle in more and more outsiders. A common example is a family in great stress that uses the triangle system to involve neighbors, schools, police, clinics and a spectrum of outside people as participants in the family problem. The family thus reduces the tension within the inner family, and it can actually create a situation in which the family tension is being fought out by outside people. (p. 479)

Therapists allowing themselves to become triangulated in such situations show little regard for the self-reliance of couples and families and their ability to grapple effectively with their own difficulties, an approach that raises the ethical issue of encouraging unnecessary client dependency.

Therapists must avoid assuming a superior position in relation to couples and families by excessively helping them cope with service systems. Hoffman and Long (1969) assert that therapists who act as "social brokers" or "advocates" in expertly mediating couple–agency or family–agency relations may become "too omnipotent a figure" in the couple's or family's affairs. Carl and Jurkovic (1983) offer a case illustration in this regard:

> Ms. James, a single parent whose 6-year-old was not participating at school . . . complained that the teacher did not understand her daughter, Angela, and even feared that the teacher was physically abusing her. With [the] mother's permission, the therapist visited the teacher at school where he learned that Angela was behaving in a listless and immature manner in the classroom. It was questionable whether she would be promoted to the next grade. Also of serious concern to the teacher was that Angela's mother did not have confidence in her teaching, although she had more than fifteen years' experience. All of the ingredients for an agency triangle were present. Both mother and teacher were complaining to the therapist about the other and clearly seeking a coalition with him. To avoid becoming part of the problem, the therapist "detriangulated" himself in a subsequent session in which he met with both the family and the teacher in the child's classroom. The strategy simply was to encourage mother and teacher to talk directly to one another and to agree on a plan for helping Angela. After a number of angry false starts in which Ms. James and the teacher attempted to speak through Angela first and then the therapist, which he stopped, they were able to make eye contact and to air their differences directly to each other. In the process, the mother learned that the teacher had Angela's best interests at heart, and the teacher came to some understanding of the mother's fears and stressful life situation. With additional prompting by the therapist, they clarified how each could appropriately help Angela in view of their different roles and also ways in which they could collaborate. (pp. 448–449)

The most respectful and productive stance by the therapist was to encourage Ms. James to deal directly with her daughter's teacher. Therapists can normally leave this task to a couple or family themselves or, if necessary, coach marital partners or family members on how to assert themselves when seeking services as well as how to protect themselves from unwarranted agency intrusions. By creating a context in which Ms. James was able to work out her concerns with the teacher in a one-to-one manner, the therapist not only aided her in resolving the current problems but also prepared her to better cope with similar future difficulties.

Bowen's (1978) comments emphasize triangulation initiated by family members. Carl and Jurkovic (1983) also address the actions of helping agents who inadvertently triangulate families. They propose the addition of a corollary to Bowen's axiom concerning the instability of two-person system conflicts: "The relationship between an agency and a family is unstable under stress and will tend to form a three-party system, often with another agency, to diffuse the stress" (p. 442). Such interagency conflicts frequently develop after difficulty arises between an agency and a couple or family (as client). Some third agency is then pulled in as an attempt to divert the original conflict. Hoffman and Long (1969) term this predicament a *systems dilemma*, describing it as follows:

> These systems seldom act collaboratively, and are more often than not in conflict with one another. As a result, a person may be caught in a paradoxical situation in a family which is in turn caught in paradoxical situations within the systems designed to help the family or person. (p. 241)

Couples and families enter therapy in many ways: referrals from family service agencies, schools, clergy, and courts; cross-referrals within mental health centers; and self-referrals. The kind of "paradoxical situation" alluded to by Hoffman and Long frequently develops when an agency refers a couple or family to another agency (e.g., a marriage and family therapist). The couple or family may have challenged the agency to be more helpful or act differently in some manner, or the agency may have felt the need for support services to carry out its functions, perhaps because its own efforts had been unsuccessful. The nature of this referral process can have a powerful effect on the therapeutic process and outcome (Selvini-Palazzoli et al., 1978).

Family service agencies, for example, may refer a family for therapy to "fix up" parents so that they can become "fit" to regain custody of their children. A court may refer a couple to therapy as a required precursor to potential divorce proceedings. Schools regularly refer children because they are acting out or doing poorly in the classroom in the belief that problems in their home environment constitute primary contributors. Carl and Jurkovic (1983) suggest that all of these situations have a common denominator: an "agenda" from the referral source that figures prominently in the development of agency triangulation. They illustrate this issue in discussing day treatment program referrals:

> Another intrasystem dilemma occurs when a day program in a mental health center refers a client family for treatment in the hope of making the client a "better-adjusted part" of the day program. Since many systems' interventions rely on reframing problems and inducing change in ways that make clients less dependent upon supporting agencies, conflictual program goals provide ample opportunity for a triangle. The day program wants a more cooperative "member." The systems therapist wants no "member" at all. The family can stay the same so that all concerned remain involved. These different "agendas" derive, of course, from the guiding philosophy, rules, procedures, and objectives of the agency. As stress develops between the agency and its charges (whether they be day program participants in a mental health center, students in the classroom, parolees, etc.), the agency may direct the client and his or her family to some other agency—often a therapist. The therapist's orientation frequently conflicts with that of the agency, and unless the two collaborate effectively, an agency triangle can result. (p. 444)[2]

In accepting referrals from agency sources, therapists are immediately faced with an ethical dilemma. The couple or family as client is entitled to expect certain things from the therapist, particularly to put their interests above all others' interest. Couples and families as clients derive intrinsic benefits from the assurance that the therapist has an undivided commitment to helping them. All these circumstances change when a third party enters the picture. The quality of the relationship between the therapist and a couple or family is irrevocably altered once the self-contained structure of that relationship is no longer intact, which inevitably is the case when agency referrals incorporate agendas emanating from

[2]*Note.* From "Agency triangles: Problems in agency–family relationships," by D. Carl and G. J. Jurkovic, 1983, *Family Process, 22*, pp. 444, 448–449. Copyright 1983. Reprinted with permission.

the referral source. Although the therapist–couple or therapist–family relationship is not necessarily invalidated and the couple or family will not stop receiving adequate services, the nature of the relationship is different.

Bourne (1982) summarizes the ethical dilemma in a biblical allusion: "No [one] can serve two masters." This principle is at the heart of the ethical issue therapists must confront in addressing agency triangulation. Carl and Jurkovic (1983) propose a number of guidelines for therapists to prevent agency triangulation:

1. *Therapists must include themselves and other nonfamily members, agencies, and institutions as parts of the presenting problem needing treatment.* The unit of treatment thus becomes the larger "suprasystem" incorporating the couple-therapist-agency or family-therapist-agency.

2. *The identification of these parts requires an ecological assessment that extends beyond the boundaries of the immediate couple or family relationship system to include other interacting systems.* (Note: Carl and Jurkovic propose that this assessment is a point where potential agency triangulation can be detected.)

3. *After conducting such an assessment, therapists' further strategies should incorporate cooperation with relevant agencies.* Successful collaboration that does not limit therapists' ability to maneuver calls for them to skillfully join with other helping agents without taking a one-up position and without implying that these agents are part of the unit of treatment. These collaborative efforts should begin early in the therapy process, preferably at the point of referral.

4. *Although it is best for couples and families to handle problematic agency contacts themselves, there will be times when therapists may wish to block or redirect subversive agency actions, especially if the couple or family is under significant stress.* Particularly at a time when publicly funded services are declining, therapists who work with couples and families receiving such services will have to resolve any quandary created by encouraging these relationship systems to be more self-reliant in the face of harsh economic realities.

5. *Therapists should always be aware of their limited power to actually control other agency interventions and policies.* At minimum, adverse agency actions can often be reframed in the interest of the couple or family. Or inventive therapists can seek out other facets of the agency operation that might offer therapeutic opportunities. For example, in special education settings, the development and updating of Individualized Education Plans require that parents meet regularly with school staff. If not invited, therapists can ask to attend these meetings to offer input as a part of family therapy efforts.

6. *Therapists must perceive themselves as active, not passive, participants in any agency triangulation process.* They may even be the primary precipitators of such processes. Therapists who refer couples or families for other services—psychological testing, medication, tutoring, and so on—must be clear

about the purpose of the referral. Is it to help the couple or family or to alleviate the therapist's own discomfort? If the former, then it is necessary to coordinate therapeutic efforts with other service providers and to reach agreement on areas of responsibility and control. Therapists' discomfort, on the other hand, is best addressed through consultation with a clinical supervisor or colleague.

SUMMARY AND CONCLUSIONS

Marriage and family therapy, as opposed to individually oriented psychotherapy, considers the couple or family as an active, whole unit. This view represents a conceptual change in therapeutic thinking: Relationship systems are seen as rule-governed, organic wholes rather than as collections of individuals interacting according to the dictates of their separate personalities. This point of view—thinking about relationship systems instead of individuals—requires that special ethical as well as theoretical dilemmas be confronted. Solutions to such dilemmas cannot necessarily be derived from individually oriented psychotherapeutic experiences.

Marriage and family therapists are faced with the challenge of coping with a plethora of thorny ethical issues that impinge on their work; they must deal with far more potential ethical conflicts in their clinical decision making than most individually oriented therapists because of the increasingly complex nature of their work (Morrison, Layton, & Newman, 1982). The ethical concerns addressed in this chapter raise questions that need to be answered by marriage and family therapists:

- Can therapists automatically assume the right to define couples' and families' presenting problems in terms of their own therapeutic orientation?
- How much concerted effort (or pressure) can therapists exert in convening all significant familial or extrafamilial members for therapy sessions?
- Should willing individual marital partners or several family members seeking assistance go untreated because one individual refuses to participate?
- Should therapists impose their control on couples and families? If so, to what extent should they impose it in seeking change in the relationship system?
- How much intrasystem stress should be engendered or allowed to materialize in the pursuit of change?
- What are the ethical implications inherent in employing paradoxical procedures?
- How can the impact of working with couples and families within the larger context of service agency impingements be ethically pursued?

Abroms (1978) asserts that ethical behavior on the part of the therapist requires more than good intentions based on personal bias and subjectivity. If therapeutic ethics involves a determination of what therapists ought to do to provide maximum benefit for the greatest number of persons, then marriage and family therapy as a treatment of relationship systems instead of individuals in relative isolation appears to be the most ethical and integrated of approaches (O'Shea & Jessee, 1982).

3

Contemporary Ethical Concerns

The importance accorded to ethical considerations by marriage and family therapists is an acknowledgment of the responsibilities inherent in the promise and process of being a health care professional. Should these responsibilities be fulfilled with less than the greatest of care, persons may suffer. For example, the actions of a therapist may determine whether a battered spouse is able to secure a safe haven or is forced to return to a potentially lethal environment. Likewise, they may determine whether a child abused through incest is accurately identified and given treatment or is left to go on suffering (Pope & Vasquez, 1999).

Few marriage and family therapists take these responsibilities lightly. Few set aside their concerns about a violent family or abused child between sessions. The very human ability to be moved by the pain and struggles of other human beings and the special sense of responsibility felt when the descriptor *client* is attached to these persons can feel like a tremendous weight at times. This weight is particularly heavy when a therapist is operating with a sense of uncertainty about what direction professional help should take.

The scope of ethical issues faced by marriage and family therapists is ever widening. This increase reflects a growing awareness among practitioners that their resources for decision making when faced with ethical concerns are limited. One element of this ambiguity is due to the general, nonspecific nature of the ethical guidelines provided by professional organizations (Green & Hansen, 1989). Another major contributor, however, is the lack of precedent for handling a number of contemporary ethical issues.

This chapter considers several of these contemporary ethical issues and offers positions currently advocated in the professional literature to address them. These issues include (a) acquired immune deficiency syndrome (AIDS) and the therapist's duty to protect, (b) dual relationships, (c) the *Diagnostic and Statistical Manual of Mental Disorders (DSM)* (American Psychiatric Association,

1980, 1987, 1994) and its use in marriage and family therapy, (d) the treatment context for domestic violence, (e) managed mental health care participation, (f) the employment of technology in therapeutic work, (g) dealing with issues of diversity, and (h) publications.

AIDS AND THE DUTY TO PROTECT

Acquired immune deficiency syndrome (AIDS), caused by the human immunodeficiency virus (HIV), is one of the most serious epidemics of this century. "Persons with HIV-positive status, compared to those with other diseases, tend to be seriously stigmatized in contemporary society" (Huber, 1996, p. 55). Researchers do not know how long it may take to find a cure for or an immunization against the disease, or even whether it will be possible to do so. Unlike other sexually transmitted diseases that typically produce visible lesions or blisters, the HIV infection frequently produces no apparent symptoms for months or even years. Thus, many HIV-positive persons are not diagnosed until they exhibit evidence of AIDS through the onset of unusual infections or cancers. Studies suggest that within 7 years after infection, 30 percent of HIV-infected persons will develop AIDS and another 40 percent will have other illnesses associated with HIV infection (Allen & Curran, 1988). As of 1999, the Centers for Disease Control reported that 733,374 AIDS cases had been reported in the United States, with 430,441 total deaths from AIDS.

The spread of AIDS has given rise to questions regarding the limits of confidentiality within the therapeutic relationship. Do marriage and family therapists have a duty to warn a potential victim when a client discloses that she or he has tested HIV-positive and has an identifiable sexual or needle-sharing partner who is unaware of the infection? A study by Kegeles, Catania, and Coates (1988) found that 12 percent of homosexual or bisexual men being tested for HIV said that they would not tell their primary sexual partners if they tested positive, and 27 percent said that they would not contact their previous partners. Almost one fifth of the sample reported that they had been engaging in high-risk sexual relations with nonprimary sexual partners. In a similarly focused study (Elias, 1988), approximately 35 percent of single, sexually active heterosexual males stated that they had lied about past sexual behaviors to female partners. Furthermore, 20 percent reported that they would lie about being HIV-positive. Thus, it cannot be assumed that HIV-positive individuals will be open and honest with others about their sexual habits or infectious state.

Gray and Harding (1988) have reviewed the limits of confidentiality with HIV-positive clients in light of contemporary ethical and legal practices. They advocate procedures to increase clients' responsibility for informing their sexual partners. Should a client refuse to do so, however, Gray and Harding propose that the therapist take action to protect potential victims. Responding to Gray and Harding, Kain (1988) emphasizes the needs of the HIV-positive client in asserting that the therapist's primary responsibility is to help clients deal with issues such as abandonment, rejection, and loneliness, as well as, perhaps, reasons for not informing their partners of their condition.

Kimberly, Serovich, and Greene (1995), in examining the reasons HIV-positive women decided to disclose their HIV status to family members, found a six-step framework for understanding the process of deciding. Each step included a proposed counseling intervention:

1. Accepting and adjusting to the diagnosis (counseling intervention—information and education)
2. Evaluating personal disclosure skills (counseling intervention—emphasis on pros, cons, difficulties, and strategies of disclosure)
3. Taking inventory of who should be told (counseling intervention—highlighting the issue of family boundaries)
4. Evaluating potential recipients' circumstances, such as health, age (counseling intervention—addressing feelings of guilt, anxiety, and sadness for telling some family members and not others; developing plans for disclosure)
5. Anticipating reactions of recipients, such as anger, support (counseling intervention—clarification of possible reactions)
6. Motivation for disclosure, such as desire for support, obligation (counseling intervention—defining personal needs and identifying family members most likely to meet those needs)

While disclosing to family members may not be the same as disclosing to sexual partners, Kimberly et. al. (1995) provide a model that may be used in understanding the HIV-positive client and how the client can be helped in making a decision regarding disclosure. This process has important ethical implications that can be translated to both family and society.

A more legally oriented ethical approach to dealing with HIV-positive clients is taken by Melton (1988) and G. D. Erickson (1998), who have proposed that the ethical dilemma involving therapists' obligations to their clients and third parties relative to the AIDS epidemic bears an apparent resemblance to the question regarding the duty to protect third parties from violent behavior by a client believed to be dangerous. The question of what to do in such situations was answered in the *Tarasoff* decision (*Tarasoff v. Regents of the University of California*, 1976). According to the *Tarasoff* decision, confidentiality within psychotherapy is to be valued highly, but it should never be regarded as absolute:

> A therapist is not to be encouraged routinely to reveal such threats since such disclosures could seriously disrupt the patient's relationship with the therapist and with the person threatened. On the contrary, the therapist's obligations to the patient require that he [or she] not disclose a confidence unless necessary to avert danger to others, and even then that he [or she] do so discreetly and in a fashion that preserves the privacy of the patient to the fullest extent compatible with the prevention of a threatened danger. (p. 337)

Schlossberger and Hecker (1996) make recommendations based on the *Tarasoff* ruling and go further in addressing the ethics of disclosure. According to Schlossberger and Hecker (1996), when there is "no legal duty to warn . . . and the information is not expressly protected from disclosure by law, therapists must struggle with the ethical aspects of disclosure" (p. 34). Among the relevant ethical factors therapists must consider are "respecting autonomy, maintaining integrity, benefiting clients, and fostering responsibility" (p. 35).

Lamb, Clark, Drumheller, Frizzell, and Surrey (1989) and Knapp and Vande-Creek (1990) encourage therapists dealing with confidentiality in an AIDS-related therapeutic situation to employ criteria resulting from *Tarasoff:* (a) the presence of a fiduciary relationship, (b) the identifiability of a victim, and (c) the foreseeability of danger. They then offer further recommendations about taking appropriate action; these are discussed next.

A Fiduciary Relationship

The first criterion is whether a fiduciary relationship—a relationship of special trust—is present between therapist and client. This relationship is inherent when a therapist agrees to work with a client. In doing so, the therapist assumes special responsibilities for the client's behavior that are not a part of everyday relationships.

Identifiability

According to the second criterion, the duty to protect extends only to identifiable victims and not to all persons whom a client could potentially harm. With HIV-positive clients, only identifiable sexual or needle-sharing partners such as spouses or monogamous lovers would be included. The duty to protect would not necessarily extend to casual sexual or drug partners unless they were readily identifiable.

Foreseeability

According to the third criterion, the danger must be foreseeable before the duty to protect is invoked. Knapp and VandeCreek (1990) identify the issue of foreseeability as being the most difficult to ascertain for therapists working with HIV-positive clients. Research has not defined all the risk factors involved in HIV transmission. With this in mind, Knapp and VandeCreek have offered direction in classifying low-risk behaviors that do not appear to give rise to a duty to protect, high-risk behaviors that clearly give rise to such a duty, and intermediate-risk behaviors for which the duty to protect may be present but the foreseeability of danger to others is less apparent.

Low-Risk Behaviors
Current evidence suggests that transmission of HIV infection cannot occur through food, tears, urine, or insect bites. Isolated reports of transmission through kissing, human bites, or tatoos have been made but not confirmed (Castro et al., 1988). Thus, casual nonsexual contact and simply living together should be considered low-risk behaviors and should not be the basis for any breach of confidentiality.

High-Risk Behaviors

Unprotected sexual contacts and sharing of needles are the primary modes of HIV transmission. Knapp and VandeCreek (1990) propose that therapists assess the presence of high-risk behaviors in the context of establishing and enhancing a therapeutic relationship, because a primary goal of psychotherapeutic efforts is to empower clients to be responsible for their own well-being and that of another.

Intermediate-Risk Behaviors

Knapp and VandeCreek identify the greatest difficulty in determining foreseeability as coming from HIV-positive clients who engage in "safe sex" but do not inform their partners of their infection. Although barrier contraceptives can reduce the risk of infection ("Condoms for Prevention," 1988), maximum protection occurs only when both partners know the risks (Kaplan, Sager, & Schiavi, 1986).

> The vulnerable partner has to make the final decision whether to continue sexual relations, engage in only completely safe sex such as parallel or mutual masturbation, or discontinue the sexual relationship completely. A unilateral decision to protect the partner through use of barrier contraceptives by a person who has already shown a lack of adequate concern in concealing the fact of the infection cannot be viewed as an acceptable resolution. This would deny the partner's right to decide what risks are acceptable. (Knapp & VandeCreek, 1990, p. 163)

Taking Appropriate Action

"A therapist should not be encouraged routinely to reveal such threats . . . unless such disclosures are necessary to avert danger to others" (*Tarasoff v. Regents of the University of California*, 1976). Less intrusive means of diffusing risks before making an exception to confidentiality should always be considered. Depending on the level of risk for transmission, clients' voluntary disclosure of their HIV status (and the processes that go with deciding on disclosure as outlined by Kimberly et al., 1995) should be a more or less immediate focus of therapy. In making a final determination, factors such as the client's credibility, perceived degree of concern for the identifiable partner, and overall sense of social responsibility must be taken into account (Silva, Leong, & Weinstock, 1989). In some situations, however, certain clients may act in ways that meet the criteria of a duty-to-protect case. Clinical experience with physically assaultive clients provides direction for making a necessary disclosure.

DUAL RELATIONSHIPS

Dual relationships are those in which marriage and family therapists assume two roles simultaneously or sequentially with a person or persons engaging their professional assistance (Herlihy & Corey, 1992). These roles may both be professional, such as therapist and supervisor, or a combination of professional and nonprofessional, such as therapist and friend or therapist and lover. "Dual relationships are problematic because they are (a) so pervasive, (b) difficult to recognize at times, (c) sometimes unavoidable, (d) sometimes harmful but may also be beneficial, and (e) the subject of conflicting advice" (B. Pearson & Piazza, 1997, p. 91). In addition, dual relationships may cause a therapist to lose impartiality as well as impair the therapist's professional judgment (McGrath, Browning, Martinek, Beck, & Culkin, 1995). Therefore, the ethical codes of virtually every mental health profession prohibit or warn of the dangers of relationships involving conflicts of interest. For example, Standard 1.2 of the *AAMFT Code of Ethics* (American Association for Marriage and Family Therapy, 2001) states:

> Marriage and family therapists are aware of their influential position with respect to clients, and they avoid exploiting the trust and dependency of such persons. Therapists, therefore, make every effort to avoid dual relationships with clients that could impair their professional judgment or increase the risk of exploitation. When a dual relationship cannot be avoided, therapists take appropriate professional precautions to ensure judgment is not impaired and no exploitation occurs. Examples of such dual relationships include, but are not limited to, business or close personal relationships with clients. Sexual intimacy with clients is prohibited. Sexual intimacy with former clients for two years following the termination of therapy is prohibited.

Despite this seemingly clear sanction, one of the most frequent ethical violation reviewed by ethics committees involves dual relationships, particularly sexual intimacy between therapist and client (Ethics Committee of the American Psychological Association, 1988), a phenomenon a former president of the American Psychological Association termed a "national disgrace" for his profession (Cummings, 1985).

Not all dual relationships can be avoided, however, nor as mentioned previously, are they all necessarily harmful (Kitchener, 1988; Koocher & Keith-Spiegel, 1998). In a survey of rural physicians, Purtilo and Sorrel (1986) have identified the overlapping of professional and personal relationships as a major ethical issue that is consistently being faced. Professionals who live and work in small or rural communities may be unable to avoid blending roles with clients. For instance, when there is only one marriage and family therapist in a community with only one grocery store, unless the grocer and his or her family go without treatment when treatment is needed or the therapist travels an inordinate distance to purchase groceries, a dual relationship may be almost impossible to avoid.

Where then is the line between those relationships that are clearly unethical and those that are acceptable if handled with due care and caution? Kitchener (1988) offers three guidelines based on role theory that can be used to differentiate between dual role relationships that will probably lead to unethical behavior and those that are less likely to be problematic: (a) compatibility of expectations, (b) divergence of obligations, and (c) power/prestige differential. Appropriate action emanating from the contemporary literature on this topic is suggested within the context these guidelines create.

Compatibility of Expectations

As the difference between the expectations of the therapist and client increases, the potential for misunderstanding and harm increases.

> Jacob has seen Dr. P. in her private practice for weekly sessions over the past 2 months following his divorce. During the most recent sessions, Jacob has asked questions about Dr. P.'s personal relationships. Dr. P. senses that Jacob is interested in pursuing a social relationship outside of therapy with her and raises the issue with him. Jacob confirms her suspicion. Dr. P. states that it would be unethical for her to pursue such a relationship with him.

Herlihy and Corey (1992) and Welfel (1998) stress the importance of clear expectations regarding the therapeutic relationship. They note that when therapists' expectations are unclear, clients' expectations are likely to be even more unclear. A survey by Borys (1988) suggests that the majority of therapists avoid social relationships with clients. The intimacy of the therapeutic relationship, however, can readily lead clients to expect a "special type of friendship" and to invite their therapists to participate in their lives outside of therapy. When such incompatible expectations are allowed to continue, the potential increases for dual relationships that promote compromising or unethical behaviors.

In the preceding case illustration, Dr. P. was very clear in her expectations for the therapeutic relationship once she suspected that her client may not have been. In the future, she might proactively forestall such potential problems by including a clear policy on social relationships as part of the informed consent information provided to clients when they enter therapy.

Divergence of Obligations

As the divergence between the obligations imposed by different roles increases, the potential for divided loyalties and loss of objectivity increases.

> Karen is a single parent experiencing significant difficulties with her two teenage daughters. She requests that Dr. K., her neighbor, see her and her daughters in family therapy. Dr. K. declines Karen's request and suggests several marriage and family therapists in the community whom she might contact. Karen implores Dr. K. to reconsider, maintaining that her daughters are more likely to agree to therapy with him because they know and like him.

The professional literature contains many cautions regarding seeing friends and acquaintances in therapy. Koocher and Keith-Spiegel (1998) put forth the position that conducting therapy with friends or acquaintances as clients potentially involves mixed allegiances and misinterpretation of motives. Likewise, Kitchener and Harding (1990) propose that therapeutic relationships and friendships differ in function and purpose. Herlihy and Corey (1992) characterize the roles of therapist and friend as generally divergent:

> Because being a counselor as well as a friend to the same person creates a dual relationship, there is always the possibility that one of these relationships will be

compromised. It may be difficult for the counselor to switch roles from friend to professional and to confront the client for fear of damaging the friendship. It may also be problematic for clients, who may hesitate to talk about deeper struggles for fear that their counselor/friend will lose respect for them. Counselors who are tempted to enter a counseling relationship with a friend might do well to ask themselves whether they are willing to risk losing the friendship (p. 137).

In the preceding case illustration, the primary obligation of Dr. K. is to promote the welfare of Karen and her daughters. It would be very difficult for Dr. K. to carry out his professional responsibilities to Karen and her daughters as clients while simultaneously attempting to maintain his relationship to them as friends.

Power/Prestige Differential

As the difference in power and prestige increases between the roles of therapist and client, the potential likewise increases for exploitation on the part of the therapist and an inability on the part of clients to remain objective about their own best interests.

A marriage and family therapist terminates therapy with a couple deciding to amicably divorce. The divorce becomes final one month after the last session is held. The therapist and former wife happen to meet at the party of a mutual acquaintance shortly thereafter. An intimate relationship between them ensues. When questioned by a colleague, the therapist states that the relationship was instituted after termination of therapy.

Ryder and Hepworth (1990) posit that differences in power and status, not specifically dual relationships, encourage exploitation. Kitchener (1992) describes this differential:

Acknowledged or not, therapists because of their prestige and personal characteristics and because of transference issues often have considerable power over their clients. This power does not necessarily end with the end of therapy and may limit a former client's ability to make clear, rational, and autonomous choices about entering into a relationship with a former therapist (p. 147).

The marriage and family therapist in the preceding case illustration would be acting in violation of the *AAMFT Code of Ethics* Standard 1.2, which prohibits sexual intimacy with former clients for 2 years following termination of therapy. Perhaps of more consequence, however, is the fundamental ethical principle that, many scholars argue, applies in such situations (Beauchamp & Childress, 1994; Kitchener, 1984b; Stadler, 1986): Agreeing to work with persons in therapy implies a contract to help them. To harm those whom one has agreed to help undermines the foundation of the profession (Kitchener, 1984b).

When the therapeutic relationship ends, does the therapeutic contract end? Evidence is accruing that sexual relationships with former clients have harmful consequences for most clients (Vasquez, 1991). Although few would suggest that therapeutic contracts ought to carry a lifelong obligation, it is equally implausible to suggest that the formal ending of a contract should entitle a therapist to engage in activities with a former client that will undo the benefits that therapy promoted. The fundamental ethical principles of helping clients and doing no harm to clients would be violated (Kitchener, 1992). Marriage and family therapists are cautioned to proceed with particular care should they ever consider entering into an intimate relationship with a former client even 2 years or more after the termination of therapy.

Taking Appropriate Action

The potential for a dual relationship to promote harm increases to the extent that therapist–client expectations become increasingly incompatible, role obligations increasingly divergent, and the power differential enlarges. In contrast, when therapist–client expectations are clearly defined and compatible, role obligations convergent, and the power differential small, there is much less danger that harm will ensue (B. Pearson & Piazza, 1997).

Marriage and family therapists have a special obligation to promote the welfare of the clients with whom they work. Consequently, even in relationships in which there is minimal danger of harm, they are ethically bound to exercise due care. Therapists exercising due care would be sensitive to potential role conflicts and work to minimize their impact should they occur; thus, marriage and family therapists must be cognizant of the potential for harm in any dual relationship, even when they determine that the potential for harm is minimal.

THE *DIAGNOSTIC AND STATISTICAL MANUAL OF MENTAL DISORDERS* AND ITS USE IN MARRIAGE AND FAMILY THERAPY

The *Diagnostic and Statistical Manual of Mental Disorders* (4th edition), known as the DSM-IV (American Psychiatric Association, 1994), and its immediate predecessors have had an enormous impact on the mental health field. The DSM "made available for the first time, diagnostic criteria that people could agree upon, based on descriptive features, rather than speculations about etiology" (Wylie, 1995, p. 25). Thus, the DSM nomenclature has come to be accepted as the common standard of language for most mental health researchers and clinicians. Indeed, most marital and family therapy educational programs train their students in the DSM if for no other reason than to be able to communicate with other professional specialists (Denton, Patterson, & Van Meir, 1997).

"Like many other classification systems, the *DSM* focuses on 'mental' disturbance that occurs *within* individuals, and relational conditions are outside this domain" (Simola, Parker, & Froese, 1999, pp. 225–226). Therefore, the use of the DSM raises several ethical concerns for marriage and family therapists. Denton

(1989) discusses four of these concerns: (a) incompatibility of orientations, (b) the stigma of diagnosis, (c) misrepresentation of diagnoses, and (d) competence to diagnose.

Incompatibility of Orientations

Although there are many approaches to the practice of marriage and family therapy, nearly all share a common basis in general systems theory, that is, an emphasis on the interactions between and among persons. In contrast, the DSM has as its basis an emphasis on the individualistic notion of "mental disorder."

Thus, no matter what may be occurring in persons' family or social contexts, any distress they experience is assumed by the DSM to be due to a dysfunction within them as individuals. This assumption is in direct conflict with marriage and family therapists' belief that such distress is due to dysfunction within the entire family system. Stevens-Smith (1997a) expresses the dilemma this conflict creates for marriage and family therapists. She notes that marriage and family therapists who work within an agency or interagency structure, or who are dependent in other ways for third-party payments requiring DSM diagnoses, frequently find themselves in an ethical conflict over how a presenting problem is to be conceptualized or defined. This conflict is particularly acute for family systems "purists," such as Haley (1987), who believe that individual and family approaches are inherently incompatible. A therapist who conceptualizes a child's behavior as only one link in a circular chain of interactions with other members of the family will have to diagnose an individual "mental disorder" if insurance reimbursement is expected.

A second incompatibility between the DSM and marriage and family therapy lies in where they locate a presenting problem. The DSM concentrates on an "identified patient"; marriage and family therapy focuses on shared responsibility, that is, the concept that family problems involve everyone in the family. When they enter family therapy, however, most family members understand and communicate their presenting concerns only from their own perspective, the same individually oriented approach taken by the DSM toward mental disorders. Children typically complain, "My father is too strict" or "My mother is unfair," while their parents in contrast protest, "She just won't listen" or "He's so self-centered." Again, if DSM diagnosis is required in the workplace or if insurance reimbursement is desired, marriage and family therapists will probably find themselves supporting family members' view that there is a scapegoat on whom to focus their complaints.

Denton (1990) has observed that, in practice, most experienced marriage and family therapists generally recognize that a "pure" family systems approach is too reductionistic for understanding complex problems. A number of marriage and family therapy writers have advocated a reconceptualization of the "systems" perspective that incorporates the interaction among different systems levels. Coyne and Anderson (1989), for example, have proposed that marriage and family therapists give due consideration in their practice to the interaction between the health care delivery system and family system as well as to the interaction between the individual system and family system. Melito (1988), M. P. Nichols (1987a, 1987b), and R. Schwartz (1987) have all stressed the role of the individual within the family system.

Marriage and family therapists whose conceptualization of systems theory includes more than just the family system and incorporates the individual, family, and larger social systems as different system levels interacting with each other will likely find greater compatibility between their views and the DSM. Family systems "purists," on the other hand, will be hard put to harmoniously handle this incompatibility in their explanations to family members. They might need to reconsider the ethics of seeking insurance reimbursement as well as their place of employment if the DSM is a requirement in the workplace.

The Stigma of Diagnosis

Marriage and family therapists need to be acutely aware of how DSM diagnoses might be perceived by family members as well as used by others. DSM diagnoses can serve useful therapeutic purposes. Providing an individual diagnosis (e.g., Major Depression) for one family member may alleviate criticism of that member, because her or his social withdrawal can be seen as "illness" and not "noncaring" (Denton, 1989). Seeing a family member as experiencing an "illness" can also facilitate family members' participation in family therapy; they will be less likely to feel blamed when a family systems conceptualization of their circumstances is further offered (C. M. Anderson, Reiss, & Hogarty, 1986).

Although a DSM diagnosis may reduce unhelpful blaming, it can also mistakenly be perceived as an excuse from taking responsibility. For example, a physically abusive spouse might seek to excuse his or her violent attacks by claiming to have "Intermittent Explosive Disorder" (Denton, 1989). Individual diagnoses can also induce persons who are diagnosed to become resigned to certain conditions; these persons can subsequently begin to despair and/or their actions become self-fulfilling prophecies (Corey, Corey, & Callanan, 1998). Such diagnoses can also damage family members' perceptions of the individuals and family interactions with them.

Another ethical quandary arises over the potential uses to which the information in a diagnosis might be put. The revelation on a job application, for example, that applicants have received mental health treatment or a diagnosis of mental disorder might preclude their being considered for a position because of the continuing stigma attached by many to mental and emotional disorders and their treatment. A diagnosis might be used to block clients in custody hearings or other legal proceedings or might prevent them from obtaining insurance.

Denton (1989) recommends that the most ethical way to approach the potential problems imposed by the stigma of diagnosis is to discuss the risks directly with clients and their family members. Marriage and family therapists should address, as part of their informed consent procedures at the beginning of therapy, both the benefits and the risks of releasing diagnostic codes.

Misrepresentation of Diagnoses

Many marriage and family therapists are relatively ignorant of the rationale and workings of health insurance coverage. One insurance company executive has addressed psychiatrists on this point:

> A . . . problem is the willingness of some psychiatrists to put an insurance-acceptable diagnosis on a condition that is not considered a covered diagnosis. Examples of this category include the problems of living: floundering marriages, trouble raising children. . . . We can understand why a person would go to an analyst to get rid of such unpleasant or unwanted human behavior . . . but insurance was never intended to cover this type of 'non-psychiatric problem.'
>
> Medical insurance should only be asked to cover medical mental disorders. Insurance is meant to pay for the sick, not the discontented who are seeking an improved lifestyle. We need your help in differentiating between those who have mental disorders and those who simply have problems. (Guillette, 1979, p. 32)

This lack of knowledge can lead to what Packer (1988) has termed "insurance diagnosis" (p. 19). Pressure from both clients and therapists themselves to obtain health insurance reimbursement increases the possibility that a diagnosis will be misrepresented and that a DSM diagnosis will be applied when none of the family members actually meets the criteria.

For example, Meg and Kevin have been married for 21 years. The past 4 years have seen their two children enter young adulthood and progressively separate from the home. Meg and Kevin are once again a couple alone and find themselves somewhat aimless. They seek the assistance of a marriage and family therapist to renew the "spark" they once had. Neither reports experiencing any major distress.

All the diagnostic classifications in the DSM have criteria that must be met in order for a specific diagnosis to be given. Diagnosis of a reimbursable mental disorder might be difficult to justify in Meg and Kevin's case. A nonreimbursable V Code classification (e.g., V62.89 Phase of Life Problem or Other Life Circumstance Problem) appears more apt. Yet some marriage and family therapists and clients do not see misrepresentation of diagnosis as a serious concern. They justify "insurance diagnosis" by noting that premiums have been paid and therefore reimbursement is deserved—despite the fact that the client may not have a covered condition (Denton, 1989, 1996).

Obviously, in many cases, one or more family members can clearly meet the criteria for a DSM diagnosis of mental disorder. When none do, the offer of a misrepresented "insurance diagnosis" constitutes fraud (Packer, 1988). The comments of Wilson (1985) apply just as much to marriage and family therapists as they do to physicians:

> The falsification of records or case reports to protect the patient's access to treatment undermines the credibility of the profession itself as well as the individual physician. . . . It is also unethical for the physician to collude with the patient to obtain, fraudulently, insurance reimbursement to which the patient is not entitled. (p. 63)

Most clients find it relatively easy to find a clinician who will provide a coverable diagnosis when it is not justified (Packer, 1988). Marriage and family therapists have a perhaps economically difficult but still ethically clear obligation not to misrepresent diagnoses.

Competence to Diagnose

Standard 3.6 of the *AAMFT Code of Ethics* (American Association for Marriage and Family Therapy, 2001) states:

> Marriage and family therapists do not diagnose, treat, or advise on problems outside the recognized boundaries of their competence.

According to a research study in 1999 by William Doherty, only 13 percent of the 352,535 mental health professionals in the United States "were specifically taught marital therapy as a part of their professional training" (K. S. Peterson, 1999, p. D2). Thus, most marriage and family therapists received their training in other disciplines (e.g., counseling, psychiatry, psychology, social work) in which the study of psychopathology and the use of the DSM were required portions of the training program. As a consequence, assessing individual symptoms and assigning DSM diagnoses are fully within their realm of competence. However, clinical membership in the American Association for Marriage and Family Therapy (AAMFT) does not guarantee this competence. Clinical membership requires 9 semester hours or 12 quarter hours of "Human Development" coursework. Although this coursework can and often does include instruction in psychopathology or abnormal behavior, these subjects are not automatically required; several other options are available (American Association for Marriage and Family Therapy, 1990).

Denton (1989, 1996) asserts marriage and family therapists' responsibility to be able to recognize and appreciate the significance of serious individual symptoms and syndromes so that they can be dealt with or the person appropriately referred. For example, Hirschfeld and Goodwin (1988) report that approximately 15 percent of persons who are seriously depressed may eventually commit suicide. Similarly, D. W. Black, Yates, and Andreasen (1988) cite an increased rate of death from suicide and accidents for persons with schizophrenia.

Marriage and family therapists who have not had training in psychopathology or abnormal behavior and the use of the DSM should therefore make every effort to increase their level of competence by acquiring these skills and knowledge. They will then be better equipped to address some of the possible ethical challenges occasioned by the interaction of the DSM and marriage and family therapy.

THE TREATMENT CONTEXT FOR DOMESTIC VIOLENCE

A growing awareness of the prevalence of abuse and violence in families began in the 1970s. Before that time, "intimate partnerships" were "believed to emanate from higher virtues like romantic love, affection, or a natural unity of interest" and thus were "exempt from considerations of justice" and ethics (Jory, Anderson, & Greer, 1997, p. 401). However, contextual therapists brought the concept of justice with its ethical implications into the field of marriage and family therapy especially through the writings of Boszormenyi-Nagy (e.g., Boszormenyi-Nagy & Sparks, 1973). The focus in this approach was the intergenerational nature of justice where justice was defined as the "long-term preservation of an oscillating balance among family members, whereby the basic interests of each are taken into account by the others in a way that is fair from a multilateral perspective" (Boszormenyi-Nagy & Ulrich, 1981, p. 160).

Nevertheless, most traditional treatment programs addressing domestic violence conceptualize the problem in terms of victims and victimizers. In most shelters for battered women, particularly those staffed by formerly abused women or women identifying with a firm feminist position, the separation of victim and victimizer is strongly advocated. In cases of child abuse, separation has likewise frequently been the norm mandated by protective service agencies, which prohibit contact between perpetrators and abused children (Shapiro, 1986).

Marriage and family therapists are increasingly being asked to intervene in cases of domestic violence (Bograd & Mederos, 1999; Eisikovits, Edleson, Guttmann, & Sela-Amit, 1991). Yet family therapy is at odds with traditional approaches in its determination that problems exist not in a single individual but between and among family members. This basic tenet of family therapy has been interpreted by many to imply that neutrality on the part of the therapist should be the norm in cases of domestic violence.

> Violence can draw the therapist into taking charge of others' lives, a role that does not enhance the process of therapy. Violence also draws in helping systems to protect the "innocent" and "powerless" members of the family. Such a band-aid approach does not begin to resolve the issues which lead to violence. Quite to the contrary, it seems to perpetuate them. (Combrinck-Graham, 1986, p. 69)

The clinical debate around what type of approach is most appropriate in cases of domestic violence has tended to be narrowly limiting, couched in terms that argue for one approach at the exclusion of another (Eisikovits et al., 1991).

To address this controversy, the use of ethical judgment by mental health professionals must be an integral part of treatment planning. Employing a guiding concept of neutrality has much to offer from an ethical standpoint. It ensures that all family members are treated as self-reliant, responsible individuals whose autonomy is recognized and respected (Willbach, 1989). However, Willbach also asserts that ethically aware marriage and family therapists actively utilize their perception of who is right and who is wrong in a family in which domestic violence is present. In doing so he notes:

> An ethically aware approach to psychotherapy points to the flexible utilization of different techniques and modalities. Because family therapy developed in opposition to a tradition of individual therapy, the limits of its appropriate use have rarely been explored, as if to do so would run the danger of conceding valuable ground to the enemy. In fact, when a potentially actively violent abuser and the abused person are in the same family, family therapy may be generally contraindicated. (p. 50)

It is valuable to recognize that Willbach employs the qualifying phrase *may be* in considering contraindications for family therapy in cases of domestic violence. Family therapy certainly has a function in the treatment of domestic violence. Willbach affirms this function, but with due consideration given to four interrelated clinical positions as a means of ensuring ethical practice:

1. The overt goal of therapy should be the complete cessation of intrafamily violence whenever it is present.
2. When intrafamily violence is the therapeutic focus, neutrality should not be a primary therapeutic procedure.
3. Therapists should use their ethical judgment in asserting individual responsibility for violent behavior.
4. Family therapy is contraindicated unless the violent family member is able to contract for nonviolence (i.e., formally agree not to use violence).

The Cessation of Violence

Among the behaviors that can contribute to harm, marriage and family therapists ought to especially strive toward eliminating violence and make a priority of eliminating it whenever it is present. Willbach makes a strong statement for this position:

> Violence is qualitatively different from other actions, in that the harm it causes is not capable of being controlled by the person harmed ("sticks and stones . . . "). Secondly, violence, in its most extreme manifestation, results in death, a most unquestionable harm. Lesser degrees of violence have a greater probability of leading to death, either accidentally or as the result of willful escalation, than does the infliction of emotional suffering. Thirdly, physical injury is a particularly blatant and obvious type of harm. For these reasons, violence is an especially condemned form of harm in our broader community's moral standards as embodied in the legal system (1989, p. 47).

The Contraindication of Neutrality

Marriage and family therapists are trained to highlight the interactive nature of family members' behaviors. For example, Sluzki (1978) states:

> The positions of "victim" and "victimizer" are the result of a punctuation in the sequence of events, that is, of an arbitrary decision on the part of one or both participants about who leads and who follows. . . . Except perhaps in the very early stages of parent–child relationships, there is no totally passive, victim-like position in interpersonal situations within small systems. All members are contributing parties to the interactional sequences, the behavior of each member being induced and in turn inducing the other. At the most, in certain circumstances one of the actors *appears* to be the victim (pp. 377–378).

Although this "powers of the weak" perspective (Janeway, 1980, p. 4) is quite valid, Willbach (1989) proposes that it is a conceptualization oversimplified in its application to cases of domestic violence. Violence signals a breakdown in the very bedrock of family life, a family's willingness to take responsibility for the safety of its members, cautions Mathias (1986), who quotes family therapist Betty Carter's admonishment: "To stop domestic violence you must intervene in the system in a dramatic way. . . . Putting the abuser in jail may not be therapy, but data shows it gets his attention and stops the violence" (p. 27).

Willbach (1989) calls for a more pragmatic model of systems theory in working with cases of domestic violence. This model assumes family relationships to be interactive, but unequally so as a consequence of gender and age power differentials in that

> it takes a certain amount of money to feed, clothe and house young children. . . . The victim is constrained by these material limitations in reacting to the activity of the victimizer. Coercive power is based, to a large extent, on the effective control of material realities. (pp. 45–46)

Thus, advocacy rather than neutrality must be employed to equalize interactions before a pure systems approach is considered.

Individual Responsibility

Some marriage and family therapists have addressed the importance of taking responsibility in cases of domestic violence, but with the proviso that neither partner should be blamed: "Violence invariably translates into victim and aggressor, right and wrong, good and bad. . . . To transcend this viewpoint is a difficult task for the therapist, yet to be fully effective, it is necessary to do so" (Shapiro, 1984, p. 118). "If the worker did think the husband to blame, she or he would not be able to help him. One of the basic tenets for therapeutic practice is freedom from judgements" (Geller & Wasserstrom, 1984, p. 39).

Willbach (1989) identifies such a position as illogical:

> If the batterer is found responsible for the violence, then, unless there are mitigating factors, such as diminished mental capacity, he [or she] is also to blame for the violence. In the normal case, it is contradictory to affirm the former and deny the latter, even if these therapists feel it would be less emotionally problematic to work with blameless perpetrators. (p. 49)

According to Bograd (1986), cases of domestic violence demand that marriage and family therapists "take unapologetically value-laden stands" (p. 47). He further states:

> Most family therapy training discourages us from advocating for just one member of a couple. . . . But when there is violence, what is good for the system is often not good for the more victimized partner. For such couples, the most crucial intervention may be giving a strong, unequivocal message about who is responsible for the violence. (p. 47)

Krugman (1986) likewise recommends that family therapists "give a clear message that the hitter is responsible for [the] hitting and that rationalizations like 'she [or he] provoked me' or 'I couldn't help it' are not acceptable" (p. 42).

In cases of mutual violence, therapists' judgments of responsibility can be critical. Women's violent behavior in most cases of domestic violence is reactive and defensive (Kemp, 1998; Saunders, 1988). The differences between aggressive and defensive behaviors needs to be accentuated and the aggressor held accountable (Willbach, 1989).

Contracting for Nonviolence

A number of marriage and family therapists have recommended family or conjoint sessions without qualification in cases of domestic violence (Madonna, 1986; W. C. Nichols, 1986; Weidman, 1986) or have offered only vague criteria as contraindications, such as the presence of "severe violence" (Bagarozzi & Giddings, 1983, p. 11; Gelles & Maynard, 1987, p. 272). Willbach (1989) strongly advocates the ability to contract for nonviolence as an essential criterion to employ in determining treatment modality. He likens such a contract to those used in cases of suicidal behavior in which the possible consequences are so ethically unacceptable that the therapist simply has to oppose it and intervene to stop it.

Bograd (1986) likewise recommends contracting for nonviolence in cases of domestic violence. Adherence to the contract establishes a safe context that enables systemic interventions to proceed more readily; the consequences of violating it constitute a powerful therapeutic intervention. Clinical evidence suggests that abusive men require strong external pressures as motivation to seek treatment. The threat by their partner to leave or the partner's actually leaving has been viewed as the most effective pressure in this regard (Roberts, 1996; Saunders, 1984). If, however, a person is unable to contract or adhere to contract terms, then individual issues become primary and must be dealt with before relationship or contextual issues (Willbach, 1989).

MANAGED MENTAL HEALTH CARE

Until the 1980s, health care was generally financed by traditional major medical insurance. In such a fee-for-service delivery system, the provider of services submitted a bill to the insurance company and was paid for services rendered after a deductible was paid by the consumer. However, the traditional insurance system has given way to other, managed health care and mental health care delivery systems. A revolution has transformed the delivery of mental health services in the private sector. Fueled by sweeping cost-containment efforts, this revolution has brushed aside almost all resistance from the various mental health care provider professions. It is called *managed mental health care (MMHC)* and involves a service delivery system that is driven more by costs than by client needs. The familiar fee-for-service system has been replaced by a system in which costs are controlled by placing limits on the amount and type of services, by monitoring services intensely, and by changing the nature of services (Foos, Ottens, & Hill, 1991).

Four common models of MMHC are employee assistance programs, utilization review, preferred provider organizations, and staff model health maintenance organizations. Each model incorporates greater or lesser intrusiveness into the procedures of treatment. For example, utilization review requires the practitioner to submit a written justification for treatment along with a comprehensive treatment plan. The justification and plan are reviewed by a utilization reviewer who, if the plan is approved, allocates a specific number of sessions; further sessions are subject to reapplication and approval by the reviewer. Only under these conditions can claims be reimbursed.

Haas and Cummings (1991) raise several questions prospective service providers should consider before participating in an MMHC program:

- Who takes the risks? (That is, who pays additional costs?)
- How much does the plan intrude into the relationship between client and service provider?
- What provisions exist for making exceptions to the rules?
- Are there referral resources if clients' needs exceed the plan's benefits?
- Does the plan provide assistance or training to help service providers achieve treatment goals?
- Is the plan open to input by providers?
- Are policyholders clearly informed of the limits of benefits?

The following discussion extends Haas and Cummings' responses and considers the ethical implications of each of the questions.

Risk Taking

Traditionally, insurance companies have taken the risk of paying for unforeseen expenses. Plans have generally factored in the probability of particular treatment needs. Should clients need more treatment, however, insurance plans usually reimburse for it. In some MMHC programs, a portion of this added cost is shifted to the client. If the client should need additional treatment past a certain point, the client pays for it. In other MMHC programs, a portion of the added cost is shifted to the service provider. If costs exceed a set limit, or if referral for ancillary treatment is required, the service provider's reimbursement drops. One potential ethical concern that can emerge here is the tendency for service providers to "hoard resources" (Morreim, 1988); this hoarding is a consequence of service providers' reluctance to refer or extend treatment if it costs them too much.

Intrusion Into the Therapeutic Relationship

In traditional fee-for-service insurance plans, there has been substantial contractual freedom. A client expresses a need for a service, selects a service provider from among existing alternatives, and has some degree of participation in the treatment-planning process. This process calls for an expression of loyalty on the part of the service provider. The provider has the freedom to accept or decline working with the client, to select that treatment method in which he or she is most competent, and then to honor his or her commitment to treat the client until the presenting complaint is resolved, an appropriate referral is made, or the client discontinues treatment. The therapeutic relationship is characterized by freedom and responsibility: freedom to treat as the service provider sees fit and responsibility primarily to the client, not the insurance company. Although some people have argued that such an arrangement offers incentives to provide more treatment than is necessary, others (Nelson, Clark, Goldman, & Schore, 1989) have contended that it also emphasizes that the primary loyalty of the service provider is to the client (Haas & Cummings, 1991).

Service providers who agree to participate in an MMHC, in contrast, incur obligations not only to clients but to the MMHC program as well. For example, if too many clients' treatment becomes too costly, the MMHC program's financial livelihood, if not its existence, is threatened. The service provider's financial livelihood would likewise be threatened. Therefore, how service providers balance their loyalty to clients with their responsibilities as an agent of the MMHC program becomes a critical ethical issue (Stevens-Smith, 1997a, 1997b).

Exceptions to the Rules

Certain clients' conditions or circumstances call for treatment beyond the prevailing norm. Some MMHC programs employ a method called *capitation* to pay for such treatment. Under a capitated system, the MMHC provider agrees, within certain parameters, to deliver all the mental health services required by a given population for a fixed cost per member or employee. In a capitated system, the MMHC provider assumes financial risk for a given population because the payment to the provider is the same regardless of the amount of service offered (Richardson & Austad, 1991). Continuing treatment past a certain point is primarily a financial consideration and a built-in risk. Other MMHC programs employ a noncapitated system wherein services are simply limited to a specific number of sessions or cost *per illness*. In such noncapitated systems, the temptation for a service provider to change a diagnosis or description of treatment for a particular client who has exceeded the benefits but requires continuing treatment is ever present and represents a potentially recurrent ethical conflict.

Referral Resources

Marriage and family therapists, like all providers of mental health services, have a responsibility to offer treatment until a presenting complaint is resolved, an appropriate referral is made, or the client or clients discontinue treatment. To do otherwise is to abandon clients, which is clearly unethical according to the *AAMFT Code of Ethics* (American Association for Marriage and Family Therapy, 2001). Although this same code calls for marriage and family therapists to devote a portion of their professional activity to services for which there is little or no financial return (pro bono service), the key question becomes "Can I avoid abandoning my clients without going bankrupt?" (Haas & Cummings, 1991). Thus, to provide continuing treatment to clients whose benefits have been exceeded, referral may frequently be necessary. Are appropriate referral resources available? It may present significant ethical conflict for most marriage and family therapists to provide extensive pro bono service if they are not.

Short-Term Treatment Competence

Mental health services under an MMHC plan must be delivered within the parameters of the plan, which typically limit the number of sessions and/or allowable treatment costs. Time limitations and monetary constraints dictate that marriage and family therapists working under such a plan be proficient in brief, time-limited therapy. Treatment plans have to be formulated rapidly and must include specified goals and number of sessions (Foos et al., 1991).

Most clinicians resent having their practices subjected to external control (Zimet, 1989). Short-term treatment, however, is not just long-term treatment squeezed into a briefer time period. Marriage and family therapists who are not trained in brief therapy and yet who work under an MMHC plan that demands short-term, cost-effective treatment are more likely to be dissatisfied with the treatment they can offer. Consequently, their clients will similarly be dissatisfied with their treatment. The treatment is more likely to be less structured and therefore less effective. These therapists, furthermore, are more likely to lack faith in their ability to obtain positive outcomes from brief treatment, a pessimism covertly if not overtly communicated to their clients (Budman, 1989).

Brief-therapy modalities are not simply abbreviated forms of long-term therapy approaches to which most clinicians were exposed in graduate school (Gladding, 1998b; Sperry, 1989). Brief-therapy modalities entail their own framework of skills and assumptions. Budman and Gurman (1988) present compelling theoretical arguments that brief, time-sensitive treatment can offer benefits that in many cases is superior to time-unlimited therapy. Furthermore, they have shown that repeated "doses" of brief therapy have the same effect as, or even a better effect than, one dose of long-term treatment. Marriage and family therapists who are not competent in brief therapy as a distinct modality should probably avoid involvement in an MMHC program (Haas & Cummings, 1991). Likewise, MMHC programs ought to select only service providers competent to offer short-term mental health treatment, or they ought to make provisions for selected service providers to receive training to gain competence in employing a short-term treatment model.

Input by Service Providers

MMHC programs have encouraged the development and use of clinical decision-making aids (e.g., diagnosis-specific treatment protocols). The majority of these aids are relatively newer to mental health care than to physical health care. They assist in controlling costs by promoting a standard quality of care, and they can be readily examined in utilization review. One of these clinical aids, the algorithm, is an outline of a methodology (usually represented in graphic form) or a prescribed procedure for diagnosis and treatment. Algorithms assist service providers in making sound clinical decisions and in providing efficient care, thereby protecting against possible claims of negligence. They also, however, tend to homogenize treatment (Grumet, 1988). Unfortunately, research into the effects of algorithms on the nature and quality of mental health care apparently does not exist (Richardson & Austad, 1991). Given the proliferation and support of such mechanisms by MMHC programs, it is essential that service providers have frequent and formal means of offering input not only about the overall MMHC plan but also about those therapeutic mechanisms it promotes. Otherwise, the service provider becomes only an employee as opposed to a mental health professional treating clients (Haas & Cummings, 1991).

Informed Consent

All the disciplines within the mental health field are clear on the issue of informed consent. Prospective MMHC clients should be given full information about the benefits to which they are entitled as well as the limits of treatment as the clinician envisions them to be. As noted before, marriage and family therapists working under an MMHC program have inherently divided loyalties to both the MMHC program and to clients. It is critical that marriage and family therapists avoid being caught in the middle, having to explain benefit limitations to naive clients after the benefit limits have been reached (Haas & Cummings, 1991).

Acting Ethically as an MMHC Service Provider

Third-party payment arrangements consistently raise ethical concerns, and ethical dilemmas are a price one has to pay if the decision is made to participate in the managed care marketplace (Golden & Schmidt, 1998). One such concern is the accurate representation of a client in formulating a treatment plan where the temptation might be to try to justify an individual diagnosis when seeing a couple or family (Bonnington, Crawford, Curtis, & Watts, 1996). Such a ploy would be a misrepresentation of the family therapist's client—that is, the couple or family—and would be unethical.

An equally difficult dilemma for family therapists who participate in MMHC programs is in regard to divided loyalties. The ethical principle of fidelity (Beauchamp & Childress, 1994) demands that marriage and family therapists as professionals be loyal to those with whom they have a contractual relationship. Therefore, marriage and family therapists agreeing to MMHC participation should believe in the service philosophy and procedures the MMHC endorses (Huber, 1995). Likewise, if a marriage and family therapist agrees to work with a certain client, she or he should be loyal to that client's interests.

Standard 6.1 of the *AAMFT Code of Ethics* (American Association for Marriage and Family Therapy, 2001) calls for marriage and family therapists to remain accountable to the standards of the profession when acting as members or employees of organizations. One such standard is that marriage and family therapists avoid dual relationships that could impair professional judgment or increase their risk of exploitation. In MMHC participation, the most likely conflict would be between the demands of the MMHC plan (e.g., that reimbursement for treatment cease beyond a specified point regardless of the client's need) and the needs of the client for continuing treatment and the ethical responsibility of the marriage and family therapist (e.g., that the welfare of the client be considered above all other concerns). Should the demands of MMHC participation conflict with a marriage and family therapist's code of ethics, that therapist should attempt to bring the conflict to the attention of the relevant parties and seek to resolve it. Establishing and maintaining support systems of informed colleagues to help generate alternatives through open discussion in such circumstances can be of immeasurable assistance.

Should the conflict remain unresolved, however, the marriage and family therapist should consider temporarily withdrawing from active participation as an MMHC service provider and pursue resolution in other ways (e.g., through professional, organizational, and/or legislative advocacy efforts on behalf of consumer-clients). To do otherwise would risk colluding with either the client or the MMHC to the detriment of the other (Haas & Cummings, 1991).

TECHNOLOGY

The growth of technology has been phenomenal in the last two decades. Technology that has "had the most impact on a therapy practice are voice mail, personal computers, e-mail, pagers, answering machines, and hand-held audio recording devices" (Caudill, 1999, p. 20). Electronic connections and transmissions have truly revolutionized the sending and receiving of information and have important ethical implications for any type of therapeutic relationship. Technology can be used well or abused in therapeutic relationships.

One area of concern in the use of technology involves confidentiality. The electronic transformation of data "has greatly increased the complexity of issues related to confidentiality" (Bonnington, McGrath, & Martinek, 1996, p. 156). Computerized records are subject to potentially less security than records kept under lock and key. "The availability of client records through computerized transmission and storage in national data banks creates a nightmare for both clients and clinicians" (Stevens-Smith, 1997b, p. 54). In fact, Freeny (1995) has stated that "computers and confidentiality may be incompatible" (p. 37). Thus, the ethical principles of nonmaleficence (do no harm) and fidelity (loyalty to the client) come under question more when technology is a part of counseling with couples and families. Even faxing information to a managed mental health care provider or to a supervisor can have profound ethical implications and ramifications. E-mails and faxes are not protected by federal law in the same way that items carried by the United States Postal Service are. Thus, if someone else, besides the intended receiver, reads them, a client's integrity and confidentiality may be compromised.

So-called "cybercounseling," or "the delivery of counseling and therapeutic services over computer and internet-based mediums" is another area in technology fraught with ethical concern (Duncan & Watts, 1999, p. 160). Counselors who wish to use computer technology to counsel must consider that the process is more potentially perilous than it appears. For instance, clients are usually restricted to a 200-word limit as to what they can ask of a cybercounselor through e-mailing his or her Web site. Therefore, they may not be able to explain their situation adequately, especially if it involves multiple family members. Another limit of cybercounseling includes an inability to access cultural variables and nonverbals. Both of these factors may be extremely important in determining what approach a marriage and family therapist should use in a situation. However, the biggest problems with Internet counseling are tied in to ethics namely protecting confidentiality and being able to warn others if there is a potential threat of harm (Frame, 1997). Also, for marriage and family therapists licensed in a specific state, ethical and legal concerns arise if the client family is in another state. Practicing across state lines may be technically possible but it may be ethically and legally prohibited because of the limits of one's license.

In short, cybercounseling and marriage and family therapy appear to be ethically if not legally incompatible in a number of areas. Certainly, therapists face a number of ethical challenges in trying to offer their services via electronic means instead of face to face (American Association for Marriage and Family Therapy, 1999). There are some exceptions to working with client families through technological means. For example, the use of technology may be most appropriate if a therapist is following up with a client family or working with a family member who cannot come to in-office sessions because of disabilities or other extenuating circumstances.

DIVERSITY

The importance of couple and family therapy from a multicultural perspective has increased in recent years as the population of the United States has become more diverse. Cultures are unique in regard to what they teach and the values they hold. Families are influenced by their cultural backgrounds in such areas as worldview, roles, lifestyles, interactional patterns, and attitudes toward problem solving (Thomas, 1998). Unfortunately, in therapy many experiences of "people of color have been ignored" (May, 1998, p. 123). This "lack of familiarity with the beliefs and customs of culturally diverse individuals and families, coupled with the tendency to look for dysfunctionality . . . [has] lead to errors in clinical assessment and unethical clinical interventions" (Kurilla, 1998, p. 207). Its over-all impact has been detrimental to the field of marriage and family therapy (Hardy & Laszloffy, 1992).

To avoid potentially unethical practices, marriage and family therapists need to cultivate greater awareness of others and themselves as well as to develop mul-ticultural counseling competencies. Furthermore, they must realize that the area of cultural diversity is fluid as well as ever expanding. Although some families have an overriding cultural orientation, many families are more diverse then they may first appear. Even when families share a similar background, they may not hold the same values, and they may identify with two or more cultures simultane-ously (Pederson, 1996). Thus, content knowledge of cultural backgrounds is not enough to ensure appropriate treatment, although without cultural awareness, family therapists are more likely than not to make errors in judgment.

In examining the issue of cultural diversity and ethics in marriage and family counseling, C. Williams (1999) states that "therapy with culturally diverse families requires rethinking what constitutes ethical practice in light of family structures, experiences, and worldviews that may diverge markedly from those on which pro-fessional ethics are based" (p. 125). In an exercise that encompassed ethical rethinking, K. Jordan and Stevens (1999) had their graduate students study the International Association of Marriage and Family Counselors (IAMFC) code of ethics (1993) and make suggestions on areas that the students believed the IAMFC needed to address. Diversity was one area where students thought that the code should be stronger. Improvements that they advocated were adding manda-tory hours of continuing education in multicultural education every 2 years, pro-moting greater awareness of self (especially biases and values) and of others, and promoting cultural considerations in the selection and interpretation of tests and assessment instruments. In addition, Thomas (1998) has recommended that mar-riage and family therapists be knowledgeable of racism and oppression in society and how these insidious and sometimes unnoticed "isms" impact family behaviors. Thomas (1998) concludes by stating that

> To provide both clinically sound and ethical treatment to families, particularly cultur-ally diverse families, the family counselor must be open, accepting, and respectful of diversity issues. Family counselors who are not competent culturally are ethically obligated to refer their diverse families to competent counselors or to seek further training and supervision to become culturally competent. (p. 51)

PUBLICATIONS

The importance of the publication of professional literature is an area vital to marriage and family therapists. Published research is a means by which therapists can (a) share information, (b) promote themselves, and (c) succeed in academia (K. D. Jones, 1999). Yet, the ethical code of the AAMFT addresses the ethics of publishing in only four articles under Section 6—Responsibility to the Profession

(American Association for Marriage and Family Therapy, 2001). These articles (6.2, 6.3, 6.4, and 6.5) address general concerns that frequently arise in publishing and that are vital to marriage and family therapists.

In articles 6.2 and 6.3, the issue of crediting those who contributed to a research or publication effort is raised. While it may seem straightforward that participants who contributed the most to a publication be listed first, such is not always the case. To avoid ethical dilemmas in multiple authorship, Goodyear, Crego, and Johnston (1992) suggest the use of an informed consent process before entering a publishing endeavor. In such a process, the roles, duties, and expectations of each participant should be spelled out. Likewise, in student/faculty publications, potential ethical problems arise because of the unequal status of the participants. K. D. Jones (1999) suggests that in these situations, students be listed as the first author if they have contributed the most to the publication. Such a listing places students on an equal footing with faculty as well as models appropriate ethical behavior.

In article 6.4, the AAMFT code addresses plagiarism and the giving of proper credit to sources. While the perils of plagiarism may seem relatively easy to avoid, in fact they are not, because of the pressure to perform and contribute to the field. Thus, marriage and family therapists who write must observe copyright laws and the temptation to promote an idea of another as their own. Adhering to article 6.4 means exercising the principle of fidelity, that is, upholding truth and maintaining loyalty. Likewise, in article 6.5, the same principle of fidelity comes into play regarding marriage and family therapists who publish, taking reasonable precautions "to ensure that the organization" that "promotes and advertises" their books and materials do so "accurately and factually."

SUMMARY AND CONCLUSIONS

Marriage and family therapists are well aware that they will constantly be challenged to address ethical concerns in their work. One means of doing so is to look to a professional code of ethics for guidance. Such a code, however, is a finite document that can cover only a limited number of issues. To a great extent, historical factors influence what is incorporated into any code of ethics. Significant changes in society can result in a code that omits issues of current concern or contains gaps in its discussion of those issues.

A limited range of topics are covered in a code, and because a code approach is usually reactive to issues already developed elsewhere, the requirement of consensus prevents a code from addressing new issues and problems at the "cutting edge" (Mabe & Rollin, 1986, p. 295).

Although these matters are eventually addressed by revision committees that meet periodically to bring a code of ethics up to date, professionals must look to the literature and consult with colleagues to find precedents on which to base their decisions. This chapter addressed eight contemporary ethically sensitive areas.

Confidentiality and the duty to protect are extensively discussed in the *AAMFT Code of Ethics* (American Association for Marriage and Family Therapy, 2001). Deciding whether to maintain (or breach) confidentiality with clients who are HIV-positive and in relationships with noninfected persons, however, is a relatively recent question about which there is still controversy. As a means of addressing this ethical dilemma, several writers have discussed applying the "duty to protect" guidelines emerging from the *Tarasoff* decision (*Tarasoff v. Regents of the University of California*, 1976). A therapist's duty to protect depends on the presence of a fiduciary relationship (a relationship of special trust), the identifiability of a victim, and the foreseeability of danger.

Likewise, dual relationships are discussed in the *AAMFT Code of Ethics*. Not all dual relationships can be avoided, however, nor are they necessarily harmful. Where the line is drawn between those dual relationships that are clearly unethical and those that are acceptable if handled with due care and caution is still a matter of controversy. Three guidelines based on role theory were offered in this chapter as one means of differentiating between dual role relationships that will probably lead to unethical behavior and those that are less likely to be problematic:

- Compatibility of expectations (similarity—or difference—between the expectations of the therapist and the client)
- Divergence of obligations (contrasts between the obligations imposed by the therapist's and the client's different roles)
- Power/prestige differential (the difference in power and prestige between the roles of therapist and client)

Some ethical issues are not covered in the *AAMFT Code of Ethics*, and some have little or no precedent. Some criteria are needed to assist marriage and family therapists in formulating an educated response to such issues. The use of the *Diagnostic and Statistical Manual of Mental Disorders* (DSM) (American Psychiatric Association, 1980, 1987, 1994) within marriage and family therapy, for example, is a contemporary concern that is not discussed in the *AAMFT Code of Ethics*. Four areas of ethical consideration were outlined in this chapter:

1. Incompatibility of orientations (conflict between the assumption in the DSM that distress in family or social contexts is due to a dysfunction within individuals and the assumption in marriage and family therapy that such distress is due to dysfunction within the entire family system)
2. The stigma of diagnosis (the possible adverse results of a DSM diagnosis)
3. Misrepresentation of diagnoses (application of a DSM diagnosis when the criteria for such a diagnosis are not met)
4. Competence to diagnose (training and experience sufficient to enable a therapist to make a DSM diagnosis)

The treatment context of family violence is also not discussed in the *AAMFT Code of Ethics*. Four interrelated principles for marriage and family therapists were considered as a means of assuring ethical practice:

1. The cessation of violence (stopping existing violence)
2. The contraindication of neutrality (advocating for the family member or members against whom violence is used in order to balance the family system)
3. Individual responsibility (holding the aggressor accountable)
4. Contracting for nonviolence (obtaining an agreement from the aggressor not to use further violence)

A fifth issue, managed mental health care (MMHC), was addressed along with its implications for ethically sensitive participation on the part of marriage and family therapists. Perhaps above all, marriage and family therapists have an obligation to help educate consumers about the potential benefits and problems inherent in mental health services rendered through managed care systems. Research ought to be pursued to separate effective from adverse treatment consequences. Only then can consumers make fully informed choices about the care they receive (Newman & Bricklin, 1991). If informed consumers and, subsequently, their employers should threaten to select other forms of insurance coverage, MMHC programs will surely determine how to strike a better balance between their financial interests and their clients' care.

Technology, while not addressed in the *AAMFT Code of Ethics*, is yet another contemporary ethical issue. Electronic devices that make work simpler and faster also raise questions in regard to ethics, especially in regard to the ethical principles of nonmaleficence and fidelity. So-called "cybercounseling" is fraught with ethical concerns especially in regard to confidentiality. The Internet is basically nonregulated, and information on it or from it that is of a personal nature is often unprotected.

On the seventh issue covered in this chapter, diversity, marriage and family therapists need to acknowledge that culture plays a major role in the worldview of client families and impacts how work with families is handled. The AAMFT ethical standards address diversity issues in article 1.1, but this article is general. Therefore, it is imperative that therapists recognize that if they are not actively thinking about diversity issues as they conduct therapy sessions, they are more likely than not to either implicitly or explicitly promote racism or oppression of families based on behaviors and background.

Finally, the matter of publications as covered in four articles of section 6 of the *AAMFT Code of Ethics* is a contemporary ethical issue mentioned here. Publishing helps therapists share information, promote themselves, and advance their careers, but a number of concerns around publishing are vital to marriage and family therapists. Giving proper credit is one. Avoiding plagiarism is a second. Upholding the principle of fidelity is yet a third, and truthfulness is a fourth.

It is easy to bypass any of the ethical dilemmas mentioned in this chapter unless a marriage and family therapist is attuned to present concerns and issues. Therefore, therapists of all ages and stages should stay abreast of current events and advancements and continuously query themselves and others regarding the proper course of action to take in novel situations.

4

Ethical Accountability: A Casebook

Several professional association ethics committees have published books on their respective codes of ethics (e.g., American Counseling Association's *Ethical Standards Casebook*, Herlihy & Corey, 1996; American Association of Marriage and Family Therapy's *Ethics Casebook*, Brock, 1998; American Psychological Association's *Ethical Conflicts in Psychology*, Bersoff, 1995). Codes of ethics are, by nature, general and often debatable. These books represent a consensus from reputable professionals and assist practitioners in understanding how best to apply the principles the codes represent.

Two primary professional affiliations for marriage and family therapists are the American Association for Marriage and Family Therapy (AAMFT) and the International Association of Marriage and Family Counselors (IAMFC). These organizations have promulgated the *AAMFT Code of Ethics* (American Association for Marriage and Family Therapy, 2001) and the *Ethical Code for the IAMFC* (International Association of Marriage and Family Counselors, 1993). Both associations maintain an ethics committee. Operating under the AAMFT bylaws, the AAMFT ethics committee interprets its code of ethics, considers allegations of violations of the codes made against association members, and, if the case is heard by Judicial Council, adjudicates the charges against the member.

Both the AAMFT and IAMFC have published an ethical casebook for the practice of marriage and family counseling (Brock, 1993; Stevens, 1999). This chapter, using a casebook format, represents our analysis of the selected standards within the *AAMFT Code of Ethics* through consultation with relevant professional colleagues. Actions recommended within each case illustration were also developed in a like manner. The *AAMFT Code of Ethics* and specific cases follow an overview of the structure and functioning of AAMFT's Ethics Committee.

The Ethics Committee is composed of six members appointed by the president of AAMFT. Four are AAMFT Clinical Members and two are "public members," representing the interests of potential clients, consumers of marriage and family therapy services. The committee ordinarily meets three times yearly at 4-month intervals. The *Procedures for Handling Ethical Matters* (American Association for Marriage and Family Therapy, 1992b) codify the manner in which the Ethics Committee and associated bodies address ethical complaints raised against AAMFT members. Figure 4–1 graphically describes the five major steps (each with substeps) in handling complaints of unethical behavior by AAMFT members.

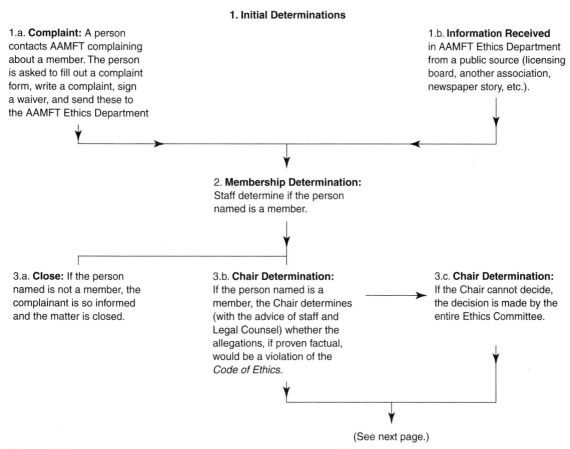

Decision tree: AAMFT Ethics Cases

AAMFT follows a process of five major steps (each with sub-steps) in handling complaints of unethical behavior by AAMFT members, Approved Supervisors, applicants for membership or the Approved Supervisor designation, or recently resigned members or Approved Supervisors (hereafter, member). After steps I, III, IV, and V, the process may be closed or may proceed to the next step.

1. Initial Determinations

1.a. **Complaint:** A person contacts AAMFT complaining about a member. The person is asked to fill out a complaint form, write a complaint, sign a waiver, and send these to the AAMFT Ethics Department

1.b. **Information Received** in AAMFT Ethics Department from a public source (licensing board, another association, newspaper story, etc.).

2. Membership Determination: Staff determine if the person named is a member.

3.a. **Close:** If the person named is not a member, the complainant is so informed and the matter is closed.

3.b. **Chair Determination:** If the person named is a member, the Chair determines (with the advice of staff and Legal Counsel) whether the allegations, if proven factual, would be a violation of the *Code of Ethics*.

3.c. **Chair Determination:** If the Chair cannot decide, the decision is made by the entire Ethics Committee.

(See next page.)

Figure 4–1

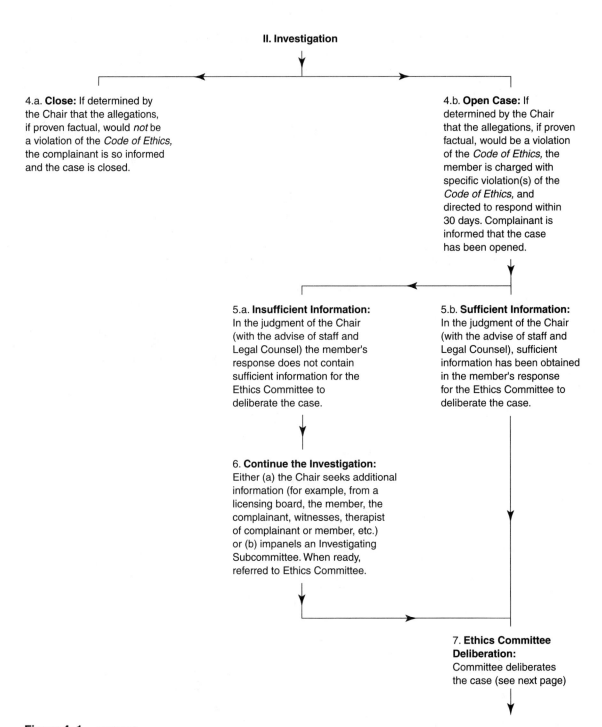

II. Investigation

4.a. **Close:** If determined by the Chair that the allegations, if proven factual, would *not* be a violation of the *Code of Ethics,* the complainant is so informed and the case is closed.

4.b. **Open Case:** If determined by the Chair that the allegations, if proven factual, would be a violation of the *Code of Ethics,* the member is charged with specific violation(s) of the *Code of Ethics,* and directed to respond within 30 days. Complainant is informed that the case has been opened.

5.a. **Insufficient Information:** In the judgment of the Chair (with the advise of staff and Legal Counsel) the member's response does not contain sufficient information for the Ethics Committee to deliberate the case.

5.b. **Sufficient Information:** In the judgment of the Chair (with the advise of staff and Legal Counsel), sufficient information has been obtained in the member's response for the Ethics Committee to deliberate the case.

6. **Continue the Investigation:** Either (a) the Chair seeks additional information (for example, from a licensing board, the member, the complainant, witnesses, therapist of complainant or member, etc.) or (b) impanels an Investigating Subcommittee. When ready, referred to Ethics Committee.

7. **Ethics Committee Deliberation:** Committee deliberates the case (see next page)

Figure 4–1 *continued*

III. Ethics Committee Action

7. **Ethics Committee Deliberation:** Committee deliberates the case.

8.a. **Close:** No violation found. Member and complainant so informed.

8.b. **Insufficient Information:** Committee directs that specific information be obtained (#6) then returned to the Committee (#7).

8.c. **Violation Found:** Committee makes a formal finding of specific violation(s) of the *Code of Ethics.*

9.a. **Mutual Settlement:** Committee offers to settle the matter with the member (for example, enter supervision and/or therapy for a stipulated period, take course(s), do community service). If accepted, the agreement goes into effect and is monitored by the committee for other action (#8).

9.b. **Recommended Action:** The committee recommends to the Judicial Committee that formal action be taken against the member (for example, termination of membership). The member is informed that he or she has the right to request a review by the Judicial Committee, but must do so within 15 days or the recommended action becomes final.

10.a. **No Review:** The Member does not request a review, and so the action is implemented. (If the action requires monitoring, this is done by the Ethics Committee.) The complainant is informed of the outcome.

10.b. **Review:** The member requests a review by the Judicial Committee. (See the next page.)

IV. Review by Judicial Committee

10.b. **Review:** The member requests a review by the Judicial Committee.

11. **Hearing:** An in-person hearing is scheduled before a Hearing Panel of the Judicial Committee. Chair of the Ethics Committee serves as prosecutor, and member presents case. Witnesses may be called.

12.a. **Close:** No violation found. Member and complainant so informed.

12.b. **Violation Found:** The Hearing Panel fully or partially upholds the findings of the Ethics Committee and orders action(s) to be taken. The member is informed that he or she has a right to appeal to the AAMFT Board of Directors, but only if the Judicial Committee's *Procedures* were violated in such a way as to prevent a fair hearing, and must do so within 15 days or the order becomes final.

13.a. **No Appeal:** The member does not appeal so the action is implemented. (If the action requires monitoring, this is done by the Ethics Committee.) The complainant is informed of the outcome.

13.b. **Appeal:** The member appeals to the Board of Directors (See the next page.)

Figure 4–1   *continued*

V. Appeal to the Board

14. **Appeal:** The Board reviews the information submitted by the member and the Judicial Committee to determine whether the *Procedures* were violated.

15.a. **Upholds Judicial Committee Decision:** The Board finds no violation of the *Procedures.* The action ordered by the Judicial Committee is implemented. (If the action requires monitoring, this is done by the Ethics Committee.) The member and complainant are informed of the outcome.

15.b. **Remands to Judicial Committee:** The Board finds that the *Procedures* were violated and orders a new hearing before a Hearing Panel of the Judicial Committee (Return to #11.)

Engelberg (1985) summarizes this process as follows:

> Cases consist of complaints brought against AAMFT members for violating the AAMFT Code of Ethical Principles. Complaints may be brought against an AAMFT member by another AAMFT member, or nonmember therapists, by clients, by members of the public, and by the Ethics Committee itself. Once a complaint is made, the AAMFT national office first determines whether the charged professional is an AAMFT member. If confirmed, the complaint is forwarded to the Chair of the Ethics Committee. The Chair then makes a determination whether the complaint, if proven, states a claim under the Code. If so, a case is opened and the complainant (if a client) is sent a waiver of the client–therapist privilege. Upon receipt of the signed waiver, a letter is written to the charged member, requesting a response. The case may be decided through further written communications between the Ethics Committee and the charged member. On occasion, the Ethics Committee impanels an investigating subcommittee before which the charged member has a right to appear.

Cases are often disposed of through a process of agreement called "settlement by mutual consent." If settlement by mutual consent is unable to be agreed upon, the Ethics Committee can recommend to the AAMFT Judicial Council that final action be taken against a member. Any proposed settlement or final action recommended by the Ethics Committee can include a requirement that the charged member seek therapy or obtain supervision. The Ethics Committee is also authorized to propose revocation of a member's approved supervisor status and, in most serious cases, termination of membership. Charged members may appeal Ethics Committee recommendations for final action; appeals are made to the independent Judicial Council. At that point, the Ethics Committee is, in effect, prosecuting the complaint, and the Judicial Council makes the final ruling on the matter.

The presence of the Ethics Committee exemplifies AAMFT's commitment to protect consumers of marriage and family therapy services from unethical practices without violating the rights of AAMFT members. The Ethics Committee, however, does not serve simply as a reactive body; proactive functions are of equal importance. The Ethics Committee also serves as a consultation source for members of the association for an opinion relative to a course of action. For example, what decision should a marriage and family therapist who is concerned with possible confidentiality violations make when considering a request to appear on a television program aimed at common problems of couples in marital therapy? Thus, the actions of the Ethics Committee are primarily constructive and educational; they are problem solving and adversarial only when the occasion arises.

PRINCIPLE 1. RESPONSIBILITY TO CLIENTS

Marriage and family therapists advance the welfare of families and individuals. They respect the rights of those persons seeking their assistance, and make reasonable efforts to ensure that their services are used appropriately.

1.1. Marriage and family therapists provide professional assistance to persons without discrimination on the basis of race, age, ethnicity, socioeconomic status, disability, gender, health status, religion, national origin, or sexual orientation.

1.2 Marriage and family therapists obtain appropriate informed consent to therapy or related procedures and use language that is reasonably understandable to clients. The content of informed consent may vary depending upon the client and treatment plan; however, informed consent generally necessitates that the client: (a) has the capacity to consent; (b) has been adequately informed of significant information concerning treatment processes, procedures, risks and benefits; (c) has freely and without undue influence expressed consent; and (d) has provided consent that is appropriately documented. When persons, due to age or mental status, are legally incapable of giving informed consent, marriage and family therapists obtain informed permission from a legally authorized person, if such substitute consent is legally permissible.

1.3 Marriage and family therapists are aware of their influential positions with respect to clients, and they avoid exploiting the trust and dependency of such persons. Therapists, therefore, make every effort to avoid conditions and multiple relationships with clients that could impair professional judgment or increase the risk of exploitation. Such relationships include, but are not limited to, business or close personal relationships with a client or the client's immediate family. When the risk of impairment or exploitation exists due to conditions or multiple roles, therapists take appropriate precautions.

1.4 Sexual intimacy with clients is prohibited.

1.5 Sexual intimacy with former clients is likely to be harmful and is therefore prohibited for two years following the termination of therapy or last professional contact. In an effort to avoid exploiting the trust and dependency of clients, marriage and family therapists should not engage in sexual intimacy with former clients after the two years following termination or last professional contact. Should therapists engage in sexual intimacy with former clients following two years after termination or last professional contact, the burden shifts to the therapist to demonstrate that there has been no exploitation or injury to the former client or to the client's immediate family.

1.6   Marriage and family therapists comply with applicable laws regarding the reporting of alleged unethical conduct.

1.7   Marriage and family therapists do not use their professional relationships with clients to further their own interests.

1.8   Marriage and family therapists respect the rights of clients to make decisions and help them to understand the consequences of these decisions. Therapists clearly advise the clients that they have the responsibility to make decisions regarding relationships such as cohabitation, marriage, divorce, separation, reconciliation, custody, and visitation.

1.9   Marriage and family therapists continue therapeutic relationships only so long as it is reasonably clear that clients are benefiting from the relationship.

1.10 Marriage and family therapists assist persons in obtaining other therapeutic services if the therapist is unable or unwilling, for appropriate reasons, to provide professional help.

1.11 Marriage and family therapists do not abandon or neglect clients in treatment without making reasonable arrangements for the continuation of such treatment.

1.12 Marriage and family therapists obtain written informed consent from clients before videotaping, audio recording, or permitting third-party observation.

1.13 Marriage and family therapists, upon agreeing to provide services to a person or entity at the request of a third party, clarify, to the extent feasible and at the outset of the service, the nature of the relationship with each party and the limits of confidentiality.

CASE 1

A female client had been seeing a male marriage and family therapist for over a year to resolve issues emanating from her divorce. When sexual desires between her and the therapist were mutually conveyed and then acted on, the therapist immediately terminated the therapeutic relationship. No referral was recommended, nor was there any time spent addressing the termination. A socially and sexually intimate relationship continued for the next 6 months. The woman eventually broke off the relationship when she began to experience the same emotional difficulties that originally led her to initiate therapy following her divorce.

Analysis

Principles 1.3, 1.4, 1.5, 1.9, 1.10, and 1.11 all come under consideration in this case. The therapist was correct in terminating the therapeutic relationship. However, by not assisting the client to obtain other therapeutic services when he decided he was no longer able to offer professional help, the therapist abandoned the client therapeutically. At the very least, the therapist could have prepared a one-page listing of resources which he could have mailed or discussed with the client. However, more serious was the therapist's lack of cognizance relative to the influence he had with the client, which suggests an exploitation of her vulnerable position. The issue of sexual intimacy is a flagrant ethical violation, as was the therapist's use of his professional position to advance his own sexual interests.

CASE 2

A marriage and family therapist with a national reputation as an expert in the area of fathers who have sole custody of their children was recommended by a lawyer to a father engaged in a custody case. The father wrote to the therapist, who resided in a neighboring state, and requested to be given any relevant information that the therapist might have. The therapist replied that some materials could be sent for a specified fee. The therapist also offered his services as an expert witness to the father for a fee, which included travel expenses. The father wrote back to the therapist, expressing anger at the therapist for "soliciting" him.

Analysis

Principles 1.3 and 1.7 are of primary consideration in this case. Although the father claims that the therapist sought to further personal financial interests, nothing directly proves this allegation. Similarly, nothing explicitly suggests that the therapist sought to exploit the father's request or create any dual therapeutic–business relationship, particularly because a relationship could not be considered as expressly present. The therapist was reasonable in requesting compensation for offering services to the father.

CASE 3

A couple sought marital therapy from a female marriage and family therapist. The therapist saw the couple conjointly and also in concurrent individual sessions for several months. The couple eventually decided on divorce and terminated their participation in therapy. Several months after the divorce was finalized, the wife discovered that her former husband and the therapist were seeing each other socially and had in fact become quite intimate. The wife confronted the therapist, charging her actions to be unethical. The therapist replied that she had not entered into a social relationship with the woman's former husband until some time after professional contact between them had ended. The therapist further responded that she had sought peer consultation with two other marriage and family therapists immediately after meeting the husband at an open social affair; afterward, he had telephoned her in pursuit of further social contact. Both therapists consulted recommended a several-month hiatus before accepting any social invitation from the husband. The therapist stated she had communicated this to the husband and followed through with her colleagues' recommendations.

Analysis

Principles 1.3 and 1.7 are of dominant concern in this case. Although the therapy had ended before the inception of the therapist's close personal relationship with the husband, concern must be raised in the case of a marriage and family therapist becoming socially and emotionally involved with a former client. Did the therapist exploit her professional position and enter into a dual relationship to further personal interests? Based on the therapist's pursuit of peer consultation and follow-through with regard to the professional cautions offered, it appears that the therapist acted in a conscientious, ethically aware manner. *A caveat:* Although the extent of the intimacy shared between the therapist and her former client is not specified, Principle 1.5 does clearly state that sexual intimacy with former clients is prohibited for 2 years following termination of therapy.

CASE 4

A 16-year-old sought the assistance of a marriage and family therapist working in a Catholic Services Center regarding her discovery that she was pregnant. The girl communicated her desire to obtain information and professional assistance in making a decision as to whether to terminate her pregnancy by abortion or offer the child for adoption. The therapist, a strong "pro-life" advocate, provided the girl with factual information and assisted her in contacting relevant referral sources to further investigate the available options. The therapist also, with the girl's permission, convened family therapy efforts to include the girl's parents and boyfriend in the decision making. At no time did the therapist personally advocate one option over the other.

Analysis

Principles 1.8 and 1.10 are of particular relevance in this case. The therapist displayed exemplary diligence in the respect shown this teenage girl. Despite strong personal views, the therapist sought only to assist the girl in arriving at a fully considered decision. Direct referral to both adoption and abortion services for concrete information and convening the boyfriend and parents in family therapy exhibited further evidence of the therapist's efforts to help the client fully comprehend the consequences of her options.

PRINCIPLE 2. CONFIDENTIALITY

Marriage and family therapists have unique confidentiality concerns because the client in a therapeutic relationship may be more than one person. Therapists respect and guard the confidences of each individual client.

2.1   Marriage and family therapists disclose to clients and other interested parties, as early as feasible in their professional contacts, the nature of confidentiality and possible limitations of the clients' right to confidentiality. Therapists review with clients the circumstances where confidential information may be requested and where disclosure of confidential information may be legally required. Circumstances may necessitate repeated disclosures.

2.2   Marriage and family therapists do not disclose client confidences except by written authorization or waiver, or where mandated or permitted by law. Verbal authorization will not be sufficient except in emergency situations, unless prohibited by law. When providing couple, family or group treatment, the therapist does not disclose information outside the treatment context without a written authorization from each individual competent to execute a waiver. In the context of couple, family or group treatment, the therapist may not reveal any individual's confidences to others in the client unit without the prior written permission of that individual.

2.3   Marriage and family therapists use client and/or clinical materials in teaching, writing, consulting, research, and public presentations only if a written waiver has been obtained in accordance with Subprinciple 2.2, or when appropriate steps have been taken to protect client identity and confidentiality.

2.4   Marriage and family therapists store, safeguard, and dispose of client records in ways that maintain confidentiality and in accord with applicable laws and professional standards.

2.5   Subsequent to the therapist moving from the area, closing the practice, or upon the death of the therapist, a marriage and family therapist arranges for the storage, transfer, or disposal of client records in ways that maintain confidentiality and safeguard the welfare of clients.

2.6   Marriage and family therapists, when consulting with colleagues or referral sources, do not share confidential information that could reasonably lead to the identification of a client, research participant, supervisee, or other person with whom they have a confidential relationship unless they have obtained the prior written consent of the client, research participant, supervisee, or other person with whom they have a confidential relationship. Information may be shared only to the extent necessary to achieve the purposes of the consultation.

CASE 5

A marriage and family therapist working within an employee assistance program in a large company received a complaint from an employee who, with his wife and children, was seeing the therapist. The employee alleged the therapist had discussed aspects of the employee's family life, as revealed during therapy sessions, with the executive vice president in charge of the employee's department. He recalled signing a release of information allowing the therapist and the department vice president to communicate about his progress, but alleged that the information shared was of a strictly personal nature and not job-related.

Analysis

Principles 2.1 and 2.2 are of primary concern in this case. Although the client had signed a waiver, it is obvious that there was some misunderstanding about the exact terms of the waiver. Whether the therapist or the client was unclear cannot be identified from the facts presented. It is a therapist's responsibility, however, to provide clients a copy of and fully explain the terms of any waiver, confirm their understanding, and then act accordingly when communicating information.

CASE 6

A marriage and family therapist received a referral of a 19-year-old client who was a niece of the referral source, a physician. The client's parents lived in another city, and the physician initiated the referral on the request of his brother and sister-in-law who were concerned about their daughter's adjustment in establishing herself away from home for the first time. Some months later, the physician contacted the therapist with the complaint that the therapist had refused to give the client's parents any indication of her well-being, despite the fact that they had made phone calls and written letters to the therapist, all of which had gone unanswered. The therapist replied that the client was an adult who requested that no information about her participation in therapy be communicated to anyone.

Analysis

Principles 2.1 and 2.2 are of primary consideration in this case. It is clear that the therapist was responding to the client's request accordingly, in line with the identified ethical principle noted. The issue of the therapist's obligation to the client's family as well as to the referral source, however, is raised in this case. The client specified that no information about her participation in therapy be divulged. Although it would have been prudent for the therapist to have asked the client to consider communicating with her parents, she still might have chosen not to do so. The therapist could be considered to have some responsibility to the client's parents because of their repeated attempts to contact the therapist. A brief return call or letter might have been appropriate, simply explaining in a general sense that no information about clients could be communicated ethically without their expressed permission, not even confirmation as to whether their daughter is or is not a client. A similar stance might have been taken with the referral source as well after the client had made her wishes regarding strict confidentiality known to the therapist.

CASE 7

A new secretary was hired by a marriage and family therapist. The therapist provided an orientation to the position, addressing the importance of confidentiality, but only in a general sense. A few days after the orientation, an attorney contacted the office with regard to a couple with whom the therapist had previously worked. The attorney requested information about the couple's participation in therapy efforts, indicating she was representing one in a divorce suit. She further noted that she would subpoena the records if she was unable to get the information requested over the telephone. The therapist was unavailable at the time, and, deciding that the information would eventually be available to the attorney anyway, the secretary provided the requested details.

Analysis

Although Principles 2.1 and 2.2 are relevant, of dominant concern is Principle 2.4. The therapist did not display sufficient attentiveness to the training of the secretary concerning responsibilities for the maintenance and communication of client records. Support staff must be trained in the importance of confidentiality and in the appropriate management of case files. The secretary should have been explicitly instructed not to reveal information regarding persons presently or previously receiving services or the nature of any services they received in response to inquiries made by phone, letter, or in person. Such inquiries or related questions should always be reviewed by the therapist before final action is taken.

CASE 8

A marriage and family therapist received a telephone call from a husband whose wife and adult children were being seen together with him in family therapy because of his alcohol abuse. The husband requested that information about his progress be communicated to his employer. The therapist was aware that the husband's job was in jeopardy but declined his request, explaining that all family members must agree to the release of information on their mutual participation in therapy. The husband became angry, stating that his job was on the line and that he was the one with the problem, not his family. The therapist reiterated the ethical importance of mutual consent; requested that the husband gather the family members together, stop by the therapist's office, and sign a waiver; and then the information might be forwarded as requested.

Analysis

Principle 2.2 is quite explicit in respect to the circumstances in this case. Without a waiver from each family member, the therapist is obliged ethically not to disclose the information. Although the client made a logical argument for his request, marriage and family therapists must be attuned to the fact that the "client" in the therapeutic relationship is the family, which calls for mutual consent for a waiver. The therapist acted in full ethical accord in this case.

PRINCIPLE 3. PROFESSIONAL COMPETENCE AND INTEGRITY

Marriage and family therapists maintain high standards of professional competence and integrity.

3.1 Marriage and family therapists pursue knowledge of new developments and maintain competence in marriage and family therapy through education, training, or supervised experience.

3.2 Marriage and family therapists maintain adequate knowledge of and adhere to applicable laws, ethics, and professional standards.

3.3 Marriage and family therapists seek appropriate professional assistance for their personal problems or conflicts that may impair work performance or clinical judgment.

3.4 Marriage and family therapists do not provide services that create a conflict of interest that may impair work performance or clinical judgment.

3.5 Marriage and family therapists, as presenters, teachers, supervisors, consultants and researchers, are dedicated to high standards of scholarship, present accurate information, and disclose potential conflicts of interest.

3.6 Marriage and family therapists maintain accurate and adequate clinical and financial records.

3.7 While developing new skills in specialty areas, marriage and family therapists take steps to ensure the competence of their work and to protect clients from possible harm. Marriage and family therapists practice in specialty areas new to them only after appropriate education, training, or supervised experience.

3.8 Marriage and family therapists do not engage in sexual or other forms of harassment of clients, students, trainees, supervisees, employees, colleagues, or research subjects.

3.9 Marriage and family therapists do not engage in the exploitation of clients, students, trainees, supervisees, employees, colleagues, or research subjects.

3.10 Marriage and family therapists do not give to or receive from clients (a) gifts of substantial value or (b) gifts that impair the integrity or efficacy of the therapeutic relationship.

3.11 Marriage and family therapists do not diagnose, treat, or advise on problems outside the recognized boundaries of their competencies.

3.12 Marriage and family therapists make efforts to prevent the distortion or misuse of their clinical and research findings.

3.13 Marriage and family therapists, because of their ability to influence and alter the lives of others, exercise special care when making public their professional recommendations and opinions through testimony or other public statements.

3.14 To avoid a conflict of interests, marriage and family therapists who treat minors or adults involved in custody or visitation actions may not also perform forensic evaluations for custody, residence, or visitation of the minor. The marriage and family therapist who treats the minor may provide the court or mental health professional performing the evaluation with information about the minor from the marriage and family therapist's perspective as a treating marriage and family therapist, so long as the marriage and family therapist does not violate confidentiality.

3.15 Marriage and family therapists are in violation of this Code and subject to termination of membership or other appropriate action if they: (a) are convicted of any felony or misdemeanor, or engage in conduct which could lead to conviction of a felony or a misdemeanor, related to their qualifications or functions; (b) are expelled from or disciplined by other professional organizations; (c) have their licenses or certificates suspended or revoked or are otherwise disciplined by regulatory bodies; (d) are no longer competent to practice marriage and family therapy because they are impaired due to physical or mental causes or due to abuse of alcohol or other substances; or (e) fail to cooperate with the Association at any point from the inception of an ethical complaint through the completion of all proceedings regarding that complaint.

CASE 9

A marriage and family therapist had given court testimony contradicting the testimony of a second marriage and family therapist in a child custody action brought by one parent against the other. The marriage and family therapist hired by the father was upset and very concerned about the ethical implications of the testimony of the mother's marriage and family therapist. The therapist's concerns emanated from the fact that the therapist hired by the mother had seen the child alone during the actual therapy sessions, communicated with the mother only very briefly before and after those sessions, and had never met with the father, yet testimony was given relative to the entire family's functioning. In contrast, the therapist hired by the father had seen the entire family together in therapy for several months.

Analysis

Principles 3.11, 3.13, and 3.14 present the primary ethical issue in this case. The marriage and family therapist hired by the mother appears to have based court testimony solely on hearsay. This therapist might have given reliable testimony relative to the child's current functioning. The ability to accurately evaluate total family functioning solely from the communications of the child or through brief encounters in a waiting room with the mother is a questionable practice, however. This therapist should be strongly urged to seek supervision from a marriage and family therapist with significant experience in family evaluation, especially before agreeing to act as an expert witness to provide similar court testimony.

CASE 10

A psychiatrist raised questions about the ethical conduct of a marriage and family therapist employed by the clinical group to which he acted as psychiatric consultant. The psychiatrist alleged that the therapist's use of intensification procedures with the family of a young boy whom he was psychopharmacologically treating for hyperactivity was having a harmful effect on his client's condition. The psychiatrist portrayed the boy as experiencing undue harassment from his parents as a result of the family therapy sessions. The therapist responded by conveying to the boy's parents that the psychiatrist had some questions about the family therapy, requesting the parents' consent to communicate with the psychiatrist in this regard. With the parents' consent, the marriage and family therapist explained to the psychiatrist the specific nature of the procedure, anticipated side effects, and the likelihood of greater improvement as a result of its use.

Analysis

Principles 3.5 and 3.8 are of direct concern in this case. The psychiatrist's inquiry was reasonable, given his apparent linear perception of his client's condition. The therapist responded conscientiously in asking the parents' permission to consult with the psychiatrist and then seeking to educate the psychiatrist on relevant ramifications of the procedures in question. The therapist presented not only the potential positive attributes of the procedures but also anticipated side effects. At no time, however, does it appear that the therapist engaged in any action that would encourage unwarranted harassment of the boy.

CASE 11

A marriage and family therapist had seen a client for a number of therapy sessions when he realized that his intimate feelings toward her were excessive and potentially harmful in their effect on the therapeutic relationship. He sought consultation from a senior colleague who recommended that the therapist refer the client to another therapist and consider the probability of similar situations occurring in the future. The therapist followed through with the suggestions of the consultant and entered into personal therapy to address his own needs in more appropriate ways. Concurrently, he also contracted with the senior colleague whom he had consulted to provide regular supervision of his work until the time his personal concerns were adequately addressed.

Analysis

Principle 3.2 states that marriage and family therapists seek professional assistance when personal issues might negatively affect their clinical practice. The therapist in this case, when he became aware of his inappropriate feelings, acted with ethical promptness in consulting a senior colleague. His further actions of pursuing personal therapy and contracting for supervision are evidence of proper ethical practice.

CASE 12

A young woman requested of a marriage and family therapist to be able to attend a therapy session with her parents, who were seeing the therapist to resolve their marital discord. The woman conveyed that she was feeling very depressed over her parents' conflicts and sought desperately to help them in any way. The parents had expressed strong feelings of anger and resentment about their daughter's continuing interference in their lives. Without considering the possible negative impact of the daughter's presence during a session or forewarning the daughter of her parents' intense hostility, the therapist agreed (with the parents' consent) to allow the daughter to attend the next session. The parents verbally attacked her and she responded immediately by crying hysterically and running out of the session.

Analysis

This case highlights the importance of preparing family members who join in the therapy some time after it has begun. Not preparing the daughter for a possible negative reaction by her parents in this case suggests a violation of Principle 3.8. The daughter communicated to the therapist that she was in a depressed mental state when she made her request to participate in therapy with her parents. The therapist should have recognized that this vulnerability, combined with the fact that the parents had conveyed intense hostility toward their daughter during sessions, could create a context for harassment of the daughter. Although the harassment came directly from the woman's parents, the therapist indirectly facilitated its occurrence, particularly by not preparing the daughter for it.

PRINCIPLE 4. RESPONSIBILITY TO STUDENTS, EMPLOYEES, AND SUPERVISEES

Marriage and family therapists do not exploit the trust and dependency of students and supervisees.

4.1 Marriage and family therapists are aware of their influential positions with respect to students and supervisees, and they avoid exploiting the trust and dependency of such persons. Therapists, therefore, make every effort to avoid conditions and multiple relationships that could impair professional objectivity or increase the risk of exploitation. When the risk of impairment or exploitation exists due to conditions or multiple roles, therapists take appropriate precautions.

4.2 Marriage and family therapists do not provide therapy to current students or supervisees.

4.3 Marriage and family therapists do not engage in sexual intimacy with students or supervisees during the evaluative or training relationship between the therapist and student or supervisee.

4.4 Marriage and family therapists do not permit students or supervisees to perform or to hold themselves out as competent to perform professional services beyond their training, level of experience, and competence.

4.5 Marriage and family therapists take reasonable measures to ensure that services provided by supervisees are professional.

4.6 Marriage and family therapists avoid accepting as supervisees or students those individuals with whom a prior or existing relationship could compromise the therapist's objectivity. When such situations cannot be avoided, therapists take appropriate precautions to maintain objectivity. Examples of such relationships include, but are not limited to, those individuals with whom the therapist has a current or prior sexual, close personal, immediate familial, or therapeutic relationship.

4.7 Marriage and family therapists do not disclose supervisee confidences except by written authorization or waiver, or when mandated or permitted by law. In educational or training settings where there are multiple supervisors, disclosures are permitted only to other professional colleagues, administrators, or employers who share responsibility for training of the supervisee. Verbal authorization will not be sufficient except in emergency situations, unless prohibited by law.

CASE 13

A licensed marriage and family therapist in private practice expanded her practice by opening satellite offices in a number of surrounding communities. She hired several school counselors on a part-time basis to assist her in offering family therapy services. None of the school counselors had any formal family therapy training. All listings and literature associated with the satellite offices claimed the offices as belonging to and being staffed by a licensed marriage and family therapist. The therapist had, however, made arrangements to meet weekly with each of her employees.

Analysis

Principle 4.4 is of direct concern in this case. The marriage and family therapist appears to have sought to expand her practice more on an economic than an ethical basis. If the satellite offices are to be identified as offering services from a licensed marriage and family therapist, then the therapist should endeavor to employ licensed marriage and family therapists. Employing school counselors to offer services relevant to their training and demonstrated competencies is ethical and appropriate as an adjunct to family therapy services. Permitting these individuals to hold themselves as family therapy providers, even though under the supervision of a trained, experienced marriage and family therapist, represents unethical practice. It is therapists' ethical responsibility to clearly state the purposes of services being offered to prospective clients, being very careful to label providers appropriately so consumers can accurately acquire desired services, and said providers can be accountable for their professional activities.

CASE 14

A professor in a graduate marriage and family therapy training program maintained a part-time private practice in addition to his university responsibilities. The professor had a reputation among colleagues and students as an outstanding clinician as well as academician. Occasionally, students in the program requested marital or family therapy services from the professor through his private practice. The professor was conscientious in explaining that such services could be obtained at the university's counseling center at minimal cost for students and their families. Some students, however, insisted, and the professor agreed to provide them the therapy services requested.

Analysis

The therapist in this case appears to be cognizant of his influential position with respect to students in the training program. His advocacy of the university's counseling center appropriately conveys this cognizance. However, he had obligations to his academic position that might create conflicts should issues of a problematic nature arise in therapy. For example, information might be shared in therapy suggesting that the student should be prevented from pursuing an internship that incorporated direct client work. The student might seek to immediately pursue that kind of internship, maintaining that information shared within the therapy be kept confidential. Or, although the student might not be ready for an internship from an academic perspective, the therapist's sympathy for the student's family circumstances generated during therapy could encourage a biased academic assessment. Principles 4.1 and 4.2 call for marriage and family therapists to avoid dual relationships that could impair their judgment and do not provide therapy to current students. The therapist in this case seems to have entered such a dual relationship.

CASE 15

Several faculty of a university training program in marriage and family therapy expressed concern to the department head about one graduate student who received satisfactory grades in his didactic coursework but exhibited extremely poor relationship skills with family members as well as individual clients in the program's in-house practicum placement. The department head did not follow up on faculty concerns, as the student had an acceptable overall grade-point average.

Analysis

Principles 4.4 and 4.5 are relevant here. Even though he is still a student, by allowing the student to provide services to family and individual clients when he was reportedly not competent at this time to do so is of concern. It is critical that marriage and family therapy trainers assist students in securing remedial assistance when needed. Also critical, however, is the potential need to screen from further training those individuals who are unable to provide competent services following reasonable remediation efforts.

PRINCIPLE 5. RESPONSIBILITY TO RESEARCH PARTICIPANTS

Investigators respect the dignity and protect the welfare of participants in research and are aware of federal and state laws and regulations and professional standards governing the conduct of research.

5.1   Investigators are responsible for making careful examination of ethical acceptability in planning studies. To the extent that services to research participants may be compromised by participation in research, investigators seek the ethical advice of qualified professionals not directly involved in the investigation and observe safeguards to protect the rights of research participants.

5.2 Investigators requesting participants' involvement in research inform them of all aspects of the research that might reasonably be expected to influence willingness to participate. Investigators are especially sensitive to the possibility of diminished consent when participants are also receiving clinical services, have impairments which limit understanding and/or communication, or when participants are children.

5.3 Investigators respect each participant's freedom to decline participation in or to withdraw from a research study at any time. This obligation requires special thought and consideration when investigators or other members of the research team are in positions of authority or influence over participants. Marriage and family therapists, therefore, make every effort to avoid multiple relationships with research participants that could impair professional judgment or increase the risk of exploitation.

5.4 Information obtained about a research participant during the course of an investigation is confidential unless there is a waiver previously obtained in writing. When the possibility exists that others, including family members, may obtain access to such information, this possibility, together with the plan for protecting confidentiality, is explained as part of the procedure for obtaining informed consent.

CASE 16

An advertisement was placed in the university and city newspapers by a marriage and family therapy graduate student and her major professor for the purpose of recruiting volunteer families to take part in a "Family Mediation Project." The research involved one-half of the families to be subjected to "very uncomfortable circumstances" when they took part in the research (i.e., the family would be kept waiting a long time before being seen, the temperature in the waiting room would be raised, there would be only two seats in the waiting room). The other half of the families would not experience these uncomfortable circumstances. Both groups would take part in family mediation with a trained therapist following their respective circumstances. The study was intended to test the efficacy of certain mediation techniques with families under stress.

Analysis

A study such as this raises several potential ethical problems, given the information offered. Principles 5.1 and 5.2 are especially relevant. In research with human subjects, investigators must take special care in their planning a study so as to avoid physical, psychological, or social harm being inflicted on the subjects. Minimally, this would include consent procedures so that subjects are fully informed of the purpose of the study and the possible risks. In studies when subjects are withheld some information or given misinformation because it is essential to the investigation, corrective action must be taken as soon as possible following completion of the study. Whether family members are being informed that some will experience "very uncomfortable circumstances" is unclear; further, there is no indication of any debriefing procedures to address any negative effects of those who do experience "uncomfortable procedures." Finally, all studies involving human subjects should be reviewed by a "human subjects committee" before being implemented to ensure that research participants' rights are safeguarded.

CASE 17

A couple participated in a research project conducted by a marriage and family therapy doctoral student. The couple filed a complaint with the university after their participation in the project stating that they were deceived by the student regarding the requirements of their participation and suffered undue stress as a result. The project did incorporate deception because participant couples were led to believe that the purpose was to rate a videotape of another couple's interaction, when the dependent variable was actually their reaction in having experienced a 2-hour delay before viewing the tape. The couple was thoroughly debriefed following their participation according to procedures incorporated in the project, which had been previewed and approved both by the student's doctoral committee members and the university's Human Subjects Research Committee.

Analysis

Principle 5.1 maintains that marriage and family therapists are responsible for making careful examination of ethical accountability in planning studies. The student's preparatory actions in seeking the preview and approval of relevant bodies suggest she took adequate precautions to minimize any stress reactions participant couples might experience. Were a significant number of the participant couples to complain that they had experienced excessive stress as a result of their participation, however, it would be ethically incumbent on the student to consider revision of her procedures in consultation with her doctoral and university research committees. Although the potential impact of the findings may be considerable, the welfare of participants must be the primary concern.

CASE 18

A marriage and family therapy professor was teaching an undergraduate course in family relations. The professor was conducting a study that required subjects to complete a family inventory. The inventory results would be compared with subjects' behavior in small-group interaction activities held during class. Participation was mandatory, as the study was related to the course content.

Analysis

Principle 5.3 is particularly applicable in this case. Participation in research must be voluntary. Further, investigators who are in positions of authority over participants such as this professor must take due care in potentially asserting their influence. Even if participation in this study was not overtly mandatory, the professor's position could influence some students to participate, although they'd rather not (e.g., fear of a lower grade, etc.). In a situation such as this, the professor might conduct the study, as it is related to course content, but offer another equally valuable way to contribute to the class for those choosing not to participate in the study (e.g., paper and/or presentation). Principle 5.4 may be applicable in this case as well, depending on the manner in which inventory results are shared or not shared during class. If they are to be shared, it is critical that participants understand the content of what may be shared and provide their written permission to do so.

PRINCIPLE 6. RESPONSIBILITY TO THE PROFESSION

Marriage and family therapists respect the rights and responsibilities of professional colleagues and participate in activities that advance the goals of the profession.

6.1 Marriage and family therapists remain accountable to the standards of the profession when acting as members or employees of organizations. If the mandates of an organization with which a marriage and family therapist is affiliated, through employment, contract or otherwise, conflict with the AAMFT Code of Ethics, marriage and family therapists make known to the organization their commitment to the AAMFT Code of Ethics and attempt to resolve the conflict in a way that allows the fullest adherence to the Code of Ethics.

6.2 Marriage and family therapists assign publication credit to those who have contributed to a publication in proportion to their contributions and in accordance with customary professional publication practices.

6.3 Marriage and family therapists do not accept or require authorship credit for a publication based on research from a student's program, unless the therapist made a substantial contribution beyond being a faculty advisor or research committee member. Coauthorship on a student thesis, dissertation, or project should be determined in accordance with principles of fairness and justice.

6.4 Marriage and family therapists who are the authors of books or other materials that are published or distributed do not plagiarize or fail to cite persons to whom credit for original ideas or work is due.

6.5 Marriage and family therapists who are the authors of books or other materials published or distributed by an organization take reasonable precautions to ensure that the organization promotes and advertises the materials accurately and factually.

6.6 Marriage and family therapists participate in activities that contribute to a better community and society, including devoting a portion of their professional activity to services for which there is little or no financial return.

6.7 Marriage and family therapists are concerned with developing laws and regulations pertaining to marriage and family therapy that serve the public interest, and with altering such laws and regulations that are not in the public interest.

6.8 Marriage and family therapists encourage public participation in the design and delivery of professional services and in the regulation of practitioners.

CASE 19

A marriage and family therapist discovered to his dismay that the publisher with whom he had contracted had changed the subtitle of his book to one that conflicted with the *AAMFT Code of Ethics* (American Association for Marriage and Family Therapy, 2001). The subtitle was altered by the publisher during editing to promise "a guarantee of family happiness" to the reader. The therapist immediately contacted the publisher on learning of the subtitle change and was informed that the first printing of the book would have to stand as is; no changes could be made until a second printing was initiated sometime in the future, depending on the book's sales.

Analysis

Principle 6.5 is of direct concern to the author in this case. Although the relevant prepublication contact between the author and publisher is not clear, the author does appear to have taken timely and appropriate action on learning of the subtitle change. Unfortunately, this case illustrates the limited control authors sometimes have with publishers and suggests a need for the marriage and family therapist to assume a more assertive stance with regard to editorial changes. Ethically, the author should have required his consent to any changes made before actual publication of the book to ensure its accuracy.

CASE 20

In a graduate course in marriage and family therapy theory, the instructor assigned students as their major project an extensive analysis of dominant figures in the field. The instructor required that the projects become the permanent property of the department and asked that students desiring feedback attach a photocopy, which was returned to them with comments. Later the instructor used the materials submitted by the students in preparing an article that was accepted and eventually published in a leading journal. No mention of the students' contribution was made.

Analysis

The instructor's actions in this case appear questionable with regard to Principles 6.2, 6.3, and 6.4. This is particularly true if the instructor used any students' original ideas in writing the article; if so, proper credit was ethically due to the students. Further, the students whose projects were used in the preparation of the article would have significantly contributed to its contents, and thus publication credit was ethically due them.

CASE 21

A marriage and family therapist employed by a county agency recognized understaffing as becoming a serious problem. As demands for services increased, therapists were being asked to carry an excessive caseload, which caused the quality of services being delivered to deteriorate. Further, more and more student interns were being recruited by the agency's administration to meet new requests for services at a time when staff members' increased caseloads allowed less time for supervision of the interns' work. This was done in lieu of hiring additional full-time experienced professionals.

Analysis

Principle 6.1 is most relevant for the marriage and family therapist experiencing this dilemma. Although the therapist should expect the agency administration to recognize and appropriately respond to concerns about the quality of services, it is ultimately the therapist's responsibility to inform the administration and other relevant sources of the ethical standards that apply. In this instance, the therapist would be ethically bound to pursue such a course of information giving. Depending on the response received, further action might include identifying relevant staff involved in the delivery of services and proposing that they organize to assess the present needs for direct client services, staffing, supervision, and the like and that they take an active stance in asserting that these needs be more adequately and ethically addressed.

PRINCIPLE 7. FINANCIAL ARRANGEMENTS

Marriage and family therapists make financial arrangements with clients, third-party payors, and supervisees that are reasonably understandable and conform to accepted professional practices.

7.1   Marriage and family therapists do not offer or accept kickbacks, rebates, bonuses, or other remuneration for referrals; fee-for-service arrangements are not prohibited.

7.2   Prior to entering into the therapeutic or supervisory relationship, marriage and family therapists clearly disclose and explain to clients and supervisees: (a) all financial arrangements and fees related to professional services, including charges for canceled or missed appointments; (b) the use of collection agencies or legal measures for nonpayment; and (c) the procedure for obtaining payment from the client, to the extent allowed by law, if payment is denied by the third-party payor. Once services have begun, therapists provide reasonable notice of any changes in fees or other charges.

7.3   Marriage and family therapists give reasonable notice to clients with unpaid balances of their intent to seek collection by agency or legal recourse. When such action is taken, therapists will not disclose clinical information.

7.4   Marriage and family therapists represent facts truthfully to clients, third-party payors, and supervisees regarding services rendered.

7.5   Marriage and family therapists ordinarily refrain from accepting goods and services from clients in return for services rendered. Bartering for professional services may be conducted only if: (a) the supervisee or client requests it, (b) the relationship is not exploitative, (c) the professional relationship is not distorted, and (d) a clear written contract is established.

7.6   Marriage and family therapists may not withhold records under their immediate control that are requested and needed for a client's treatment solely because payment has not been received for past services, except as otherwise provided by law.

CASE 22

A family initiated therapy services with a marriage and family therapist. In completing a written intake form, the parents noted having mental health benefits as part of their insurance coverage. When they requested information with regard to the therapist's fees, they were told not to be concerned, as insurance would cover the costs.

Analysis

Principle 7.2, which clearly states that a therapist's fee structure be disclosed to clients at the onset of treatment, is of specific concern in this case. Adherence to this standard allows clients to make a fully informed choice regarding the pursuit of treatment. The client is not the insurance company or any other third-party payer. Consequently, the family (parents in the present case) must be informed of the session fees before being rendered services. This ethical obligation still stands, even though services are paid for by a third party.

CASE 23

A marriage and family therapist was frequently called on by a group of pediatricians to provide family therapy services in cases where family dynamics appeared to be negatively affecting children's physical conditions. In return, the marriage and family therapist regularly referred families to this particular medical group because of their enlightened position on the value of family therapy for their patients.

Analysis

Violation of Principle 7.1 is the major concern in this case. The primary ethical question revolves around the presence of any formal agreement regarding compensation for referrals. Although the marriage and family therapist accepted referrals from the group and referred in turn, the facts suggest that this was done due to the professionals' mutual confidences in each other, not because a specific agreement had been made to offer remuneration in return for referrals. Thus, the marriage and family therapist's actions represent appropriate ethical practice.

CASE 24

A marriage and family therapist had been working with a family whose insurance benefits expired. Both she and the family recognized the need for further sessions to achieve the goals they had mutually established. The family could not, however, afford to pay the therapist's fees.

Analysis

Principle 7.2 calls for marriage and family therapists to disclose their fees to clients at the beginning of services. The preamble for Principle 7 states that financial arrangements with clients should be reasonably understandable. In establishing a fee agreement with this family, it does not appear that the limitations of insurance benefits were considered, or at least discussed. Such possibilities should be addressed with clients at the onset of services with alternative courses of action (e.g., referral, pro bono sessions, etc.) that might be pursued if the need for continuing therapy exceeds the benefit period.

PRINCIPLE 8. ADVERTISING

Professional advertising is discussed in Chapter 9. Principle 8 and relevant case illustrations are considered in Chapter 9 and again in Chapter 10.

II

Legal Issues in Marriage and Family Therapy

Law and therapy go hand in hand. What are some of the obvious areas in which legal input would be essential to the therapeutic or counseling process? When should the therapist be sensitive to legal issues? What problems can exist where therapy and law must co-exist? Can a therapist afford to be ignorant of the law? Can such ignorance ever be excused?

(Bernstein, 1982, p. 10)

The Marriage and Family Therapist: Roles and Responsibilities Within the Legal System

Contemporary public policy has evolved from a progressive merger of legal principles and social science conceptualizations. As with most mergers, these two factions have come to pursue similar ends. For years the legal system has sought to maintain the family as the primary building block of the social order. Likewise, over the past century, mental health professionals became increasingly influential in helping to create laws aimed at facilitating healthy, stable family functioning (Mulvey, Reppucci, & Weithorn, 1984). Today, the knowledge and assistance of legal services and mental health professionals are inextricably linked to most aspects of public policy, so much so that there is presently an active use of the legal system to promote goals deemed desirable by the mental health profession and vice versa.

Marriage and family therapists need to know the law (Riley, Hartwell, Sargent, & Patterson, 1997). For instance, marriage and family therapists are regularly being called as expert witnesses to assist the legal system; effective testimony implies familiarity not only with marital and family understandings but also with the legal issues in question and the process by which they will be decided. Similarly, the principles on which judgments of professional legal responsibility and liability are based have seen many changes in recent years. Marriage and family therapists must keep abreast of these changes to protect themselves and their clients. For example, familiarity with relevant law will allow them to make more sophisticated decisions about when confidentiality applies as opposed to circumstances mandating disclosure of information (e.g., child abuse, suicidal threat).

Involvement with the legal system calls for conceptual changes by many marriage and family therapists. In contrast with professionals from other disciplines, marriage and family therapists may find movement into legal matters more difficult because of their philosophy and methods. Most marriage and family therapists' training is heavily influenced by goal-oriented notions of "what should be"; as a result, they are often unprepared for the "what is" emphasis of the courtroom. The legal system aims not at helping clients progress and become better but rather on reaching a fair decision that solves a practical problem in the here and now, one that can be applied to similar situations in the same way. The philosophy of the courtroom process frequently contradicts the therapy process (Woody & Mitchell, 1984).

Methodologically, marriage and family therapists' major therapeutic role is to facilitate individuals and families in functioning better. In legal proceedings, marriage and family therapists' primary role is simply to tell the truth. The attorneys' role is to promote their particular client's interest within the boundaries of the law and rules of the court. The attorney is not there to discover the truth; the court will determine the truth by weighing all evidence within the context of an adversarial struggle between attorneys. Marriage and family therapists are placed in the middle and sometimes mistakenly take an opposing attorney's activities as a personal attack against themselves or the best interests of their client. This makes it difficult to remain objective in an atmosphere accentuating any tendency, conscious or unconscious, for personal bias as well as actual abuse of behavioral science data.

An understanding of the law and legal system as relevant to areas concerning marriage and family therapy can relieve many of the pressures potentially confronting therapists in these circumstances. It is obviously not necessary or possible for therapists to possess the knowledge of an attorney; rather, they should have a basic comprehension of legal processes and procedures, information necessary to pursue elementary legal research efforts, and access to an attorney when legal advice is necessary.

Ruback (1982) asserts that marriage and family therapists may assume three major roles within the legal system: (1) a source of information leading to intervention by the state, (2) a resource for therapy services, and (3) an expert witness. Following an introduction to the basics of legal education, this chapter considers each of these roles as well as the increasingly pertinent issue of marriage and family therapists' professional liability under the law. A bibliography of recommended resources at the end of the chapter provides a more extensive exploration of the topics addressed.

LEGAL EDUCATION

Marriage and family therapists need to be familiar with the basics of legal research so they can educate themselves in matters relevant to their professional practice. Shea (1985) asserts that researching a particular point amid the expanse of the law is generally not beyond the ability of the competent layperson. For marriage and family therapists—legal "laypersons"—several distinctions are of particular concern.

Common Law

Common law is the fundamental law of the United States. Derived from the English Common Law, its authority stems from tradition and usage, not from legislation. Common law is regarded as expressing "the usage and customs of immemorial antiquity" common to the people of England. Conceptually, common law represents the belief that law does not have to be derived from only written sources (Reed, 1985). American law in the 1800s took pride in its common law arrangement. In the 1900s, legislation has modified and often supplemented the common law.

Constitutional Law

The U.S. government and each of its states and territories have a constitution. Constitutions provide basic principles that cannot be violated by other types of law.

Statutory Law

Statutory law consists of those laws passed by a legislative body, such as a state legislature or Congress, and signed into law. Statutory laws exist in each of the 50 states, in the U.S. territories, and at the federal level. The statutes are binding only in the jurisdiction where they are passed.

Administrative (Regulatory) Law

Administrative agencies have grown rapidly in this country, beginning with the New Deal legislation of the 1930s. At that time it became clear that Congress and state legislatures could not effectively promulgate rules on all areas of government control. Highly specialized areas required knowledge and time beyond the limits of the average legislator. Consequently, Congress or state legislatures passed laws delegating broad rule-making authority to specialized agencies (Knapp, Vandecreek, & Zirkel, 1985).

Case Law (Court Decisions)

Case law is a body of legal decisions that, when taken collectively, create rules for decision making. Typically, statutes prescribe certain legal principles. Legislation, however, is frequently written in broad terms, and thus courts apply, interpret, and fill in the intricacies in the statutes. Courts consider a statute and its legislative history and decide what the legislators actually intended. Court opinions take into account any bearing that higher laws (such as the state or federal constitution) may have on the interpretation of the statute in question (Knapp et al., 1985).

Many nuances enter the process. A determination must be made as to whether federal or state law applies. In general, state law must be considered first; if a federal issue is raised, such as a constitutional right or a conflict between states, federal law will come into play. Depending on the nature of a case, a federal court may apply a state law, even when considering a federal issue (Woody & Mitchell, 1984).

Case law accumulates on the basis of *stare decisis* (let the decision stand). Under this doctrine, when a court interprets and applies common law, statutes, and/or regulations to the facts of a case, that court and lower courts in the same jurisdiction are bound to apply that precedent to future cases with similar facts (Kempin, 1982). Other courts may regard such decisions, depending on their number and reasoning, as persuasive, albeit not binding. Reed (1985) described this process:

> The fashion in which one case governs another is elusive of description. In retrospect, the process is seen to constitute a form of logic, but a logic which often deals with principles that are imperfectly expressed, even in the court's opinion in the case at hand. Indeed, merely because a case has been decided in a given direction and because a legal principle applying to the case has been enunciated, the law on the point is, by no means, necessarily established. The saying, "Hard cases make bad law," illustrates a common failing of judges to overgeneralize a legal principle in rationalizing a case which, because of its one-sidedness, is easy to resolve. But one case does not establish the law; others come along which test declared legal principles and, consequently, lead to refinement.
>
> Typically, case law originates with a case; for example, in Oklahoma, the Supreme Court in that State formulates a legal principle that will be considered binding in Oklahoma (until it is successfully challenged). But the lawyers in an adjoining state might say that they are from Missouri and that they, themselves, have to test such a finding in their own courts. (A precedent in a neighboring state is bound to carry some weight in a jurisdiction, but it is not binding as precedent.) Missouri, with a somewhat similar fact situation as that in the Oklahoma case, will be likely to deal with the Missouri facts in the light of the decided case from Oklahoma, but may find different conclusions and somewhat different case law. Ultimately, several states, and perhaps even the courts of the Federal system, will formulate principles dealing with the same type of related cases, and a "weight of opinion" will have been achieved. The weight of opinion, expressed in differing ways and perhaps binding with somewhat differing nuances in different states, is considered to be the law. If the original decision on a case, as in Oklahoma, should, in retrospect, be seen as countering the trend of opinions, it is likely that that viewpoint will be challenged in the original state. The highest appellate court may overrule its original opinion, usually in some face-saving manner, or the state may continue in a maverick status with respect to that particular legal point. The trend is for some homogeneity to evolve over the various states and over Federal jurisdictions. The process of this evolution takes place over time and over several regions.[1]

Cases may be decided in the trial, intermediate, appellate, or highest court levels within the state or federal system. Although the nomenclature may vary from one

[1]*Note.* From "The Origin and Functions of American Law," by J. M. Reed, in *Law and Ethics: A Guide for the Health Professional* (pp. 4–5), edited by N. T. Sidney, 1985, New York: Human Sciences Press. Copyright 1985 by Human Sciences Press. Reprinted with permission.

Figure 5–1 Typical Court Names
in Federal State Systems

Note. From "Legal Research Techniques:
What the Psychologist Needs to Know" by S.
Knapp, L. Vandecreek, and P. Zirkel, 1985,
Professional Psychology: Research & Practice, 16, pp. 363–372. Copyright 1985 by
American Psychological Association.
Reprinted by permission of the author.

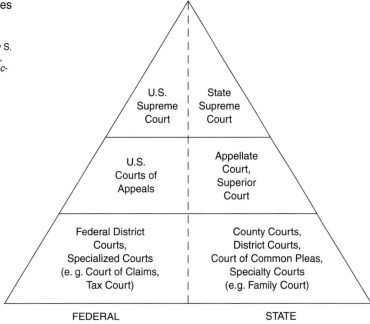

jurisdiction to another, the typical designations for various court levels are listed
in Figure 5–1.

Trial courts determine facts in disputes and apply appropriate rules of law. In
the trial court, parties first appear, witnesses testify, and other evidence is presented. The losing party on the trial level may appeal the decision to an appellate
court. Appellate courts do not hear new testimony, but rather decide whether the
law was properly applied at a lower level in the court system. A higher level of
appeal is typically available, depending on the issue, as a matter of right (the legal
privilege due each person as a citizen) or as a result of an upper court's discretion. It is important to reiterate that even a minor change in the facts can change
the decision of the court.

An understanding of five component parts is helpful in interpreting court
decisions (Shea, 1985):

1. *Facts.* The facts of a case form the basis for a court's decision. In a jury
   case, it is the jury who decides what are the facts; in a nonjury case, it is
   the trial judge who makes these determinations.
2. *Issue.* An issue of a case is its decisional focus. The parties attempt to
   focus a judge's attention on the issues of a case most favorable to their
   position. Ultimately, the judge decides what the issues in a case are
   regarding his or her decision.
3. *Rule.* A rule is a statement of the law that is applied to the facts. Often
   rules are incomplete or ambiguous, requiring the court to interpret them.

Such an interpretation then becomes a rule in being a statement of law developed by the court. The rule of a decision, especially of an appellate court, serves as a precedent. Once a rule is stated in a decision, only that court or a higher court may alter it.

4. *Holding.* The holding of the decision is its outcome, the result of the rule applied to the facts, and who wins or loses.

5. *Dicta.* In a decision, a court may discuss rules that are not directly related to the facts of present case. When a court states a rule that is not necessary for deciding a case, the rule is referred to as an *obiter dictum*. Dicta (plural) serve as guidance but do not constitute binding precedent for lowercourts.

Criminal vs. Civil Law

Although their basic purposes are similar, that is, to promote social order and to provide a system of dispute resolution, civil and criminal law differ in one significant way. *Civil law* pertains to acts offensive to individuals, *criminal law* to acts offensive to society in general. The ultimate remedy for harms inflicted in violation of criminal laws is punishment of the violator in the name of the state. Civil law provides a framework within which claims by one party or parties against another are adjudicated before a court. In civil law, the remedy is some compensation to the victim (Keary, 1985).

Marriage and family therapists who seek to supplement their therapeutic expertise with specific legal understandings should become familiar with the major types of legal sources. Woody and Mitchell (1984) offer an orientation for doing so in Figure 5–2.

This orientation should provide sufficient information to enter a law library. Law libraries are maintained by law schools, whose official policies vary; however, most will give permission for legal research by professionals such as marriage and family therapists. State, county, and city law libraries, although intended for judges and lawyers, are generally available to the public. Although their collections are probably less extensive than a good law school library, most civic law libraries are quite willing to provide assistance to nonlawyers. Local bar associations can be contacted for the location of these libraries. Private law libraries provide another research source. Larger law firms and office complexes catering to attorneys often have fairly extensive libraries. Access may prove more difficult, however (Shea, 1985). Finally, many university, college, and public libraries have good legal collections.

In most locations, law librarians are available to assist researchers, including marriage and family therapists. Furthermore, many attorneys typically welcome giving free advice for bona fide research efforts; such contacts frequently facilitate future referral relationships. Last, seminars, symposia, and workshops on relevant legal issues are regularly sponsored by colleges and universities, public and private agencies, and various professional organizations.

It would be unrealistic to expect the human services professional to acquire the same facility at locating and understanding legal information as would be commonplace for the legal scholar. On the other hand, the human services professional can supplement his or her behavioral or health science expertise with legal ideas, albeit in a somewhat rudimentary fashion. The human services professional can achieve an adequate orientation by becoming familiar with the major types of legal sources. This fundamental orientation can be augmented by guidance from a professional legal librarian.

United States Supreme Court decisions are reported by official and unofficial reporters. The official reporter, created by statutory authority, is the *United States Supreme Court Reports* (cited as U.S.). The unofficial reporters, products of commercial publishers, are the West Publishing Company's *Supreme Court Reporter* (S.Ct.) and the Lawyers Co-operative Publishing Company's *Lawyers' Edition of United States Supreme Court Reports* (L. Ed. or L. Ed. 2d). All these editions are authoritative as to text, but the unofficial versions may also contain supplemental information (such as summaries of the attorneys' arguments or abstracts on specific legal points). If a Supreme Court case has not yet appeared in these publications, it might be found in *United States Law Week* (U.S. L.W.), a looseleaf service.

Decisions on cases from the U.S. Courts of Appeals appear in the *Federal Reporter* (F. or F.2d). U.S. District court decisions appear in the *Federal Supplement* (F. Supp.) and *Federal Rules Decision* (F.R.D.).

State court decisions (except in a few states) are disseminated by an official state reporter, such as *Michigan Reports* (Mich.) or *California Reports* (Cal., Cal.2d, or Cal.3d). There will also be a regional reporter, such as *Northwestern Reporter* (N.W. or N.W.2d), which includes important cases from Michigan, Wisconsin, Minnesota, Iowa, North Dakota, South Dakota, and Nebraska.

Contrary to popular belief, not all court cases are published. That is, most cases at the federal level are published (especially those decided by the U.S. Supreme Court or a U.S. Court of Appeals); at the state level, most jurisdictions publish appellate decisions, but other cases (for instance, those decided at the trial level) may not be published unless they have special legal importance. Cases that are unreported elsewhere (as well as recent cases that have not yet appeared in the various reporters) may sometimes be found in separately paginated "advance sheets," in "looseleaf services" (such as the *Criminal Law Reporter,* the *Family Law Reporter,* or the *Labor Law Reporter*), or in legal periodicals.

Federal statutes appear, among other sources, in the *Statutes at Large* (these "session laws" are arranged in the order in which they are enacted); this source (cited Stat.) also includes congressional resolutions, select presidential proclamations, and treaties and other international agreements. *The United States Code* (U.S.C.) is published by the U.S. Government Printing Office and is the primary authority on final legislative law.

Federal administrative rules and regulations appear in the *Federal Register* (Fed. Reg.). The *Code of Federal Regulations* (C.F.R.) cites (by title and section) all federal administrative rules and regulations, except Treasury materials. Federal administrative decisions are published by various agencies, such as the Federal Trade Commission and the National Labor Relations Board.

Figure 5–2 An Orientation to Legal Research Sources

State statutes—for example, the *Arkansas Statutes Annotated* (cited Ark. Stat. Ann.)—are published in bound volumes periodically. In between issues, a statute may be eliminated, amended, or added, and will be found in supplemental editions. It is always necessary to check in the back of a bound volume to see whether a "pocket supplement" reflects any revision of a statute.

Municipal and county ordinances appear in many forms but are usually confined to local distribution. The variations in form preclude detail herein. In general, however, these ordinances are similar in form to the statutes.

Legal research is blessed with encyclopedic sources. For example, the *American Law Reports* (A.L.R., A.L.R.2d or A.L.R.3d) include selected cases and annotations on specific subjects, along with historical background, current law, and probable future developments. Similarly, the *Corpus Juris Secundum* (C.J.S.) series cites case authority; presents a researched summary of the law, and so on. *Words and Phrases* contains more descriptive and extensive definitions than the well-known *Black's Law Dictionary.*

An often-used legal research method is to "Shepardize" a case—that is, to use *Shepard's Case Citations* to follow the judicial history of a targeted case, learn the contemporary status of the case, locate other cases that have cited it, and acquire research leads (such as where to look in *American Law Reports*). The *Shepard* volumes are divided by jurisdiction. Statutes may also be researched in *Shepard's United States Citations,* and law review articles may be located in *Shepard's Law Review Citations.* Municipal charters and ordinances may be cited in *Shepard's Ordinance Law Citations.*

Legal materials follow a special referencing or citation system. For example, cases are cited as follows (with minor variations in type style used in different publications):

Tarasoff v. Regents of the University of California, 17 Cal.3d 425, 551 P.2d 334, 131 Cal. Rptr. 14 (1976).
("Cal.3d" is the third series of *California Reports,* the state reporter for California Supreme Court cases; "17" is the volume where the *Tarasoff* case is reported, and "425" is the first page where the case appears. "P.2d" is the *Pacific Reporter,* the regional reporter for California state court cases; and again, "551" is the volume number and "334" the first page where the case appears. "Cal. Rptr." is *West's California Reporter,* an unofficial reporter for California court cases.

Muller v. Oregon, 208 U.S. 412, 415 (1908).
("U.S." is *United States Supreme Court Reports,* and "415" is the page where a specific quoted passage, presumably just cited in the text, appears. If the case has previously been cited, this citation may appear as *"Muller v. Oregon,* 208 U.S. at 415.")

Driver v. Hinnant, 356 F.2d 761 (4th Cir. 1966).
("F.2d" is *Federal Reporter,* publisher of U.S. Court of Appeals cases; "4th Cir." indicates that the case was heard by the U.S. Court of Appeals for the Fourth Circuit.)

Figure 5–2   *continued*

Greenberg v. Barbour, 332 F. Supp. 745 (E.D. Pa. 1971).
("F. Supp." is the *Federal Supplement,* reporter for U.S. District Court Cases;
"E.D. Pa." indicates that the case was heard by the U.S. District Court for the
eastern district of Pennsylvania.)

In addition, books, periodicals, newspapers, statutes, legislative materials, and other
specialized materials are cited in prescribed ways. An authoritative source for learning
legal citations is *A Uniform System of Citation* (12th ed., 1976), created by law
review groups at Columbia, Harvard, Pennsylvania, and Yale (distributed by the Harvard Law Review Association, Gannett House, Cambridge, Massachusetts 02138.

Note. From "Understanding the Legal System and Legal Research" (pp. 30–33), by R.H. Woody & R.E. Mitchell. In
The Law and Practice of Human Services by R.H. Woody (Ed.). 1984, San Francisco: Jossey-Bass. Reprinted by
permission.

THE MARRIAGE AND FAMILY THERAPIST AS A SOURCE OF INFORMATION

Marriage and family therapists have an obligation to provide information leading
to intervention by the state. The two most frequently encountered situations in
which therapists need to serve as sources of information involve their duty to protect third parties from actions by a client believed to be dangerous (R. E. Watts,
1999) and statutes requiring the reporting of child abuse and neglect. Both of
these requirements can pose painful professional dilemmas for therapists, as discussed in earlier chapters on ethical obligations. The present discussion, however,
highlights only the legal obligations.

The Duty to Protect

In 1976, the California Supreme Court handed down a decision in *Tarasoff v.
Board of Regents of the University of California* that signaled a trend toward
protection of the public's safety in preference to client confidentiality in psychotherapy. The case involved a client who threatened during therapy to kill his
girlfriend and did so 2 months later:

> In August 1969, Prosenjit Poddar, a voluntary outpatient at the student health ser-
> vice on the Berkeley campus of the University of California, informed his therapist,
> a psychologist, that he was planning to kill a young woman. He did not name the
> woman, but as was established later, the psychologist could have easily inferred
> who she was. The murder was to be carried out upon the woman's return to the uni-
> versity from her summer vacation. Following the session during which this informa-
> tion was given, the therapist telephoned the campus police, requesting that they
> observe Poddar for possible hospitalization as a person who was "dangerous to him-
> self or others." The therapist followed up his telephone call with a formal letter

requesting assistance from the chief of the campus police. The campus police did take Poddar into custody for the purpose of questioning, but later released him when he gave evidence of being "rational." Soon afterward, the therapist's supervisor asked the campus police to return the letter, ordered that the letter and the therapist's case notes be destroyed, and directed that no further action be taken to hospitalize Poddar. No warning was given to the intended victim or her parents. The client, understandably, did not resume therapy. Two months later Poddar killed Tatiana Tarasoff. Her parents filed suit against the Board of Regents of the university, several employees of the student health service, and the chief of the campus police plus four of his officers for failing to notify the intended victim of the threat. A lower court dismissed the suit, the parents appealed, and the California Supreme Court upheld the appeal and later reaffirmed its decision that failure to warn the intended victim was irresponsible.

In *Tarasoff* the court held that a therapist who knew, or by the standards of his or her profession should have known, that his or her client posed a threat to another, had a duty to exercise reasonable care to protect the intended victim. Several other courts in jurisdictions outside California have since adopted the *Tarasoff* reasoning, subsequently further narrowing and refining it.

Three factors emanating from the *Tarasoff* decision have come to embody the findings regarding therapists' duty to protect. First, the court noted that generally one person does not have a duty to control the conduct of another. However, an exception to this was established for instances wherein one person has a "special relationship" either to the person whose conduct needs to be controlled or to the foreseeable victim of that conduct. This special relationship must be found to exist in the factual context of the case. In *Tarasoff*, the court held that the therapist–client relationship met the test of being a special relationship.

The second condition required to create a duty to protect is a determination that a client's behavior "needs to be controlled." Again, in the factual context of *Tarasoff*, the court found that the client, Prosenjit Poddar, was a threat. It was noted, however, that determining whether an individual's conduct needs to be controlled is frequently a difficult prediction to make.

While there is no definitive formula for determining whether an individual is at risk for violence, Beck and Baxter (1998) have suggested both internal (related to the person's thoughts, perceptions, feelings) and external (related to environmental or other situations that exist outside the individual) factors must be considered in assessing a person's potential for violence. These authors caution that a client has the potential for dangerousness if he or she (a) is angry; (b) has a motive, either delusional or realistic, for harming someone; (c) drinks (Rice & Harris, 1995; J. W. Swanson, 1993), or (d) is now or has been delusional, especially if the delusions involve influence or control. Kausch and Resnick (1998) have declared, "Risk factors for violence include a past history of violence, young age (early 20s), gender (male), lower social class, low intelligence quotient (IQ), major mental illness, organic brain disorder, a history of violence, suicide attempts, a history of prior criminal acts, access to lethal weapons, and use of drugs and alcohol" (p. 334).

In *Tarasoff*, the court identified a "reasonableness" test as the standard for determining if a client's conduct could result in a threat to a third person. In determining reasonableness, the court considered within the context of the specific case "that reasonable degree of skill, knowledge, and care ordinarily possessed and exercised by members of (that professional specialty) under similar circumstances" (*Tarasoff v. Regents of the University of California*, 1976, p. 345). The court further pointed out within that standard, opinions might differ and thus therapists are free to exercise judgment without fear of liability: "Proof aided by hindsight, that he or she judged wrongly is insufficient to establish negligence" (p. 345).

The third and final condition that gave rise to the duty to protect was a "foreseeable" victim. Tatiana Tarasoff, while not specifically named, was readily identifiable as the proposed victim. Thus, the facts of *Tarasoff* satisfied the three conditions creating a duty to protect for the therapist: a special relationship, a reasonable prediction of conduct that constituted a threat, and a foreseeable victim.

In *McIntosh v. Milano* (1979), a New Jersey court ruled on a factual situation similar to that found in *Tarasoff* and similarly addressed a therapist's duty to protect:

> In this case, the client was an adolescent boy referred by a school counselor to the therapist, a psychiatrist. The boy informed the therapist of several fantasies he had including a fear of others, being a hero or important villain, using a knife to threaten those who might intimidate him, and having sexual experiences with Kimberly, the girl living next door to him. The boy also informed the therapist of having shot at Kimberly's car with a BB gun when she left for a date and showed the therapist a knife he had bought. The therapist was well aware of the boy's possessive feelings for Kimberly. The boy further told the therapist that he wanted Kimberly "to suffer" as he had and showed anger when Kimberly moved out of her parents' home. He was hateful toward Kimberly's boyfriends and upset when he could not obtain her new address. The boy killed Kimberly. Although the therapist had spoken to his client's parents on a number of occasions about their son's relationship to Kimberly, he never addressed the issue with either Kimberly or her parents.

Lane and Spruill (1980) asserted that dangerousness cannot be accurately predicted and that errors in making this decision are likely. The prediction of dangerousness in *Tarasoff* did not seem to be a questionable factor. Based on the testimony of another psychiatrist, dangerousness was not a question in *McIntosh v. Milano* but rather considered a fact based on a violent act (firing a weapon at Kimberly's car) and on the therapist's statement that his client had admitted fantasies of violence and feelings of retribution. The client had also verbalized threats toward Kimberly and her boyfriends. The court pointed out that "a therapist does have a basis for giving an opinion and a prognosis based on the history of the patient and the course of treatment" (*McIntosh v. Milano*, 1979, p. 508). In *Davis v. Lhim* (1988), the Michigan Supreme Court specified factors that should be considered by a mental health professional in seeking to determine whether a client might act on a threat to a third party. These included the client's clinical diagnosis, manner and context in which the threat was made, opportunity to act on the threat, history of violence, factors provoking the threat and whether threats are likely to continue, relationship with the potential victim, and the client's response to treatment.

In *Thompson v. County of Alameda* (1980), the court was asked to decide if there was a duty to protect the parents of a child who was murdered by a released juvenile offender. The juvenile had been in the custody of Alameda County and confined to an institution. He was known to have "latent, extremely dangerous and violent propensities regarding young children and that sexual assaults upon young children and violence connected therewith were a likely result of releasing (him) into the community" (p. 72). Within 24 hours of his temporary release to his mother, the boy killed a child who lived a few doors away. The foreseeability of the victim was the predominant question. The court referred to the language of *Tarasoff* and held that although the victim need not be directly named, he or she must be "readily identifiable." The court thus refused to impose liability on the involved county officials for failing to give a blanket warning to all neighborhood parents, the police, or the juvenile's mother.

Although the courts in other states have similarly declined to impose liability in the absence of an identifiable victim (*Brady v. Hopper*, 1983; *Leedy v. Hartnett*, 1981), the Vermont Supreme Court in *Peck v. Counseling Service of Addison County, Inc.* (1985) ruled that a mental health professional who knows that a client poses a risk to an identifiable person *or group* has a duty to protect that person or group. Other courts (*Hedlund v. Superior Court*, 1983; *Jablonski v. United States*, 1983) have held that the duty to protect extends to "foreseeable" victims who may not be specifically identifiable but nevertheless would be probable targets if the threatening client were to become violent or carry through on threats. For example, in *Hedlund v. Superior Court*, a woman was assaulted in the presence of her child by a client who had threatened to harm her. The mother alleged that the child had sustained "serious emotional injury and psychological trauma" as a consequence. The California Supreme Court held that a duty to "exercise reasonable care" needed to be fulfilled, which would have been satisfied by warning the mother that both she and her child might be in danger (Corey, Corey, & Callanan, 1993).

Although generally no legal obligation is imposed on a person to control the conduct of another, there is an exception. When an individual has a special relationship to either the one whose conduct needs to be controlled or to the intended victim of that conduct, the law imposes a duty to protect the victim (Serovich & Mosack, 2000). This is particularly relevant for marriage and family therapists because their relationship with their clients fulfills this "special relationship" condition. Given this, marriage and family therapists are expected to apply a standard of reasonableness in determining a threat posed by clients' conduct. It is important to remember that reasonableness is not a fixed concept but a standard comparing an individual therapist to others in the same profession with similar knowledge, skills, and training. Finally, when these two conditions occur and there is an intended victim or victims who are foreseeable, the marriage and family therapist has a duty to protect that victim or be liable under the law for negligence.

In an article entitled *"Tarasoff:* Ten Years Later," Fulero (1988) proposes that the issues raised by the *Tarasoff* decision are likely to continue to generate litigation, legislation, and controversy for some time into the future. Fulero strongly urges that clinicians seek consultation whenever necessary to clarify the soundness of their professional practices. As discussed earlier, a marriage and family therapist would not be liable for any negative outcome unless his or her actions fell below a reasonable standard of care. This book advocates the position put forth by Fulero in that marriage and family therapists should be competent relative to assessing and dealing with dangerousness as well as maintain a current understanding of statutes and case law in their own states.

McIntosh and Cartaya (1992) have suggested that there is a trend in case law to acknowledge the difficulty of predicting aberrant behavior. Although this is a welcomed development, marriage and family therapists must strive to protect others from the acts of dangerous clients.

Child Abuse and Neglect

There are no reliable statistics regarding the exact extent of child abuse and neglect in the United States. This uncertainty is likely caused by inconsistencies in definitions of what child abuse and neglect represent, variations in reporting laws from state to state, and the different methods of data collection commonly used. Nevertheless, the U.S. Advisory Board on Child Abuse and Neglect (1990), established by Congress to evaluate the nation's effectiveness in accomplishing the purposes of the Child Abuse Prevention and Treatment Act of 1974, declared that the problems still present relative to the treatment and prevention of child abuse and neglect in this country are so extreme as to constitute a national emergency. L. Davis (1991), for example, estimated that one in four girls and one in seven boys are sexually abused by the time they reach the age of 18.

The Child Abuse Prevention and Treatment Act of 1974 (PL 93-247) defines abuse and neglect as follows:

> Physical or mental injury, sexual abuse or exploitation, negligent treatment, or maltreatment of a child under the age of eighteen or the age specified by the child protection law of the state in question, by a person who is responsible for the child's welfare, under circumstances which indicate that the child's health or welfare is harmed or threatened thereby.

Although a clarifying definition, because child abuse is not a federal crime, federal law does no more than make money available to the states that meet its reporting guidelines and other qualifications, such as agreeing to set reporting standards. Thus, state definitions become very important as they provide the basis for abuse and neglect as a crime within a particular jurisdiction. Although state laws vary, most use a combination of two or more of the following elements in defining child abuse and neglect: physical injury, mental or emotional injury, and sexual molestation or exploitation. Fischer and Sorenson (1985) note that although some states have separate definitions for abuse and neglect, others do not. They assert it is unimportant to be able to distinguish between abuse and neglect.

> The time and effort spent in trying to distinguish between abuse and neglect serves no useful purpose. A child may suffer serious or permanent harm and even death as a result of neglect. Therefore, the same reasons that justify the mandatory reporting of abuse require the mandatory reporting of child neglect. (p. 183)

All states require that child abuse and neglect be reported to the proper authorities, particularly if physical injury is present. Other aspects of mandatory reporting laws may differ from state to state. For example, in Pennsylvania, therapists are required to file a report if their client is a child who has been abused; if their client is the abuser, however, the mandatory reporting law does not apply. New York state law requires that therapists report abuse whether they learn of it from a child in therapy, abuser in therapy, or a relative. Maryland law requires therapists to report both present and past cases of child abuse that have been revealed by adult clients in therapy (Corey et al., 1993).

State statutes mandating that marriage and family therapists report cases of suspected child abuse or neglect vary substantially in their content. As a result, it is imperative that therapists read and understand the exact language of the reporting statutes that govern mandatory reporting in their states. Volumes containing state statutes are available in all public and educational libraries.

When reading the language for their state statute that mandates suspected child abuse reporting, therapists should make the following determinations: (a) which categories of professionals must make suspected abuse or neglect reports; (b) whether reports are required only for current abuse or whether reports are required for suspected past abuse as well; (c) whether statutes exist requiring that reports of suspected abuse or neglect be made for adults who are elderly, developmentally disabled, residents of institutions, or otherwise vulnerable; (d) whether reporting suspected abuse or neglect to a therapist's supervisor is sufficient to satisfy the law or whether direct reports are required to child protection agencies; (e) whether oral reports must be followed by written reports; (f) the types of specific information that must be included in reports; and (g) circumstances under which reports must be made.

To be eligible for federal funds under the Child Abuse Prevention and Treatment Act, states must grant immunity to reporters. All states have complied with this requirement and therefore provide immunity by law from civil suit and criminal prosecution that might arise from the reporting of suspected child abuse or neglect. Such immunity applies to all mandatory or permissible reporters who act "in good faith." In many states, good faith is presumed; therefore, the person seeking to sue a reporter has the burden to prove that the reporter acted in bad faith. Clearly, any marriage and family therapist who, mandated by law, acts in good faith in reporting suspected cases of abuse or neglect is immune from suit.

No state requires that the reporter be absolutely certain before filing a report of abuse or neglect. It is sufficient that the reporter has "reason to believe" or "reasonable cause to believe or suspect" that a child is subject to abuse or neglect. As noted with respect to the duty to protect, the standard applied is what the reasonable person (professional) would believe under similar circumstances. As abuse rarely occurs in the presence of witnesses and because the protection of children is the primary purpose of reporting laws, reporters are not held to unduly rigorous standards as long as they act in good faith. Some states even require one to report when he or she "observes the child being subjected to conditions or circumstances which would reasonably result in child abuse or neglect" (Fischer & Sorenson, 1985, p. 184).

Marriage and family therapists are trained observers of children and their interactions with significant adults. There are, however, various symptoms that should alert therapists that some form of abuse or neglect is taking place. Table 5–1 lists in chart form some of the most common indicators of child abuse and neglect. These signs are of course only indicators that should alert marriage and

Table 5–1 Physical and Behavioral Indicators of Child Abuse and Neglect (CA/N)

Type of CA/N	Physical Indicators	Behavioral Indicators
PHYSICAL ABUSE	Unexplained Bruises and Welts: — on face, lips, mouth — on torso, back, buttocks, thighs — in various stages of healing — clustered, forming regular patterns — reflecting shape of article used to inflict (electric cord, belt buckle) — on several different surface areas — regularly appearing after absence, weekend, or vacation Unexplained Burns: — cigar, cigarette burns, especially on soles, palms, back or buttocks — immersion burns (sock-like, glove-like, doughnut shaped on buttocks or genitalia) — patterned like electric burner, iron, etc. — rope burns on arms, leg, neck or torso Unexplained Fractures: — to skull, nose, facial structure — in various stages of healing — multiple or spiral fractures Unexplained Lacerations or Abrasions: — to mouth, lips, gums, eyes — to external genitalia	Wariness of Adult Contacts Apprehensiveness When Other Children Cry Behavioral Extremes: — aggressiveness — withdrawal Fear of Parents Fear of Going Home Reports of Injury by Parents

Table 5–1   continued

Type of CA/N	Physical Indicators	Behavioral Indicators
PHYSICAL NEGLECT	Consistent Hunger, Poor Hygiene, Inappropriate Dress Consistent Lack of Supervision, Especially in Dangerous Activities or Long Periods Unattended Physical Problems or Medical Needs Abandonment	Begging, Stealing Food Extended Stays at School (early arrival and late departure) Constant Fatigue, Listlessness, or Falling Asleep in Class Alcohol or Drug Abuse Delinquency (e.g., thefts) Statements That There Is No Caretaker
SEXUAL ABUSE	Difficulty in Walking or Sitting Torn, Stained, or Bloody Underclothing Pain or Itching in Genital Area Bruises or Bleeding in External Genitalia, Vaginal or Anal Areas Venereal Disease, Especially in Preteens Pregnancy	Unwilling to Change for Gym or Participate in Physical Education Class Withdrawal, Fantasy, or Infantile Behavior Bizarre, Sophisticated, or Unusual Sexual Behavior or Knowledge Poor Peer Relationships Delinquency or Running Away Reports of Sexual Assault by Caretaker
EMOTIONAL MALTREATMENT	Speech Disorders Lags in Physical Development Failure to Thrive	Habit Disorders (sucking, biting, rocking, etc.) Conduct Disorders (antisocial, destructive, etc.) Neurotic Traits (sleep disorders, inhibition of play) Psychoneurotic Reactions (hysteria, obsession, compulsion, phobias, hypochondria) Behavior Extremes: — compliant, passive — aggressive, demanding Overly Adaptive Behavior: — inappropriately adult — inappropriately infant Developmental Lags (mental, emotional) Attempted Suicide

Note. From *The Educator's Role in the Prevention and Treatment of Child Abuse and Neglect*, by D.D. Broadhurst, 1979, Washington, D.C.: National Center on Child Abuse and Neglect, U.S. Department of Health, Education and Welfare, Publication No. 79-30172.

family therapists to the possibility of abuse or neglect. They do not prove the existence of abuse or neglect. The therapy setting provides further clues to confirm suspicions or present satisfactory explanations for a child's condition.

Marriage and family therapists have criminal liability, usually at a misdemeanor level, for failure to report suspected abuse or neglect in the overwhelming majority of states. The penalty might range from a low of a 5- to 30-day jail sentence and/or a fine of $10 to $100 to a high of a year in jail and a fine of $1,000. Criminal prosecution for failure to report a case of child abuse or neglect usually occurs after a child has been seriously injured or murdered and a later investigation reveals that a mandated reporter knew or should have known that abuse was occurring.

Fischer and Sorenson (1985) attribute this lack of enforcement to the fact that state laws sometimes require a "knowing" or "willful" failure to report. They note the difficulties involved in proving, beyond all reasonable doubt, that someone knowingly or willfully failed to report. For example, a limited-license psychologist in Michigan was prosecuted for failure to report suspected child abuse. Part of the psychologist's defense was the argument that the Michigan reporting law (i.e., "reasonable cause to suspect") was vague and not objective. The psychologist was ultimately acquitted at a jury trial (Kavanaugh, 1989).

THE MARRIAGE AND FAMILY THERAPIST AS REFERRAL RESOURCE

As a referral resource, marriage and family therapists are called on by the courts for informational as well as therapeutic intervention assistance. Primarily within the juvenile justice system and in civil actions addressing issues ranging from adoption to divorce to child custody, marriage and family therapists assume the role of referral resource. This referral resource role reflects a growing recognition of marriage and family therapists' expertise in offering preventative as well as rehabilitative services to youthful offenders and their families. Likewise, it has long been recognized that every civil action reflects the failure of a relationship. The parties involved are not capable of satisfactorily resolving their own disputes. All things considered, it is almost always more advantageous for two disputing parties to come to their own resolution rather than run the risk of losing control of their situation by having a third party (judge or jury) decide for them. This is in addition to the costs and time involved with a court encounter (Sidley & Petrila, 1985). Marriage and family therapists have thus taken on the roles of treatment specialist, particularly within the juvenile justice system, and mediator in averting civil court actions.

The Treatment Specialist

Evans (1983) described the role of mental health professionals aiding the courts within the criminal justice system as that of treatment specialist. Marriage and family therapists have the clinical and academic training as well as the experience and are currently acting in some capacity as a treatment specialist predominantly within the juvenile justice system. Marriage and family therapists are also acting in like manner in civil hearings relative to cases involving divorce, child custody, visitation, and such.

Diagnostician

A primary function of marriage and family therapists within the juvenile system is to provide diagnostic evaluations for rehabilitative decisions. Although judges make the final decisions about what will happen to a youthful offender, information made available through evaluations of identified youth and their families has a heavy impact on those decisions.

Initially the court must decide whether it has jurisdiction to act; that is, it must decide if the youth falls within a prescribed statutory classification. Although there is variance from state to state, typical statutory classifications and dispositional alternatives that marriage and family therapists can provide diagnostic input within the juvenile justice system include juvenile delinquency, having been identified as a person in need of supervision (PINS), and child abuse and neglect (Kissel, 1983). The role of marriage and family therapists as diagnostician in civil hearings involving child custody and visitation is discussed next.

Juvenile Delinquency

Juvenile courts generally have jurisdiction over youth accused of committing a crime if they are under 18 years of age on the date of the commission of the act. Some state laws treat children as adults if they are age 13 or older and are charged with murder, forcible rape, robbery while armed, first-degree burglary, or assault with intent to commit any of the aforementioned (Guggenheim, 1979). State laws sometimes specify that juveniles age 15 and over at the time of the offense who are charged with a felony, as well as juveniles age 16 or over who have previously been committed to an institution and are charged in a new delinquency petition for any offense, may be transferred to the appropriate criminal division for trial.

The court's relationship to youthful offenders is a meld of providing for "the best interests of the child" along with protection for the community. The court can decide to dismiss a youth, that is, grant an outright dismissal of the charge. This motion might be considered when a minor offense is charged against a first offender and court supervision of the child is perceived as unnecessary. A consent decree can also be granted by the court and may be entered if the youth has not been previously adjudicated a delinquent by the court, or if such adjudication has been sealed (is not available to the court). Under a consent decree, a juvenile is put on probation for up to 6 months without a finding of guilt. Thus, the court provides supervision without stigmatization. After successful completion of the specific terms of the decree (therapy, community work hours, restitution, etc.), the original petition is dismissed. If the conditions of the decree are violated, the original petition may be reinstated and the juvenile forced to stand trial.

Person in Need of Supervision

A PINS is typically a youth who is habitually truant from school without justification or is habitually disobedient of the reasonable and lawful commands of his or her parents, guardians, or other custodians and is thus ungovernable and in need of care and supervision. When parents and social agencies are unable or unwilling to find a solution for a troubled or troublesome child, it is in society's interest to try, through its legal system, to prevent crime and delinquency via an attempt at rehabilitation rather than wait to punish its occurrence.

The court normally has at its disposal an array of social services as well as traditional judicial remedies. Referral to court is not meant for children with inconsequential discipline problems at home or minor school difficulties. Only when youth are at risk of becoming delinquent should this step be taken. The court has considerable leeway when fashioning a plan for disposition. Youth typically are placed in facilities for delinquents only if they have been adjudicated a PINS more than once.

Child Abuse and Neglect

The primary aim of the court is to preserve the family bond unless such preservation endangers the welfare of a child. Consequently, the court attempts to arrange dispositions when abuse and neglect allegations are brought before it that permit parents to maintain custody of their children unless such custody is harmful to the child. The judge can also order families to seek medical, psychiatric, or other treatment services if parents want to maintain custody of their child.

If the court finds that placement with the parents is not possible, then relatives, other qualified individuals, or commitment to that agency charged with foster placement will be sought. When more than one child is involved, courts generally prefer to keep siblings together to preserve whatever family bonds remain as well as to ease the transition to an alternative home environment. The court can also free a child for adoption by termination of parental rights in severe cases. It is important to know, however, that unless abused/neglected children are also found to be delinquent, they cannot be committed to or confined in an institution for delinquent children.

Child Custody and Visitation

In Domestic Relations Courts throughout the country, seemingly unresolvable disputes between parents and, increasingly, grandparents (Thompson, Tinsley, Scalora, & Parke, 1989) over custody and visitation are commonplace. It is difficult for the court to determine child custody and visitation both at the time of divorce and when brought back for potential amendment. The testimony presented by the two parents is obviously weighted toward what each one wants. The standard employed by the court is what constitutes "the best interests of the child(ren)." To help make this determination, the court often relies on the testimony of an evaluator representing the child(ren) and the court, not the parents (Stevens-Smith & Hughes, 1993).

As a diagnostician in such cases, the marriage and family therapist conducts an assessment, offers a detailed view of the family dynamics, and provides recommendations regarding the form of custody and/or visitation in a report addressed primarily to the judge and attorneys. Although the specifics of law and expectations for such reports vary among jurisdictions, most reports are expected minimally to include recommendations about the structure of how decisions should be made, the primary residence for the child(ren), and time to be spent with each parent. Other recommendations might include such things as the need for therapy by family members. Typically, the attorneys and parties use the report as a fulcrum for further discussion. If an agreement cannot be reached, however, the report and its recommendations can become a central focus of the court in its decision making (Lebow, 1992).

Lebow (1992) proposes guidelines for marriage and family therapists to consider in systemically evaluating custody disputes. These are offered in Figure 5–3.

---

1. Don't try to do this without special training.
2. Establish your independence. If you conduct an evaluation at the behest of one party, you are likely to be treated as biased and of limited credibility. Always look to be appointed by the judge or at the agreement of both parties.
3. Develop at least a cursory understanding of the law about custody and visitation in your state.
4. Get in writing the parameters of your role and an agreement about who pays your fee.
5. See parents alone, children alone, and each parent with children. Pay a home visit if you can.
6. Always balance. Never do something with one parent you are not prepared to do with the other.
7. Listen with an open mind, while remembering the power of personal construction.
8. Encourage the presentation of simple information, like police reports, that confirms or disputes the occurrence of events.
9. Employ standardized tests. Not only can these offer valuable information, they increase credibility considerably.
10. Don't try to be a detective or the judge.
11. Make recommendations that promote the long-term welfare of children. In almost all cases, our knowledge base tells us this involves the inclusion of both parents in some shape or form in the children's lives.
12. Remember the focus of your evaluation: a recommendation for custody and visitation that is in the best interest of the children.
13. Look to research data whenever it is possible to support your recommendations.
14. If you can't decide about something, say so.

Figure 5–3   Some Guidelines for Custody Evaluation

Note. Reprinted from Volume 23 Number 2 of *Family Therapy News,* Copyright 1992, American Association for Marriage and Family Therapy. Reprinted by permission.

15. Make your recommendation clearly. Always speak to custody, residence, visitation, and other needs of the family (e.g., therapy. . . . Always explain why you are deciding what you are deciding).
16. Be prepared for cases to take a long time to reach resolution through the court. Although some court systems are quite quick to adjudicate matters, many are slow; even when the court itself moves for speed, lawyers may move slowly. Take thorough notes that will help you recall your process a year or two later. Take comfort in the fact that in most jurisdictions, 80%–90% of these cases settle before trial.
17. If asked or subpoenaed to appear before the court for deposition or trial, cooperate; but know and assert your rights. You usually can establish a good amount of control over scheduling. Answer questions as best you can. Don't try to answer questions you can't.
18. Employ a lawyer to help you prepare for testimony. Court appearances should only be undertaken with careful preparation.
19. Know thy biases. These cases pull for massive countertransference. Some parents are truly monstrous; many are in the process of using their children as self-objects in the pursuit of their battles with their spouses. Gender bias also needs to be explored.
20. Use every opportunity to explicate and promote a systemic viewpoint. Lawyers, judges, and others who work in the area of family law are the first and often most influential contact point for a wide array of distressed families. Typically, their training offers them little background in systemic understanding or the role of marital and family therapists. The evaluator is perfectly positioned to educate these professionals about family systems, not only specifically about the cases served but also with regard to others.

Resource Expert

A second major function of marriage and family therapists serving in the role of treatment specialist is that of resource expert. Courts are continually in need of information regarding referral resources, particularly for use in the disposition of youth and their families. Identification and categorization of referral resources require knowledge of treatment modalities and a constant updating of information on the facilities providing treatment. To the court, it is the quality of the information and the credibility of the treatment specialist that are crucial. Evans (1983) asserts that the following information regarding referral resources should be submitted to the court.

"Primary" Program Characteristics

The treatment specialist should be prepared to offer his or her "primary" recommendation given the circumstances of the case and his or her understanding of the way the recommendation will fit with available referral resources. This includes the services offered by the recommended program, clients served, referral procedure, cost and duration of structured programs, funding sources and location, director or contact person, and telephone number.

The Relationship of the Facility to the Court

It is important that it be clear whether there can be an ongoing contact with the court, probation department, or other relevant personnel. Is the program willing to accept court referrals requiring reports back to the court and possible court appearances? There may also be questions of payment, the acceptance of juvenile offenders, and the ethical implications of accepting a court-ordered referral.

An Inventory of Other Available Programs

This up-to-date list of other available programs should include some subjective and evaluative comments regarding reputation, outcome of program involvement, and treatment modality used in addition to the typical objective data as just outlined. With some youthful offenders, the court may be highly sensitive to security issues, for example. Thus, the presence of a secure facility that is fully accredited and licensed may be of paramount importance and override the recommendation for an innovative drug program that may appear ideal as a primary recommendation to the treatment specialist.

Treatment Provider

The third function of marriage and family therapists as treatment specialists is that of providing direct treatment services to families and their individual members at various points during the court process. Shrybman and Halpern's (1979) summarization of a child-abuse–related hearing process in juvenile court illustrates these intervention times in that setting:

Utilizing the instance of a complaint of abuse and neglect, said complaint can be initiated by the filing of a petition (written complaint) in the juvenile court alleging that a child has been abused or neglected. The petition may be written and filed by the county attorney, the juvenile probation officer, and/or county social worker according to state law and local court procedures. (Some states allow anyone to file a petition alleging a child has been abused or neglected.)

In emergency situations where there is imminent danger to the child in remaining with the parent(s), the child may be removed from the custody of the parent(s) and placed in protective custody pending the outcome of the juvenile court proceeding. This decision may be made by the police, juvenile probation, child protective services, and/or a physician, depending on state law. Whenever a child is placed in protective custody, a petition must be filed in juvenile court, usually within 24 to 48 hours, and a hearing must be held soon thereafter (usually within 48 to 72 hours, depending upon state law), to allow a judge to review the decision.

There must be an evidentiary trial in which the state must prove to a judge that a child has been abused or neglected. Unless the parent(s) admit to abusing or neglecting their child, it is necessary to call witnesses to substantiate the allegations of abuse or neglect. This is called an *adjudicatory hearing* and normally occurs from 2 to 6 weeks after the initial petition is filed. Because dependency (the idea that the child is in need of services that the parent(s) cannot provide and therefore is dependent upon the state to see that they are provided) is technically a civil rather than criminal issue, the state need not prove abuse or neglect beyond a reasonable doubt, only by a preponderance of evidence, a somewhat lower standard of proof.

Child abuse and neglect proceedings are usually "bifurcated proceedings," meaning the decision as to what should be done with the child occurs in a separate hearing from that which determines whether the child is, in fact, abused or neglected. A dispositional hearing, analogous to the sentencing hearing in a criminal case, may occur on the same day as the adjudication hearing or be held at another time, sometimes weeks later. The dispositional hearing generally focuses on those recommendations made to the judge regarding the appropriate order for the child. An important point to understand regarding the disposition order is that the court has leverage over parents only by its jurisdiction over their child. Thus, the court cannot directly enforce its orders against parents of a child by fines, imprisonment, or threats of either. The court can, however, after finding that a child has been abused or neglected, order that the child remain in the home of the parents on the provision that the entire family participate in therapy efforts. If the parents fail to comply, the court can then order the child removed from the home and placed in a foster home or other care setting.

In some states, no review hearings are held. In others, they are an integral part of the hearing process. After a child has been declared dependent by the court, the court retains jurisdiction over that child until the child reaches adulthood or until the dependency status is ended by the court. In order to measure the progress of the case and determine any need to modify a previous order, courts will generally hold periodic hearings to review the case every 6 months to a year.

In their function as treatment providers, marriage and family therapists work closely with the court and associated state social service personnel to formulate and facilitate families' follow through on treatment plans designed to protect their children and improve the family situation with the primary purpose of preserving the family system. Intervention can come at any point in the process beginning with the initial petition and concluding with successful treatment outcome culminated with dependency status being terminated by the court at a follow-up hearing sometime subsequent to the disposition order.

Mediation

For some time, marriage and family therapists have had fundamental questions about the legal system's response to families experiencing divorce. Therapists who have seen family conflicts exacerbated by courtroom experiences have sought alternatives to the traditional procedures for legally dissolving marriages. The central issue raised has been the adversarial orientation embedded within the very structure of the court system.

Trained to operate within this adversarial system, divorce lawyers typically see their job as getting the best possible settlement for their particular client, while remaining relatively unconcerned about the impact of the settlement on the entire family system. Nor do they see their role as including helping a family to negotiate the emotional minefield of divorce. Law schools do not pretend to prepare their students to appreciate the psychological dilemmas divorcing families must face. Although family law constitutes a primary component of most law programs, there is rarely more than a passing reference to the personal and family trauma involved or to the effect of divorce on children (Vroom, 1983).

Mediation is an increasingly used alternative to court action (Hahn & Kleist, 2000). A cooperative dispute resolution process in which a neutral intervener helps disputing parties negotiate a mutually satisfactory settlement of their conflict, mediation stresses honesty, informality, and open and direct communication. It also facilitates emotional expressiveness, attention to underlying causes of disputes, reinforcement of positive bonds, and avoidance of blame (Deutsch, 1973; Felstiner & Williams, 1978). Many lawyers believe, however, that individuals seeking a divorce must have attorneys involved in a fair mediation process (N. J. Foster & Kelly, 1996; Gangel-Jacob, 1997).

According to proponents, mediation relieves court dockets that are clogged with divorce and child custody actions, reduces the alienation of litigants, inspires durable consensual agreements, and helps families to resume workable relationships even though the parents are legally divorced. Further, the process itself is significantly less traumatic and less costly to the participants (Blades, 1984; DelCampo & Anderson, 1992). Comparisons of mediation and court adjudication have shown that mediation encourages settlement, generates a higher degree of user satisfaction, improves communication and understanding in families, results in more cooperative coparenting, and reduces the incidence of divorce relitigation (J. Pearson & Thoennes, 1982). Conciliation courts in many states offer mediation as a court-related service for families with parents seeking divorce. The family sits down with a mediator to resolve disputed areas rather than have a judge impose a resolution. For years, the Family Court System in Australia has used such court-related mediation services as the primary method of working out visitation, child custody, spousal maintenance, and child support questions (McKenzie, 1978).

In actual practice, divorce/family mediation can look much like couples counseling or family therapy. As in family therapy, husband and wife sit together in a room with a third person who facilitates their communication (although some mediators may see each party separately and perform a kind of "shuttle diplomacy"). When appropriate, children are brought into the decision making. There are some differences, however, the primary one being that the mediator begins with the understanding that it is the clear intention of the family to physically break up (Vroom, 1983). The task of the mediator is then to create an environment where productive negotiation in areas of conflict can occur.

Generally, the mediation process is viewed as progressing in stages. These might include the following:

1. Setting the stage by providing a neutral setting, introducing oneself as a mediator, establishing ground rules, and gaining the disputants' commitment to mediation.
2. Defining the issues by eliciting facts and expression of needs, desires, and feelings.
3. Processing the issues by managing emotions, encouraging empathy, narrowing differences, exploring solutions, and maintaining positive momentum.
4. Resolving the issues by offering concessions, evaluating alternative solutions and tentatively coming to an agreement.
5. Formalizing an agreement that is realistic and positively framed; details are specified in a concrete, understandable manner to ensure implementation by all concerned (DelCampo & Anderson, 1992; New Mexico Center for Dispute Resolution, 1990).

This type of stage conceptualization is used by virtually all the practitioners who have developed and published model approaches to divorce/family mediation. For example, Kessler (1978) emphasizes the need to systematically progress from the beginning to final stage. Rules need to be established at the beginning to create a secure atmosphere and avoid the violation of "unspoken" rules by either party at critical moments later in the mediation. Processing and resolving issues prior to their proper definition may result in wasted energy. Kessler clearly defines specific mediator goals, focuses, and techniques appropriate to each mediation stage.

M. Black and Joffee (1978) outlined a stage approach to mediation comparable to Kessler's, although they also delineated a division of labor for attorney–mental health professional teams. With the attorney focusing on settlement details and the mental health professional dealing with emotional and communication issues, the team helps families to simultaneously achieve a legal and psychological divorce.

Milne (1978), a social worker, outlined a very specific procedure that involves extensive information gathering and emotional ventilation prior to the generation of a mediation settlement. Believing that emotional issues are at the root of most custody battles, Milne advocates instructing each disputant to prepare an autobiography and spend one mediation session reviewing the marriage and decision to divorce. During following sessions, the parties describe existing and desired custody and visitation arrangements. The mediator also meets with the children and communicates the information to the parties. The mediator then solicits resolution proposals from the parties and helps them combine these proposals and/or generate new ones.

In contrast, Coogler (1978), a lawyer with training as a therapist, identified economic issues as underlying most custody battles. His model calls for extensive information gathering on financial matters and property issues. After an orientation to the mediation process, the disputants work out a temporary arrangement regarding child and financial issues. Next, they do homework that involves identifying assets and preparing budgets and income statements. Subsequent sessions are devoted to dividing property and generating acceptable maintenance and child support arrangements. Custody and visitation matters are tackled last. Each party submits two property settlement plans: one in the event they receive custody, the other in the event they do not. The goal of the process is to prevent children from becoming pawns in their parents' financial battles. The resolution of financial issues is believed to lead to resolution of emotional issues.

Another mediation model was developed by Haynes (1981), a social worker with experience in labor mediation. Haynes also offers a stage approach. Initially, the process is explained and basic data on the marriage and impending divorce collected. The parties then meet with the mediator individually to assess their areas of agreement and disagreement, power relationship, communication style, and potential divorce adjustment. At this time too, the mediator seeks to balance the couple's power relationship by educating the weaker party about negotiation strategies, divorce finances, and the adjustment process. The mediator then meets with the parties jointly to identify points of agreement and narrow the issues in dispute. The parties are then separated, and the mediator uses shuttle diplomacy techniques to relay trial proposals, encourage trade-offs, and suggest compromises. The parties are brought together when it seems they have reached a settlement.

DelCampo and Anderson (1992) propose that adversarial court proceedings only produce increased stress among already stressed families. They cited Kass (1990) and Gardner (1989) in asserting that such adversarial proceedings encourage family members to turn against each other and force win–lose situations. Although the court may order a decision, its decision does not necessarily stop the fighting and disagreements. Instead, the conflict frequently becomes intensified, particularly over the long term. As DelCampo and Anderson state, "Only the disputing family members can fully resolve their conflicts" (p. 77). Mediation offers a milieu where this can occur.

THE MARRIAGE AND FAMILY THERAPIST AS EXPERT WITNESS

Recognition by the courts that family influences play a significant part in determining litigants' behavior has expanded the role of marriage and family therapists to encompass that of expert witness. For many marriage and family therapists, however, the courtroom may be an unfamiliar environment with different ground rules and basic assumptions. Testifying as an expert witness may call for a reconsideration of those situational role demands normally encountered in usual therapeutic settings. Although marriage and family therapists have the knowledge and expertise necessary to serve in courts as expert witnesses, they should attend training seminars and read materials on the topic (e.g., Gould, 1998; Weikel & Hughes, 1993) before accepting cases.

Brodsky and Robey (1972) identify the ideal role of the expert witness as "that of a detached, thoroughly neutral individual who simply and informatively presents the true facts as he sees them" (p. 173). Likewise, others have asserted that the position of the mental health professional as expert witness should be to strive to be impartial, free from prejudice, and not act as an advocate for either side (Bromberg, 1979; MacDonald, 1969; Slovenko, 1973). The expert witness is specifically defined as one who "formulate[s] a presented opinion in court based on [his or her] specialized knowledge" (Remley, 1991, p. 39). When a marriage and family therapist is called on to testify as an expert witness, he or she is explicitly appointed by the court to prepare and provide a professional opinion relative to the case in question emanating from his or her specialized knowledge.

The Rules of Evidence

Understanding the rules of evidence employed in the courtroom is the most fundamental issue marriage and family therapists must consider. These rules have evolved to promote the goals of the law, specifically, to facilitate a fair trial. The marriage and family therapist can tailor a therapeutic plan to the needs of clients; if one intervention does not produce the desired results, intervention efforts can be redirected. The court cannot afford this luxury. It must solve the presenting problem in a timely manner, and its solution must be applicable to persons with similar problems. The court reaches its solution to the problem on the basis of presented evidence. The rules of evidence are, therefore, of utmost importance because they determine what will be allowed to come before the court. No professional function in the legal system can occur without an allegiance to the rules of evidence (Woody & Mitchell, 1984).

Almost anyone who is "professionally acquainted with, skilled, or trained in some science, art, trade, and thereby has knowledge or experience in matters not generally familiar to the public" can serve as an expert witness (Schwitzgebel & Schwitzgebel, 1980, p. 238). The expert witness may offer opinions or inferences and may respond to hypothetical questions. The lay witness must have had direct contact with the action or expression—otherwise, the testimony would be hearsay and not admissible.

The expert witness may be allowed to offer testimony based on indirect observation. For example, many jurisdictions will allow a professional to testify about data collected by another professional who is part of a team effort; in a child custody case, for example, a marriage and family therapist may be allowed to cite a home visitation report made by a child services worker. Usually, however, any source of information, such as the child services worker, is expected to be personally available for testimony to accommodate cross-examination by the attorney for the party being testified against (Woody & Mitchell, 1984).

Opinion testimony must be directly aligned with the issue in question. There must also be a concrete description of facts. Opinion evidence must also be such that the state of the present scientific body of knowledge permits a reasonable opinion to be asserted by an expert (Cleary, 1972). Examining attorneys will frequently preface or summarize their questioning of an expert witness by asking, "Have you derived or formed an opinion based on your professional knowledge and with a reasonable degree of professional certainty?" Because experts must be qualified by a judge before they testify, expert witnesses are usually asked to cite their qualifications relevant to their professional knowledge on the subject and to enter a copy of their professional credentials into the court record.

Hypothetical questions comprise another area where experts may be allowed to testify without firsthand, observation-based knowledge of the parties involved (Woody & Mitchell, 1984). Judges are free to decide whether to allow testimony based on hypothetical facts (which closely parallel the characteristics of the parties or circumstances of the current case). If such testimony were erroneously admitted, however, it would present the probable basis for an appeal. For example, a judge could be led to believe that certain data were obtained through normally accepted data collection methods of a profession and therefore qualified as an exception to the hearsay rule. If the methods were not commonly used, the information would definitively be hearsay. Were the case determined by that evidence, an appeal would be in order.

Some jurisdictions allow reports to be submitted as evidence, whereas others will not allow reports unless the author is available for in-court cross-examination (or is available for cross-examination under oath via a deposition). There are some exceptions, such as illness, incapacitation, and death. Cross-examination, however, maintains strong traditional importance:

> For two centuries, common law judges and lawyers have regarded the opportunity of cross-examination as an essential safeguard of the accuracy and completeness of testimony, and they have insisted that the opportunity is a right, and not a mere privilege. . . . And the premise that the opportunity of cross-examination is an essential safeguard has been the principal justification for the exclusion generally of hearsay statements, and for the admission as an exception to the hearsay rule of reported testimony taken at a former hearing when the present adversary was afforded the opportunity to cross-examine. Finally, state constitutional provisions guaranteeing to the accused the right of confrontation have been interpreted as codifying this right of cross-examination. (Cleary, 1972, pp. 43–44)

Courtroom Testimony

An expert witness generally testifies at the request of a representative attorney, although an expert can be requested to give testimony by both attorneys or by the court. Irrespective of the basis of the expert's entry into a case, however, testimony should reflect expertise, preparation, and perhaps most importantly, complete candor. Sidley and Petrila (1985) outlined a slate of strategies applicable to marriage and family therapists serving as expert witnesses.

Preparation

The successful presentation of testimony depends to a large degree on the willingness of the witness and requesting attorney to prepare for court. There are a number of preparatory steps that expert witnesses should concern themselves with.

1. Provide the requesting attorney with a written list of qualifications, for example, education, years in practice, publications, and other pertinent

information that demonstrates familiarity with the subject of the upcoming testimony.

2. If the testimony will involve a particular client, review and become familiar with the client's records. Particularly be aware of the frequency of sessions with the client.

3. Acquire at least a rudimentary understanding of the legal issues involved in the case. This information can be most readily obtained from the requesting attorney.

4. Insist that the requesting attorney take the time to prepare and discuss the questions he or she intends to ask on direct examination. The attorney should also assist in anticipating and discussing questions that are likely to be asked on cross-examination. Issues of information protected by confidentiality or privilege particularly need to be addressed at this time.

5. If you are going to testify for the first time as an expert witness, visit a court in session in advance and observe the examination and cross-examination of a number of witnesses.

Direct Examination

The requesting attorney presents his or her side of a case through direct examination of the expert witness. The goal of the requesting attorney and expert witness on direct examination is to present the technical aspects of the case in layperson's terms so that the judge and, when present, jury may understand. In direct examination, the attorney cannot "lead" the witness; that is, the witness must testify without the aid of suggestions from the attorney conducting the examination. This is one example of why precourt preparation is so valuable. In-court considerations are also of paramount importance as well.

1. The expert witness must remember that the judge or jury is the ultimate decider of what is "fact" in a given case. Thus, in presenting testimony to the fact finder, the witness may enhance effectiveness and credibility by carefully attending to his or her courtroom image.
   a. Arrive on time.
   b. Concentrate on courtroom etiquette, especially in addressing the judge as "Your Honor."
   c. Dress conservatively and neatly.
   d. Maintain a generally serious demeanor; do not talk about the case in hallways, restrooms, or other public places.
   e. Avoid displaying nervous mannerisms (e.g., wringing hands or pencil tapping).
2. The manner in which the expert witness listens and responds to the requesting attorney's questions is similarly important.
   a. Listen carefully to each question, and be certain that you understand the question. If necessary, request that the question be repeated.
   b. Directly and simply, in appropriate layperson's language, answer the question asked and then stop. Do not volunteer information.

    c. Address the judge or jury when responding, rather than the attorney asking the question. Never forget that it is the jury or judge who weigh the testimony.

    d. Speak clearly, slowly, and sufficiently loud so all present can hear, remembering that the court reporter is recording the proceedings. "Yes" and "no" responses must be verbalized, not given as head shakes.

    e. Questions should never be answered in a joking or arrogant manner.

    f. Pointedly avoid exaggeration and misrepresentation in answering.

    g. Answers should be given as confidently as possible: Language such as *perhaps* or *possibly* presents problems.

        (1.) Mere speculation or possibility is usually not relevant to a legal decision, which demands at least a preponderance of the evidence, which means that any proposition presented is more probably true than not. Therefore, in any situation involving less than certainty in an expert witness's testimony, the expert must be prepared to give a reasonable appraisal of how probable the proposition is. The usual, still ambiguous standard sought is "to a professional certainty."

        (2.) Qualifying words like "possibly" suggest uncertainty and lack of confidence.

    h. If the answer to a question is unknown or can only be estimated, you should clearly state such. The expert witness is only human, and fact finders appreciate an honest recognition of this point.

    i. Avoid looking at the examining attorney or judge in a manner that suggests seeking their assistance.

    j. When an objection is made by the nonexamining attorney, stop until the court or that attorney indicates it is acceptable to continue.

Cross-Examination

After direct examination, in which the expert witness has usually been questioned in a sympathetic manner by the requesting attorney, the opposing attorney cross-examines the witness. During cross-examination, the opposing attorney will attempt to discredit the expert witness by asking leading questions and framing questions in a manner that requires a "yes" or a "no" answer favorable to that attorney's position on the case. The opposing attorney will generally seek to test the credibility of both the substance of the expert's testimony and the expert as well.

    Common methods of attempting to discredit the expert witness include the following:

1. Challenging the thoroughness of an evaluation by asking whether the examiner was aware of certain facts when performing an evaluation. Sometimes, certain facts that may bear on the expert's opinion surface only during the court proceedings. It is, of course, perfectly reasonable on cross-examination to ask if those facts change the expert's opinion, as indeed they might. The requesting attorney calling the expert should

apprise him or her of those facts; otherwise, the opposing attorney may take the expert by surprise, with potentially disastrous consequences for the requesting attorney's case.

2. Challenging the witness by the use of treatises giving an opinion contrary to that of the witness.

3. Challenging the witness by attempting to demonstrate that his or her viewpoint, as presented on direct examination, is either internally inconsistent or has changed over time.

4. Challenging the expert by attempting to show that he or she is incompetent because of a lack of necessary training or experience. Although this will not serve to disqualify the expert after having been qualified previously, it may reduce the value in the fact finder's eyes of any testimony given. For example, the cross-examiner may deliberately ask obscure questions from the witness's field.

5. Challenging the expert by attempting to show that he or she has a financial interest in the outcome of the case.

The opposing attorney may ask one or more trick questions in an effort to discredit the expert witness. Examples are as follows.

1. "Have you talked to anyone about this case?" A response of "no" is easily disproved, because inevitably the witness has discussed the case with others, normally including the requesting attorney for whom he or she has already testified. A response of "yes" may lead the opposing attorney to suggest that the witness was told what to say. The best response is to simply acknowledge that the case was discussed. If the cross-examiner persists, the witness can mention that he or she was advised only to tell the truth.

2. "Are you being paid to testify in this case?" This question implies that the expert's testimony is for sale. An appropriate answer to this question is, "I am not being paid to testify. I am being compensated for time I have spent on this case and for my expenses associated with it."

The expert who is undergoing cross-examination must remember that his or her demeanor and style of presentation are even more important on cross-examination than on direct examination. Further considerations in this regard include the following:

1. Above all, remain calm and answer the opposing attorney's questions in a courteous manner. Nothing is worse than emotionalism on the witness stand. A cross-examiner able to provoke an expert to an emotional display has scored a major triumph.

2. Ask to have a question repeated if it is not clearly understood.

3. Indicate when a "yes" or "no" answer is insufficient and that an explanation is necessary by answering, "That requires more explanation than a simple 'yes/no' answer." (Remember that the cross-examiner will attempt to restrict the witness to "yes" or "no" answers.)

4. Refrain from asking the judge if you must answer a given question. If the question is improper, the requesting attorney should object to it. Remember that the court proceedings are primarily orchestrated by the attorneys. If the attorney who requests the expert's presence is at all competent, he or she will know better than the expert whether to object to a question or allow it to be presented to the expert without challenge. It is advisable for the expert and the requesting attorney to discuss in advance how to deal with such questions on cross-examination.

Redirect Examination

After cross-examination is concluded, the requesting attorney who originally called the expert witness will have the opportunity to *redirect examination.* This gives that attorney and the witness the opportunity to offer clarification on any points made by the opposing attorney during cross-examination. A further round of cross-examination may follow the redirect examination.

Marriage and family therapists must prepare themselves for the emotional experience of having their opinions discredited and their credentials questioned. Lawyers have at their disposal professional materials designed to assist them in attacking the testimony of mental health experts (e.g., Becker, 1997; Hagan, 1997; Ziskin, 1995). Considerable preparation is advised before marriage and family therapists make themselves available for expert testimony.

Systemic Understandings and Expert Testimony

Meyerstein and Todd (1980) assert that marriage and family therapists who can transfer their systemic understandings from the therapy context to the courtroom significantly enhance their effectiveness as expert witnesses. These authors paralleled the courtroom context with a family environment. For example, they noted the unique physical arrangement seen on entering a courtroom that graphically conveys the hierarchy of positions and nature of the contest. Likewise, the activities of the courtroom are governed by rules that possess their own internal logic and order; a system based on a theory predicating that the truth will emerge from the oppositional presentation of the best arguments that can be made for each side of the conflict.

Meyerstein and Todd (1980) propose that marriage and family therapists enter the courtroom and redefine the setting as simply a different kind of system. Although different, it is still a system where certain predictable phenomena occur. The therapist's task is to apply available information and transfer it to the interactional skills within the court context. Particularly valuable strategic suggestions in this regard included redefining the problem and dealing with resistance.

Redefining the Problem

Perhaps the key technique of a skilled marriage and family therapist is the art of redefining the problem, or *reframing* (P. Watzlawick, Weakland, & Fish, 1974). The therapist challenges the couple's or family's view of a problem and presents an alternative explanation of the same set of facts in a way that facilitates change through a shift in context. By using reframing, the witness should feel free to engage in a persuasive teaching and advocacy of his or her position (Brodsky & Robey, 1972). This often entails elaboration, systematic repetition, and intensification of ideas using commonsense examples familiar to laypersons to clearly illustrate concepts.

Meyerstein and Todd (1980) described the case example of a marriage and family therapist called to give testimony as an expert witness in a civil commitment suit filed against an adult male by his parents. The prosecutor portrayed the defendant as insane and beyond rehabilitation. His advocating for an indefinite commitment to a state institution suggested a belief that contextual family and community factors were irrelevant both to the defendant's emotional disturbance and his treatment. The therapist as expert witness sought to provide a clearer, more encompassing contextual view:

> **Question:** Are you saying that the blame can't really be placed on either side?
>
> **Answer:** All of them participated in this situation and the outcome was a result, but it's not really one party's fault. The parents have a good deal of love for both their boys, but in their parenting approach they had been so lenient with them that they never put any regulation on them, and they were so worried about their welfare that they could never leave them alone. If he was six or eight I would say that he was a bad boy, that he was disobedient, stubborn and childish. He's not six or eight or 10, but 29. Perhaps he should be seen as an ungrateful son. No doubt, in recent events the defendant equally participated in maintaining the closeness in the family which became detrimental to his and the parents' growth. The defendant has continued to reinvolve his parents and they comply. There is no question . . . the difficulty separating has been a two-sided thing. (p. 47)

The therapist viewed her task as one of illustrating an interactional picture of the problem by highlighting, in a sympathetic manner, participation of family members in maintaining the defendant's problem. Furthermore, the witness used developmental analogies to reframe the behavior in question from "sick" to "immature" and "disobedient" to construct a more normalized and, thus, treatable view of the disability.

Dealing With Resistance

The marriage and family therapist is no stranger to the strategic handling of resistance in therapy situations. The most effective path is to initially go with and then redirect the resistance. This skill is particularly relevant during cross-examination in the courtroom setting as well. The cross-examining attorney ordinarily has a well-practiced repertoire consisting of clever phrasings. The grammatical logic of these phrases intend to create doubt and rejection of the expert witness' testimony in the minds of the judge or jury. Any discrepancy uncovered in the testimony given may cause the witness to redouble efforts at explaining apparent inconsistencies. Backtracking and correcting misimpressions may leave the witness looking flustered and defensive.

A common tack used by cross-examining attorneys in this regard is: "Would you be surprised if I were to tell you that . . .?" Meyerstein and Todd (1980) offered the following example taken from a right-to-treatment suit on behalf of mental hospital patients:

Question: So, would you assume that the people in the higher staff positions are basically unfamiliar with the community based programs, that sort of orientation?

Answer: I would suspect that, yes.

Question: Would it surprise you if I were to tell you that [the hospital superintendent] is a former Executive Director of [a] community mental health center?

Answer: Yes, that would surprise me.

Question: Would it surprise you to know that he was a consultant to the Department of Health, Education, and Welfare, in community mental health, from 1970 to '74?

Answer: Based on the operation he's running at [the mental hospital], that surprises me a great deal. (pp. 49–50)[2]

Being opaque and calling the questioner's bluff with a calm "Yes, that would surprise me" is obviously preferable to equivocating and attempting to reconcile apparent inconsistencies. And, if the cross-examining attorney does procure contradictory evidence to compromise the witness, it is still possible for the witness to have an opportunity to explain on redirect examination. The expert witness should pursue proper preparation to be sure of his or her facts and conclusions.

PROFESSIONAL LIABILITY UNDER THE LAW

Always implicit, and frequently explicit, in legal discussions regarding the practice of marriage and family therapy is the concept of therapists' responsibility and professional liability. Most legal authorities agree that if a therapist is to act legally, then he or she must behave responsibly. Responsible behavior seems clearly to be at least a necessary, if not a sufficient, condition for legal behavior (Widiger & Rorer, 1984). Legally, therapists have a responsibility to communicate to their clients an honest representation of their skills and methods, along with the conditions of treatment, fees, appointment schedules, and any special obligations incumbent on either the therapist or client. Clients' informed consent should always be obtained. The understanding that develops during the initial contacts becomes, in effect, an unwritten agreement. (The terms of therapy may be agreed to in a written document as well.) Each party has a responsibility to abide by the agreement. If the agreement is breached, the remedy may be legal action (Van Hoose & Kottler, 1985). Marriage and family therapists' major areas of legal

---

[2]*Note.* From "On the Witness Stand: The Family Therapist and Expert Testimony," by I. Meyerstein and J. C. Todd, 1980, *The American Journal of Family Therapy, 8*(4), pp. 47, 49–50. Copyright 1980. Reprinted with permission.

responsibility and thus liability are centered on civil liability, including contract law, unintentional torts or malpractice, and intentional torts (Lifson & Simon, 1998; Remley & Herlihy, 2001; Schultz, 1982).

Contract Law

Contractually, marriage and family therapists' legal responsibility to their clients and thus their liability comes from a conception of the therapist–client relationship as a fiduciary one. *Black's Law Dictionary* (1968) says a *fiduciary* relationship "exists where there is a special confidence reposed in one who in equity and good conscience is bound to act in good faith and with due regard to interests of one reposing the confidence" (p. 753). B. S. Anderson (1996) suggests that a fiduciary relationship fosters the highest level of trust and confidence.

A fiduciary relationship is, in essence, based on trust; the therapist, as fiduciary of the client's trust, cannot serve his or her own needs in preference to those of the client. Schultz (1982) stated that a therapist is not strictly a fiduciary because the commonly called-for requirement of absolute candor is normally not present: "The therapeutic privilege—instances where the therapist withholds information in the interest of the patient and the treatment—may contraindicate it; and the maintenance of early rapport, so that later confrontations may be handled, also cuts into the degree of candor that best serves the patient" (pp. 12–13). Despite this concept of therapeutic privilege, the therapeutic relationship is still a fee-for-services relationship. It has implied contractual elements and legal responsibility and thus liability is present through contract law.

Schultz (1982) raised a number of situations in which therapists might be liable under contract law. For example, the fee-for-services aspect of the therapeutic relationship can be conceived as creating circumstances wherein the therapist has a compelling personal interest taking precedent over the client's, namely, preserving his or her income. Marriage and family therapists could be open to a charge of fiduciary abuse in recommending that a couple or family not terminate treatment or that the frequency of sessions be increased without a sound therapeutic rationale. Likewise, the therapist who tells clients that treatment will be successful can be sued for breach of warranty if the predicted outcome does not occur. Reassurances should always be couched in probabilistic terms. Therapists who hold themselves out as guarantors of success can be held to that, even though it is not a normally expected responsibility.

Marriage and family therapists can more definitively carry out their legal responsibilities by the use of explicit, written contracts specifying roles and duties. They can shape such contracts to accurately reflect what they can provide for a fee. At the same time, however, precisely because of their clarity, expressed contracts can make breach of contract or warranty easier to prove (Malcolm, 1988). Moreover, reducing the complexity involved in the therapeutic enterprise to the confined context of an explicit contract may reinforce clients' tendency to view the relationship solely in terms of the conditions described in the contract, therefore increasing the likelihood of litigation (Schultz, 1982). The contract can be pointed to, noting, "We didn't get what we paid for." On the other hand, research has indicated that clients want information about their prospective counselors (Braaten, Otto, & Handelsman, 1993) and that clients perceive counselors who provide information as being more expert and trustworthy (Waltor & Handelsman, 1996).

Although contractual liability is potentially a source of litigation, it is a relatively infrequent approach to legal liability for psychotherapeutic dissatisfaction (Hendrickson, 1982; Schultz, 1982). Primary liability has been through tort liability.

In general, tort liability is a civil wrong that does not arise out of contractual liability (Hendrickson & Mangum, 1978). Torts arise out of a responsibility to protect individuals from harm resulting from socially unacceptable behavior. A tort is a type of harm done to an individual in such a manner that the law orders the person who inflicts the harm to pay damages to the injured party. Torts may be intentional or unintentional.

Unintentional Torts: Malpractice

Corey, Corey, and Callanan (1984) defined malpractice as "the failure to render proper service, through ignorance or negligence, resulting in injury or loss to the client" (p. 229). In order to prove malpractice, four key elements must be shown to be present (Prosser, Wade, & Schwartz, 1988; Schultz, 1982):

1. A therapist–client relationship was established.
2. The therapist's conduct fell below the acceptable standard of care.
3. This conduct was the cause of an injury to the client.
4. An actual injury was sustained by the client.

Professional Relationship
The existence of the therapist–client relationship is usually the easiest of the four elements to prove; normally, a bill for the therapist's services is sufficient evidence. Casual conversations could be interpreted by courts as professional relationships if marriage and family therapists listen to a person's personal problems and offer advice regarding the situation.

Standard of Care
Establishing the acceptable standard of care in a given case is a more difficult undertaking. First, there are numerous schools within the psychotherapeutic community advocating different treatment approaches to the same presenting problem. With the variety of schools in existence, almost any treatment activity will probably be endorsed somewhere. In writing on tort liability, Prosser (1971) clarifies this, however, in stating:

> A "school" must be a recognized one with definite principles, and it must be the line of thought of at least a respectable minority of the profession. In addition there are minimum requirements of skill and knowledge as to both diagnosis and treatment,

> particular in light of modern licensing statutes which anyone who holds himself out as competent to treat human ailments is required to have, regardless of his personal views. (p. 163)

Schultz (1982) highlighted two situations in which therapists might *not* be judged according to the tenets of a particular school: (1) if the therapist does not profess membership (if, for example, he or she advocates a professional eclecticism), he or she will then be held to the standard of care of a therapist "in good standing" who will be called on to testify as an expert witness in the case; and (2) if the approach is so innovative that the therapist is the only person capable of expert testimony, then his or her testimony will be held to a general standard of reasonableness, as evaluated by the judge and/or jury. Obviously, marriage and family therapists who adhere to a particular school carry less liability in that the scope of a standard of care is clarified. Such clarity will aid those therapists falling within the scope, but it may hurt when practices employed are at odds with the school's principles or with commonsense expectations; innovation *could* appear as negligence.

Traditionally, the standard of care for psychotherapeutic practice has been based on what other practitioners in the same geographical area would do under similar circumstances. This is still the predominant frame of reference; however, with knowledge increasingly more accessible, this "locality rule" is being replaced by national standards of practice. In addition to expert testimony, published professional standards are allowed as a yardstick in a number of states, particularly if they are standards of a school or group with whom the therapist identifies.

Once a standard of care has been determined, the plaintiff must show that a breach of this standard occurred in that the therapist did not exercise (a) the minimally accepted degree of knowledge or skill possessed by other practitioners or (b) the minimally accepted degree of care, attention, or diligence exercised in the application of that knowledge or those skills.

Proximate Cause

Once a breach of standard of care has been shown to have occurred, then that breach must be proved to be the proximate cause of the injury. *Proximate cause* is considered to be a cause that produces the injury in question in a natural and continuous sequence, unbroken by any independent intervening causes. Thus, the breach must be the direct cause of the injury.

Proximate cause is easiest to prove if the acts and the injury in question are closely related in time. As the time draws on from act to injury, the opportunity for intervening variables to intercede increases. States arbitrarily set statutes of limitations on negligence cases, thereby setting a limit on liability. It is important to know the statute of limitations in one's own jurisdiction and whether it is dated from the day of the actual injury or of the *discovery* of the injury. It should also be noted that a minor's right to sue begins when he or she comes of age, so that a therapist might be sued by a child's parents, or, depending on the age of the child and statute of limitations, some years later by the child, now an adult.

The major defense against allegations of malpractice is the concept of contributory negligence on the client's part as an intervening cause, breaking the chain of causality between the therapist's acts and the injury. What must be proved is that the client's acts fell below the level of self-care that the average person would have exercised under the same or similar circumstances. This defense is not normally applicable to children or to clients whom a judge has declared as mentally incompetent.

Injury

If proximate cause is proved, an injury must have resulted from it. Strupp, Hadley, and Gomes-Schwartz (1977) offered a partial list of negative effects:

1. Exacerbation of the presenting symptoms (including increased depression, inhibitions, extension of phobias; increased somatic difficulties; decreased self-esteem; paranoia; obsessional symptoms; guilt; decrease in impulse control)
2. Appearance of new symptoms (including severe psychosomatic reactions, a suicide attempt, development of new forms of acting out, disruption of previously perceived stable relationships)
3. Client misuse or abuse of therapy (settling into a dependent relationship, increased intellectualization with concomitant avoidance of action, therapy as a place to ventilate and rationalize hostility, increased reliance on irrationality and "spontaneity" to avoid reflection on real-world limits)
4. Clients' overextending themselves in taking on tasks before they can adequately achieve them, possibly to please the therapist or due to inappropriate directives, leading to failure, guilt, or self-contempt
5. Disillusionment with therapy, leading to feelings of hopelessness in getting help from any relationship

Other negative effects often cited by plaintiffs as injuries emanating from psychotherapeutic malpractice include damages due to reliance on a therapist's directives leading to divorce, job loss, economic loss, emotional harm, suicide or death of a third party, and self- or nonself-inflicted injuries (Schultz, 1982).

Damages

If the four key elements of malpractice are proved, then damages will be awarded to the plaintiff. The standard of proof in civil cases is a "preponderance of the evidence." Numerically, this may be conceived of as at least a 51 to 49 split of the evidence, a lower standard than the criminal one of "beyond a reasonable doubt." Damage can be of two types, either compensatory for the injury or punitive as punishment for wanton or reckless acts. Compensatory damages generally consider past earnings lost, future earnings lost, pain and suffering, restitution to undo the damage, and/or the cost of the therapy itself (Schultz, 1982).

Intentional Torts

A number of difficulties arise when plaintiffs seek to prove the four elements in a malpractice action. These difficulties center primarily on the inherent vagueness in the elements of standard of care and proximate cause. Barring gross misconduct, the large range of treatment options allows for great latitude in acceptable care. Also, because the "natural" course of "mental illness" is a still-uncertain conception, it is difficult to prove that a therapist's action or inaction caused an alleged injury; the injury might just as easily be explained as a natural consequence of the illness. This vagueness of the elements of proof in negligence cases invites more suits than other tort actions but, at the same time, makes them harder for plaintiffs to win. In contrast, the relative clarity of the elements of proof for intentional torts makes them easier to prevent but harder to defeat in court when reality-based allegations are made (Schultz, 1982).

Generally, expert testimony is not required in cases involving intentional torts. The questions raised are more clear-cut "yes" or "no" as opposed to variable assessments of acceptability or proximate causation. The major intentional tort actions normally filed are discussed in the following paragraphs.

Battery

Schwitzgebel and Schwitzgebel (1980) stated with regard to *battery:*

> The unconsented touching of a person gives rise to a legal action in tort, even though that touching as a treatment is for the welfare of the patient and actually benefits the patient. . . . If the person consents to the touching, then there is no battery. (p. 274)

The standard of care is not a question in battery. Although the act must be willful on the part of the therapist, it does not have to be based on proving intent to harm the client. Proximate cause, injury, and most importantly, lack of informed consent are the elements needed to be proved in this tort. It should be noted, however, that consent obtained without imparting adequate information nullifies the consent. Therapists must fully explain their particular treatment procedures and any possible adverse or negative consequences that may result from clients' participation. The reasoning of this requirement is that clients who know the risks involved in certain procedures would elect not to participate. Sex therapy represents an area of potential liability of particular relevance for marriage and family therapists.

Defamation

Black's Law Dictionary (1968) defines *defamation* as: "The offense of injuring a person's character, fame, or reputation by false and malicious statements" (p. 505).

Defamation may be oral, as in slander, or written, as in libel. It must be made public, and it must be injurious to the reputation of the plaintiff. There are three avenues of defense in this tort (Schultz, 1982): (a) An absolute bar to liability is that the statement is true; (b) an informed consent to release the information would indicate that the plaintiff had no reason to bar the information from being made public; and (c) the defendant can invoke the doctrine of "qualified privilege," or overreaching social duty to release the information. *Berry v. Moensch* (1958) elaborated on this latter point in setting forth the following four conditions:

1. The information must be presented in good faith and not in malice.
2. There must be a legitimate social duty to release the information.
3. The disclosure must be limited in scope to what is necessary to discharge the duty.
4. The disclosure must be only to the appropriate parties with a right to know.

Marriage and family therapists who act in a professional manner and are cautious about client information communicated to third parties will generally be protected from defamation actions because of the doctrine of qualified privilege (Hopkins & Anderson, 1990).

Invasion of Privacy

Invasion of privacy is a violation of the right to be left alone. It requires that private facts be disclosed to more than a small group of persons and that the information must be offensive to a reasonable person of ordinary sensibilities (Schultz, 1982). Invasion of privacy can be distinguished from defamation in that even complimentary statements can be considered an invasion of privacy and such invasion need not require publication of the information, only an intrusion into an individual's private spheres. It is the fact of the invasion itself that is the question in this tort, regardless of the intent or negligence. The certain defense in this tort action is informed consent by the client.

Invasion of privacy requires unreasonable or offensive conduct. Schultz (1982) identified a number of examples in this regard:

> A therapist who makes phone calls to a patient's place of work, identifying himself as a therapist, or who sends bills and correspondence to a patient, with an identification of his relationship to the patient, might give grounds for an invasion of privacy action. The presence of nonessential staff in treatment settings has been viewed as an intrusion on the patient's seclusion. The patient has an absolute right to refuse to be interviewed as a "case conference." (p. 11)

It is obviously important from not only an ethical but also a legal standpoint that client confidentiality be carefully maintained. The implications for this tort reach into office practices such as record keeping as well as the professional realms of research, training, and supervision.

Infliction of Mental Distress

The tort of *infliction of mental distress* normally requires outrageous conduct by the defendant. The harm done is the infliction of emotional pain, distress, or suffering. Schwitzgebel and Schwitzgebel (1980) noted that most cases have required the existence of physical injury resulting from the distress as well.

Malicious Prosecution and False Imprisonment

The tort of *malicious prosecution* is relatively difficult to prove, as it requires the plaintiff to prove malicious intent on the part of the plaintiff or prosecutor of the underlying case. Even grossly destructive behavior can occur without the requisite malice (Schultz, 1982). *False imprisonment* normally is brought as an action when the sufficiency of an examination or treatment are questionable, particularly in cases of involuntary commitment (Schwitzgebel & Schwitzgebel, 1980). The injury in both of these torts is usually deprivation of liberty.

Diligence and a reasonable belief on the part of the therapist that a client may be harmed or harmful should serve as adequate protection against this tort action. Completeness in examinations and regular evaluations should be standard procedure so any necessary confinement is kept to a required minimum.

Professional Liability Insurance

Therapist–client relationships resulting in court action, although infrequent, are always possible, with subsequent risks to the contemporary marriage and family therapist (Appleson, 1982). Certainly such risks can be minimized by acting responsibly and in concert with the ethical standards of the profession and accepted practices within the field. Although risk can be minimized, it cannot be eliminated and insurance coverage is therefore advisable (Hendrickson, 1982).

It is important to remember that even a marriage and family therapist who is innocent might still be sued. Bennett, Bryant, VandenBos, and Greenwood (1990) estimated that costs including legal fees, expenses such as telephone calls and photocopying, expert witness fees, transcript fees, and court costs typically amount to approximately $20,000; and this amount does not even consider the million or so dollars an award might theoretically be if a suit is lost.

Professional liability insurance will be necessary for most marriage and family therapists to afford to pay the costs of litigation, should they be sued, as well as pay any damages, should a court find liability. Some states have indemnification statutes that provide that state or private institutions pay for damages and legal fees of employees at the end of litigation. Insurance is also advisable for these professionals as well. Because litigation may be frequently drawn out over several years, professional liability insurance will prevent these therapists from having to use their own personal assets to pay legal expenses during the litigation.

In purchasing professional liability insurance, it is critical that the kinds of policies and coverages available be carefully considered. For example, there are typically two very different types of policies: claims-made policies and occurrence-based policies. *Occurrence-based* policies cover against any claims that may be filed for acts that *occurred during the policy period covered,* even if one is no longer insured by that policy or the insurance carrier who provided it. In simple terms, the insured is covered forever for acts that occurred during the policy coverage period. This form of coverage is generally more expensive than claims-made policies.

Claims-made policies protect the insured against a claim only if he or she were covered at the time the alleged act occurred and had been *continuously insured with that same carrier* up to the time the claim is filed (Bennett et al., 1990). This means that once the annual policy is not renewed, even if one is no longer in practice (e.g., retired), any subsequent claims will not be covered. Bennett et al. (1990) commented on this more specifically:

> If you are insured under an employer's claims-made policy, you are in effect tied to that employer forever, even if you stop working for the employer. If you have chosen a claims-made policy, it may be necessary to purchase a special kind of coverage to protect you after you retire, stop working, change jobs, or change insurance carriers. The cost of this special coverage—referred to as *tails, riders,* or *reporting endorsements*—could offset any savings achieved when you chose the claims-policy. You buy the tail to cover a particular period of time . . . between 1 and 5 years and even longer. (p. 107)

Although most insurance carriers offer occurrence-based coverage, many are attempting to switch their clients to claims-made coverage. It is important to note, however, that the average time lapse between events precipitating a malpractice claim and the claim report is 2 to 3 years; some suits have been brought 10 years after the events in which they are based (Bennett et al., 1990).

Professional liability insurance is available through most national and regional professional associations. The American Association for Marriage and Family Therapy, American Psychological Association, American Counseling Association, and others offer a group liability insurance plan for members. Again, as with any insurance, the policy should be studied and exclusions taken due consideration of.

SUMMARY AND CONCLUSIONS

Legal roles and responsibilities have become more important in the practice of marriage and family therapy as consumer advocacy and stress on accountability have grown along with changes in judicial attitudes toward mental health professionals. These roles and responsibilities influence every aspect of practice and must be addressed by all marriage and family therapists.

The courts are finding an increasing number of uses for the opinions, recommendations, and therapeutic resources offered by marriage and family therapists—as a source of information leading to needed intervention by the state, as a resource for therapy services, and as an expert witness. It is clear that training in this psycholegal interface must be a significant part of marriage and family therapy training. Relative to other participants in the courtroom drama, marriage and family therapists will otherwise be underprepared, however expert they are in clinical confines. The legally naive therapist will likely experience frustration and embarrassment at the hands of a skilled and well-prepared attorney within the adversarial system of the court. Moreover, his or her responsibility to best serve clients' welfare may be seriously compromised in the process because of improper preparation.

The first four chapters of this book addressed ethical responsibilities incumbent on marriage and family therapists. There is a strong relationship between ethics and the law. Codes of ethics reflect statements by professions with respect to acceptable standards of practice; they outline members' basic responsibilities. Ethically responsible therapist behavior relating to client welfare, confidentiality, and especially informed consent not only maintain professional standards but help avoid unnecessary legal actions.

Van Hoose and Kottler asserted one major reason for the professional codes of ethics is to protect the profession from governmental regulation. Ethical codes foster professions' internal regulation of themselves rather than risk being regulated by governmental bodies. A therapist's failure to follow the published code of his or her primary professional association may result in disciplinary action and/or expulsion from that group. Van Hoose and Kottler (1985) noted, however:

> Professional societies have no legal power per se, and their standards, however appropriate, may be unenforceable without statutes to back them up. Thus, laws may become necessary to prevent practice by unqualified persons, to prevent abuses, to protect the general public and the professions from charlatans and quacks, and to discipline offenders. (p. 70)

Ultimately, ethical responsibilities thus equate with legal responsibilities; neither can be ignored. Marriage and family therapists need to educate themselves with regard to both. Chapter 6 looks specifically at family law and Chapter 7 provides case examples and critiques offering further opportunities to expand one's knowledge base in this area.

RECOMMENDED RESOURCES

Bennett, B. E., Bryant, B. K., VandenBos, G. R., & Greenwood, A. (1990). *Professional liability and risk management.* Washington, DC: American Psychological Association.

Cohen, R. J., & Mariano, W. E. (1982). *Legal guidebook in mental health.* New York: The Free Press.

Coogler, O. J. (1978). *Structured mediation in divorce settlement.* Lexington, MA: D. C. Heath.

Gould, J. W. (1988). *Conducting scientifically crafted child custody evaluations.* Thousand Oaks, CA: Sage.

Haynes, J. M. (1981). *Divorce mediation. A practical guide for therapists and counselors.* New York: Springer.

Hopkins, B. R., & Anderson, B. S. (1990). *The counselor and the law.* Alexandria, VA: American Association for Counseling and Development.

Lifson, L. E., & Simon, R. I. (Eds.). (1998). *The mental health practitioner and the law.* Cambridge, MA: Harvard University Press.

Remley, T. P., Jr., & Herlihy, B. (2001). *Ethical, legal, and professional issues in counseling.* Upper Saddle River, NJ: Merrill/Prentice Hall.

Reppucci, N. D., Weithorn, L. A., Mulvey, E. P., & Monahan, J. (Eds.). (1984). *Children, mental health and the law.* Beverly Hills: Sage Publications.

Schultz, B. M. (1982). *Legal liability in psychotherapy.* San Francisco: Jossey-Bass.

Sidley, N. T. (Ed.). (1985). *Law and ethics: A guide for the health professional.* New York: Human Sciences Press.

Stevens-Smith, P., & Hughes, M. M. (1993). *Legal issues in marriage and family counseling.* Alexandria, VA: American Counseling Association.

Woody, R. H., & Associates. (1984). *The law and the practice of human services.* San Francisco: Jossey-Bass.

6

Family Law

The life circumstances confronting all couples and families and their thoughts and feelings concerning these circumstances must be considered in light of reality. Legal issues represent a major portion of that reality. Since the 1970s, legal doctrines relating to intraspousal and interfamily immunity have been weakened or stricken in many states. Spouses may now testify against each other, and children may now sue their parents. Many are actively doing so (Kaslow, 1990a).

When legal problems arise within the therapeutic context, clients are usually advised to consult with an attorney. Yet there can be several significant stumbling blocks in gaining meaningful assistance with the "this is a legal problem—see a lawyer" approach. Some lawyers may not be aware of, understand, or even care about relevant psychosocial or psychiatric difficulties underlying any legal problems. Consulting an attorney could initiate the involvement of marital partners or family members in a bitter adversary process, resulting in the downfall of therapeutic efforts. Once begun, litigation could become difficult to directly channel or affect in a manner conducive to originally sought-after treatment goals (Bernstein, 1982).

Marriage and family therapists need to be familiar with these stumbling blocks and the law that affects couples and families if they are to effectively work with cases requiring the input of both legal and therapeutic objectives. Many problems that couples and families present for therapy have legal implications that cannot be ignored. Therapists must be able to effectively address both legal and therapeutic problems when they exist in tandem. Marriage and family therapists should recognize and understand relevant legal issues—not to practice law, but rather to provide basic, therapeutically relevant information—and to refer or seek appropriate consultation. Bernstein (1982) summarized this position most aptly:

> Ignorance of the law may be an excuse in the malpractice area in the sense that therapists are not liable for failure to offer legal advice nor would they be liable for failure to refer a client to an attorney. But, certainly, effective therapy must at least consider the options that are allowable and involve these options in the therapeutic process. (p. 100)

This chapter presents an overview of relevant issues in family law. However, contemporary family law in the United States is far too complex a subject to detail in depth in a single chapter. Changes in the law are constantly occurring, individual states have different rules and procedures, and courts can interpret the meaning of the law in contrasting ways. When applicable, the primary references employed for the information presented in this chapter are "uniform" acts put forth by professional bodies for the purpose of providing common provisions for state legislatures. For example, the Uniform Marriage and Divorce Act was promulgated by the National Conference of Commissioners on Uniform State Laws in 1971. The American Bar Association approved this act and recommended it for passage by the states in 1974. Acceptance by the American Bar Association does not imply that the act has been equally accepted by all state legislatures; however, it does provide the model most frequently used by states to revise or prepare their own statutory provisions. To clarify specific laws in their own state, marriage and family therapists must consult that state's statutes and cases. With regard to particular legal problems, therapists are urged to consult an attorney with a reputation of specializing in family law. For a more thorough presentation of the issues addressed in this chapter, a bibliography of recommended resources concludes the chapter.

MARRIAGE AND COHABITATION

The two major forms of legal marriage are ceremonial marriage and common law marriage. *Ceremonial marriage* is performed in a ceremony before a religious or civil authority, and *common law marriage* results from partners living together as husband and wife for a specified minimum period of time without having participated in a marriage ceremony. For both forms of marriage, partners must have the legal capacity to enter into a contract and actually have made an agreement to marry (Clark, 1974).

Most marriages are ceremonial marriages. In the majority of states, there is no specified procedure for the ceremony, although most require witnesses (usually at least two) and that a marriage license has been obtained and recorded in the appropriate civil office. Section 203 of the Uniform Marriage and Divorce Act (Bureau of National Affairs, Inc., 1982) outlines this licensing procedure:

> When a marriage application has been completed and signed by both parties to a prospective marriage and at least one party has appeared before the (marriage license) clerk and paid the marriage license fee of ($. . . .), the (marriage license) clerk shall issue a license to marry and a marriage certificate form upon being furnished:
>
> (1)   satisfactory proof that each party to the marriage will have attained the age of 18 years at the time the marriage license is effective, or will have attained the age of 16 years and has either the consent to the marriage of both parents or his guardian, or judicial approval; (or, if under the age of 16 years, has both the consent of both parents or his guardian and judicial approval); and

(2) satisfactory proof that the marriage is not prohibited; and

(3) a certificate of the results of any medical examination required by the laws of this State.

Requirements relating to Subsection 2 prohibiting marriage have been the subject of significant judicial scrutiny. The Supreme Court has established persons' marital choice as a fundamental right: "The freedom to marry has long been recognized as one of the vital personal rights essential to the orderly pursuit of happiness by free men" (*Loving v. Virginia,* 1967). The Supreme Court held in *Loving* that the state of Virginia could not prohibit interracial marriage between whites and members of other races because such racial classifications violated the equal protection clause of the Fourteenth Amendment and because marriage is a basic right:

> Marriage is one of the "basic civil rights of man," fundamental to our very existence and survival. To deny this fundamental freedom on so insupportable a basis as racial classification embodied in these statutes, classifications so directly subversive of the principle of equality at the heart of the Fourteenth Amendment, is surely to deprive all the state's citizens of liberty without due process of law. The Fourteenth Amendment requires that the freedom of choice to marry not be restricted by insidious racial discriminations. Under our Constitution, the freedom to marry, or not to marry, a person of another race resides with the individual and cannot be infringed by the state.

Given that the right to marry is fundamental, the extent to which states may infringe on that right has been incorporated in a number of judicial decisions. For example, in *Zablocki v. Redhail* (1978), the Supreme Court held a Wisconsin statute as unconstitutional. The statute required state residents who were under a court order to support minor children not in their custody to prove, before being permitted to marry, that the children were not likely to become public charges. In a similar stance, the Court of Appeals of California ruled against prison officials who sought to prevent prisoners from marrying (*In re Carrafa,* 1978). *In re Carrafa* affirmed the right to marry as a fundamental one, especially considering that many of the civil rights normally available to citizens convicted of criminal action may be curtailed.

Because the right to marry is a basic one, states can significantly interfere with this right only in the presence of a "compelling state interest" (Glendon, 1976). Prohibitions against bigamy and close incestuous marriage have been upheld consistently.

Although the federal government passed the Defense of Marriage Act (1996), which supports states in refusing to allow same-sex marriages or refusing to acknowledge such marriages performed in other jurisdictions (Polikoff, 1993) and most state courts have held that gay and lesbian marriages can be prohibited, two state supreme courts (Hawaii and Vermont) have held that denying the right to marry to gay and lesbian couples violates the constitutions of those states (*Baehr v. Lewis,* 1993; Sneyd, 2000; Thompson-Schneider, 1997). In addition, the Vermont legislature has passed a law creating "civil unions" that are available to gay and lesbian couples that are equivalent to marriages (Sneyd, 2000). While many authors have argued that gay and lesbian marriages should be permitted because gay and lesbian individuals are discriminated against if they are not given the protections and benefits available to heterosexual citizens (Eskridge, 1993; Hunter, 1991; Thompson-Schneider, 1997), Kovacs (1995) has suggested that the children of gay and lesbian couples need to be protected by allowing their parents to marry.

Clearly, the structure of the family in America has dramatically changed since the 1970s. In a parallel process, the nature and functions of marriage as a legal and social institution have seen a similar evolution. Although this evolution is ongoing, particular patterns can be discerned. A family based on marriage is still perceived as the most desirable and productive unit of society, although no longer necessarily the most stable. Although procreation may continue to be a predominant purpose of marriage, other forms of productiveness are being increasingly recognized; for example, the financial or educational advancement of both partners by joint effort. With such ends in view, parties to a marriage are paying closer attention to the economics of the relationship than they might have in the past. Thus, marriage can be seen as acquiring many of the characteristics present in a pooling of resources for speculative investment, or as a co-ownership in gaining present and future property similar to a business partnership for profit (Weyrauch & Katz, 1983).

As a result, prenuptial agreements have taken on increased importance and recognition. A *prenuptial agreement* is a contract made by a couple before their marriage in order to modify certain legal repercussions that would otherwise occur as a result of marrying (Krause, 1977). In the past, such agreements were a rare practice confined to the elderly and rich who sought to preserve their assets. Prenuptial agreements today are being entered into by many couples attempting to articulate their mutual expectations. Reversing the common law principle that contracts between husband and wife interfered with the marital commitment and were therefore not recognized, courts are tending to accept the validity of prenuptial agreements even if they contemplate and regulate the possibility of future divorce or dissolution of a marriage. The courts are increasingly leaving the nature and terms of marriage to the parties themselves rather than imposing restrictions by a formal pronouncement of policy by the state (Weyrauch & Katz, 1983).

This increased acceptance of prenuptial agreements by the courts has particular relevance for marriage and family therapists. Religious mandates frequently call for couples contemplating marriage to seek premarital counseling from the clergy. Likewise, many couples considering marriage, especially for a second or third time, sensibly seek therapeutic input (from marriage and family therapists) prior to entering into marriage to address potential problems they may encounter. In this era of the blended family, while an early marriage was likely entered into basically unencumbered, second or third relationships should be entered only with reasonable caution regarding legal and property rights before, during, and perhaps even following the marriage, should it end in divorce. Bernstein (1982) characterized these possible circumstances in stating:

One can easily picture the typical American family of "your" children, "my" children, and possibly "our" children. Then there is your property before marriage, my property before marriage, and our property during marriage. Then, in a later marriage there are children and grandchildren as well, often former spouses, and business or financial arrangements and obligations of various degrees of complexity. Likewise, there might also be items of inheritance from either side of the family that can cause ownership problems. One can easily envision two parties immediately prior to marriage who have real and personal property, children, insurance, family obligations, and perhaps properties secured by substantial debts. (p. 96)

Couples entering into marriage should be forewarned about the legal complexities and potential consequences arising from their union in the same manner as they need to understand and address emotional and developmental tasks. Therapists who participate in premarital therapy efforts with couples should present legal issues that may impinge on their emotional well-being. The possibility of preparing a prenuptial agreement should accompany such a discussion. Each party may clearly desire the marriage. One or both partners, however, may fear the real or imagined hazards inherent in negotiating finances and other sources of contractual conflict during this sensitive time. One or both partners may be so enamored that emotion overrules thought that should be given to realistic, concrete planning for the future.

Bernstein (1982) proposed that, at minimum, each party entering into marriage should prepare an inventory of their present assets. He recommended an accompanying prenuptial agreement that can then provide that, in the event of divorce, each partner will leave the marriage with the property they brought into it. Further, the ownership, control, and characterization of property gained during the marriage can also be fixed. Thus, each partner can be secure in understanding that the interest in his or her property and monies earned from that property during the marriage remain personal, individual, and apart from that of his or her spouse. Finally, a full review of each party's insurance and estate plan should be made so each party can be comforted by the knowledge that loved ones will not be isolated and that prior family expectations and obligations will be respected.

Most states require that prenuptial agreements be in writing. Ruback (1984) reported that prenuptial agreements that concern the transfer of property before a marriage have generally been considered valid, although federal tax consequences were applicable. Similarly, agreements relating to the distribution of property on the death of one spouse have also been generally validated, assuming there was full disclosure of the spouse's financial circumstances at the time of the contract and the other spouse was fairly provided for. Ruback cautioned, however, that prenuptial agreements relating to the distribution of property and support obligations that a partner would receive in the event of a divorce have been struck down by the courts as being against the public policy of state. This suggests that such agreements encourage divorce.

To assist attorneys in drafting premarital agreements that will withstand later legal challenges, Belcher and Pomeroy (1998) have developed the following suggestions: (a) Each partner should have his or her own attorney who will give independent advice on the terms of the agreement. (b) Enough time should be allowed to draft and negotiate the agreement before the wedding to avoid the appearance of duress. (c) Each partner should fully disclose his or her assets and obligations rather than asking a partner to waive the disclosure requirement. (d) Personal obligations such as requiring a partner to live in a particular location after the marriage should be avoided. (e) Any marital rights that are waived, such as a probate homestead or serving as a personal representative, should be clearly specified rather than waived with a general statement. (f) Recitals (which include, among other things, that the agreement is freely and voluntarily entered into without duress or undue influence, each partner is represented by independent legal counsel, and full disclosure of assets and obligations have taken place) should be read by each partner and his or her lawyer before execution of the document.

Weyrauch and Katz (1983) advocated the increasing importance and acceptance of prenuptial agreements relating to potential divorce settlements. They cited *Posner v. Posner* (1979) as a leading case in support of the proposition that parties should be able to regulate incidents of marriage breakup. According to the viewpoint alluded to as background for the case, such regulation was traditionally identified as against public policy; the conception of marriage as a personal relationship entered into for life made any contemplation of divorce seem an impairment to the marital intent. Also noted was the traditional notion of the state as a third party to the marriage contract, intervening with party autonomy. In its final decision the court stated:

> We cannot blind ourselves to the fact that the concept of the "sanctity" of a marriage—as being practically indissoluble, once entered into—held by our ancestors only a few generations ago, has been greatly eroded in the last several decades. This court can take judicial notice of the fact that the ratio of marriages to divorces has reached a disturbing rate in many states; and that a new concept of divorce—in which there is no "guilty" party—is being advocated by many groups and has been adopted by the State of California in a recent revision of its divorce laws providing for dissolution of a marriage upon pleading and proof of "irreconcilable differences" between the parties, without assessing the fault for the failure of the marriage against either party. With divorce such a commonplace fact of life, it is fair to assume that many prospective marriage partners whose property and familial situation is such as to generate a valid antenuptial agreement settling their property rights upon the death of either, might want to consider and discuss also—and agree upon, if possible—the disposition of their property and the alimony rights of the wife in the event their marriage, despite their best efforts, should fail.

Prenuptial agreements concerning obligations and duties during marriage are also increasingly being prepared. These agreements attempt to regulate areas such as sexual practices, finances, and religious upbringing and education of children. These latter agreements, however, have been rarely enforceable because of courts' increasing reluctance to intrude in ongoing marriages (Ruback, 1984).

Given this shifting emphasis toward marriage as a legal partnership with a corresponding acceptance of prenuptial agreements, marriage, except in the formal legal sense as a symbol, has been increasingly viewed as decreasingly necessary. Although the practice of living with someone of the opposite sex without being married is old, it has become more commonly practiced in contemporary society over the past several decades (Glendon, 1980). Lavori (1976) offered a number of reasons to explain this increase in cohabitating couples:

1. The desire by couples to avoid the sex-stereotyped allocation of roles associated with marriage
2. The feeling that unless children are involved, marriage is unnecessary or irrelevant
3. A lack of readiness to commit oneself completely
4. The idea that one cannot predict how he or she will feel in the future and so promises should not be made that potentially cannot be kept or may not promote desirable outcomes
5. The desire to avoid the legal involvement and expense inherent in a possible divorce
6. A conscientious objection to marriage on the part of some couples
7. The belief that legal sanction of a relationship is irrelevant and meaningless

Corresponding to this increase in cohabitation among couples has been a trend for individuals to seek court action when the relationship ends to divide property that was obtained during the period of cohabitation (Cruchfield, 1981). This was exemplified in the well-publicized case of *Marvin v. Marvin* (1976) in which the California Supreme Court held that the cohabitating couple, actor Lee Marvin and his partner, could make an express contract affecting their property rights as long as sex was not part of the consideration for the agreement. In responding to the question of precedence in legal theory and practice set by *Marvin v. Marvin*, Weyrauch and Katz (1983) concluded:

> An express contract of cohabitation is not likely to raise serious problems; courts will be increasingly inclined to enforce well-drafted ones. Since one of the many functions of express contracts of cohabitation is to refute any presumption of marriage, as well as limit judicial discretion, express contracts may become an alternative available to the literate American middle classes. That is, if they choose not to protect themselves by formal marriage, they will be able to protect themselves through written contractual stipulation. (p. 204)

Not all states have followed the decision handed down in *Marvin v. Marvin*. Where not, however, the general trend has been to incorporate concepts from other areas of the law to address the obvious fact that a legal remedy is often needed to divide property obtained by couples cohabitating without being married. Such borrowed concepts include implied contract, implied partnership, and constructive trust (Douthwaite, 1979; Hennessey, 1980). The position of the prudent practitioner of marriage and family therapy in all of these instances is a recommendation to formalize relationship interests whether through ceremonial marriage or legal contract. Still, equitable legal remedy might be available, although more questionable in its ultimate outcome as well as the effort necessary to secure a successful decision.

PARENT–CHILD RELATIONSHIPS

Ruback (1984) identified five frames of reference for considering parent–child relationships under the law: legitimacy, paternity, adoption, surrogate parenthood, and abortion.

Legitimacy and Paternity

Legitimate children are those who are held as having a "full legal relationship" with both of their parents (Krause, 1977). Generally, the marital status of the parents determines legitimacy of children. Because of the importance of identifiable and stable family relationships for society, the law presumes that children born to married women are the offspring of their husbands (Ruback, 1984).

Children identified as illegitimate were, until relatively recently, denied benefits relating to such things as support, inheritance, and wrongful death claims. Although discrimination is still present to some degree in cases of legitimacy determination, the Supreme Court has offered judicial opinions that have struck down most legislation denying benefits to nonmarital children. For example, in *Trimble v. Gordon* (1977), the Supreme Court ruled as unconstitutional an Illinois statute that only allowed illegitimate children to inherit from their mothers, but not their fathers. Similarly, the Supreme Court found in *Weber v. Aetna Casuality & Surety Co.* (1972) that there is no justifying state interest for denying workers' compensation benefits to the dead father's unacknowledged, illegitimate children. In *Gomez v. Perez* (1973), the Supreme Court decided that illegitimate children are guaranteed a right of support from their father in striking down a Texas statute that granted legitimate children a judicially enforceable right to support from their natural fathers but denied that right to illegitimate children. In its decision, the court stated:

> Once a State posits a judicially enforceable right on behalf of children to needed support from their natural fathers there is no constitutionally sufficient justification for denying such an essential right to a child simply because its natural father has not married its mother. For a State to do so is "illogical and unjust."

The different states vary in the types of proceedings used to make paternity determinations. Some states settle paternity issues in civil proceedings. Other states determine paternity as an adjunct to a criminal proceeding. As a result of contrasting types of proceedings, various standards of proof and presumptions of paternity are employed. Section 4 of the Uniform Parentage Act (Bureau of National Affairs, Inc., 1976) is that portion of the act dealing with the ascertainment of parentage and provides a common statutory framework that has been presented to the states by the National Conference of Commissioners on Uniform State Laws:

(a) A man is presumed to be the natural father of a child if:
    (1) he and the child's natural mother are or have been married to each other and the child is born during the marriage, or within 300 days after the

marriage is terminated by death, annulment, declaration of invalidity, or divorce, or after a decree of separation is entered by a court;

(2) before the child's birth, he and the child's natural mother have attempted to marry each other by a marriage solemnized in apparent compliance with law, although the attempted marriage is or could be declared invalid, and,

    (i) if the attempted marriage could be declared invalid only by a court, the child is born during the attempted marriage, or within 300 days after its termination by death, annulment, declaration of invalidity, or divorce; or

    (ii) if the attempted marriage is invalid without a court order, the child is born within 300 days after the termination of cohabitation;

(3) after the child's birth, he and the child's natural mother have married, or attempted to marry, each other by a marriage solemnized in apparent compliance with law, although the attempted marriage is or could be declared invalid, and

    (i) he has acknowledged his paternity of the child in writing filed with the (appropriate court or Vital Statistics Bureau),

    (ii) with his consent, he is named as the child's father on the child's birth certificate, or

    (iii) he is obligated to support the child under a written voluntary promise or by court order;

(4) while the child is under the age of majority, he receives the child into his home and openly holds out the child as his natural child; or

(5) he acknowledges his paternity of the child in a writing filed with the (appropriate court or Vital Statistics Bureau), which shall promptly inform the mother of the filing of the acknowledgment, and she does not dispute the acknowledgment within a reasonable time after being informed thereof, in a writing filed with the (appropriate court or Vital Statistics Bureau). If another man is presumed under this section to be the child's father, acknowledgment may be effected only with the written consent of the presumed father or after the presumption has been rebutted.

(b) A presumption under this section may be rebutted in an appropriate action only by clear and convincing evidence. If two or more presumptions arise which conflict with each other, the presumption which on the facts is founded on the weightier considerations of policy and logic controls. The presumption is rebutted by a court decree establishing paternity of the child by another man.

Section 12 of this same Uniform Parentage Act identifies evidence courts can be expected to employ relating to paternity cases:

(1) evidence of sexual intercourse between the mother and alleged father at any possible time of conception;

(2) an expert's opinion concerning the statistical probability of the alleged father's paternity based upon the duration of the mother's pregnancy;

(3) blood test results, weighted in accordance with evidence, if available, of the statistical probability of the alleged father's paternity;

(4) medical or anthropological evidence relating to the alleged father's paternity of the child based on tests performed by experts. If a man has been identified

as a possible father of the child, the court may, and upon request of the party shall, require the child, the mother, and the man to submit to appropriate tests; and

(5)   all other evidence relevant to the issue of paternity of the child.

In paternity suits, a judgment that a man is a child's father usually incorporates an order that the father pay periodic support for the child. Also included may be an order for the father to pay the mother's expenses for the pregnancy and birth, as well as expenses incurred in prosecuting the paternity suit (Krause, 1977).

Adoption

Adoption is the legal process by which children acquire parents other than their natural parents and parents acquire children other than their natural children (Clark, 1968). In the event of adoption, the rights and duties between a child and his or her natural parents are ended and replaced by rights and duties between the adoptive parents and the child. All states permit adoption of children and minors (Krause, 1977).

Most adoptions of children by nonrelatives are supervised and take place through adoption agencies. Private adoptions are legal in certain states; however, some contact with a public child welfare agency is still required before a legal adoption can occur. The extent of this required contact varies. Some states merely require that parents provide notification of the prospective adoption to the appropriate regulatory agency. In other states, the agency investigates the prospective parents. In still others, it totally controls the adoption process. Criminal prosecution is possible in some states if an adoption takes place without the requisite agency involvement, particularly if the natural parents receive compensation beyond what is required for medical, legal, and appropriate administrative expenses (Krause, 1977).

Despite the threat of criminal prosecution, there is an extensive black market in "desirable" (usually meaning healthy and white) babies. Likewise, independent adoptions, where available, are also steadily increasing. It is often more advantageous for natural mothers to participate in a private as opposed to public adoption. The former process is often viewed as less demeaning, and mothers who give their children up for public adoption are not likely to be reimbursed for medical and living expenses as they are with private adoptions. Further, the natural parent can occasionally meet the adopting parents, a practice that is almost impossible in public adoptions (Ruback, 1984).

Two points currently lack clarity with regard to the adoption: (a) the rights of a nonmarital father in proceedings by others to adopt his children and (b) an adoptee's right to know the identity of his or her natural parents. The Supreme Court in *Stanley v. Illinois* (1972) held that an unwed father was entitled to notice and a hearing concerning the disposition of his children. A major factor in this decision, however, was the fact that the father had lived with the children in a de facto family unit (Krause, 1977). Following *Stanley*, the Supreme Court extended constitutional protection to unwed fathers in the adoption process in the case of *Caban v. Mohammed* (1979). In *Caban* the Court considered the constitutionality of a New York law that permitted an unwed mother but not an unwed father to block the adoption of their children by withholding consent. In this case, the unwed father challenged the adoption of his two natural children by their natural mother and stepfather without his consent. The Supreme Court struck down the New York law in stating:

> The effect of New York's classification is to discriminate against fathers even when their identity is known and they have manifested a significant paternal interest in the child. The facts of this case illustrate the harshness of classifying unwed fathers as being invariably less qualified and entitled than mothers to exercise a concerned judgement as to the fate of their children.

Several years later, the Supreme Court again ruled on unwed fathers' rights in *Lehr v. Robertson* (1983). In *Lehr*, the Court found that the mere existence of a biological link is insufficient to merit constitutional protection. An unwed father must demonstrate a full commitment to the responsibilities of parenthood by coming forward to participate in the rearing of his child. It is this exhibited interest and personal contact that allow him protection under due process. Given these decisions by the Supreme Court, many states have statutes that require some form of notice be given to unwed fathers before their children can be adopted. The exception to this general rule, however, is when the father never had or sought custody or did not exhibit interest in their children's well-being (S. E. Friedman, 1992).

Courts and state legislatures have long recognized that ensuring the sealing of adoption records serves a number of vital interests. These include (a) preventing natural parents from interfering with adoptive parents' raising of the adoptee, (b) protecting the adoptee from the potential stigma of illegitimacy, and (c) protecting the natural parents from the unwanted intrusion that might arise in the event of the sudden appearance of their natural child. Virtually every state provides that records relating to adoptions are confidential and can be examined only on establishing good cause and securing judicial approval (S. E. Friedman, 1992). Although adoptees have instituted constitutional challenges to sealed records laws on the theory that they have a right to know their origins, these challenges have tended to be rejected by the courts (e.g., *In re Roger B.*, 1981).

In response to these court decisions, some states have implemented voluntary registries that authorize the release of sealed records in the event that both the natural parents and the adult adoptee consent. One drawback, however, is that these acts typically do not allow the solicitation of a person's registration. An alternative response has been the enactment of what are termed *consent statutes*. Under these statutes, an adult adoptee may request a state agency to locate his or her natural parents, and once identified, seek their consent to be identified to their natural child (S. E. Friedman, 1992).

Surrogate Parenthood

Recent years have seen a pronounced increase in the number of instances where only one member of a marital dyad is the natural parent of their child (Ruback, 1984). With regard to artificial insemination of the mother from a donor who is not the husband, presumptions as to legitimacy and paternity are relatively clear. Section 5 of the Uniform Parentage Act (Bureau of National Affairs, Inc., 1976) precisely specifies:

(a) If, under the supervision of a licensed physician and with the consent of her husband, a wife is inseminated artificially with semen donated by a man not her husband, the husband is treated in law as if he were the natural father of a child thereby conceived. The husband's consent must be in writing and signed by him and his wife. The physician shall certify their signatures and the date of the insemination, and file the husband's consent with the [State Department of Health], where it shall be kept confidential and in a sealed file. However, the physician's failure to do so does not affect the father and child relationship. All papers and records pertaining to the insemination, whether part of the permanent record of a court or of a file held by the supervising physician or elsewhere, are subject to inspection only upon an order of the court for good cause shown.

(b) The donor of semen provided to a licensed physician for use in artificial insemination of a married woman other than the donor's wife is treated in law, as if he were not the natural father of a child thereby conceived.

In re Adams (1990) represented an Illinois case brought by a woman seeking to dissolve her marriage and obtain financial support for her child conceived in Florida by artificial insemination during the marriage. Her husband contested the claim for child support on the grounds that the Illinois Parentage Act, modeled on the Uniform Parentage Act, required the written consent of the husband to establish paternity. Both parties agreed this had never been given. In its finding, the Illinois Appellate Court found that even though the written consent of the husband was absent, 35 other facts contested the husband's current disclaimer of parental responsibility (e.g., the husband taking an active part in selecting the child's name, his never objecting to his designation on the child's birth certificate as the father, his listing the child as a dependent on the couple's federal income tax return).

Clearly, identifying parenthood is difficult when a surrogate mother bears the child of a father whose wife is unable to. Major questions regard financial considerations, possible criminal penalties, and the unenforceability of the contracts between the parties (Ruback, 1984). Financial considerations involve the surrogate mother's medical expenses (including prepregnancy, medical, and psychological screening) and compensation to her for the pregnancy. Paying the surrogate mother for her services can make the procedure a crime in some states where statutes have been enacted outlawing payments to parents for their consent to an adoption of their children. Handel and Sherwyn (1982) assert that these statutes are likely unenforceable because of their vagueness and the fact that they may violate constitutional guarantees of privacy.

A potentially more volatile concern is the question of surrogate mothers who ultimately decide to keep their children. To overcome this possible circumstance, prospective parents and surrogate mothers often sign contracts prior to the pregnancy designed to allay this problem. Handel and Sherwyn (1982) caution, however, that such contracts are likely unenforceable. The Uniform Status of Children of Assisted Conception Act (USCACA), promulgated in 1988, has been approved by the American Bar Association. The act provides two basic options for states considering its implementation. Option one provides that surrogate mother agreements must be approved by a court if they are to be held valid. The second option voids all surrogate motherhood agreements.

Another area of parenthood that is still legally unsettled is donor egg in vitro fertilization (IVF). In donor egg IVF, an egg that has been removed from one woman is fertilized and then implanted in another woman. The birth mother then carries and gives birth to a child who is not genetically related to her. In donor egg IVF, the donor's role ends when the egg is retrieved, and the mother who gives birth performs most of the creation process. The donor has no emotional ties to the child, which might develop during gestation.

Henry (1994), after reviewing the law related to donor egg IVF, concluded that no model statutes, actual state statutes, or case law have given any legal rights to or imposed any legal responsibilities on women who provide donor eggs that result in a later birth. Birth mothers are sometimes protected in statutes from unwanted interference from the donor. All existing U.S. statutes establish the birth mother as the natural and legal mother.

Abortion

Roe v. Wade (1973) represented a landmark Supreme Court decision on the subject of abortion. In it, the Court examined the state's interests in regulating abortion. The Court held that during the first 3 months of pregnancy, a mother's right to privacy is paramount and the state has no compelling interest that outweighs this right; during the second 3 months, the state has a compelling interest in the mother's health and therefore can establish reasonable regulations for the abortion procedure; during the last 3 months, the state has a compelling interest in safeguarding the life of the fetus. Thus, the Supreme Court asserted that the state can regulate and even ban abortion. However, in *Doe v. Bolton* (1973), a companion case to *Roe v. Wade*, the Court declared unconstitutional a Georgia statute that was too restrictive of abortion. Among other things, this law required that abortions be performed only in accredited hospitals and only after approval by a hospital abortion committee.

The Supreme Court addressed the issue of whether consent from a woman's husband or parent is required prior to an abortion being performed in *Planned Parenthood of Central Missouri v. Danforth* (1976). The Court held that both adult and minor women have a constitutional right to reproductive privacy; no spousal or parental consent is thereby necessary for the woman to procure an abortion. However, the Court also suggested that the constitutional right may be restricted in the case of minors. Justice Blackmun, writing for the Court, described the right as extending to the "competent minor, mature enough to have become pregnant." Shortly thereafter, however, he further noted that "not every minor regardless of age or maturity may give effective consent for the termination of her pregnancy."

Thus, the extent to which a state might involve parents in their child's reproductive decision was left unsettled in *Planned Parenthood of Central Missouri v. Danforth* (1976). In *Bellotti v. Baird (II)* (1979), the Supreme Court held that although a state may require parents' consent as one form of access to abortion, an alternative, either a judicial or administrative proceeding, must be available to the minor woman who is reluctant to approach her parents. If she demonstrates that she is "mature and competent to make the abortion decision," to the satisfaction of a judge or other state decision maker, she must be allowed to act independently. Even if she fails to establish her capacity to make a mature decision, the abortion should be authorized if it is determined to be in her best interest.

In *Planned Parenthood Association v. Ashcroft* (1983), the Supreme Court affirmed the revised parental consent clause of *Bellotti v. Baird (II)*. Although this represents an avenue to abortion for the minor woman who does not want to seek parental permission, it still offers a forbidding path to the teenager who lacks experience or knowledge of legal procedures. A requirement that minors pursue a legal remedy to prove their ability to make an abortion decision potentially can lead to delayed decisions (and hence more risky abortions), illegal abortion, and an increased incidence of unwanted childbirth (Torres, Forest, & Eisman, 1980).

These Supreme Court decisions have established that states may not require that minor women must have parental consent to obtain an abortion. Notice to parents of any abortion, however, may be an acceptable restriction. In *H. L. v. Matheson* (1981), the Supreme Court held constitutional a Utah law requiring physicians to give notice to parents when performing an abortion on a minor. The Court suggested several significant state interests were served by the statute. These included encouraging pregnant minors to seek advice from their parents, preserving the integrity of the family, and protecting the adolescent. The assumption that all informed parents will respond in a manner beneficial to their daughter's interests has been questioned. Although many parents may be supportive, it seems equally plausible that others will respond negatively (Scott, 1984).

The Supreme Court reconsidered the abortion issue again in 1989 in *Webster v. Reproductive Health Services* (1989) in upholding a Missouri statute restricting the availability of publicly funded abortion services. The Missouri statute also required physicians to test for fetal viability at 20 weeks, two thirds of the way through the second trimester of a pregnancy. Furthermore, the preamble of the Missouri statute expressed the intention of stopping abortions. The Court stated that the language in the preamble was not binding on anyone, and the public funding of abortion services has never been constitutionally protected. This decision highlighted that states do have the right to regulate abortions (Hopkins & Anderson, 1990).

After reviewing the *Planned Parenthood of the Blue Ridge v. Camblos* (1998) decision, McLaughlin (1999) concluded that the U.S. Supreme Court, "still requires parental consent, parental notification, or judicial bypass for minors seeking an abortion, thus infringing on this very private right of a minor's autonomy" (p. 150). The U.S. Supreme Court's position on abortions for minors has been consistent since 1980 (Vitiello, 1999).

PARENTAL RIGHTS AND RESPONSIBILITIES

The area of primary legal impact on parents' rights and responsibilities relative to their children are those state statutes addressing child maltreatment: neglect and abuse. Rosenberg and Hunt (1984) characterized legal issues in cases of child maltreatment as "an evolving attempt to balance the often competing interests of state, parent, and child" (p. 83). They described the interests of the state and the child as requiring that children be protected from serious harm, such as might result from abuse or neglect. Parent and child interests require that the family be free from unnecessary intrusion by the state. In circumstances when parents act in ways inconsistent with their children's best interests, the state can assume the role of parent in protecting children's welfare, thereby overriding parental authority. There has been ongoing debate, however, as to the state's ability to provide alternatives that are as good or better than children's own family situation (S. E. Friedman, 1992; Mnookin, 1973; Wald, 1976, 1982).

The state's right to intrude on a family derives from two distinct sources: its police power and the concept of parens patriae. The *police power* is the state's inherent power to prevent its citizens from harming one another as well as its mandate to promote all aspects of the public welfare. *Parens patriae* is the limited paternalistic power of the state to protect and promote the welfare of certain individuals (e.g., children) who lack the capacity to act in their own best interests (Rosenberg & Hunt, 1984). The state's exercise of parens patriae over children, however, is limited: it is used solely to further the best interests of children. Before intervening, the state must show that children's parents or guardians are either unfit, unable, or unwilling to care for them (Mnookin, 1973).

Determining this unfitness has been most controversial, becoming associated and further delimiting parens patriae by the "void for vagueness" doctrine. As applied herein, this doctrine concerns potential infringement of parents' due process rights and is composed of three distinct, yet related, components providing the basis for judicial consideration (Day, 1977). The concept of "fair warning" comprises the central component of the doctrine and requires that a statute be worded clearly so that parents are given adequate notice of what behaviors are considered illegal. The second component, an antidiscretionary element, concerns the potential for arbitrary judicial enforcement of ambiguously worded statutes. The third component considers whether a component is too broad; that is, there is a strong potential that legal as well as illegal behavior might be prosecuted.

Alsager v. District Court of Polk County, Iowa (1975) was a precedent-setting family law case that illustrated the importance of the void for vagueness doctrine as well as the tension between the state's parens patriae interests and parents' autonomy. In this case, the Supreme Court of Iowa acted "in the best interest of the child" to terminate the parents' rights with respect to five of the six Alsager children. The stated grounds for doing so were that the parents "substantially and continuously or repeatedly refused to give the child necessary parental care and protection" and that they were "unfit parents by reason of . . . conduct . . . detrimental to the physical or mental health or morals of the child."

The parents successfully appealed this initial decision; the appeals court held that the evidence presented in the termination proceeding was insufficient to warrant severing the parent–child relationship. For example, evidence entered into the proceedings identified that the parents "sometimes permitted their children to leave the house in cold weather without winter clothing on, allowed them to play in traffic, to annoy neighbors, to eat mush for supper, to live in a house containing dirty dishes and laundry, and to sometimes arrive late at school." The decision to order the initial temporary removal of the children from the home was based on a 20-minute visit by a probation officer who found that the only occupants at that time included the mother and her youngest child, who was less than a year old. Further, following the children's removal from the home, they spent the next 5 years in a total of 15 separate foster homes and 8 juvenile home placements. The decision to terminate the parental rights was determined to have failed to provide the children with increased stability or improved lives.

Although few would argue that severe, purposefully inflicted physical injury or a clear diagnosis of failure to thrive constitutes abuse in the first instance and neglect in the latter, the majority of reported abuse and neglect cases fall somewhere along a continuum of "potential" child maltreatment. The importance of clearly defining and delineating instances of abuse and neglect was aptly noted by Wald (1975) in considering psychological harm to children emanating from abusive and neglectful caretaker behaviors:

> While emotional damage to a child should be a basis for intervention in some cases, it is essential that laws be drafted in a manner consistent with our limited knowledge about the nature and causes of psychological harm. Intervention should not be premised on vague concepts like "proper parental love," or "adequate affectionate parental association." Such language invites unwarranted intervention, based on each social worker's or judge's brand of "folk psychology." Although such language might clearly apply to parents who refuse to hold, talk to, or engage in any contact with their children, it could also be applied to parents who travel a great deal and leave their children with housekeepers, who send their children to boarding school to get rid of them, or who are generally unaffectionate people. (pp. 1016–1017)

Ruback (1984) proposed that court procedures are usually in the best interests of allegedly abused or neglected children. In child protective court proceedings in most states, involved children are provided representation by an independent agent, an attorney or lay guardian ad litem ("in a law suit") appointed by the court. This party represents the child's interests as opposed to the parents or the state. Prior screening tends to eliminate the majority of those cases that do not belong in court and often acts as a precipitant for families to seek therapeutic assistance and/or change their potentially destructive interactions. Court proceedings are generally dismissed when there is insufficient evidence of abuse or neglect, the child is in no danger of further harm, the harm from potential state intervention outweighs any dangers posed by the parents, a mature child asks that a petition be dismissed, and the parents voluntarily accept treatment (Besharov, 1982).

"Voluntary" acceptance of treatment services is frequently the result of pressures from professionals to "take advantage" of these services in lieu of threatened court action (Rosenberg & Hunt, 1984). Further, most families who proceed through court action find participation in treatment to be embodied in consequent court orders, particularly in cases where children are temporarily removed from their parents' custody. Thus, these families' contact with marriage and family therapists is common.

If a court does find that parents have abused or neglected their children, several options are available. The children may be temporarily or permanently removed from the custody of their parents. If so, a temporary or permanent guardian (an individual or a state or private agency) is appointed to take responsibility for the child's well-being. Although it depends on the facts present in individual cases, parents do not necessarily lose their parental rights (e.g., visitation) when a guardian is appointed. In severe cases of abuse or neglect, however, the state may initiate proceedings to terminate parents' rights to the custody of their children and permit the children to be adopted (Chemerinsky, 1979).

ANNULMENT AND DIVORCE

A marriage can be terminated in three ways: death, divorce, or annulment. Because the overwhelming majority of unsuccessful marriages are dissolved through divorce as opposed to annulment, the former will be given the greater emphasis.

Annulment

Annulment is a declaration by the court that *for reasons existing at the time of a marriage*, the marriage was invalid from its inception. Common grounds for annulment include factors affecting parties' ability to enter a legal contract (such as fraud, duress, insanity, and immaturity) and factors about the parties' marriage proscribed by law (such as incest or bigamy). The traditional difference between court actions initiated for annulment and those initiated for divorce is that the grounds for annulment must have occurred prior to the marriage, such as preexisting insanity or fraud, usually combined with an allegation that marital consent had been impaired as a result. In contrast, divorce conceptually requires grounds that occurred after the marriage.

Weyrauch and Katz (1983) reported that requests for annulment have tended to become increasingly rare and frequently involve cases in which one party, because of strong feelings, is particularly aggrieved. Allegations necessary to obtain an annulment can be difficult to adequately prove to a court's satisfaction. For example, in *Larson v. Larson* (1963), the Appellate Court of Illinois ruled that the plaintiff, the husband, had not clearly and definitively satisfied the burden of proving that his wife was insane at the time of their marriage even though she had numerous inpatient hospitalizations during their 10 years of marriage. In commenting on this case, Weyrauch and Katz (1983) emphasized that insanity as used for purposes of an annulment action is not necessarily identical with common psychiatric conceptions of mental illness. Specific complications in this case surrounded the psychiatric classification of schizophrenia.

Because of the difficulty in obtaining annulments and to avoid the need for filing new complaints, many attorneys are inclined to combine requests for annulment with alternative requests for divorce. There are situations, however, wherein obtaining an annulment as opposed to a divorce can be critical. Examples include efforts to receive a pension or Social Security benefits from a preexisting marriage.

Divorce

Many couples initially seek therapy in the hope of preserving and enhancing their marriage. The result of therapeutic efforts is often a more vibrant, healthier marriage. By contrast, however, therapeutic efforts also can create an increased awareness in one or both partners that the costs of maintaining the marriage greatly outweigh the potential benefits. Should this be the case, the therapist involved with the couple leading up to their decision to divorce is then often excluded from the divorce proceedings as the couple seeks legal assistance. It is important that marriage and family therapists work with couples past the point of deciding to divorce; a couple must be prepared to deal with the win–lose legal process they are about to enter.

Most couples, particularly those seeking an amicable divorce, seldom consider in advance that they might be thrust into a bitterly competitive struggle. Although they have heard stories of divorce and custody battles, they may have agreed not to let it happen to them. After all, "We've gone through enough pain" or "We've got to work things out peacefully for the children's sake." They might even have worked out an agreement in advance on everything they thought was necessary. What they did not realize is that the legal system they are entering is by its nature adversarial and can work against their well-intentioned, cooperative endeavors. Coogler (1978) addressed this issue:

> The lawyer, as an advocate, is required to represent, or advocate, *solely* the interest of his client. *He cannot represent both parties*, as is commonly supposed. The lawyer represents his client within the "light of his professional judgment." But the client's interest is always perceived as being in opposition to the interests of the other party. The lawyer cannot and does not regard the parties as having a common problem which he or she will help resolve. (p. 7)

Lawyers are ethically bound to represent their own particular client to the best of their abilities, regardless of the effect it might have on the other party. As a result, each tends to push his or her own client to win every possible advantage (Haynes, 1981). The retaining of one attorney leads to the retaining of a second for the unrepresented partner. These circumstances certainly do not support the give and take required to gain a mutually satisfying settlement. Further, much of the decision making is taken out of the couple's hands.

The battle between attorneys normally occurs outside of the courtroom. However, if attorneys cannot agree on an out-of-court settlement, the matter goes before a judge who makes the final decision. Unless they are prepared to individually and assertively push for a concerted and active involvement, neither husband nor wife will have much of an effect on the outcome. This lack of involvement often leaves both partners dissatisfied and angry at the court, the attorneys, and even more antagonistic toward each other. These potentially bitter and hostile responses frequently continue long after the marriage is legally ended, not because of the fact that it did end, but because of the way it ended. The resulting negative effects can be devastating, especially for children (Hammond, 1981; Schoyer, 1980).

Traditionally, obtaining a divorce required that one party be at fault. The original fault grounds were adultery and physical cruelty. These were later expanded to include habitual drunkenness, willful desertion, mental cruelty, and conviction of a felony. Because the assumption was that only the innocent party was entitled to a divorce, if it could be proved that both parties were at fault, neither one could receive a divorce. This reasoning, called the *doctrine of recrimination*, made contested divorces difficult to win. Proof of collusion between the two parties was also sufficient to bar the action for a divorce. This action was based on the state's interest in protecting marriages (Ruback, 1984).

Recent years have evidenced a significant trend away from requiring fault in divorce actions. Almost every state allows for some type of no-fault divorce, although traditional fault ground may still be alleged. The grounds in these no-fault actions are best represented by Section 305 of the Uniform Marriage and Divorce Act (Bureau of National Affairs, Inc., 1982):

(a) If both of the parties by petition or otherwise have stated under oath or affirmation that the marriage is irretrievably broken, or one of the parties has so stated and the other has not denied it, the court, after hearing, shall make a finding whether the marriage is irretrievably broken.

(b) If one of the parties has denied under oath or affirmation that the marriage is irretrievably broken, the court shall consider all relevant factors, including the circumstances that gave rise to filing the petition and the prospect of reconciliation, and shall:

(1) make a finding whether the marriage is irretrievably broken; or

(2) continue the matter for further hearing not fewer than 30 nor more than 60 days later, or as soon thereafter as the matter may be reached on the court's calendar, and may suggest to the parties that they seek counseling. The court, at the request of either party shall, or on its own motion may, order a conciliation conference. At the adjourned hearing the court shall make a finding whether the marriage is irretrievably broken.

(c)   A finding of irretrievable breakdown is a determination that there is no reasonable prospect of reconciliation.

Although finding fault is no longer required, in most states, divorce is not immediately granted merely on the parties' filing a petition. Many states have a mandatory minimum waiting period after the action is filed before the court may grant a divorce. Further, there normally must be some evidence to support the finding that the marriage is irretrievably broken (Freed & Foster, 1981). In addition, in many states, courts have at their discretion the ability to require couples to attend counseling and conciliation sessions. The stated purpose of these barriers to automatic divorce is to avoid hasty dissolution of marriages. For liberalized divorce procedures, the barriers might also still be viable and remain intact (Ruback, 1982). Such statutes that delay but do not deny access to divorce have been ruled as constitutional, the assumption being that the delay is reasonable and the state has legitimate interests protected by the requirements (Strickman, 1982). For example, in *Sosna v. Iowa* (1975), the Supreme Court upheld Iowa's requirement of a year's residency in the state for a divorce action. This requirement could be justified in several legitimate ways, other than budgetary considerations or administrative convenience (e.g., confirming that the party seeking divorce had sufficient contact with the state before important questions such as child custody were decided by the courts; Ruback, 1984).

The requirement of counseling and conciliation sessions prior to the granting of divorce has obvious implications for marriage and family therapists. For example, an Iowa statute allows judges the power to require parties to participate in conciliation efforts conducted by the domestic relations division of the court or its representative. Orlando (1978) reported that, in those areas where required conciliation counseling outcome has been studied, a majority of participating couples reconcile and stay together for at least a year. Even when reconciliation was impossible, however, the required counseling was successful in reducing the number of custody disputes and contested divorces. Others have disputed the value of required conciliation efforts, suggesting them to be expensive, to have a low probability of success, and to generate overexpectations due to the shortage of trained personnel (Krause, 1977).

Given that no-fault divorce is the avenue of choice for most divorcing couples, problems relative to divorce tend to center almost completely on matters relating to property and children. Thus, marriage and family therapists seeking to prepare couples to amicably, yet assertively, address issues relative to their divorce proceedings need to be aware of matters relating to spousal maintenance (alimony) and the division of property as well as custody and support of dependent children.

Spousal Maintenance

Although newspaper headlines are sometimes made by alimony awards, even in 1981 only about 14% of all divorces involved alimony (U.S. Bureau of the Census, 1981). Moreover, the amount of alimony awarded is relatively small. Statutory guidance is provided in most states for awarding alimony; however, some states provide no clear guidelines beyond considering the "wife's needs" and the "husband's ability to pay" (Ruback, 1984). Section 308 of the Uniform Marriage and Divorce Act (Bureau of National Affairs, Inc., 1982) offers a common denominator for marriage and family therapists to consider concerning alimony awards:

(a) In a proceeding for dissolution of marriage, legal separation, or maintenance following a decree of dissolution of the marriage by a court which lacked personal jurisdiction over the absent spouse, the court may grant a maintenance order for either spouse, only if it finds that the spouse seeking maintenance:

   (1) lacks sufficient property to provide for his reasonable needs; and
   (2) is unable to support himself through appropriate employment or is the custodian of a child whose condition or circumstances make it appropriate that the custodian not be required to seek employment outside the home.

(b) The maintenance order shall be in amounts and for periods of time the court deems just, without regard to marital misconduct, and after considering all relevant factors including:

   (1) the financial resources of the party seeking maintenance, including marital property apportioned to him, his ability to meet his needs independently, and the extent to which a provision for support of a child living with the party includes a sum for that party as custodian;
   (2) the time necessary to acquire sufficient education or training to enable the party seeking maintenance to find appropriate employment;
   (3) the standard of living established during the marriage;
   (4) the duration of the marriage;
   (5) the age and the physical and emotional condition of the spouse seeking maintenance; and
   (6) the ability of the spouse from whom maintenance is sought to meet his needs while meeting those of the spouse seeking maintenance.

Required alimony payments generally end with the death of the supporting exspouse or with the remarriage of the supported ex-spouse. In some states, alimony can be discontinued with the submission of proof that the supported ex-spouse is cohabitating with a person of the opposite sex. Further, permanent or open-ended alimony awards are significantly declining, likely reflecting the belief that alimony should be used to obtain education and training leading to self-sufficiency (i.e., rehabilitative alimony). In most states, alimony is paid only for a brief period of time (typically no more than 5 years) after the divorce (Sack, 1987). Increasingly, however, the trend among states is away from alimony and toward a division of property. Alimony is being seen as a supplement to the division of property occurring on divorce (Ruback, 1984).

Division of Property

One of two basic systems of marital property rights are usually operational in divorce proceedings: common law and community property (Krause, 1977). In those states where common law property rights laws are present, each spouse separately owns the property that he or she brought into the marriage and that came to him or her during the marriage by personal income, interest, or dividends from separate property; by inheritance; or through gifts. Problems arise in deciding on the division of property primarily in regard to property bought during the marriage with money from both spouses but with the title taken in the name of only one spouse or when property is purchased with money from only one spouse but title is taken in the name of both. Courts frequently have difficulty deciding who owns what property. They attempt to answer this by reconstructing the parties' intent at the time the property was purchased (Ruback, 1984).

As is the case with spousal maintenance, statutory guidelines available to judges with regard to the division of marital property have been relatively unclear. Most often those factors taken into account relate to an evaluation of marital assets (Connell, 1981). Section 307, Alternative A of the Uniform Marriage and Divorce Act (Bureau of National Affairs, Inc., 1982) provides a common set of considerations for adoption in this regard:

(a) In a proceeding for dissolution of a marriage, legal separation, or disposition of property following a decree of dissolution of marriage or legal separation by a court which lacked personal jurisdiction over the absent spouse or lacked jurisdiction to dispose of the property, the court, without regard to marital misconduct, shall, and in a proceeding for legal separation may, finally equitably apportion between the parties the property and assets belonging to either or both however and whenever acquired, and whether the title thereto is in the name of the husband or wife or both. In making apportionment the court shall consider the duration of the marriage, any prior marriage of either party, any antenuptial agreement of the parties, the age, health, station, occupation, amount and sources of income, vocational skills, employability, estate, liabilities, and needs of each of the parties, custodial provisions, whether the apportionment is in lieu of or in addition to maintenance, and the opportunity of each for future acquisition of capital assets and income. The court shall also consider the contribution or dissipation of each party in the acquisition, preservation, depreciation, or appreciation in the value of the respective estates, and as the contribution of a spouse as a homemaker or to the family unit.

(b) In the proceeding, the court may protect and promote the best interests of the children by setting aside a portion of the jointly and separately held estates of the parties in a separate fund or trust for the support, maintenance, education, and general welfare of any minor, dependent, or incompetent children of the parties.

In contrast to states where common law property statutes operate, courts in states emphasizing community property rights rule that all property coming to spouses during their marriage belongs equally to the husband and to the wife. On divorce, community property is divided equally between the two spouses. Courts are, however, free to divide the community property as they see fit (Ruback, 1984). Section 307, Alternative B of the Uniform Marriage and Divorce Act (Bureau of National Affairs, Inc., 1982) seeks to offer a set of common considerations relative to the division of marital property where community property laws are in effect:

In a proceeding for dissolution of the marriage, legal separation, or disposition of property following a decree of dissolution of the marriage or legal dissolution by a court which lacked personal jurisdiction over the absent spouse or lacked jurisdiction to dispose of the property, the court shall assign each spouse's separate property to that spouse. It shall also divide community property, without regard to marital misconduct, in just proportions after considering all relevant factors including:

(1)   contribution of each spouse to acquisition of the marital property, including contribution of a spouse as homemaker;

(2)   value of the property set apart to each spouse;

(3)   duration of the marriage; and

(4)   economic circumstances of each spouse when the division of property is to become effective, including the desirability of awarding the family home or the right to live therein for a reasonable period to the spouse having custody of any children.

Ruback (1984) reported two important contemporary developments regarding the division of marital property. The first relates to property "earned" but not received during the marriage; this includes pensions and training, the latter especially through a formal education. With regard to pensions, particularly in states with community property laws, the trend has been to give the spouse (generally the wife) a property interest in the husband's pension proportional to the amount of the pension earned during the marriage (Krause, 1977). An exception has been made for military pensions. In *McCarty v. McCarty* (1981), the Supreme Court held that these pensions are controlled by federal law, not state property laws.

The second type of property earned, but not received, during the marriage is a professional degree, normally obtained by one spouse while the other works to pay for the education and support the dyad during the schooling period. Several state courts have held that the spouse who worked has an equitable interest in the value of the professional degree. For example, in *Reen v. Reen* (1981), a Massachusetts probate and family court held that a wife who sacrificed her own education and the prime child-bearing years of her life to put her husband through dental school and orthodontic training was entitled to part of the value of the degree in orthodontia.

CHILD CUSTODY AND SUPPORT AFTER DIVORCE

In the past, parents usually entered divorce proceedings believing that single-parent custody with tightly regulated visitation rights was the only option. Parents, angry with each other particularly given the potential hostility emanating from the adversarial legal process, frequently used custody controversies over children to provide a structure for dealing with their anger. In the past, most states gave physical custody only to mothers and put sole responsibility for child support on fathers. Times have changed, however. Mothers are working and fathers are mothering. Parenting roles have lost their gender identity as parents are increasingly becoming equally involved in raising their children, though their children are likely spending greater amounts of time in the care of others. Likewise, the male's image as breadwinner has been considerably blemished by the developing evidence that women have been and are providing substantially to the support of the family. These developments have had a significant impact on child custody and support determinations in divorce proceedings.

Child Custody

Ruback (1984) proposed that child custody after divorce is best seen as a continuing problem rather than a one-time determination. He partitioned the issue into initial determinations and changes in custody.

In the past, initial custody decisions have been based on a conceptualization termed the *tender years doctrine*, which was an assumption that preadolescent children benefit most from being with their mother because only their mother could provide the particular nurturance they needed during their "tender years." Mothers were generally awarded custody of younger children unless ruled by the court to be "unfit." The term *unfit* referred to moral fitness. It was and occasionally still is an attack on a mother's morals and represented the only successful way of overcoming the tender years presumption. Children beyond their tender years were presumed to benefit more from being in the custody of their same-sex parent, thus fathers were awarded custody of sons and mothers the daughters. Exceptions usually occurred only in cases when courts were reluctant to separate siblings (Krause, 1977).

In the past several decades, the tender years doctrine has been officially discarded by the courts or legislatures in most of the states (Freed & Foster, 1981). Replacing it is the "best interests of the child" standard. Section 402 of the Uniform Marriage and Divorce Act (Bureau of National Affairs, Inc., 1982) offers guidelines delineating the best interests standard:

> The court shall determine custody in accordance with the best interest of the child. The court shall consider all relevant factors including:
> (1) the wishes of the child's parent or parents as to his custody;
> (2) the wishes of the child as to his custodian;
> (3) the interaction and interrelationship of the child with his parent or parents, his siblings, and any other person who may significantly affect the child's best interest;
> (4) the child's adjustment to his home, school, and community; and
> (5) the mental and physical health of all individuals involved.
> The court shall not consider conduct of a proposed custodian that does not affect his relationship to the child.

Although the tender years doctrine has been superseded in most states by the best interests standard, judges still tend to have a bias that children's best interests are served by awarding custody to their mother. Other problems that arise in the application of the best interests standard include children's natural unwillingness to express a preference for one parent and thereby offend the nonchosen parent, and judges' subjectivity and/or lack of professional training regarding adjustment, interactional, and mental health variables. The best interests standard also requests that judges ignore conduct of a parent that does not affect his or her relationship with the child. This provision was included to discourage parties from spying on each other to prove marital misconduct (usually sexual) for use as evidence in a custody case. Some authors have suggested, however, that marital misconduct is very often paralleled by poor parenting practices. Such misconduct might include serious emotional problems, habitual drunkenness, adultery, and gross immorality (Weiss, 1979).

In determining child custody under the best interests standard, judges often need to rely on the advice of experts. Marriage and family therapists' testimony in this regard can be very persuasive. Very frequently, parents seek the services of marriage and family therapists as do the courts themselves. For example, were testimony to be rendered by a marriage and family therapist asserting that a child's emotional needs were best met by one parent over another or that the parent's marital behaviors did not affect his or her parenting practices, that parent will obviously have a stronger case. This would be particularly so if the testimony was perceived to be objective. In fact, expert testimony regarding the emotional needs of a child is generally superior to the expressed wishes of the child (Kazen, 1977).

Mnookin and Weisberg (1995) have distinguished between physical and legal custody. In initial custody determinations, four forms of legal custody are available today: sole custody, split custody, divided custody, and joint custody (Folberg, 1984).

1. *Sole custody* is still the most common form of custody determination after divorce. One parent is awarded sole legal custody of the child with visitation rights allowed to the noncustodial parent. The noncustodian, by informal agreement, may have a voice in important decisions affecting the child, but ultimate control and legal responsibility rest with the custodial parent.
2. *Split custody* is a custody award of one or more of the children to one parent and the remaining children to the other. Courts tend, however, to generally refuse to separate siblings unless for compelling reasons. Intense hostility or competition between siblings may be one such reason. Another reason might be the inability of either parent to care for all of the children at once.
3. *Divided custody* allows each parent to have primary custody of the child for a part of the year or every other year. This form of custody is also referred to as *alternating custody*. Each parent has reciprocal visitation rights under this arrangement, and each exercises exclusive control over the child while the child remains in his or her custody. Courts tend to most often award divided custody that provides for residence with one parent during the school year and the other during vacations. When parent's homes are separated by greater geographical distances, making frequent visitation impossible, divided custody is generally an approved award. In contrast, courts have also tended to award divided custody on

the grounds that both parents live in close proximity. In these cases, this proximity was seen as minimizing the strains that divided custody might place upon children (Folberg & Graham, 1979).

4. Joint custody goes beyond the concept of divided custody and may also be referred to as *shared parenting, shared custody,* or *concurrent custody.* Both parents retain legal responsibility and authority for the care and control of their child, much as in an intact family unit. The parent with whom the child is residing at a specific moment must make immediate, day-to-day decisions regarding discipline, diet, emergency care, and so on. Both parents in joint custody awards have an equal voice in their child's education, upbringing, religious training, nonemergency medical care, and general welfare. Joint custody is most often applicable where parents are able to give priority to their children's needs, are willing to negotiate differences, and can arrange their life-styles to accommodate their children's needs.

Joint custody awards are controversial (Kramer, 1994). Some state courts have stated a preference for joint custody (*In re marriage of Kovash,* 1993), while other state courts have determined that joint custody should be avoided (*Petrashek v. Petrashek,* 1989).

How children and their parents react to the aftermath of divorce and initial custody determinations is relevant to the law in that any problems that children experience may initiate and thus affect judgments concerning modifications of custody. The primary consideration in calling for a custody change is proof that there have been substantial changes in the custody situation that affect the welfare of the child and that have arisen subsequent to the initial award of custody (Ruback, 1984). What constitutes sufficient evidence to justify a decision to alter an initial custody determination varies from state to state. Further, changing societal values have created a mirroring change in what constitutes an unfit parent. For example, although the appeals court in one state approved a change in custody because the mother was cohabitating with a man who was not her husband (*Sims v. Sims,* 1979), in other states, such behavior is not likely to result in a change in custody. Correspondingly, a parent's homosexuality has traditionally been a bar to custody. More recently, however, many courts are requiring evidence confirming a connection between the parent's homosexuality and likely harm to the child before deciding custody (Guernsey, 1981).

Interstate custody disputes are more common. Direct attempts to alter custody decisions by seeking proof that substantial changes have occurred following the initial award emanate from violations of prior determinations of custody. Increasing mobility is a reality in American society. In 1981, over 47% of the population moved at least once within the past 5 years (U.S. Bureau of the Census, 1981). Thus, many divorced parents are moving to different states. Noncustodial parents have kept their child after a visitation period has ended, or simply snatched their child from the custodial parent's home and taken him or her to a second state and entered a court action there to change custody.

Before the adoption of the Uniform Child Custody Jurisdiction Act (UCCJA) by the vast majority of the states, it was relatively easy for an abducting parent to find a court in a second state that would not enforce a first state's custody decree. The reasons for this were based in states' sovereignty issues, judicial jurisdictional contradictions, and the fact that child custody decrees are never final (S. N. Katz, 1981). The UCCJA was designed to prevent conflicting custody decrees in two or more states. To ensure that only one state makes an official custody determination, the act requires that parties notify the courts of any pending custody proceeding in another state and that the courts involved determine the more appropriate forum, so that the actual custody determination will be made in only one court. Thus, the predominant emphasis of the UCCJA is that only one state and one court will make a final judgment. Since being drafted and approved by the American Bar Association in 1968, the UCCJA has been enacted in varying forms by every state (S. E. Friedman, 1992).

The federal government became deeply involved with the enforcement of child custody decrees with the enactment of the Parental Kidnapping Prevention Act of 1980 (PKPA). The PKPA establishes rules to decide jurisdictional disputes that arise in interstate custody disputes. Under the PKPA, every state court is required to enforce custody orders entered by other states that were issued consistently with this act. The scope and limits of the PKPA were considered by the Supreme Court in *Thompson v. Thompson* (1988). In its finding, the Court affirmed the significance of the PKPA. The Court explained that the UCCJA, drafted to address the problem of jurisdictional conflicts concerning custody disputes, had not proved fully effective, because a number of states had, at the time the PKPA was enacted, failed to enact the UCCJA or to enact it with modification. The PKPA thus provided for nationwide enforcement of custody orders made in accordance with the terms of the UCCJA (S. E. Friedman, 1992).

Child Support

Section 15 of the Uniform Parentage Act (Bureau of National Affairs, Inc., 1976) summarizes major factors to be considered by judges in deciding on child support awards:

> In determining the amount to be paid by a parent for support of the child and the period during which the duty of support is owed, a court enforcing the obligation of support shall consider all relevant facts, including:
> (1)   the needs of the child;
> (2)   the standard of living and circumstances of the parents;
> (3)   the relative financial means of the parents;
> (4)   the earning ability of the parents;
> (5)   the need and capacity of the child for education, including higher education;
> (6)   the age of the child;
> (7)   the financial resources and earning ability of the child;
> (8)   the responsibility of the parents for the support of others; and
> (9)   the value of services contributed by the custodial parent.

Child support awards remain in effect until a child reaches the age of majority. Complete and continued follow-through on payment of support obligations, however, represents a major problem. This is particularly the case when the parent making support payments remarries and becomes obligated to provide support to a second family. Generally, support obligations can be enforced through either civil or criminal contempt proceedings. Contempt proceedings call for the parent seeking support payments to show that the supporting parent has not complied with the support order and that this failure was intentional and without justification (Harp, 1982). Given evidence of willful contempt, the amount of money owed must be proved. The court will then order some method of repayment and pronounce a penalty of a fine and/or jail sentence.

Ruback (1984) suggested that, although imposing a fine is an available remedy, it makes little sense if a defaulting parent could not make the original support payment. Neither is it sensible to put the offender in jail, where he or she will be unable to earn the money needed to pay the support and will be costing the state money, in addition to the money the state might have to pay to support the family. Of course, these latter caveats are likely to become secondary in circumstances when a supporting parent arrogantly refuses, overtly or covertly, to comply with a court order. Aimed at motivating rather than seeking revenge, a judicial penalty may be most appropriate.

In cases when a supporting parent has remarried and has taken on obligations to a second family, it is not always clear whether obligations to the first family should be reduced because of the new obligations to the children of the second family. The courts have generally not found such changes in circumstances to justify a reduction in previously ordered child support awards (Ruback, 1984). Further, many state courts maintain priority for the children of a first marriage, although it has been strongly suggested that all the children involved should be considered on an equal basis (Krause, 1982).

The majority of states have tended to enforce support obligations ordered in another state. The primary means of enforcing out-of-state support obligations is the Uniform Reciprocal Enforcement of Support Act (URESA) and its later revision, the Revised Uniform Reciprocal Enforcement of Support Act (RURESA). All of the states have adopted URESA or RURESA in some form. Under the provisions of this act, the parent claiming support can bring an action in a court in his or her state of residence. The action is then forwarded to a court located in the supporting parent's home state, under whose law the case will be tried. The case is heard and a judgment rendered and enforced in this second court. Monies collected under the judgment are sent to the first court and disbursed to the claimant.

The federal government is also involved in the problem of nonpayment of child support by a parent who resides in a different state or whose whereabouts are unknown. Under legislation passed in 1975 and amended in 1984, the Office of Child Support Enforcement operates as an agency within the Department of Health and Human Services. This agency assists states to find absentee parents, establish paternity, and obtain child support from the absent individuals.

LEGAL ACTIONS BETWEEN PARENTS AND CHILDREN

Historically, the law has failed to recognize civil suits by minor children against their parents for personal injuries wrongfully inflicted (Stack, 1993; Vance, 1995). This prohibition was generally referred to as the *parent–child immunity doctrine*. The Washington Supreme Court, ruling in *Roller v. Roller* (1905), addressed the public policy undergirding the parent–child immunity doctrine:

> The rule of law prohibiting suits between parent and child is based upon the interest that society has in preserving harmony in the domestic relations, an interest which has been manifested since the earliest organization of civilized government, an interest inspired by the universally recognized fact that the maintenance of harmonious and proper family relations is conducive to good citizenship, and therefore works to the welfare of the state.

Despite this long-standing legal assumption that parents act in the best interests of their children, statistical data collection has increasingly revealed this assumption to be oft contradicted. The spiraling amount of sexual abuse and incest, for example, clearly confirm this (Kaslow, 1990a). The result has been a progressive erosion of the parent–child immunity doctrine. Courts have acknowledged that absolute parental immunity may not be justifiable in all circumstances (S. E. Friedman, 1992).

A case frequently cited relative to the erosion of the parent–child immunity doctrine is *Chaffin v. Chaffin* (1964). In ruling on this case, the Oregon Supreme Court stated:

> Each parent, in the rearing of the child, is required under the law to provide maintenance and guidance for that child, and, so long as that parental duty is performed, the family unity is maintained and the parent is entitled to the custody of the child. This family unity the law recognizes and protects against invasion insofar as the parents' duties are concerned. It is only when a parent acts to cause a child to become or when a child becomes a "dependent" or "delinquent" child that the law recognizes a breach of parental duty that will deprive the parent of custody of the child.
>
> Necessarily then, a parent in performing his duties of providing support, discipline and education to his children must have wide discretion. Wealth or poverty, physical strength or weakness, wisdom or mental incapacity are not in themselves criteria for fixing guidelines by which the law judges the performance of parental duties.
>
> Physical, mental or financial weakness may cause parents to provide what many a reasonable man would consider substandard maintenance, guidance, education and recreation for their children, and in many instances to provide a family home which is not reasonably safe as a place of abode. But it would be clearly wrong to permit the minor child to hold the parent liable for these intended injuries.

The Court then concluded that ordinary negligence would not override the parent–child immunity doctrine; something "crueler" was required:

> We conclude that an act by a parent, whether described as willful or malicious or wanton, which will pierce the veil of parental immunity, is an act which is done with an intention to injure the child or is of such a cruel nature in and of itself as to evidence not a reasonably normal parental mind, but an evil mind, *malo animo*. That a negli-

gent act which, although intentionally done, does not disclose an evil mind, but merely a willingness to take great risk in the face of conditions that should warn a reasonably prudent person that there is likelihood of injury is insufficient.

A 1988 Virginia case, *Samantha Baskin v. Peter Baskin,* highlights not only the potential liability a parent faces but also the damages that may arise as a result thereof. In this case an 11-year-old girl obtained a judgment against her father in the amount of $300,000 for his excessive use of discipline. The girl had attempted to intervene to stop her parents fighting. In response, her father dragged her upstairs by her hair, pounded her on the back, and slapped her across the face several times.

SUMMARY AND CONCLUSIONS

Family law matters account for over 50% of civil law filings in this country (Hennessey, 1980). Families are increasingly turning to the legal system for help in their problem-solving processes. Part of this willingness can be explained by the confidence expressed toward that system. Yet this often tends to be a false confidence, frequently shattered within the confines of the adversarial system of legal actions. Judges and attorneys are increasingly realizing that many of the problems presented to them are often more likely within the province of mental health rather than the law (Ruback, 1982). Thus, marriage and family therapists are being called on to assist legal professionals.

More pressing from marriage and family therapists' perspective, however, is the need of their clients to understand and prepare for potential legal interventions into their personal problem-solving processes. For therapeutic efforts to be effective, questions of psycholegal interface must be addressed. As is evident in this chapter, family law encompasses a number of extensive and fluctuating topics. It is vital that marriage and family therapists gain some knowledge in family law to adequately assert themselves, and therefore allow their clients to do so in this regard.

The following is a list of recommended resources for marriage and family therapists. Chapter 7 provides several case examples and critiques that show how family law issues affect therapeutic experience.

RECOMMENDED RESOURCES

Areen, J. (1978). *Cases and materials on family law.* Mineola, NY: Foundation Press.

Friedman, S. E. (1992). *The law of parent–child relationships: A handbook.* Chicago: American Bar Association.

Green, S., & Long, J. V. (1985). *Marriage and family agreements.* Colorado Springs, CO: Shepard's/McGraw-Hill.

Kramer, D. T. (1994). *Legal rights of children* (2nd ed.). New York: McGraw-Hill.

Krause, H. D. (1977). *Family law in a nutshell.* St. Paul, MN: West Publishing.

Krauskopf, J. (1983). *Marital and non-marital contracts.* Chicago: American Bar Association.

Sack, S. M. (1987). *The complete legal guide to marriage, divorce, custody, & living together.* New York: McGraw-Hill.

7

Legal Considerations

M arriage and family therapists need to understand the basic legal issues that affect their professional practices. They also need to learn when to seek the advice of attorneys. This chapter is structured to make marriage and family therapists more aware of the legal environment in which they function. Case illustrations involving guiding legal principles are presented and explained with reference to leading laws and cases. There is no effort, however, to present an exhaustive analysis of all relevant laws and cases. Practicing attorneys may have need for all such cases, but marriage and family therapists do not.

Although this sampling represents a cross section of cases, individual state laws may differ. In addition, these cases can contain complex issues, especially as related laws and court case findings are changing. New laws are passed, regulations change, courts are persuaded by novel legal arguments, and the Supreme Court can declare a policy or law unconstitutional. Therefore, no writing related to the law is a final, definitive word at the time of its publication or a substitute for competent legal advice when specific considerations arise.

Knowing when to ask for legal advice is important. Marriage and family therapists need to be able to distinguish among ethical, professional judgment, and legal issues.

Ethical issues require the application of ethical principles that do not also include legal issues that require the advice of an attorney. An example of an ethical issue without legal implications is when marriage and family therapists are trying to determine whether to accept couples for counseling when the therapists are associated with the couples in some other way, such as going to the same church, having children in the same school classroom, or belonging to the same civic organization.

Professional judgment issues require marriage and family therapists to apply their knowledge to particular therapy situations and then make important professional decisions. When marriage and family therapists are trying to determine whether particular clients are at risk for suicide, they are dealing with professional judgment issues.

Legal issues exist for marriage and family therapists when the therapists cannot come to a conclusion regarding particular issues unless they know the law. An example of a legal issue is when marriage and family therapists receive subpoenas for therapy records that were sent by a wife's attorney and the husband does not want the records disclosed. In situations like this, marriage and family therapists must seek independent legal advice and follow the advice they receive.

When faced with ethical and professional judgment issues, the best course of action for marriage and family therapists is to review written materials such as ethical codes and advice from noted authorities on the issue to determine whether answers to their questions can be found there. If not, the next step should be to confer with their direct administrative supervisor for advice and support. Finally, consulting with peers who have the same knowledge, training backgrounds, and work settings can be very helpful in resolving ethical and professional judgment dilemmas. Proof of such consultations, such as written documentation, is very helpful if the final decisions of the therapists ever lead to negative results or are questioned later by an ethics panel or a court.

When marriage and family therapists need advice on legal issues, it is essential that the advice come from attorneys rather than from other marriage and family therapists (Remley & Herlihy, 2001). Employed marriage and family therapists should pose any legal questions they have to their direct administrative supervisors. The supervisors then have an obligation to either obtain the legal advice for the therapists and relate the information to them, or to give the therapists direct access to an attorney who represents the employer. In rare instances when the best interests of therapists are in conflict with their employers, such as when supervisors are directing therapists to perform illegal activities, then therapists should consult independent attorneys.

Marriage and family therapists who are in private practice have no alternative when they need legal advice except to pay for it from lawyers in private practice (Remley & Herlihy, 2001). Some professional liability insurance policies or professional association memberships provide limited legal consultation services that might be utilized, but in most cases, therapists in private practice will have to pay for legal advice they receive. It is best for marriage and family therapists to develop relationships with attorneys before problems arise. The best attorneys for private practice marriage and family therapists are those who represent other mental health professionals in the community because they already understand legal issues such as privileged communication, duty to warn intended victims, reporting suspected child abuse, and other important mental health issues that have legal implications.

Once administrators have passed legal advice obtained from lawyers to therapists, an employer's attorneys have given therapists advice, or private attorneys have given advice to therapists, the legal directives must be followed. Of course, therapists should give attorneys full information and even express their views regarding a particular situation. In the end, however, therapists must follow the legal advice they are given even if they do not like it. If legal advice obtained is wrong or is flawed, the attorneys who gave the advice will be legally responsible for any harm experienced by therapists as a result of the bad advice. If legal advice is obtained and not followed, therapists will not have the support of their attorneys if they have to later defend themselves against allegations of wrongdoing.

CASE 1
Ethics and the Law

Dr. D., a marriage and family therapist, is visited by a process server, who hands him a subpoena issued by an attorney representing the husband of a couple he had seen in therapy. Therapy had been prematurely terminated by the couple at the husband's insistence some months earlier. The couple has now separated and is waging a bitter battle over the custody of their two children. The subpoena directs Dr. D. to appear at the attorney's office in 10 days, with all files and notes about treatment of both the husband and wife. In contacting the wife to apprise her of the subpoena, she explicitly states to Dr. D. her desire to maintain the confidentiality of the session records.

CONSIDERATIONS

The potential for conflict between the ethical principles and practice guidelines of marriage and family therapists and the law (local, state, and federal) is ever-present. Such conflicts are manifestations of the temporal and cultural relativity of ethical codes (Mappes, Robb, & Engels, 1985) as well as the fact that laws and the regulations that aid in their implementation are often written in ways that do not take into account the nuances or complexities of marriage and family therapy practice (Bennett, Bryant, VandenBos, & Greenwood, 1990). Strict compliance with the spirit and letter of one's professional code of ethics provides no certainty of freedom from legal difficulties. Diligent adherence to their professional code of ethics may, in fact, directly lead marriage and family therapists into legal quagmires.

Clients' rights of access to their files constitutes one particular area of potential conflict between marriage and family therapists' ethics and the law. It is critical that marriage and family therapists recognize that there are both ethical and legal reasons to maintain accurate records and a corresponding duty to keep such records confidential. Marriage and family therapists must be reminded, however, that circumstances may arise when these records may be required to be disclosed to clients or third parties (Hopkins & Anderson, 1990).

The majority of marriage and family therapists will, like Dr. D., work with couples who are considering, currently involved in, or may at a later time enter divorce and/or child custody proceedings. Ethically, and under most state laws, clients are entitled to their records. Therefore, if Dr. D.'s client were seen as an individual and the client requested that treatment records be provided to his or her attorney, Dr. D. would be acting legally and ethically in accommodating the request. A dilemma arises, however, when a marriage and family therapist has worked with a couple or family and only one party authorizes a release of the records.

In most states privileged communication statutes would not apply to this situation, because privilege is waived when two persons are counseled at the same time. In other states, privilege laws specifically cover relationships between marriage and family therapists and couples or family members (Knapp & VandeCreek, 1987). In situations such as this one, marriage and family therapists must seek and obtain legal advice from an attorney who represents the therapist or the agency for which the therapist works (Boughner & Logan, 1999).

The *AAMFT Code of Ethics* is quite clear in calling for each member of the couple or family to agree to a waiver; without a waiver from each family member, a therapist cannot disclose information received from any family member. Many marriage and family therapists take a position that they should defy a court order to release client records as they believe that such a release would violate their ethical responsibility to clients to maintain confidentiality. Remley (1990) responded to this position in stating:

> Although counselors certainly should protest such orders, refusing to comply will result in the counselor being held in contempt of court and either fined or imprisoned. Legally, the client should be the one protesting such orders, not the counselor. Judges do not allow contrary ethical standards of a profession to interfere with provisions of the law. Our laws of discovery state that litigants should have access to all information relevant to a case being litigated. When a court order is issued in our society, it supersedes any professional rule to the contrary. When citizens believe laws are wrong, they should become involved in the legislative process to have them changed. Counselors do not have the option of defying laws when they do not agree with them. (pp. 166–167)

The *AAMFT Code of Ethics* is also clear, however, in noting certain exceptions to the dictate that therapists not disclose client confidences. The first noted exception is "as mandated by law." A court order to make records available would constitute such a mandate.

CONCLUSIONS

Of primary importance in this case, given the information presented, are two points: (a) Dr. D. does not have both the husband's and the wife's waiver to release the records, and (b) Dr. D. has received a subpoena, not a court order. The second point is possibly more crucial to consider in responding to the current dilemma. A subpoena is not a court order. A subpoena is simply an order filed with the court by an attorney requesting information or testimony. The order to *appear* in a subpoena must be followed. A court order is a directive by the court to *comply* and also must be followed (Stevens-Smith & Hughes, 1993). It is recommended that marriage and family therapists always consult with their own or their employer's attorney to determine whether a subpoena is valid and to obtain advice on how to proceed (Woody, 1988).

At this point, Dr. D. has only received a subpoena. The following guidelines extracted by Arthur and Swanson (1993) from M. A. Fisher (1991) and Remley (1991) would be most apt for Dr. D. to first consider in responding to the subpoena:

1. Determine if the client wants the subpoenaed information disclosed. Ensure that he or she fully understands all the ramifications of such disclosure.
2. If the client does not wish the information to be released or the therapist believes that disclosure may not be in the client's best interests, the therapist should recommend that the client consult his or her own attorney. The attorney may agree to withdraw his or her subpoena or file a motion to quash a subpoena issued by an opposing legal counsel. Such motions are generally based upon arguments of privilege protection or relevancy to the pending case. Occasionally, a motion to quash may be partially successful, with a judge agreeing to view the information in private to determine if the records are admissible.
3. If concerns remain, seek legal advice from your own independent attorney or from your employer's attorney regarding available appropriate alternatives.
4. Do not simply defy a subpoena. Take definite legal steps through the client's attorney or by securing personal legal counsel.

Given these suggestions, Dr. D. might first contact both the husband and the wife and discuss the potential ramifications of disclosure with each of them, particularly the husband. Perhaps the session records will not serve the husband as well as he might imagine; they might even display him in a poorer light than his wife relative to the custody issue. Should the husband still request that the records be disclosed (and the wife maintain her position that they not be disclosed), Dr. D. should recommend to the wife that she speak to her attorney relative to the subpoena. Should the wife's attorney be unable to have the subpoena quashed, Dr. D. should show up at the time and place the subpoena establishes and bring his own lawyer to the proceeding and follow the advice given. Should a judge specifically order that the records be produced, Dr. D. will be required to provide the records despite not having the wife's waiver to do so. Dr. D. would be both legally and ethically mandated to do so.

Several concluding points to consider in this regard include the following:

1. Subpoenas typically identify the date, place, and time to appear or present records. This is frequently flexible. A telephone call to schedule a more convenient time is common. It is best to have your own personal attorney make such requests.

2. Some therapists maintain private or unofficial notes, separate from official records. Although this practice is acceptable, it does not shield the notes from a subpoena for records (Arthur & Swanson, 1993). Further, the failure to produce all records (including private notes), if so specified by a subpoena, may subject a therapist to contempt of court charges. In addition, should the therapist testify that all records have been furnished, he or she could be charged with perjury, a criminal offense (Remley, 1990).

3. Copies of subpoenaed records and notes should be made. Originals should be retained if at all possible.

4. Never alter or destroy a document that has been subpoenaed. The potential negative consequences of such an action can not be understated (Stevens-Smith & Hughes, 1993).

5. A therapist subpoenaed to testify will be testifying as a lay witness. This type of witness, also referred to as a *factual* or *general witness* is only responsible to report his or her professional impression of what occurred in the past and should refrain from giving any professional opinions (Remley, 1991).

CASE 2
Divorce Mediation

A marriage and family therapist, Mary E., all too often had observed the negative results for families traveling through the emotional grinder of divorce and child custody court battles. Having read about divorce mediation as a potentially more positive alternative, she considered seeking training for the purpose of offering this service as a part of her practice. In discussing this pursuit with several attorneys, however, questions of significant concern arose for her. "Isn't divorce basically a legal process involving the application of legal rules and principles to the facts of the parties' lives?" She wondered. "If so, then how appropriate is it for a marriage and family therapist to offer such services?"

CONSIDERATIONS

The basic issue confronting Mary E. is her belief that divorce is first and foremost a legal event. It has become increasingly evident over the past decade that mental health professionals are taking a more active role in helping families resolve the personal and financial issues incidental to divorce. In doing this, they have found themselves moving into an area once occupied exclusively by attorneys. Marlow

(1985), an attorney, argued that viewing divorce as a legal event ignores the fact that it is more importantly a personal event in a family's life. His major points are summarized in the following paragraphs as an alternative for Mary E.

In What Real Sense Is Divorce a Legal Event?

The decision to divorce, like the decision to marry, can be viewed as primarily a personal as opposed to a legal decision. Many couples seek premarital counseling from marriage and family therapists; very infrequently do they consult attorneys when deciding to marry (unless legal rights and obligations between them are created). If the parties treat such matters as personal at the time of their marriage, deciding on them without resorting to legal counsel, can they not continue to do so when divorcing? This is not to mean that there are no legal implications whatsoever, simply that personal aspects of the event should take precedence.

What Has Prevented This "Personal Event" Concept of Divorce From Becoming the Dominant View?

Marlow (1985) asserted that the idea that divorcing parties must seek legal counsel, first to determine their legal rights, and then to protect those rights—that this is a prerequisite to any resolution of their dispute—is a myth. Many mediators and lawyers insist, however, that attorneys must be a part of divorce mediation if it is to be fair and withstand any later legal challenges (N. J. Foster & Kelly, 1996; Gangel-Jacob, 1997). The divorce process mistakenly has been represented to be more than the resolution of a dispute between a couple; divorcing couples are erroneously perceived to be unable to protect their respective rights and obligations without resorting to the law.

How Does the Law Offer This Protection?

For example, a husband is told by his wife that she is considering divorce and has consulted an attorney. He immediately assumes that his wife and her attorney are planning to get him for everything they can (a reasonable assumption, given the adversarial structure of the legal system). These concerns are further fed by the fact that legal ethics demand that he and his wife cannot be represented by the same attorney; she meets with her attorney "in confidence." To protect himself, he too retains an attorney and thus feeds the adversarial cycle. This phenomenon is referred to as a self-fulling prophecy in psychology.

Doesn't a Divorcing Family Need Attorneys to Advise Them of Their Legal Rights?

Again, the very idea that the determination of the couple's respective legal rights is an issue in the divorce is more myth than fact. This myth has stemmed from a failure to distinguish between two types of laws. The first type is usually constitutional in nature and guarantees such rights as voting, free speech, and practicing the religion of one's choice. Such laws can appropriately be labeled *legal rights*. The second type, however, contains those laws that regulate society's conduct or simply resolve personal disputes. Although these laws may embody society's conception of what is fair and appropriate at any given time, to speak of them as legal rights is to endow them with exaggerated significance.

Most people want their disagreements to be resolved in a fair manner, to represent what is just. Those rules society adopts in the form of laws to resolve disputes between people are just "rules" and no more. Legal rules are applied by society, not because they do justice, but because they are a means of ending disputes that parties are unable to end themselves. The prevailing belief, although a mistaken one, is that divorcing families must use a dispute resolution procedure that emanates from traditional legal regulation, whether they need this regulation or not. That couples may ultimately be required to resort to the law and the application of legal rules to resolve personal disputes does not change them into legal disputes. They remain personal problems that are still best resolved by relevant personal decision-making strategies, not necessarily by the application of legal rules.

Are There Times When Legal Rules Should Legitimately Take Priority in a Divorce Dispute?

Primary legal intervention is relevant in one situation: if one or both partners wish to use the agreement to divorce not as a vehicle to resolve their mutual problems, but rather as a means for venting hurt and anger. If one partner seeks to discredit the other from what is rightfully his or hers, then quite obviously both need to be apprised of legal rules and equally may need to have those rules applied to their dispute.

There is an important point to further consider, however. Families in the process of divorce generally have little accurate understanding of why and how they have gotten to this point in their lives. Frequently both partners tend to idealize themselves as victims; they want the other to pay and look to the divorce agreement as the vehicle to accomplish this. Divorce offers an opportunity to help them put their pasts behind them and to get on with the important business of their future. Divorce agreements that seek to correct past wrongs, whether real or imagined, block this potential opportunity.

CONCLUSIONS

Divorce, like marriage, is an important transitional event in the life of a family. As such, it concerns issues that are primarily personal and not legal. What the law only offers is a procedure for resolving a family's dispute if all other dispute resolution mechanisms fail. Given this fact, and contrary to a self-perpetuating myth, the law has little to contribute to the resolution of disputes between divorcing families.

After consulting with attorneys on the relevance of divorce mediation for the practice of a marriage and family therapist, Mary E. saw that the mental health community has not overstepped its boundaries and entered into the legal world in assisting divorcing families to resolve their disputes through mediation. Rather, the legal profession has for years taken mostly personal decisions in the lives of divorcing families and, by the blanket imposition of legal rules and principles, converted them into legal problems.

Mary E. can equally assert that divorce mediation represents more than an alternative procedure to help families resolve issues in a less destructive manner. She can affirm a view of divorce as a personal, not a legal, problem to which mediation represents a better means of dispute resolution. What keeps divorcing families from resolving their disagreements is their fear, hurt, and anger; the adversarial procedures inherent in legal rules almost guarantee an exacerbation of these feelings. If families are to experience a psychological as well as a legal divorce, they must be helped to put these destructive emotions into proper perspective and resolve them.

Mary E. might be more accurate in generally viewing divorce mediation based on her own understanding of family functioning. The specialized training she is considering will add to these understandings by offering pragmatic procedures to aid divorcing families making concrete decisions after they have been helped with their emotional confusion.

CASE 3
Liability in Crisis Counseling

Lou was a 16-year-old who had been seen together with his parents in family therapy for a few sessions over a year ago. Originally therapy was initiated because Lou had been experiencing problems with regard to peer pressure to engage in drug use. The family prematurely terminated therapy efforts after some early positive changes. More recently, feeling alienated, Lou had turned to drugs to alleviate his anxiety and provide himself with a greater sense of belonging. Paradoxically, he developed a barbiturate dependency, creating depression and feelings of isolation. After an especially hostile interchange with his parents over his drug use, Lou, in a hysterical frenzy, telephoned the therapist, crying that he was going to kill himself. The therapist remembered Lou and attempted to calm him, but Lou responded negatively, perceiving the therapist as preaching to him like his parents. The therapist had taken Lou's call between sessions and had someone waiting to see him. Feeling rushed, impatient with Lou, and not accurately perceiving Lou's desperation, the therapist lashed out at Lou, telling him to "grow up," whereupon Lou hung up. Feeling further rejected, Lou took an overdose of barbiturates and died. Later that day, feeling guilty about his response to the situation, the therapist called Lou's parents, hoping he might get the family to come in for further therapy. The parents were enraged that the therapist had reacted in a way that added to their son's problems. They accused the therapist of "killing" their son and filed suit against the therapist, claiming negligence that resulted in wrongful death.

CONSIDERATIONS

The law of negligence, which comprises a large part of the law of torts, includes various kinds of wrongful acts that result in injury or damages. As a general rule, liability for negligence will accrue if one person causes damage to another through a breach of duty owed to that person. To hold a therapist liable in a tort action for negligence, the court must find the following:

1. A duty was owed by the therapist to the client; that a therapist–client relationship had been established.
2. The duty was breached; that the therapist's conduct fell below an acceptable standard of care.
3. There was a sufficient legal causal connection between the breach of duty and the client's injury.
4. There was an actual injury sustained by the client.

As there had been a previous therapist–client relationship, the first major inquiry in the present case seeks to determine if the therapist's conduct fell below an acceptable standard of care. Concurrently, does the fact that this was a "crisis or emergency" situation have additional bearing on the issue? What standard of care does the law require of therapists in such special situations?

Fischer and Sorenson (1985) quoted former Supreme Court justice Oliver Wendell Holmes, Jr., in this regard: "Detached reflection can not be expected in front of an uplifted knife" (p. 48). What Holmes sought to convey is that in emergency situations, the same degree of care and thoughtful action cannot be expected as would be in ordinary affairs. This principle particularly applies to telephone crisis counseling when the therapist does not typically have real control over the client or the situation. The guiding legal principle in such situations has tended to be this: A person is responsible for harm to another only if failure to exercise reasonable care increases the risk of harm to that other person (Negligence § 1, 2000). A failure in crisis counseling requires that the therapist reject the client's cry for help in a way indicating that the therapist did not exercise reasonable care in doing so. If the therapist so acted, the next major question to consider would be whether such action by the therapist had indeed increased the risk of harm to the client.

CONCLUSIONS

Clearly, a crisis was at hand when the therapist received Lou's phone call. Lou was in an extremely distraught emotional state. It might still be argued his emotional state was not sufficiently dangerous that, considered alone, it could be construed as the cause of his death. It could be asserted, however, that the last straw for Lou was the therapist's rejection of his cry for help. Taken in that light, the therapist not only may have failed to alleviate an impending crisis, but he also may have actually made it worse.

An added factor in the therapist's scope of liability was the fact that Lou had been a client and the therapist was aware of his problems. Because the therapist was better informed about Lou's situation than a professional Lou might have selected from the *Yellow Pages*, a higher standard of care could be expected. The presumption is that increased knowledge about a situation renders an increased capability to give real assistance. As a result, it is possible that a court might find that the therapist's actions did constitute negligence that resulted in wrongful death. On the other hand, additional facts in this case could lead to a different result.

CASE 4

Informed Consent?

David K. has developed an approach to group couples therapy that includes a number of touching activities that he has found to help couples understand the importance of their primary and friendship relationships. The activities require couples to massage their partners and other group members, to physically embrace a third member of the group in some instances, and to spend substantial amounts of time in sessions holding hands with, embracing, and standing close enough to touch the bodies of members other than their partners. David has found that his approach is very effective in helping couples strengthen their commitment to each other. However, he has also discovered that if he describes the activities in his sessions in detail, very few people participate. As a result, he now advertises his workshops as "experiences that help couples appreciate their partners and be in touch with themselves and others." Recently, a couple participated in David's therapy experience. The wife had an affair with another group member, left her husband, and told her husband that she had discovered how unhappy she was in her marriage as a result of David's therapy. The husband has sued David, claiming that David never disclosed the nature of the physical contact in David's therapy sessions, that he would have never signed up for therapy with David if he had known what would happen there, and that his wife left him because of David's approach to therapy and David's failure to disclose the therapeutic approach before his agreeing to participate.

CONSIDERATIONS

Basic to all treatment is professionals' and clients' discussion of the nature of the problem and possible treatments for it. Before treatment begins, the client must consent to it, thus giving the therapist power to act (Kaplan & Culkin, 1995). Two notable cases are relevant in this regard. In the 1957 case of *Salgo v. Leland Stanford, Jr., University Board of Trustees*, tort liability was established for the failure of a physician to explain the risks and benefits of a medical procedure. The court declared that not all risks need be explained but that the practitioner should use discretion in explaining risks based on each person's mental and emotional status. Initiation of the doctrine of informed consent has been attributed to the 1960 case of *Nathanson v. Kline*. Negligence in informing the client of possible risks was the basis for the tort liability. Further, this case changed the standard for assessing liability from the "reasonable person doctrine" to the doctrine of deviation from the standard of conduct of a reasonable and prudent medical doctor of the same school of practice as the defendant under similar circumstances (H. H. Foster, 1978; J. Katz, 1977). This distinction between the "reasonable person" and "reasonable medical doctor" standards was an important one for establishing evidence and proof in a malpractice action. The conduct of a marriage and family therapist is measured against the standard of the average, reasonable person who is a marriage and family therapist (i.e., the average, reasonable person who has superior knowledge and skills as a result of training and experience and whose knowledge and skills are commonly possessed by members in good standing of the profession).

Consent to act is simply willingness that treatment can occur and will prevent liability in a tort. Consent is manifested by words or actions that a "reasonable person" would understand to be consent. Silence or inaction have been held to be consent in cases in which a reasonable person would have spoken if he or she objected. In legal actions seeking damages, the principle of informed consent of the person damaged will ordinarily void liability for intentional interference with a person or property (Prosser, 1971). Typically, consent is usually implied in clients' initiation of therapy. Such a general consent may, however, have no legal force if a client had no opportunity to compare the risks of participating in therapy with the dangers of foregoing it (Dooley, 1977).

Systemically oriented marriage and family therapists maintain the assumption that any procedures they employ may have an impact well beyond the identified client. The work they might do with individual clients is likely to affect not only the client but also those persons in contact with him or her. The legal requirement of obtaining informed consent before beginning actual treatment applies, however, only to those persons who have direct contact with the therapist. Further, *legally adequate consent* of those in direct contact with the therapist has been defined as "consent by a person who has the following characteristics: legal capacity, comprehension of informatic and voluntary agreement" (Bray, Shepherd, & Hays, 1985, p. 54). *Legal capacity* means that the person giving consent is of minimum legal age and has not been adjudicated as incompetent to manage his or her affairs. *Comprehension of information* means that the person giving consent must have been given information relating to the risks and the benefits of the procedure, the risks of forgoing the procedure, and the procedures available as an alternative to the proposed treatment (Applebaum, Lidz, & Meisel, 1987; Bray, Shepherd, & Hays, 1985).

The type and amount of information to discuss with clients have been subjects of controversy for some time (Behnke & Saks, 1998; Berner, 1998; *Canterbury v. Spence*, 1972). Clients want information about their therapists and perceive those who provide details about themselves and their procedures as more expert and trustworthy than those who do not (Braaten, Otto, & Handelsman, 1993; Handler, 1990; Hendrick, 1998; Walter & Handelsman, 1996). Johnson (1965) suggests that the only potential risks that need to be disclosed are those that would cause the client to forgo therapy. Yet Oppenheim (1968) argues for the disclosure of any risk that might influence, however slightly, the clients' decision to accept therapy. In general, therapists need not disclose every risk. In deciding what risks to discuss with clients, therapists should balance clients' desires and the right to make their own decisions regarding therapy with the therapist's own desire to withhold information about potential risks when disclosure might harm a client's well-being. This balancing calls for an exercise of professional judgment that is an exception to the basic principle of disclosure of all potential risks (Waltz & Scheuneman, 1969). Waltz and Scheuneman expressed their belief that the ideal informed consent rule calls for risks being disclosed when a client would find them important in deciding whether or not to consent to therapy. In resolving the question of what to disclose, the therapist can apply the standard of the reasonable person who finds himself or herself in the position of the client. The value of the "Professional Disclosure Statement" presented in Chapter 1 is most relevant regarding this.

Given the legal requirements for informed consent, it has been recommended to ensure proof of such procedures by having clients sign a form during an initial session, indicating that appropriate information was provided and consent is thus given for treatment (Cohen, 1979; Glosoff, 1997; Haas & Malouf, 1995; Welfel, 1998; Weinrach, 1989). An example of such a form is the "Therapeutic Contract," also discussed in Chapter 1. Failure to obtain informed consent leaves therapists liable and subject to legal action. The proof required to show consent when not in written form is unclear. In many cases, practitioners have been asked to prove that the client consented, and in others, the issue of consent was so vital to the case that the lack of consent must be proved by the client (Prosser, 1971).

CONCLUSIONS

Three possible legal actions can be taken in cases of informed consent. The first and most common is *negligence*. In this instance, the failure to make a complete disclosure can result in a judgment of negligent practice (*Cobbs v. Grant*, 1972). The second potential legal action is *battery*. If the client's bodily integrity is invaded without consent, battery occurs. Cases of this nature are characterized by absence of informed consent and do not require proof of negligence. The reasoning of this rule is that, had the client known about the risks involved, he or she would not have agreed to the procedure. A third type of possible liability is *breach of contract*. If a marriage and family therapist guarantees that a certain treatment will "cure" the client and it does not, the therapist is liable for breach of contract (Slovenko, 1978). As in battery complaints, proof is not needed, because it is in the domain of contractual law and not a breach of tort liability.

In the present case, the husband can complain of negligence and breach of contract, in that David never secured the husband's informed consent to the treatment the husband and wife received in the couples therapy sessions. In addition, the husband might argue that battery occurred, in that the husband never specifically agreed to the touching that took place in the sessions. The husband might point to his wife's leaving the marriage as damages that were a specific result of David's negligent provision of therapy services.

David's defense to these charges of wrongdoing might be that touching exercises were explained to participants before they occurred, that no clients were forced to participate, and that the lack of any objection constituted consent. David might also argue that the wife's decision to leave her husband was based on factors other than the therapy sessions and that the therapy sessions were not the cause of the breakup of the marriage.

Whether the negligence suit against David would prevail would depend on additional facts of the case and the response of a judge or jury to hearing the facts. Cases like this could be decided either way.

CASE 5
Criminal Liability

Melissa J. is a novice marriage and family therapist employed by a community-funded child guidance clinic. Cindy is a 15-year-old client Melissa has been seeing because of family conflicts. Cindy's parents were recently divorced, and she was having problems coping with their breakup. Neither parent was willing to participate in therapy with their daughter, seeing her concerns as "things she needs to work out on her own." Cindy confides to Melissa that she and her boyfriend had stolen a car the past weekend. They still have the car. Having no one else to turn to, Cindy asks Melissa's help in returning the car to the owner without involving the police.

CONSIDERATIONS

Marriage and family therapists such as Melissa J. who work with minors can encounter situations that might cause the therapist to incur criminal liability. Therapists must be aware of areas of possible danger. Three particular areas to consider include reporting known crimes, contributing to the delinquency of a minor, and being an accessory to a crime before or after the fact (Fischer & Sorenson, 1985).

Reporting Known Crimes

Private citizens have no legal duty to report crimes they know about. Persons cannot attempt to conceal criminal activity, assist a criminal in avoiding prosecution, or refuse to answer questions regarding crimes. However, they do not have to tell anyone about crimes they have observed or know about.

Based on the same principle, marriage and family therapists generally do not have to report criminal activities that clients report in therapy sessions. But, if therapists determine that clients are a danger to themselves or to others, therapists must take actions to prevent harm. As a result, a danger to self or others determination would require marriage and family therapists to report criminal activity of a client, not the criminal activity itself. In addition, marriage and family therapists are prohibited from purposefully concealing crimes from authorities or assisting clients in avoiding being discovered or arrested. If a privileged communication statute protects the relationship with the client, but a legal exception exists to privilege, then marriage and family therapists would be required to repeat to authorities information related by clients related to criminal activities. Statutes vary by state.

Contributing to the Delinquency of a Minor

Each state defines the meaning of "minor" for purposes of its own laws. Although there are variations among states, a *minor* is generally defined as a youth subject to the control of a parent or guardian or under a specified age (usually 16). Likewise, individual states have their own laws concerning what constitutes contributing to the delinquency of a minor. There are several common elements, however. The generally cited purposes of such laws are to protect minors from the negative influence of adults who might lead them astray and to prevent conduct that would lead to delinquency. Massachusetts law provides a typical illustration, stating in part, that:

> Any person who shall be found to have caused, induced, abetted, encouraged or contributed toward the waywardness or delinquency of a child, or to have acted in any way tending to cause or induce such waywardness or delinquency, may be punished by a fine of not more than five hundred dollars or by imprisonment for not more than one year, or both. (Massachusetts General Laws, ch. 119, §63)

Contributing to the delinquency of a minor is frequently associated by the general public with sexual interactions. The law identifies a much broader range of actions that might adversely affect the welfare of the public or the healthy development of a minor. Consequently, the meaning of contributing to the delinquency of a minor could encompass a wide variety of behaviors that injure the morals, health, or welfare of minors, or encourage their participation in activities that would lead to such injury.

Fischer and Sorenson (1985) offer case examples of therapists found facing a charge of contributing to the delinquency of a minor:

- The therapist who chaperoned a school-sponsored weekend trip and helped students procure beer and wine for the cookout
- The therapist who chaperoned a Friday-evening party and was aware of several youths smoking marijuana but did nothing about it

Even though there may be no intention to commit a crime, a marriage and family therapist could still be found guilty of contributing to the delinquency of a minor. In general, for a person to be guilty of a crime, there must be a concurrence of an act and an intent. The law generally requires mens rea (guilty intent) for an act to be a crime. For example, if a pedestrian is hit by an out of control car because of a tire blowout, the driver has not committed a crime. If it can be proved that the driver intentionally sought to run down a pedestrian, a crime would have been committed.

In cases involving delinquency, however, individual states differ with regard to proof of guilty intent. Some states require proof of guilty intent, and others do not require the presence of such intent. It is important that marriage and family therapists know the specific provisions in the laws of their respective states to adequately address activities that might be construed by their state courts as contributing to the delinquency of a minor.

Accessory to a Crime

Marriage and family therapists can be in a difficult position if their clients discuss either a plan to commit a crime or a crime they have already committed. Therapists' duty to protect probable victims of a dangerous crime supersedes any claim of confidentiality or privilege. Therapists' obligations are fairly clear in such instances. There is less clarity, however, when a client seeks a therapist's help after a crime has been committed.

Not all crimes involve danger to persons; some crimes are against property. For example, a client might confide a plan to destroy some equipment or building related to racist or antireligious activities. The mere knowledge that a crime will occur, if there is no special duty to prevent it, does not incur guilt. However, if a therapist were to accompany a client to the scene of a crime with knowledge that it likely will be committed, or assist a client in getting away after committing the crime, he or she will become culpable in the eyes of the law (Fischer & Sorenson, 1985). Any person who aids in the commission of a crime, even if he or she is not present when it takes place, may be as guilty as the instigator or an accessory before the fact. This will depend on the laws of the particular state.

An accessory after the fact is generally a person who, knowing that a crime was committed, receives, relieves, comforts, or assists the perpetrator or somehow aids the perpetrator in escaping arrest or punishment. Thus:

1. A crime must have been committed.
2. The accessory must know that the perpetrator committed the crime.
3. The accessory must harbor or protect the perpetrator.

If, during a session, the therapist learns that the client committed a crime, and if, thereafter, the therapist helps the client hide or otherwise offers protection from law enforcement authorities or assists the client in escaping detection, the therapist may be guilty of being an accessory to a crime after the fact (Fischer & Sorenson, 1985).

It is important to note that there may be differences relative to whether the crime is a felony or misdemeanor. Common law identifies no accessory to the commission of a misdemeanor. Individual states, however, may create such a category.

CONCLUSIONS

Marriage and family therapists who act with a reasonable degree of care should have few occasions to be concerned about criminal liability. This is not to say, however, that marriage and family therapists are immune from criminal prosecution. Intentional actions or even some careless, unintentional behaviors may constitute contributing to the delinquency of a minor or being an accessory to a crime. Burgum and Anderson (1975) described an illustrative case relating to criminal liability of a school counselor that somewhat parallels Melissa J.'s situation:

> A boy in the custody of a juvenile court had developed a good relationship with his school counselor. The boy, with two companions, robbed a service station and then, realizing the gravity of his actions, went to the counselor for help. The counselor convinced the boy that he should turn himself in to the police. It was late at night, however, so they agreed he would go to the police the next day. Meanwhile, the counselor committed a series of acts that made him an accessory to a felony. He denied to the police that the boy was in his home. He gave the boy money, which was found in the youth's possession when he tried to skip town the next morning rather than reporting to the police. The counselor would have been well-advised to have reported the matter to the boy's juvenile court representative and/or the police. Instead, he inadvertently helped the boy avoid arrest.

In this case illustration, the school counselor was clearly an accessory after the fact: (a) a crime was committed; (b) the counselor knew that the boy committed the crime; and (c) the counselor harbored and protected the boy from police.

In this situation, the best course of action would be for Melissa to convince Cindy to inform one or both of her parents about the car theft. Melissa should tell

Cindy to follow her parents' advice in handling the situation. In the event Cindy refused to tell her parents, Melissa should inform one or both parents of the theft over Cindy's objection. By ensuring that one or both of Cindy's parents are informed of the car theft by either having Cindy tell or by Melissa telling, Melissa will have turned the situation over to the parents and transferred responsibility to one or both parents. Only if the parents are incapable of handling the situation in a reasonable or appropriate manner should Melissa tell anyone of the situation beyond the parents.

CASE 6
Parental Rights and the Buckley Amendment

Aaron M. is a marriage and family therapist who regularly receives referrals from public school personnel. He works with families in which the children are experiencing emotional difficulties affecting their ability to perform adequately in the classroom. His common practice has been to provide written reports to the referral source (with the child's and parents' permission) at regular intervals and on completion of therapy efforts.

The Kent family was initially referred to the therapist because their 13-year-old son David was displaying significant acting-out behaviors with both peers and school personnel. In consultation with David's teacher, the school guidance counselor suspected that David was having these behaviors modeled at home and thus the referral was made to Aaron M. The therapist structured the therapy so that total family sessions would be alternated weekly with individual sessions for David (primarily because the parents were unable to participate every week because of work schedules). In discussing the therapist's latest report with the parents, David's teacher made particular reference to the therapist's notation that "David perceives his parents' general hostility toward each other as the way all people are." The parents became incensed, as they had not heard their son say this in their presence, assumed that he had done so during an individual session, and demanded that Aaron M. share all information from the individual sessions. The therapist politely declined, explaining the therapeutic need to allow David the opportunity to feel safe in sharing himself. The parents sought the aid of their attorney, who telephoned the therapist requesting that the parents be allowed to review the therapist's session records, citing the Buckley Amendment.

CONSIDERATIONS

It had long been common practice among mental health personnel to clearly mark or otherwise indicate that all client notes, reports, letters, and charts are "confidential." Access to or communication of the materials is generally shared only with relevant professionals directly concerned with the client. Thus, such materials are typically not intended to be seen or used by clients themselves. Such materials could be subject to misinterpretation and misunderstanding by clients and therefore could possibly have negative or harmful effects.

The Family Educational Rights and Privacy Act of 1974 (FERPA, or The Buckley Amendment, 20 U.S.C. §1232g) and the regulations promulgated for its implementation guarantee to parents and to "eligible students" (18 and over) certain rights with regard to the inspection and dissemination of educational records. Because it is a federal law, it applies to all school districts and schools that receive federal financial assistance through the U.S. Department of Education. Since most private and parochial schools receive federal assistance in some form, they generally are governed by the Buckley Amendment. Although state departments of education or private schools, at least theoretically, could decide not to accept federal money, the guarantees of the Buckley Amendment are not really rights in the fullest sense. As one court noted however, the Buckley Amendment is not necessarily binding on a particular school district, but because federal funding might otherwise be discontinued, the court enforced the provisions of the law (*Sauerkof v. City of New York*, 1981). Pragmatically, the Buckley Amendment does create rights for parents and students, that most, if not all, schools will be responsible for ensuring (Fischer & Sorenson, 1985). Further, this law is quite consistent with legislative trends in several other areas and thus grants legal support to persons (parents') right to know and to challenge personal and evaluative material maintained by various agents of society (McGuire & Borowy, 1978).

The minimum requirements of the law call for the adoption of policies and practices that meet the following criteria ("Final Regulations," 1976):

1. Parents and eligible students be informed of their rights.
2. Parents and eligible students be permitted to review educational records, request changes, request a hearing if changes are disallowed, and add their own statements by way of explanation, if necessary.
3. Ensure that the institution does not give out personally identifiable information without prior written, informed consent of a parent or eligible student.
4. Maintain and allow parents and eligible students to see the institution's record of disclosures.
5. Facilitate parents' and eligible students' access to records by providing information on the types of educational records and the procedures for gaining access to them.

Education records under the law are defined as those records that (a) are directly related to the student and (b) are maintained by the educational agency or institution or by a party acting for that agency or institution ("Final Regulations," 1976). Although educational records that must be made available on parents' request include a wide variety of materials, some exceptions are especially relevant to the present case. One record not subject to disclosure is that made by a relevant professional remaining in "the sole possession of the maker thereof" and is not "accessible or revealed to any other individual except a substitute" ("Final Regulations," 1976). The legislative history of the Buckley Amendment makes clear that educational records do not include the "personal files of psychologists, counselors, or professors if these files are entirely private and not available to other individuals" (120 Cong. Rec. 27. 365 55, 1974). However, Senator James Buckley, for whom the law is named, stated that this "memory aids" exception was not intended to allow either regular school personnel or a variety of substitutes to "rotate through courses and classes . . . for the purpose of effectively gaining access to another's notes and evaluations" (120 Cong. Rec. 31, 41381, 1974). This is reinforced by the definition of *substitute:* "An individual who performs on a temporary basis the duties of the individual who made the record and does not refer to an individual who permanently succeeds the maker of the record in his or her position" ("Final Regulations," 1976).

CONCLUSIONS

Parental rights are an important issue in this situation. Generally, a therapist's legal obligations are to a parent or guardian, rather than to a client, when a client is below the age of 18 (Orton, 1997). The clients (or in this case, the parents of a client) do have a legal right to see records kept by a therapist related to the therapist's treatment (Application of Striegel, 1977; Claim of Gerkin, 1980; *People v. Cohen,* 1977). Although the parents do not have a legal right to the records under the Buckley Amendment (as is explained below), they would have a legal right to the records if they were to pursue their rights through court proceedings. So, while Aaron M. might "politely decline" to give copies of his records regarding David's treatment to David's parents upon their demand, the parents do have a legal right to the records and could pursue this legal right through their attorney. Even though the Buckley Amendment does not provide access to the records, general legal principles regarding patient access to health care records do.

What constitutes eligible educational records is an additional issue in this case. The definition hinges not so much on the nature of the material as on the primary purposes of the material and who may have access to it. Aaron M.'s personal session notes are likely *excluded* from the definition of educational records, provided he prepares and maintains them solely for his own purposes; for example, the session notes themselves are not available to the referral source to review.

The letters communicating feedback to the referral source are a different matter. Materials accessible to other personnel (i.e., the referral source) would be considered part of David's educational record and must be made available to his parents on their request.

One path that David's parents do have access to, however, regards the contents of the therapist's report. Several provisions in the law guarantee the right to challenge information that parents or eligible students believe is "inaccurate or misleading or violates the privacy or other rights of the student" (Family Rights and Privacy Act, 1997). If the school personnel decline to change the records, there is a further right to a hearing, where parents or eligible students are allowed to bring an attorney or other representative. If, after this hearing, the school still declines to change the record, the complaining party is permitted to add a statement to the record explaining the disagreement. The school is then obliged to give out this explanation any time the part of the record it refers to is disclosed to anyone, including other school personnel.

CASE 7
The Premarital Agreement

Jan and Howard have lived together for the past 11 months. Both are divorced and have children by previous marriages. Jan's daughter lives with her and Howard. Howard's son and daughter live with their mother. The couple initiated therapy efforts to attempt to work out several problems they are experiencing between themselves and Jan's daughter. A dominant difficulty revolves around Jan's guilt feelings over the "negative" role model she sees herself as providing by living with Howard without benefit of formal marriage. Howard clearly states his love for and desire to marry Jan, but equally identifies his fear that, should the marriage fail, he would be overwhelmed if he had to pay support for Jan and any children they might have, in addition to the support he pays his first wife and two children. The issue of a premarital agreement to circumvent this concern is raised.

CONSIDERATIONS

The number of marriages between persons previously married is steadily increasing. For this and other reasons, it is becoming more common for couples contemplating remarriage to attempt to forestall any future problems by creating a premarital agreement. Despite a lengthy legal history of premarital agreements, however, there is still substantial uncertainty as to the enforceability of all, or a portion, of the provisions of such agreements (Belcher & Pomeroy, 1998). Further, there has been a significant lack of uniformity in the treatment of these agreements among the various states. The problems caused by this uncertainty and nonuniformity are exacerbated even more by the mobility of today's population. Nevertheless, this reflects not so much basic policy differences among states but rather spontaneous and reflexive responses to various factual circumstances at different times (Bureau of National Affairs, Inc., 1984).

Accordingly, the Uniform Premarital Agreement Act was adopted by the National Conference of Commissioners on Uniform State Laws in 1983 and was approved by the American Bar Association in 1984. It was felt that the act would provide a model for state governing bodies to conform to modern social policy, providing sufficient certainty yet flexibility to accommodate different circumstances. Its derivation from a consensus of state laws suggests it is a utilitarian model for the purposes of the present case.

Comprised of 13 sections, the act is relatively limited in scope. Section 1 defines a premarital agreement as "an agreement between prospective spouses made in contemplation of marriage and to be effective upon marriage" (Bureau of National Affairs, Inc., 1984). Section 2 requires that a premarital agreement be in writing and signed by both parties. Section 3 provides an illustrative list of those matters that may be properly dealt with in a premarital agreement. Section 4 states that the premarital agreement becomes effective on the marriage of the parties. Sections 1, 2, and 4 in particular establish significant parameters. The act does not deal with agreements between persons who live together but who do not marry or contemplate marriage. Nor does the act provide for postmarital, separation, or oral agreements.

Section 5 prescribes the manner in which a premarital agreement might be amended or revoked. Section 6 is the key operative of the act and sets forth the conditions under which a premarital agreement is not enforceable. Such an agreement is not enforceable if the party against whom enforcement is sought proves that he or she did not enter the agreement voluntarily or that the agreement was one-sided, oppressive, or unfair when it was entered. Also, before the agreement was entered, he or she (a) did not have access to a fair and reasonable disclosure of the property or financial obligations of the other party; (b) did not voluntarily and explicitly waive, in writing, any right to the disclosure of property or financial obligations; and (c) did not have, or reasonably could not have had, an adequate knowledge of the property and financial obligations of the other party. Even if these conditions are not proved, if a provision of a premarital agreement modifies or eliminates spousal support, and that modification or elimination causes a party to be eligible for public assistance should a future separation or divorce occur, the court is authorized to order the other party to provide support to the extent necessary to avoid that eligibility (Bureau of National Affairs, Inc., 1984).

Sections 7 and 8 address more tangential issues. Section 7 provides for very limited enforcement when a marriage is subsequently determined to be void. Section 8 tolls any statute of limitations applicable to an action asserting a claim for relief under a premarital agreement during the parties' marriage. Sections 9 through 13 simply address very minor points such as the act's "short title," "time of taking effect," and "repeal."

Of the greatest relevance to the present case is Section 3 relating to areas of contract in a premarital agreement. These include

1. Rights and obligations of each party in any of either or both the property whenever and wherever acquired or located.
2. The right to buy, sell, use, transfer, exchange, abandon, lease, consume, expend, assign, create a security interest in, mortgage, encumber, dispose of, or otherwise manage and control property.
3. Disposition of property upon separation, marital dissolution, death, or the occurrence of any other such event.
4. Modification or elimination of spousal support.
5. The making of a will, trust, or other arrangement to carry out the provisions of the agreement.
6. Ownership rights in and disposition of a death benefit from a life insurance policy.
7. Choice of law governing construction of the agreement.
8. Any other matter, including personal rights and obligations, not in violation of public policy or a statute imposing a criminal penalty.
9. The right of a child to support may not be adversely affected by a premarital agreement. (Bureau of National Affairs, Inc., 1984).

CONCLUSIONS

Section 3 of the Uniform Premarital Agreement Act permits parties to contract in a premarital agreement on any matter listed and any other matter not in violation of public policy or imposing a criminal penalty. Point 4 specifically deals with spousal support obligations.

It is important to remember that this act is a model advanced by the National Conference of Commissioners on Uniform State Laws and the American Bar Association for states to adopt. States have differed as to whether a premarital agreement may control the issue of spousal support. Some states have not permitted a premarital agreement to control this issue (e.g., Iowa: *In re Marriage of Winegard*, 1979; Wisconsin: *Fricke v. Fricke*, 1950). The more common and growing trend, however, has been to permit premarital agreements to govern this matter if such agreements and the circumstances of their execution satisfy certain standards (e.g., Colorado: *Newman v. Newman*, 1982; Connecticut: *Parniawski v. Parniawski*, 1976; Massachusetts: *Osborne v. Osborne*, 1981). Thus, it is likely that the couple in the present case, Jan and Howard, might enter into a premarital agreement, eliminating spousal support should their marriage ultimately end in divorce.

Point 9, by contrast, makes clear that any premarital agreement may not adversely affect what would otherwise be this couples' obligation to children born of their marriage. This latter point of concern will not be resolved through any premarital agreement.

CASE 8
Privileged Communications

A couple had been seeing a therapist for marital discord during the fourth year of their marriage. The couple met with the therapist for five conjoint sessions. During these sessions, the husband was open in sharing his self-perceived faults. The wife was rather guarded. The wife's lack of commitment to the therapy added much to create a context wherein the couple was unable to accommodate their differences and thus led to a decision to divorce. Now, some months after the last session with them, the therapist receives a subpoena to appear in court to testify relative to the custody of the couple's daughter. In contacting both parties, who are now living separately, the therapist learns that the wife's attorney is requesting to have the therapist testify to what her husband had shared about himself. The therapist is requested by the husband to keep what he had stated confidential, recognizing that revealing it might adversely affect his custody chances.

CONSIDERATIONS

According to common law, courts should have broad access to evidence. Citizens should present their evidence to the court because all of society benefits from the proper administration of justice. Privileged communication laws run contrary to common law in this respect because they exclude evidence from the courts (*Harvard Law Review*, 1985). Yet the need for a therapist–client privilege is an obvious one. Successful therapy efforts require the establishment of trust between therapists and clients. Fear of potential disclosure before a court would obviously deter many persons from seeking needed treatment, impair the course of therapy, or foster premature termination when issues of risk arose (H. H. Foster, 1976; Kennedy, 1973).

State legislatures have consequently enacted privileged communication laws to protect consumers of psychotherapy. The application of such privileges vary from state to state or even within the same state according to the professional training or credentials of the therapist. Generally speaking, however, courts tend to strictly interpret privileged communication laws. The traditional view holds that the statutes must specify any exception to the common law duty to provide testimony to the court. The privilege has existed only for clients of professionals specifically named in the statutes. Hence, the definition of the terms *psychologist, social worker, marriage and family therapist,* or *counselor* in statutes will determine whether a specific therapist is included. In the absence of a statute, courts have tended to refuse to extend the privilege (e.g., social workers: *State v. Driscoll,* 1972; unlicensed psychologists: *State v. Vickers,* 1981).

Several states extend privileges to associates working under the direction of a protected professional. For example, a Wisconsin law has held that the privilege extends to persons "who are participating in the diagnosis and treatment under the direction of the . . . psychologist" (*Wisconsin Statutes Annotated,* 1981–1982). This would cover marriage and family therapists, social workers, unlicensed psychologists, and other relevant professionals working with the protected therapist. Of course, the courts have the discretion of interpreting the words *under the direction* (Knapp & VandeCreek, 1985). Further, the privilege applies only to psychotherapy and not to court-ordered evaluations. When the court orders parents to undergo psychiatric or psychological evaluation, the results are always available to the court (e.g., *New Mexico ex rel. Human Services Department v. Levario,* 1982). The failure of parents to comply has severely damaged their position in court (e.g., *In re Marriage of Gove,* 1977).

Courts have always valued the welfare of children very highly and attempt to include all testimony that may help them make a proper placement in custody cases. Usually, courts value the welfare of children more than the privacy of their parents (H. H. Foster, 1978). Unless a statute clearly protects the privacy rights of parents, courts tend to rule in favor of admitting testimony. The ruling judge in *Atwood v. Atwood* (1976) reflected this most explicitly in writing: "Regardless of the desires of the parents in making an award of custody, the polar star is to determine what is for the best interest of the child."

Even in the presence of a privileged communication statute, the court may obtain a therapist's testimony in four ways:

1. A client may waive the privilege and permit testimony in court.
2. The court may nullify the privilege for communications made in the presence of third parties.
3. The wording of the state statutes may allow for waiver of the privilege in certain cases.
4. The privilege may be waived if clients introduce their mental condition into the court proceedings.

Knapp and VandeCreek (1985) offer an analysis of each of these waivers.

Client Waiver

Traditionally, the right to waive the privilege belongs to the client. The therapist has no independent right to invoke the privilege against the wishes of the client. Other interested parties, including payers for the therapy of another, have no right to the privilege. For example, in *Bieluch v. Bieluch* (1983), a father tried to prevent the testimony of a psychologist who was treating his wife and children. Although the father had paid for many of the sessions, he was not allowed to invoke the privilege, because he had no professional relationship with the therapist.

The waiver may be implied or expressed. In an *implied waiver*, the actions of the client imply that the communications were not confidential. For example, in *In re Fred J.* (1979), a mother requested that two psychiatrists examine her children and report the findings to a social service agency. In a later custody hearing, the court concluded that the psychiatrists' evaluations were not privileged because the reports had been divulged earlier to the agency. In an *expressed waiver*, the client explicitly allows the testimony of the therapist. Waivers are absolute; the client may not selectively agree that only one portion of communications be open and another portion withheld.

Third-Party Waiver

Most privileged communication controversies have dealt with situations in which only one person was the client. There have been substantially fewer cases in which families or couples were being treated together and disagreement about the waiver emerged in court. No consistent principles have been established as a result. In a number of jurisdictions, however, the privilege has been waived in such cases, not because one party or the other controls the waiver, but because the presence of a third person in therapy was alleged to indicate that the communications were not intended to be confidential or privileged.

The privilege has thus been waived or maintained according to a court's interpretation of the "third-party rule." Common law tradition holds that the presence of third persons suggests that communications were not intended to be confidential. This rule is obviously reasonable when applied to casual conversations made in public places. Not so obvious, however, is its applicability to communications made during therapy in the presence of a marital partner or family members (Meyer & Smith, 1977).

The application of the third-party rule has tended to depend on the wording of specific state statutes. For example, a Delaware statute has stated that "A communication is 'confidential' if not intended to be disclosed to third persons except persons present to further the interests of the patient in the consultation . . . including members of the patient's family" (*Delaware Rules of Evidence*, 1981). When the statutes fail to specify any rule for family psychotherapy, some courts have ruled on therapist–client privilege using the attorney–client model (DeKraai & Sales, 1982). Communications between therapists and clients are placed on the same legal ground as communication between attorneys and clients. According to this model, when two or more persons consult the same attorney about a common matter, communications made by them are not privileged among themselves (Witnesses, §190, 1976). Applying this principle, the Arizona Supreme Court ruled in *Hahman v. Hahman* (1981) that the communications made to a psychologist by a husband and wife were not privileged.

In other states, court decisions have reflected a mixture of findings. Some courts upheld the privilege when parents have been present in therapy with their children (*Grosslight v. Superior Court*, 1977) and when spouses have been seen together (*Yaron v. Yaron*, 1975). Some courts have, however, held otherwise and waived the privilege because a spouse was present (Herrington, 1979). In summary, no consistent judicial trend has emerged in this area. When there is no protective legislation, the ruling depends on the interpretation of the court and/or on the unique circumstances of the case (Knapp & VandeCreek, 1985).

Statutory Waiver

The most common statutory waiver relating to child custody cases is when suspected child abuse is a factor in the proceedings. Almost all states have child abuse reporting laws that waive the privilege in court cases that arise out of reports of suspected child abuse.

A number of states have waiver rules that apply particularly to child custody cases. A Massachusetts law, for example, has specifically allowed a waiver if the judge, on a hearing in chambers, "determines that the psychotherapist has evidence bearing significantly on the patient's ability to provide suitable custody, and that it is more important to the welfare of the child that the communications be disclosed than the relationship between the patient and psychotherapist be protected" (*Massachusetts General Laws*, 1980).

Several other states, including New York, New Hampshire, and Virginia, have allowed judges to waive the privilege when they believe that the interests of justice outweigh clients' need for privacy (DeKraai & Sales, 1982). New York state courts have specified, however, that the privilege may not "cavalierly be ignored or lightly cast aside" (*Perry v. Fiumano*, 1978). To permit the waiver, the mental health of parents must be raised as a relevant issue in a child's placement, and that this information is unavailable from other sources (*State ex rel. Hickox v. Hickox*, 1978). Also, the courts must attempt to look for a less intrusive means of acquiring the information, such as requesting the parents undergo an evaluation, or by viewing relevant records in the privacy of the judge's chambers to first determine its relevance to the case.

Mental Health as a Condition Waiver

Clients waive the privilege when they enter their mental health into the proceedings. States have disagreed, though, on whether or not the mental condition of parents is automatically entered into litigation in child custody cases. Most states have held that the privilege is maintained and the mental condition of parents does not automatically enter in such cases (e.g., Florida: *Kristensen v. Kristensen*, 1981; Michigan: *Matter of Atkins*, 1982; Texas: *Gillespie v. Gillespie*, 1982).

Courts in Kentucky (*Atwood v. Atwood*, 1976) and Delaware (*Shipman v. Division of Social Services*, 1981), however, have ruled that parents automatically enter their mental health into litigation in child custody cases. In the *Atwood* case, the mother had been awarded custody of her three children. She remarried and later obtained therapy with her children and new husband. Her first husband then sought custody. The Kentucky Supreme Court refused to exclude the testimony of the therapist, concluding that custody investigations needed to be extensive and accurate and that the mental condition of the parties involved must be considered an issue.

CONCLUSIONS

The same issues exist in this case that were discussed in Case 1. The application of privilege varies greatly according to the wording of state statutes, the common law traditions within each state, and the interpretations made by courts; prime illustrations being the *Atwood* and *Shipman* cases. The decisions in these cases were binding only in Kentucky and Delaware, respectively. Most states will not automatically waive the privilege in child custody cases. A specific response herein therefore cannot do justice to the myriad nuances of laws among the states. Consequently, the therapist in question must of necessity consult a local attorney.

Depending on the state in which they practice, most marriage and family therapists will likely find themselves operating under a patchwork of existing laws and judicial interpretations. As discussed in Case 1 in this chapter, therapists subpoenaed to court to provide testimony that they believe could ultimately harm a child or family or that represents an unreasonable waiver of privilege need not passively submit to the subpoena. Instead, through their own attorney, they may ask the court to pursue a less intrusive means of acquiring the information. They may suggest that the judge require a court-ordered examination. Or, if the therapist's records are deemed important, the attorney for the therapist can request that the judge screen the records privately in chambers before allowing them into the court proceedings. Obviously, there are no guarantees that the court will be amenable to an attorney's proposals. Nonetheless, such initiatives may create a context wherein judges will be able to more prudently balance the need for information in court with the need to protect the confidentiality of therapeutic efforts.

CASE 9

Legal Responsibility of Clinical Supervisors

One state's licensure for marriage and family therapy requires that unlicensed graduates of marriage and family therapy training programs complete 2 years of clinically supervised postdegree experience. Part of the position agreement for entry-level therapists at a Family Services Agency is that they receive regular supervision by the senior level therapist at the agency. The designated supervisor has not been able to provide what he considers to be adequate supervision. He has had to leave two entry-level therapists mainly on their own with rather difficult caseloads. The staff members at the agency are all overloaded; the supervisor is feeling overburdened by his supervisory responsibility in addition to his regular heavy caseload. Thus, quality supervision time is rare. The supervisor is preparing to bring the situation to the agency's Board of Directors and seeks to identify his legal liability as one justification for a reduced client caseload so he can adequately attend to his supervisory responsibilities.

CONSIDERATIONS

Recent years have seen a gradual and profoundly important change in the attitudes of clients toward helping professionals. Clients have become more consumer-oriented with respect to accountability; this has become a critical concept for both marriage and family therapists and supervisors. From the supervisory standpoint, the legal doctrine of respondeat superior (also known as vicarious liability) has consequently become of significant relevance (Christie, Meeks, Pryor, & Sanders, 1997; Cohen, 1979). According to this doctrine, someone in a position of authority or responsibility, such as a clinical supervisor, is responsible for acts of those individuals under his or her supervision. Stated another way, supervisors are ultimately legally responsible for the welfare of clients seen in therapy by their supervisees (Cormier & Bernard, 1982; Snider, 1985).

There are a number of implications inherent in this principle as applied to clinical supervision. The first demands that supervisors ensure that supervision actually occurs and that meetings are documented (Harrar, VandeCreek, & Knapp, 1990; Welfel, 1998). Supervisors must avoid delegating all responsibility to a supervisee because negligence may occur. Therefore, a supervisor must be familiar with each case of every supervisee. This can be established by conducting (and documenting) that face-to-face contacts with supervisees regularly take place.

It is important that supervisors observe the actual work of supervisees through audiotapes, videotapes, or observations rather than relying exclusively on the supervisees' reports of their own work (Navin, Beamish, & Johanson, 1995). Cormier and Bernard (1982) reported an attorney's advice that supervisors also conduct one face-to-face meeting with each supervisee's clients sometime during the initial stages of therapy. Such a contact allows clients the opportunity to meet the supervisor and discover how their therapist is being supervised. This information can assist clients in providing informed consent to their therapist for his or her services. Also, a face-to-face contact with clients allows supervisors to gain additional information about them, the possible management of their cases, and to better determine the amount of supervision need. Slovenko (1980) restated a comment made by the attorney in the *Tarasoff* (1974) case appropriate to consider in this regard:

> It is my view that if the supervisor of the clinic had personally examined the patient Poddar and made an independent decision that the patient Poddar was not dangerous to himself or his victim, Tatiana Tarasoff, there would be no cause of action based on foreseeability. However, the supervisor never saw the patient Poddar and ignored the medical records developed by his staff. (p. 468)

Thus, it may be of significant importance from a legal standpoint for supervisors to make contact with supervisees' clients.

Van Hoose and Kottler (1985) identified failure to supervise a therapist working with a disturbed client as one of the leading causes of psychological malpractice suits. The supervisor is legally responsible to know when supervisees are insufficiently prepared to deal with certain situations and need assistance. Knowledge that a supervisee is having difficulties in working with particular clients may call for closer supervision, cotherapy, or possibly reassigning the case to a more experienced person.

A further implication of the respondeat superior doctrine addresses supervisees' competence to provide adequate services. Some formal assessment of competence should be conducted prior to assuming an independent caseload. If a supervisor has reservations about a supervisee's clinical abilities, supervision should not be agreed on until remedial training activities are undertaken and completed and/or the supervisor seeks to protect himself or herself from liability by stating reservations about the supervisee in writing to relevant parties (Cormier & Bernard, 1982).

Finally, the respondeat superior doctrine also suggests certain responsibilities supervisors have to clients to ensure appropriate referral and termination procedures. Dawidoff (1973) noted that supervisors are liable if treatment is terminated or a referral is made without due cause. Referrals and terminations must be handled in a way that meets the recognized standard of care.

Although the respondeat superior doctrine creates legal liability for the supervisor, the supervisee is not necessarily absolved. Clients have the option of bringing action against the supervisor, the supervisee, or all parties. Cohen (1979), for example, reported the case of a supervisee, who away from the formal clinical setting and without the supervisor's knowledge, allegedly engaged in sexual relations with a client. Under the doctrine of respondeat superior, a lawsuit was brought against the supervisor rather than the supervisee. The plaintiff claimed that the supervisor was negligent by allowing an unlicensed person, not competent of providing due care, to treat her.

In a contrasting case, a supervisee rather than the supervisor was sued for failure to more closely monitor a client who committed suicide. The supervisee, a student intern, was found to be negligent (*Eady v. Alter*, 1976). Exactly who is named as defendant in such cases obviously depends on the circumstances, setting, alleged acts, plaintiff, and perhaps above all, who is seen as having the most to lose (Cormier & Bernard, 1982).

CONCLUSIONS

Slovenko's (1980) warning that "litigation involving supervisors may be the 'suit of the future' " (p. 468) can be best addressed by well-informed and conscientious supervisors. The supervisor in the present case should assert the need for regularly scheduled supervision based on a careful assessment of the needs of both supervisees and their clients. The amount and frequency of the supervision will be best determined by an accurate knowledge of the supervisees' strengths and deficits, as well as the difficulties likely to be presented by their caseloads. The supervisor should be careful to document how supervision is scheduled and what occurs during supervisory sessions.

Beyond this, the supervisor must actually provide the supervision. Negligence is based on the idea that the professional has departed from what is considered acceptable in terms of the standards of the profession. Consultation with professionals in similar situations and professional association standards can provide a recommended minimum; anything above that can take place as warranted by the results of the supervisor's assessments.

A supervisor should consider professional liability insurance. The agency might provide such coverage, but few do. It is important to identify in advance of purchase, however, what a policy actually covers. Occasionally, policies will not cover damages from either negligent supervision or acts of supervisees with less than a master's degree.

Finally, if the supervisor is not able to provide adequate supervision, or if some undesirable consequences befall clients being seen by a supervisee, the supervisor must take appropriate action. Although an important goal of providing supervised practice is to produce more effective practitioners, the supervisor must protect his or her own welfare, and most importantly, the welfare of clients.

CASE 10
Insurance Fraud?

During their initial session with a newly licensed marriage and family therapist in private practice, a couple asks the therapist if her services are covered by their health insurance. The therapist asks that they bring a copy of their policy manual to the next session for her to review. The couple forgets to bring the policy manual not only that next session, but also the following session as well. It is only after the fourth session that the therapist is able to review the policy's provisions, which allow for individual psychotherapy on an outpatient basis for a maximum of 20 sessions within 1 calendar year; marital therapy is specifically stated as not being covered. One of the couple's primary stressors is financial problems. The therapist submits a claim for reimbursement for individual psychotherapy and is reimbursed by the insurance company for the alleged services.

CONSIDERATIONS

Third-party reimbursement and managed health care dilemmas (Bittner, Bialek, Nathiel, Ringwald, & Tupper, 1999; Bonnington, Crawford, Curtis, & Watts, 1996; Huber, 1995) can generate a complex set of issues for marriage and family therapists, particularly in early experiences. Third-party reimbursement entails an individual (or his or her employer) purchasing an insurance policy to cover *specific* medical or psychiatric conditions. By accepting third-party reimbursement, providers (i.e., the marriage and family therapist in this case) agree to provide whatever documentation an insurance company deems necessary to *substantiate* treatment (Fong & Sherrard, 1990).

Intentionally reporting to an insurance company that a condition was present and/or was treated when in fact either the condition was not present or the treatment noted was not actually administered is considered fraud (Remley & Herlihy, 2001). Abuse of health insurance through fraudulent claims is prohibited by law. Uncovering such fraudulent actions could result in an insurance company filing civil suit for recovery of funds misspent, as well as the insurance company requesting criminal action be brought by appropriate legal authorities. Further, the relevant state licensing board might be contacted and sanctions imposed on a therapist's license to practice, or the license possibly revoked entirely (Stevens-Smith & Hughes, 1993).

The law identifies five elements as necessary to be present for fraud to have occurred ("Case Notes," 1985–1986):

1. There is concealment or false representation of a material fact.
2. This concealment or false representation is reasonably calculated to deceive.
3. There is an intent to deceive.
4. There is, in fact, deception.
5. The deception results in damage to the injured party.

CONCLUSIONS

It is not difficult for most marriage and family therapists to empathize with the therapist in this case. She is newly licensed and in private practice. Her training has been steeped with assertions about the value of marriage and family therapy. It is obviously frustrating that this couple identifies financial problems as a major stressor, that they have insurance coverage ostensibly to limit the negative impact of such a stressor, and yet the coverage does not directly apply. Despite this, the laws are relatively clear in this regard, and the marriage and family therapist here must abide by them.

Considering the elements required by law to be present for fraud, it seems likely the marriage and family therapist in this case is acting in a fraudulent manner under the law: (a) She is falsely representing a material fact in that marital, not individual psychotherapy is the treatment; (b) the false representation is calculated to deceive the insurance company so that the treatment falls under its coverage; (c) there is an intent to deceive for purposes of being reimbursed; (d) there is, in fact, a deception in that the reimbursement forms were submitted to the insurance company; and (e) the deception has resulted in damage to the insurance company in that it reimbursed for specific treatment that had not occurred.

Stevens-Smith and Hughes (1993), in discussing the issue of insurance fraud, noted three areas they described as practiced but forbidden: (a) claiming that a covered provider (e.g., psychiatrist or psychologist) is providing services when a different person is actually doing so, (b) ignoring the requirement of an accurate diagnosis by giving most or all clients the same diagnosis, and (c) intentionally waiving clients' share of a stated fee while reporting the full fee amount to an insurance company. Smith-Stevens and Hughes (1993) cautioned therapists considering "bending the rules" to carefully contemplate the potential long-term legal and ethical consequences before doing so.

III

Professional Issues in Marriage and Family Therapy

Professionalism . . . an attitude that motivates individuals to be attentive to the image and ideals of their particular profession.

(VanZandt, 1990, p. 243)

8

Valuing and the Professional Practice of Marriage and Family Therapy

Marriage and family therapy, indeed, any type of counseling or psychotherapy, cannot be value-free or neutral (Shulte, 1990). "Even trying to avoid a particular value choice by being noncommittal amounts to taking a value position" (Bergin, 1985, p. 107). Values are a core component of any professional therapeutic endeavor. "As long as one distinguishes between desirable and undesirable change, one is invoking values" (Welfel, 1998, p. 208). Most professional helping organizations build their codes of ethics around values. For example, the National Association of Social Workers (1996) bases its ethical principles on six core values: service, social justice, dignity and worth of the person, importance of human relationships, integrity, and competence.

Values are particularly critical to the professional practice of marriage and family therapy. Indeed, the field of marriage and family therapy "now recognizes the inescapability and importance of values" (Fowers & Wenger, 1997, p. 153). For instance, assessment and treatment directions advanced by the different approaches to marriage and family practice reflect the dominant values of clinicians practicing these models (Doherty, 1992). Values are like a compass in that they promote a direction that therapeutic practice should take (Darom, 1988). Therefore, "it is important that marriage and family counselors be in touch with their values" (Kaplan, 1999, p. 13).

Rokeach defined a *value* as "an enduring belief that a specific mode of conduct or end-state of existence is personally or socially preferable to an opposite or converse mode of conduct or end-state of existence" (1973, p. 286). Anthropologists (e.g., Kluckhohn & Strodtbeck, 1961) have identified a great similarity among predominant values orientations found in diverse cultures, suggesting a universal dimension in all human efforts to cope with life's events. These broadly accepted values address a belief in the desirable; an affective component is elicited when this belief is accepted or challenged, and an action component cues behaviors considered congruent or incongruent with the belief (Stuart, 1980).

All human events are guided by the interaction of the values of the parties concerned. This interaction of values determines those aspects of human experience labeled as events, the significance ascribed to those events, the ways persons select and pursue goals, as well as the manner in which goal attainment is evaluated. People cannot interact independently of their values, even if those values are not explicit. Professional therapeutic practice is particularly shaped by value interaction among therapists, societal institutions, and clients.

Institutional representatives of society, including governmental bodies, clinics, hospitals, social agencies, insurance companies, academic and training facilities, and professional associations, formally and informally hold out values for professional therapeutic practice. These values define professional therapeutic services, who is eligible to receive them, and who is qualified to offer them. They also decide the conditions under which such services will be financed, whether through direct fee payments, insurance coverage, tax deductions, or other subsidies and which professionals will be approved for these remunerations. In making these determinations, societal representatives assert their values about the nature of mental illness, marital and family problems, and treatment alternatives (Aponte, 1985).

Values can describe either means or ends to actions. In each case, values determine efforts to make discriminations among alternative courses of actions. Values that prescribe ends contribute to attitudes about all facets of society (Rokeach, 1968). Values that prescribe means provide the basis for professional norms (R. M. Williams, 1968). Professional norms are hierarchically organized (Maslow, 1959) and relate to a series of beliefs about all phases of therapeutic practice (Stuart, 1980). Marriage and family therapists' values thus provide the basis for their professional practice (B. Carter, 1986). Values gained from personal life experiences and professional training interact with and filter societal values about professional practice to influence every therapeutic decision. These decisions may govern who will be offered services, the goals of those services, the procedures used to achieve identified goals, and the criteria by which therapeutically mediated changes are evaluated. A further interaction with clients' values (the therapeutic process) is framed by the parameters of therapists' values. Thus, this values interaction, or *valuing*, is an essential aspect in the professional practice of marriage and family therapy.

After briefly introducing values clarification, we address systemic epistemology as a basis for the professional practice of marriage and family therapy. We espouse the need for an evolving epistemology within marriage and family therapy and offer valuing as a framework for promoting this evolving epistemology. We then identify and discuss several practice implications of valuing for marriage and family therapists. We conclude by directing attention to specific valuing components for marriage and family therapists to consider.

VALUES CLARIFICATION

In an article appropriately entitled, "Counselor: Know Thyself," Hulnick (1977) posited the inescapable need for therapists to clarify their own values if they are to assume a distinct professional identity. Similarly, Pell (1979) concurred with an earlier position asserted by Bergantino (1978) that lack of self-awareness by therapists represented a "fatal flaw." Such self-awareness must entail a clear understanding of the bases on which therapists choose to assume their professional identity.

Values clarification has been suggested as a means for therapists to clarify their professional position (Glaser & Kirschenbaum, 1980). Inherent in the values clarification perspective is the assumption that thoughtfully reflecting on one's beliefs is better than not doing so, that considering alternatives and their consequences is better than not considering them; and that acting consistently with one's most cherished beliefs—one's values—is important.

Values clarification represents a consideration of the *process* of valuing as opposed to simply identifying the *content* of values. It is an active process composed of seven subprocesses, each eliciting questions that need to be answered in a developmental sequence (Glaser & Kirschenbaum, 1980):

Choosing Basic Beliefs

1. Choosing from alternatives:
    a. Have a number of alternatives been considered?
    b. Has sufficient time been given to identifying possible alternatives?
2. Choosing after considering consequences:
    a. What are the most valuable aspects of the belief?
    b. What if everyone held the belief?
3. Choosing freely:
    a. How was the belief first procured?
    b. How freely is it now being chosen?

Prizing Basic Beliefs

4. Prizing and cherishing:
    a. Does the belief hold significant importance?
    b. Is it one to be proud of?
5. Publicly affirming, when appropriate:
    a. Is there a willingness to share the belief with others?
    b. Who would it be appropriate to share the belief with?

Acting on Beliefs

6. Acting:
    a. Is the belief one that can be readily acted on?
    b. Is there a willingness to act on it?

7. Acting with a pattern of consistency:
   a. Is the belief one that is typically acted on?
   b. Is there a willingness to consistently act on the belief?

Seymour's (1982) injunction identifying regular values clarification as essential to professional therapeutic practice aptly addresses the importance of this process:

> We do become emotionally invested in our values, we do hold some of them to be unquestionably right, and we do act in counseling in accordance with what we believe. We, as counselors, must be aware of the emotional investment, admit to, and hopefully question those values that have been previously unquestioned, and then examine closely how what we believe influences how we act as counselors. If our values are, in fact, the lenses through which we view the world, then we need to have our vision checked as a part of the selection and training process, and at regular intervals thereafter. (p. 45)

Many hold that the very essence of marriage and family therapy depends on a therapist's choosing, prizing, and acting on certain predominant beliefs of a systemic nature. They posit a systemically oriented epistemology as delineating the difference between doing marriage and family therapy and simply seeing marital partners and family members in the same room and dealing with their individual concerns.

SYSTEMIC EPISTEMOLOGY

Epistemology is a branch of philosophy that investigates the origin, nature, methods, and limits of human knowledge. For the professional practice of marriage and family therapy, the term has come to mean a formal worldview—a framework for thinking and conceptualizing (Sauber, L'Abate, & Weeks, 1985). Anthropologist Gregory Bateson (1979) first addressed epistemology as a professional issue within marriage and family therapy, and others have built on his work. Bateson saw epistemology as rules for making sense out of the world.

Marriage and family therapy as a professional practice initially grew from an intuitive or experiential awareness that families of patients were somehow implicated in the problems being experienced by patients. Patients increasingly came to be viewed by early "family therapists" as being more of a family scapegoat than singularly sick individuals. Initially, there was a tendency to flip-flop blame from child to parents, one marital partner to another, and vice versa. Soon, however, systems theory was discovered as a means of articulating family involvement without simply shifting blame from one individual to others. Eventually, blame, and with it responsibility, was shifted away altogether from the individual and onto the "system" (Cottone & Greenwell, 1992).

The traditional psychotherapeutic perspective has been founded on what has been described as the *psychological* worldview. This perspective focuses on the individual and on traits or conditions of an individual. As Cottone (1988) stated:

> Traditionally in counseling, individuals are treated primarily as independent entities, having identities all their own and problems bounded to a large degree by their individual identities. Individuals are viewed as having intelligence, skills, abilities, personality traits, interests, self-concepts, mental disturbances, adjustment disorders, etceteras. Counseling goals, likewise, are viewed as primarily "self" oriented. (p. 359)

Cottone (1991) summarized the psychological worldview according to four general propositions:

1. The focus of study is the individual.
2. Individuals are assumed to possess characteristics and traits, both learned and unlearned, that endure and represent predispositions to act (e.g., interests, attitudes, self-concepts, disorders). These traits and characteristics can be isolated and influenced in a therapeutic context.
3. Causes can be clearly defined, and symptoms (e.g., inappropriate behavior) and conditions (e.g., disturbance) can be treated directly through a therapeutic relationship.
4. One person can affect change in a second person only to the degree that the first person influences the traits and characteristics or the psychological conditions (internal or external) of the second person.

The psychological worldview thus focuses on the individual client. The individual client is viewed as able to be assessed and treated. Interventions attend primarily to the client rather than to social or cultural factors that might be affecting the client.

In the early development of the professional therapeutic practice of marriage and family therapy, more extreme and clear-cut interpretations of systems theory prevailed. The early *systemic* worldview was based primarily on a relational-ecological perspective. Becvar, Becvar, and Bender (1982) expounded on this worldview in stating:

> Previously we studied and treated the person in isolation. Our inquiry consistent with the theoretical models then in use was concerned with the nature of the individual's pathological condition and, in a wider sense, with the nature of the human mind. Consistent with our new models derived from ecology, ethology, cybernetics, systems theory, and structuralism, our inquiry is now extended to include the effects of an individual's behavior on others, their reactions to it, and the context in which all of this takes place. Our focus has shifted from the isolated monad to the relationship among the components or members of a system. We have turned from an inferential study of the mind to a concern with the observable manifestations of relationships. (p. 386)

Cottone (1991) summarized four basic propositions of the systemic worldview:

1. Relationships represent the focus of study.
2. Relationships can be isolated for study and defined, but only with the understanding that this isolation and definition are relative to the observer and his or her system (relationships) of reference.

3. Causation is circular (nonlinear) within the confines of specified relationships of significance.
4. Therapeutic change occurs through social relationship.

Two additional systemic propositions tended to underlie early family therapists' systemic worldview, particularly in explaining and validating their position in contrast to the traditional psychological worldview dominant at the time. These were (a) the whole is greater than the sum of its parts; and (b) linear thinking is an epistemological mistake. The first proposition, holism, asserts that the parts are not as important as the larger system of significance. "Why bother with the individual when it is the family or the system that has overriding influence?" (Cottone & Greenwell, 1992, p. 168). The second proposition, antilinearity, considers any attempt to identify specific sequences of causation in a linear fashion (A leads to B leads to C) as wasted effort (Fish, 1990).

Early family therapists took great pains to stress this emphasis on the larger context. Hoffman (1981) interpreted this stance in stating:

> To "chop up the ecology" is what one does when one takes the parts and pieces of what one is describing and decides that one part "controls" another or one part "causes" another. (pp. 342–343)

The psychological worldview's position of *linearity* was portrayed as resembling, for example, a pair of binoculars that a spectator at a sporting event uses to observe only one player on the field. The spectator can see the player's movements and expressions in fine detail. Yet the drawback of using binoculars eventually becomes clear: The interaction between one player and the others on the field is screened out. The spectator fails to take in the overall action among all participants, particularly important when the primary action of play occurs away from the single player. This oversight was highlighted by those advocating a systemic worldview that calls for widening the spectator's field of vision, so to speak, in an effort to consider the total context.

The systemic worldview was primarily portrayed through the concept of *circularity*. Mental illness had traditionally been perceived in linear terms, with historical, causal explanations given for the distress. Etiology was conceived primarily in terms of prior events—disease, emotional conflict, or learning history—that caused symptoms in the client. Using circularity as a core concept, the systemic worldview represented mental illness not as something that is caused but, rather, that is part of an ongoing, circular fit. Dell (1982) described this in stating:

> Without reference to etiology or causation, fit simply posits that the behaviors occurring in the family system have a general complementarity, they fit together. *Causation*, on the other hand, is a specified type of interpretation of fit that considers the observed complementarity to have the form A causes B; for instance, bad parents make their children sick. (p. 25)

Of those who originally addressed the professional impact of this epistemology that included a circular understanding of behavior, Bateson (1979) made a distinction between the world of physical objects and the world of living forms in contrasting linearity and circularity. Linearity applied to the physical world assumes that the world is like a billiard table in which the balls go in one direction when hit. Bateson believed that the world of living things is poorly represented by such a model because it neglects to account for communication and relationships; simple force alone is not enough.

Hoffman (1981) further contrasted linearity and circularity in describing what may occur as a result of kicking a stone and kicking a dog. In the case of a stone, the energy transmitted by the kick will move the stone a certain distance, depending on the force of the kick and the weight of the stone. But in kicking a dog, the outcome is not so simply predicted. What happens depends on the relationship between the person and the dog. The dog may respond in any number of ways. It may cringe, run away, or bite the person, depending on how the relationship is defined and how the dog interprets the kick. Moreover, the behavior of the dog will send back information that may modify the person's subsequent behavior. If the dog bites, the person will give greater thought before he or she kicks the dog again.

It must be remembered that these basic propositions represent early systemic epistemology. They represented the core components of marriage and family therapy as a unique professional therapeutic practice. By the end of the 1970s, marriage and family therapy had, however, moved from being a radical new approach to becoming an established force within mainstream mental health practice. The 1980s and 1990s ushered in a new stage in which marriage and family therapy's blind spots and biases have been and are being challenged. These challenges have come in a number of forms. Two of the most pointed are the feminist critique of family therapy and the self in the system (M. P. Nichols & Schwartz, 1998).

The Feminist Critique of Systemic Epistemology

The feminist critique of systemic epistemology has been characterized as representing a "rude awakening" (M. P. Nichols & Schwartz, 1998, p. 326). The critique began in the late 1970s when Betty Carter, Peggy Papp, Olga Silverstein, and Marianne Walters formed a coalition called the Women's Project in Family Therapy to "openly and publicly challenge the field's patriarchy and conventional wisdom" (Simon, 1997, p. 60). These feminists and others have called on family therapists to "recognize gender as a central organizing feature of family life and to challenge traditional ways of working which ignore, and therefore reinforce, gender-based power imbalances" (Leslie & Clossick, 1996, p. 253). Such a position is "political" in that it "refers to those processes maintaining or changing power relations within any social or interpersonal system" (Knudson-Martin, 1997, p. 421). It is also ethical in that approaches to gender within marriage and family therapy raise issues that are ethical in nature, such as beneficience, justice, and autonomy.

The feminist critique can be summarized by two basic positions. The increasing awareness, if not increasing number, of reported incidents of family violence has led to the first point. Systemic epistemology has been criticized in that circular causality is often employed to present violence as serving a functional role in the maintenance of the family system. Bograd (1984) stated in this regard:

> Feminist values are clear regarding the allocation of responsibility for wife battering incidents: 1) no woman deserves to be beaten; 2) men are solely responsible for their actions. Careful analysis of prevailing explanatory frameworks of wife battering reveals that there is little logical and empirical support for the prevalent assumption that women provoke men into abusing them. . . . From a feminist perspective, a systemic formulation is biased if it can be employed to implicate the battered woman or to excuse the abusive man. (p. 561)

The second point also criticizes circular causality but as it relates to social context. In particular, patriarchal society is seen as limiting the choices women can make related to possible life roles and therefore limits their ability to be causal agents. As Walters, Carter, Papp, and Silverstein (1988) asserted:

> Systems therapy discriminates against women by seeking balance and equilibrium for the family system as a unit, without addressing the unequal access of each individual to choice or role. The pretense that men and women are genderless cogs in the system prevents us from noticing that women are held more responsible than men for making it work, in the family and in family therapy, and that the "complementary" roles, tasks, and rewards of the stable system are allocated by gender, unequally, to its male and female members. (p. 23)

These two points have represented a credible attack on systemic epistemology. In essence, accommodating to this critique calls for a return to linearity (Cottone & Greenwell, 1992). It accentuates the fact that "local" or specific intuitions ought not be swept aside by broader philosophies (Cambien, 1989). One local intuition of concern here is that spouse abuse is wrong, that therapists should take action to stop it, and that the abuser is responsible for eliminating the abusive behavior apart from whatever nonphysical incitement to abuse may have occurred (Cottone & Greenwell, 1992). Likewise, a second intuition cautions marriage and family therapists to be more than simply sensitive to gender issues in working with families. Instead, they should assert that issues of gender, or more specifically patriarchy, permeate therapeutic practice and go on to organize concrete interventions around that understanding (May, 1998).

Only when we look through this lens of gender can we effectively stop blaming mothers, or stop looking to them to do most of the changing simply because they are the most invested in change or the most cooperative. Only then will we be able to fully counter our unconscious biases toward seeing women as primarily responsible for child rearing and housekeeping, as needing to support their husbands' careers by neglecting their own, as needing to be married, or at least, to have a man in their lives. Only then can we stop relying on traditionally male traits like rationality, independence, and competitiveness as our standards of health and stop denigrating or ignoring traits traditionally encouraged in women like emotionality, nurturance, and relationship focus (Giblin & Chan, 1995).

If these two intuitions are lost in, or negated by, systemic epistemology, then feminist intuition argues against the validity of this epistemology (Cottone &

Greenwell, 1992). As Taggert (1989) observed, "By continuing to produce 'family therapy' as if the feminist critique did not exist, family therapy theorists intensify the patriarchal project of presenting as comprehensive and normative that which is partial and atypical" (p. 101).

The Self in the System

A second major challenge to systemic epistemology has been its perceived overemphasis on the family-as-a-system, thereby overlooking the importance of the intrapsychic functioning of the individual. M. P. Nichols and Schwartz (1998) described several events signaling this challenge:

1. Family therapy as a field had grown strong and confident enough to admit it may not have all the answers; intrapsychic considerations may thus be important.
2. The constructivist movement (i.e., therapy occurs when therapists and clients together "co-create" new meanings of experience; Gladding, 1998b; Held, 1990) refocused the family therapy field from a primary emphasis on behavioral sequences, in which insight or awareness is discounted, to an emphasis on the meanings that individual family members maintain about each other and their problems.
3. Increasing numbers of psychodynamically trained clinicians have immigrated into the family therapy field as it has established itself in mainstream mental health practice. This has led to an increasing desire for models that bridge the gap between self and system.
4. Popular offshoots of psychoanalysis, notably self-psychology and object relations theory, have evolved in a manner that suggests their compatibility with family therapy.

To use the latter event as a focus of illustration here, object relations theory in essence purports that persons relate to each other in the present partly on the basis of expectations formed by early experience. The past is alive—in memory—and significantly affects a person's present existence. Mental images, called internal objects, are formed during early childhood interactions with significant others. As adults, individuals' reactions to others depend to a large degree on how much those persons resemble one's internal objects rather than on the actual characteristics of the persons in the present.

Applied to family therapy, object relations theory posits that dysfunctional patterns of behavior among family members are maintained by the internal object relations of family members. Through a process of projective identification, the images of certain internal objects are projected onto other family members. Therapy involves interpreting these projections to the family so that family members can be more aware of the unseen forces behind their patterns and be better able to change them.

M. P. Nichols and Schwartz (1998) note that some family therapists have advocated giving up systems theory and replacing it with object relations as the foundation for family therapy. Others seek to use both, keeping them separate and using them sequentially or to complement each other. Still others look to integrate the concepts of object relations and systems theory.

Evolving Epistemology

The circular emphasis within systemic epistemology recognizes that individuals are not unrelated atoms motivated only by internal urges and instincts; rather, they are parts of larger systems that exert considerable influence on their thoughts, feelings, and actions. Nonetheless, couples and families are composed of individuals, an understanding that tended to be minimized or ignored by early systemic writers in their zealousness to assert their perspective. It is little wonder that challenges to this worldview such as those just discussed eventually appeared and were followed by comments like G. D. Erickson's (1988):

> None of the major human problems of our era can be adequately addressed by, or treated within, a systemic paradigm. . . . [T]he neglect of social context and persons qua persons is inherent in the theory and noncorrectable. (p. 226)

Inherent in any discussion of epistemology, however, is also the issue of evolution. The belief that patterns of connectedness are dynamically unfolding rather than structurally based is at the heart of the matter (Taggart, 1982). Structural, fixed worldviews propose an ultimate, objective knowledge. Evolutionary worldviews emphasize that knowledge can never be entirely stabilized. Brown (1977) proposed the only permanent aspect of science as being the process of research, and it is only the current consensual agreement of the scientific community that determines the research findings that have validity, not the findings themselves. Thus, one discovery sets the stage for another, like the ever-widening ripples occasioned by the proverbial pebble thrown into the pond.

M. P. Nichols's (1987a) admonition relative to the need for openness to continuing discovery aptly summarizes the need for an evolving epistemology by marriage and family therapists:

> Over the past 30 years we have learned that there is a vast range of difficulties which respond quickly to family therapy interventions. At the same time, all family therapists know that many problems don't yield to our most ingenious methods. Clearly family treatment is not a cure-all for all the problems people bring to us. As we continue to examine our practices and note where what we do doesn't work, we need to deepen our ability to listen to our clients and explore the forces that keep them stuck. . . . Unless we do, we may find that, rather than continuing to expand, the boundaries of our understanding will begin to constrict. (p. 85)

NEGOTIATION: THE NATURE OF VALUING

The negotiation of values is increasingly central to the professional practice of marriage and family therapy. Today, less is accepted on the strength of tradition and precedent and more is open for debate. Both within the field and in society as a whole, technological and social changes are occurring at a greater rate than at any previous period. Moreover, people are actively seeking ways to determine the terms of these changes.

One major reason for this progressive acceleration of change has been an explosion in the amount and quality of information available through the media and increased opportunities for education, communication, and travel. All this has led to an escalation in the rate of change among traditional racial, socioeconomic, transgenerational, sex role, and other social network relationships. Traditions, customs, and roles within relationships must contend with mounting pressures to change. They resist, accommodate, mutate, or vanish in this swirl of social movement. Currently, people have gained greater autonomy, flexibility, and power over their own lives and in relation to the rest of society. This phenomenon, although resulting in more choice, has also created more sources of stress. Marriage and family therapy is one of the means societal institutions have identified to assist people in more successfully negotiating this social evolution (Aponte, 1985).

Systemic epistemology represents the basic core of marriage and family therapy as a professional therapeutic practice. Given that systemic epistemology, as a fixed worldview at least, is no longer acceptable to many marriage and family therapists as a framework for their practice, then the field has come to a crossroads. Should that which has been an intellectually attractive, useful, and dependable theoretical rudder be let go of (Fish, 1990)?

Traditional approaches to values have promoted a view of reality marked by a content rather than a process orientation. Put in its most basic terms, there is a "right" way that is usually presented as contrasting to a "wrong" way. The only legitimate response to such an approach is adaptation (Taggart, 1982). A more modern variant of this position is the view that social change is permitted only within the restraints of unchanging social values; the institutions that support and promote these unchanging values must themselves survive without changing (Jantsch, 1980).

This distinction of opposites results ultimately in rigidification of existing professional practice. Values within this perspective are often seen as the only things that last; to tamper with the methods embedded within those lasting values is to risk being accused of seeking to overturn them (Taggart, 1982). Thus, an unnecessary dichotomy is created. Valuing suggests that values need not be static entities denoting a right or wrong way; rather, there exists an ongoing negotiation of values resulting in an evolving epistemological process that continually balances between confirmation and novelty. Total confirmation identifies a static, rigid epistemology; for living systems, this equals death. Total novelty, by contrast, identifies a chaotic epistemology; in living systems, this heralds disintegration. Life is a dance between the two (von Weizsacker & von Weizsacker, 1974).

A. Watts (1961) uses language as a metaphor for the continuing negotiation between novelty and confirmation. A language that becomes too innovative in either time or space is at risk of losing its coherence. A language that stops growing is in danger of becoming a relic. Likewise, valuing suggests an evolving epistemological process of unfolding within the context of negotiating older beliefs, thus ensuring both debate and a common task.

A particularly cogent therapeutic illustration here is the notion of a therapeutic opposition known as resistance. The term *resistance* represents a conceptual wall between the client's and the therapist's values. Traditional views have held that this wall must be broken down for change to occur (Searight & Openlander, 1984). De Shazer (1999) notes how resistance is often used as an explanatory device to account for situations in which clients do not respond to therapeutic interventions in a manner desired by their therapists. Resistance represents attributions made by therapists to account for this "difficulty." Dell (1982) sees this notion as epistemologically mistaken: "People and systems do not resist; they simply are what they are" (p. 22). Likewise, valuing asserts that clients' and therapists' values are not inherently right or wrong, correct or incorrect; they simply are.

As strategically oriented marriage and family therapists have noted, clients traditionally seen as "resistant" will generate a different orientation than when therapists "go with reality"—when therapists accept clients' values as they are and negotiate their own values with clients' values. Andolfi, Angelo, Menghi, and Nicolo-Corigliano (1983) emphasize a somewhat similar negotiation process, resulting in clients evolving a different "script." In the valuing process of Andolfi and colleagues, a therapist negotiates with a client in emphasizing certain values previously deemphasized and at the same time in relegating other values to the background. Within the context of the therapist–client negotiation, values evolve with accompanying behavioral changes that are compatible with values changes. Essentially, the therapist and client come together in negotiating a common world of less pain and conflict.

Valuing recognizes that when therapist and client come together, they can negotiate a new, common system containing elements of both subsystems as well as unique properties arising from their interaction. Similarly, when traditional systemic epistemology is challenged, it need not be discarded but rather a context negotiated that contains said challenges. As M. P. Nichols (1987a) stated

> We do not have to choose between a theory of persons and a theory of persons in relationship. We may need both the wide-angle lens of an interactional view and the ability to use the magnifying glass of individual psychology when necessary. (p. 85)

Valuing then essentially consists of negotiating the context that surrounds systemic epistemology and the challenges that confront it. Marriage and family therapists can thus maintain the importance of an epistemology that recognizes the benefits of understanding the shapes and patterns of interaction and simultaneously augmenting and deepening that understanding.

THE PRACTICE IMPLICATIONS OF VALUING

For years, therapists have debated whether professional psychotherapy represents art or science. Many marriage and family therapists' opinion is on the side of art, yet their terminology often suggests science. To measure human exchange, couples and families have been compared to the cybernetic working of machines, the organization of solar systems, the interplay of chemical compounds, mathematical equations, and more. The language of science offers a definitive way to describe human functioning. It eliminates, however, many of the political and psychological interchanges in human systems as well as peculiarly human qualities—imagination, creativity, and unpredictability (Papp, 1984). It also represents a static value, rather than a valuing perspective for addressing therapeutic change.

As art, the major goal of marriage and family therapy is to negotiate basic perceptions so that participants see differently. Through the introduction of the novel or unexpected, a frame of reference is broken and the content of reality is rearranged. This artistic focus does not represent a solely creative act. Something is not created from nothing; rather, there is an uncovering, selection, reshuffling, combination, and synthesis of already existing facts, ideas, and skills (Gladding, 1998a). Valuing as presented in this chapter mirrors the idea of psychotherapy as an artistic endeavor.

One predominant implication of valuing for marriage and family therapists is its affirmation of marital and family relationships as pluralistic and multidimensional. As Huntley and Konetsky (1992) stated, however:

> The areas of family therapy and clinical psychology, in particular, have focused on disturbed family functioning and led professionals to look for pathology in all families and individuals. Additionally, many traits observed in families in treatment become identified as indicators of maladaptive behavior, even though these same traits are observed in people who do not need any psychological intervention. So we are presented with a dilemma. Professionals in the mental health field are looking for any signs of abnormality and are ready to interpret even normal or benign behaviors as symptoms to be treated, and we have a bias toward psychopathology because the families we observe or see in treatment are not healthy, well-adjusted families. (p. 62)

All mental health professionals have had to address in their educational and clinical training the questions of "What is normal?" and "What is abnormal?" Valuing calls for the full consideration of healthy as well as symptomatic behaviors. Dell (1983) proposed that professionals normally behave as if pathology is objective and obvious, when pathology is actually only a projection of their own values and intentions. He noted in this regard:

> When we "see" pathology as having an objective existence in the world, then we are projecting our values about how we think the world ought to be. We have shifted from, "I don't like it to be that way" (an explicit statement of personal values) to, "That's sick; that shouldn't be that way" (a statement that implies that the sickness is objective—independent of the observer's values). (p. 30)

Dell (1983) discussed a number of implications for the professional practice of marriage and family therapy that mirror those implications emanating from a valuing perspective. Four of these include the following: (a) living without objective knowledge, (b) taking personal responsibility, (c) taking responsibility for pathologizing, and (d) accepting what is.

Living Without Objective Knowledge

Dell (1983) asserted that objectivity is impossible. This is not to say, however, that human beings are passive, innocent recipients of information about the world. Rather, "the world bumps up against us and we each have our own reaction to it" (p. 31). Absolute, static values do not objectively exist. A person does not simply receive a system's values; he or she reacts to those values. Even if values did represent an objective, absolute reality, a person could not attain objective knowledge of them. Interaction can only provide one with his or her reaction to them, not how they objectively exist (Maturana, 1978). Thus, valuing represents the "bumping" together of values, with the outcome always being negotiated around any reactions to that collision. The absolute adoption of "a" value is virtually impossible.

Taking Personal Responsibility

If other systems' values cannot be taken as absolutes, then persons must realize some responsibility for their own values. Systems cannot completely determine each others' values and the manner they are acted on. For example, who is responsible for the reader's reaction to a book? The reader or the authors? Does a book determine what a reader's reaction to it will be? Both contribute, but ultimately as the age-old adage suggests, "Beauty is in the eye of the beholder." Dell (1983) referred to this as an *epistemological responsibility*.

This epistemological responsibility must be contrasted, however, with a more familiar kind of responsibility that occurs in the everyday give-and-take of human interaction. This social form of responsibility is also more active: People hold each other responsible for many different things. Valuing posits the fruitlessness of marriage and family therapists' thinking that they can take total responsibility for clients' changing their values. Both therapists and clients can present and be presented with alternatives, with their ultimate adoptions being a reflection of both; in the final analysis, they will be personal positions. However, both therapists and clients have to be held responsible for their alternatives and ultimate adoptions.

Taking Responsibility for Pathologizing

A primary illustration of the implications inherent in therapists' epistemological responsibility is the matter of "seeing pathology." If, as Dell (1983) proposed, we live without objective knowledge, then marriage and family therapists who "see" pathology are projecting certain values. He further asserted:

> We are attached to pathology, I think, because it allows us to disown responsibility for our values. We wish to imply our values are really objective or universal. I believe that many of the protests to my deconstruction of pathology originated in peoples' unwillingness to substitute the personal, "I don't like that," for the objective, "That is sick." (p. 31)

Valuing as a manner of "seeing" is represented by, "I don't like that behavior, view, emotion, and so on"—a personal reaction, rather than asserted "fact."

Accepting What Is

Dell (1983) referred to the idea of "what is, is." He took pains to assert that he was not alluding to an overly optimistic "everything is fine because everything is the way it should be," nor any fatalistic, ideological brainwashing to take no action because "what is, is." Instead, Dell described a distinction many marriage and family therapists already recognize—the difference between Murray Bowen's "taking an I-position" and not doing so. Dell described this, stating:

> If I say that I dislike something—and explicitly base my dislike on my own values (i.e., take an I-position)—then I am taking responsibility for my disliking. I am not blaming my dislike on an intrinsic wrong or sickness in the object of my dislike. By taking responsibility for my disliking, I am simultaneously accepting myself, i.e., admitting that my feelings are *mine*, and accepting that the disliked thing is the way it is. Conversely, if I were to refuse to take responsibility for how I should feel by saying, "That's sick," or, "That shouldn't be that way," then I would be refusing to accept both myself and the disliked thing. (p. 64)

From a valuing perspective, "what is, is" does not mean marriage and family therapists should take no action. It means that when marriage and family therapists do seek to change something they don't like, they should take that position from an I-position (i.e., "I don't like that") as opposed to a stance advocating objective pathology (i.e., "You're sick"). Further, "what is, is" means that on taking a position, marriage and family therapists should seek to observe what happens. If the position fails to achieve the intended result, they must identify and accept what has happened: a particular action did not achieve the desired result. For a marriage and family therapist to refuse to accept "what is, is" is to blame the thing (which he or she tried to change) for the therapist's difficulty in changing it.

VALUING COMPONENTS

Most discussions of values have tended to focus on content as opposed to process. For example, marriage and family therapists have been urged to be intimately aware of personal and professional values associated with divorce, dual careers, birth control, sexual dysfunction, abortion, child rearing, extramarital affairs, sex roles, and child and spouse abuse (Bird & Sporakowski, 1992; Margolin, 1982; Seymour, 1982). The content of values is obviously important and cannot be ignored. As noted throughout this chapter, however, values all too often are represented as static stances construed as right or wrong. Valuing proposes that values, the beliefs and resultant actions they encompass, should regularly be reconsidered, reclarified, and renegotiated.

Ivan Boszormenyi-Nagy and his colleagues have been in contrast to those who have predominantly addressed the content of values in marriage and family therapy. They have framed their process-oriented discussions in the context of ethical accountability, stressing that satisfying family relationships requires ethical behavior among family members, that is, consideration of each other's welfare and interests. In describing a type of therapy, Contextual Family Therapy, family members are facilitated in addressing relational commitments and balances of fairness (Boszormenyi-Nagy & Ulrich, 1981). The aim of the approach is a loosening of static values so family members become better able to shift their intentions and interactions toward more satisfying life experiences. What occurs is the development of a greater balance of fairness.

The ethical dimensions centering Contextual Family Therapy represent process-oriented elements of equal utility. Employed as *valuing components*, reconciliation of issues of concern can be facilitated. Regardless of the content of values, the use of these process-oriented components allows valuing to generalize to any specific issue arising in marriage and family therapy.

Obligation and Entitlement

Valuing begins with a recognition of two primary components: the mutual obligations and entitlements within all relationships. These components have been frequently minimized, overlooked, or contested in the professional literature. For example:

> I do my thing and you do your thing.
> I am not in this world to live up to your expectations.
> And you are not in this world to live up to mine.
> You are you and I am I.
> And if by chance we find each other, it's beautiful.

This "Gestalt Prayer," originated by Frederick Perls, represents an overt statement of a value that permeates much of professional therapeutic practice. It is derived from a recognition that many personal and interpersonal problems appear to emanate from destructive and unrealistic obligations in relationships. Consequently, freedom from obligations is sought. Although the intention may be freedom from only *destructive* obligations, the implication in practice has often resulted in encouraging persons to free themselves from all obligations (Karpel & Strauss, 1983).

This focus on retreating from relationships with destructive obligations offers little to describe how persons might move back into more or less satisfying, nondestructive relationships. People should take responsibility for themselves instead of trying to get others to take responsibility for their lives, but much of what individuals find important in their lives depends on the willingness of people to assume some responsibility for one another.

Karpel and Strauss (1983) expounded on the work of Boszormenyi-Nagy and his colleagues in describing a vocabulary to better comprehend the underlying structure of balanced, fair, mutually satisfying, growth-producing relationships. Karpel and Strauss asserted the inherent presence of obligations in relationships, emphasizing that not all obligations are destructive. They further offered the following illustrations:

- A wife is grateful for her husband's having gone out of his way to purchase something she wanted. She, in turn, offers to make a phone call both of them have been avoiding.
- An adolescent boy feels sad at having made fun of his younger sister in front of her peers. He apologizes to her and offers to let her use his previously off-limits record player.
- A young man with severe diabetes feels indebted, literally, for his life, to his sister who donated one of her kidneys for a transplant operation.
- A man feels a sense of debt to his parents for the physical and emotional support they offered him in building the satisfying, productive life he has come to enjoy.

These illustrations all involve at least one person's obligation based either on the *merit* of the other person (depending on his or her helpful actions or sacrifices) or the *debt* of the person (contingent on his or her actions having in some way harmed the other). This valuing component for achieving a balance of fairness relative to obligation is called *entitlement*. Obligation and entitlement represent the ends of a valuing continuum. If it is agreed that one is obliged to another, there follows an agreement that the other is entitled to something.

In any relationship, recognition of obligations and entitlements constantly fluctuates. Fulfilling obligations results in decreasing one's own obligations, yet simultaneously increasing one's entitlement as well as the obligations of others. Ignoring obligations tends to increase one's obligations as well as others' entitlement. "Give and take" underlies most of the valuing process.

Acknowledgment and Claim

Closely related to obligation and entitlement are acknowledgment and claim. *Acknowledgment* refers to "the willingness of one party in a relationship to recognize and 'give credit for' the entitlement of the other" (Karpel & Strauss, 1983, p. 34). Acknowledgment calls for a willingness to seek a balance of fairness in a relationship. Withholding acknowledgment in a relationship creates an imbalance. This is so even when such withholding is preceded by a refusal to provide acknowledgment. This second refusal only compounds the initial imbalance. Two examples illustrate withholding of acknowledgment:

- An elderly couple anticipate and make daily reference to their son's upcoming visit from his distant home. The weekly visits of their daughter who lives locally, however, are ignored or minimized.
- Two young children's efforts to clean up the kitchen receive ridicule and rebuke from their parents when some dishes are accidentally broken in the process.

Resentment and bitterness tend to be evoked by withholding acknowledgment. The likelihood of an in-kind response (concurrent withholding of acknowledgment by the opposite party) is thus increased. Mutual accusation, deafness, mistrust, and stagnation characterize such situations.

Acknowledgment is paired with claim on a valuing continuum for seeking a balance of fairness. *Claim* refers to "one person's asking for something from the other" (Karpel & Strauss, 1983, p. 35). Examples of claims include the following:

- A woman postpones completing her graduate degree program so she can work to provide income for the family while her husband pursues his professional education. She now requests that the husband assume a greater child-rearing and bread-winning burden so she can complete her own professional educational objectives.
- A single parent, who has provided well for her two teenage children in the past, is temporarily unemployed. She asks that they contribute a portion of their earnings from part-time jobs to support the running of the household during this time of financial crisis.

Claims are not inherently valid. Persons frequently do make unwarranted claims in relationships. Therefore, the willingness of one party to capitulate to unilateral, excessive claims can be as harmful to a relationship as an unwillingness to consider any claims (Karpel & Strauss, 1983).

Balance of Fairness

In an ideal sense, beneficial valuing within, between, or among persons is that outcome wherein entitlement/obligation and acknowledgment/claim stand in relative balance with each other. There is a balance of fairness. Of course, no perfect, static balance can exist. Any balance of fairness achieved through valuing efforts can and will be altered by a variety of factors. One person may momentarily refuse to acknowledge the contributions of others. His or her entitlement to an acknowledgment may have been inadvertently ignored. Involved parties may have to redefine what they consider a balance of fairness if circumstances drastically alter the entitlement of one or more of them, for example, if one family member becomes seriously injured in an auto accident.

Pursuing a balance of fairness through valuing involves ongoing efforts to consider mutual obligations and entitlements and to make realistic acknowledgments and claims. There is no perfect continuing parity. Seeking a balance of fairness thus requires commitment by all involved to try to correct imbalances. Boszormenyi-Nagy and Ulrich (1981) referred to this as *rejunction*—persons connecting with each other for the purpose of rebalancing fairness in their relationships. This may take the form of willingness to sit in a room together to reassess certain of their values, to surface claims, and to hear one another's sides. This may also call for an acknowledgment of the sacrifice or merit of others, admitting to an obligation (and therefore acknowledging the legitimacy of others' claims) or taking the factors that may limit others' ability to acknowl-edge certain claims more seriously (e.g., a strong obligation to another relation-ship, such as a newly married child's significant obligations to his or her new spouse).

In seeking a balance of fairness through valuing, the question often arises, "Who is to say what is fair and what is unfair?" The answer is rarely simple. Karpel and Strauss (1983) suggested several guidelines to make this determina-tion more manageable. They first asserted the importance of accepting that final word on what constitutes fairness and unfairness in a particular relationship comes from those who are directly involved in the relationship. There are no objective, external criteria to compare against. The only factor that might be introduced is an asserted effort to reassess the balance of fairness. This is not a fixed code with universal application; rather, it is an interchange during which involved members can seek movement toward in the context of the specifics of their relationship. This process is facilitated by asking questions that encourage the consideration of obligations and entitlements and statements of acknowledg-ment and claim.

The process of give-and-take that this common examination requires—assert-ing and considering claims, seeking to see another's side, and presenting one's own side—marks the beginning and the most important part of valuing aimed at achieving a balance of fairness. Frequently, this balance is gained in ways quite different from what might have been expected. This is natural because only the participants can truly gauge the meaning of events and considerations for them-selves, and even these assessments may significantly change as new factors are introduced into ongoing interactions (Karpel & Strauss, 1983).

A second guideline identified by Karpel and Strauss (1983) for arriving at a balance of fairness involves what they referred to as *realistic accountability*. This concept suggests the greatest benefits for all members in a relationship as being derived from mutual efforts to carry out reasonable obligations without either shortchanging others or paying excessively or destructively. Realistic accountability encourages persons neither to ignore their entitlement nor to tol-erate unreasonable obligations, but rather to look for ways to balance entitle-ment and obligation. In this sense, realistic accountability proposes that people face obligations in relationships but also puts some ceiling on how much they will ask of themselves and how much they will tolerate being asked by others. The height of the ceiling will be determined by involved members' consideration of obligations and entitlements in the context of their present situation.

Realistic accountability applies equally to all members in a relationship. Thus, a ceiling also exists on the extent to which others can be held accountable. An elderly parent may, for example, desire perfect or total accountability from his or her adult children but should also consider the limitations, lack of resources, and other problems the children face. Put simply, one needs to recognize the impor-tance of judging others' beliefs and actions by the same standard of accountability by which one judges one's own.

SUMMARY AND CONCLUSIONS

Valuing has significant implications for the professional therapeutic practice of marriage and family therapy. Valuing is a means by which marriage and family therapists can maintain a systemic worldview while incorporating challenges to it within an evolving epistemology. Practice implications of valuing, as well as specific valuing components, have been discussed.

Valuing represents a process similar to that suggested by students of ethnicity: Respect for ethnicity involves initial acceptance of cultural differences, polite exploration of those differences, and subtle explanations of how a given ethnic group's customs differ from the larger culture. The marriage and family therapist assumes the role of "culture broker," helping couples and families negotiate the traditional values they wish to retain and discard (McGoldrick, Giordano, Pearce, & Giordano, 1996). With respect to gender issues, Pittman (1985) advocates that marriage and family therapists assume a parallel role as "gender brokers":

> As a gender broker, I show initial respect for each person's efforts in playing out the gender role they have been taught, as well as sympathy for the difficulties and limitations they encounter in doing so. I try to make these people aware that they have choices about how and whether they will play out their gender stereotypes, and I am determined that they will get an equal voice in that choice. While I am personally uncomfortable with some of the arrangements my patients choose, I try to make sure that gender issues will never again go unquestioned in their relationship. And, I try to help them realize that whether someone is male or female does not mean that they must be Masculine or Feminine. (p. 31)

The essence of marriage and family therapy as a professional therapeutic practice from this perspective is to participate with persons in relationships so that their interactions within themselves and with each other can move in directions they prefer. The focus of marriage and family therapists is to find out what their clients are trying to conserve, and participate in their attempts to conserve it while seeking to maintain that balance of fairness necessary for more satisfying experiences.

Efran and Lukens (1985) propose that marriage and family therapists do not give "treatment"—something applied like a mudpack—to a waiting, passive organism. They referred to Kelly (1955), who warned against the term *patient*, implying someone who sits patiently, waiting for something to happen or something to be done to him or her. Efran and Lukens stated:

> Families do not *start* changing at the therapist's office. They are always changing, and the visit to the therapist's office is simply the next step in their process. . . . It is arrogant of us to think that we "control" other people's lives. Even court-adjudicated cases and other so-called "unwilling" clients cannot be sold anything against their will. Because people's structures keep changing as we spend time interacting with them, it seems to us as though they bought something from us that was incompatible with their beliefs. What was bought may have originally been incompatible, but at the point of sale, by definition, there could not have been an incongruity. Neither salespeople nor therapists *ever* sell their customers anything they do not want. To buy is to want. (1985, p. 72)

Professional Identity as a Marriage and Family Therapist

Professional identity is a process that evolves. In family therapy, a survey study on developmental stages in achieving a competent sense of self as a family therapist was conducted by Kral and Hines (1999). They found empirical evidence supporting D. Friedman and Kaslow's (1986) six-stage developmental model for gaining an identity as a competent family therapist. The entire process took about 5 years.

In stage 1, anticipation, new therapists learn they will be working with clients and supervisors. In stage 2, dependency, novice therapists depend on supervisors for answers. In stage 3, new therapists demonstrate continued dependence on supervisors for answers with some movement toward independence. Stage 4 marks a major transition and is characterized by new therapists' taking charge of therapy sessions; this leads to stage 5, which involves therapists' developing a sense of independence and identity. The last stage is characterized by a sense of calm and congeniality. The point is that identity as a marriage and family therapist takes times and is sequential.

This developmental sequencing of identity has not always been viewed as a part of marriage and family therapy. In fact, the advent of marriage and family therapy was initially viewed as simply another means of treating problems and was not radically different from individual approaches (M. P. Nichols & Schwartz, 2001). Thus, identifying oneself as a marriage and family therapist in the beginning days of the profession did not require a radical change in identity for those who practiced it from any previous therapeutic identity they embraced. The individual was still the client, although treated in a couple or family setting (Okun & Rappaport, 1980). Marital partners, for example, were seen separately to deal with their individual concerns. This perspective and way of working emanated from the dominant epistemological perspective of the time, which was linear in nature.

However, marriage and family therapy changed in the late 1960s and 1970s (Atwood, 1992; W. C. Nichols, 1992). It became and remains a new way of defining a problem and working through it. The "client" and the "problem" are not the individual alone, but include the client's marital, familial, or social context. This more comprehensive concept calls for a redefinition of fundamental beliefs, as well as an expanded epistemology to consider the dynamics of evolving systems, not simply the vicissitudes of individual rights (L'Abate, 1982). Marriage and family approaches generally give attention to relationship dynamics in diagnosis and share similar therapeutic goals (Gladding, 1998b; Liddle, 1991b; Olson, Russell, & Sprenkle, 1980). They are primarily systemic in their epistemological perspective.

In this chapter, we examine several major issues relating to professional identity as a marriage and family therapist, including professional affiliation, state licensure and marriage and family therapy, promoting professional identity through research, and associated pragmatic concerns. First, however, we consider the continuing debate relative to whether marriage and family therapy is a profession or a professional specialty.

PROFESSION OR PROFESSIONAL SPECIALIZATION?

Marriage and family therapy initially was and continues to be considered by some as an area of specialization within other professional disciplines. This view is reflected vividly in the professional association membership of practitioners espousing marriage and family therapy. Many therapists who practice marriage and family therapy subscribe their allegiance to the American Association for Marriage and Family Therapy (AAMFT). However, many others identify primarily with professional associations representing psychiatry, psychology, social work, and counseling: the American Psychiatric Association, the American Psychological Association, the National Association of Social Workers, and the American Counseling Association (Atwood, 1992). These latter groups maintain that marriage and family therapy is a therapeutic modality, a professional specialization, within psychiatry, psychology, social work, or counseling. This is a continuing and important debate, because the way marriage and family therapy is conceptualized influences the practice of the profession (Canfield & Locke, 1991). (See Figure 9–1.)

Marriage and Family Therapy as a Separate and Distinct Profession

Those who believe marriage and family therapy is a separate and distinct profession stress that it has clearly acquired those characteristics that are hallmarks of a profession unto itself (Winkle, Piercy, & Hovestadt, 1981). Ard and Ard (1976) were among the earliest to assert this position:

> Marriage and family counseling is a profession . . . with a scientific body of knowledge, some relevant theory, a code of ethics, and some specific techniques. (p. xv)

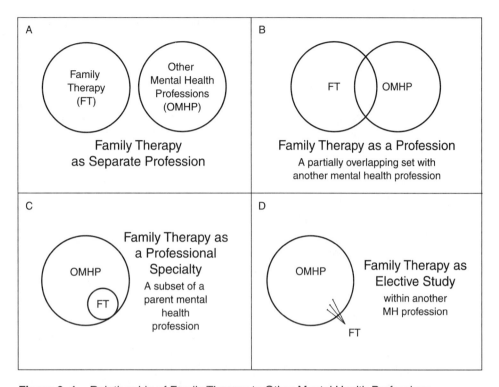

Figure 9–1　Relationship of Family Therapy to Other Mental Health Professions

Note. From "Family Therapy as a Profession or Professional Specialty: Implications for Training," by D. L. Fenell and A. J. Hovestadt, 1986, *Journal of Psychotherapy and the Family, 1* (4). © Copyright 1986. Reprinted with permission.

Since the late 1970s, this view and the data supporting it have significantly broadened. For instance, in a March 1998 public opinion telephone interview conducted by the AAMFT, 6 in 10 respondents polled disagreed with the statement that "any mental health professional can conduct marriage and family therapy" (AAMFT, 1998c, p. 5). Furthermore, almost 9 of 10 respondents were of the opinion that "it is important for mental health professionals who work with couples and families to have a special license to practice marriage and family therapy" (p. 5).

Those who voice the opinion that marriage and family therapy is a distinct profession see marriage and family therapy as an independently identifiable entity, a "sibling" to psychiatry, psychology, social work, and counseling. The growth in membership and influence of the AAMFT and the development of educational and training standards and formal accreditation of programs promoting to these standards is one indication that marriage and family therapy is a distinct profession. Legislative efforts creating government-regulated licensing and research showing the efficacy of marriage and family therapy as a profession are additional indicators of its distinction (Bowers, 1992a). As Haley (1984) asserted:

> The issue of whether to organize the family therapy field has been resolved. This organization [AAMFT] has accomplished that. . . . All of us face the accomplished fact that the field is organized and ready for the benefits that follow to those who belong to the club. A certain point is reached, as in nuclear fission, when the outcome is inevitable. As therapists join an organization and are licensed, other therapists must do the same to compete. The supervisors and teachers come under pressure to be properly approved, or their trainees cannot share in the financial benefits of membership. (p. 12)

Marriage and Family Therapy as a Professional Specialization

Those who view marriage and family therapy as a professional specialization hold that marriage and family therapy is a special way of providing mental health service but in and of itself is not a profession. They point out the prevailing majority of professionals practicing marriage and family therapy received their education as psychiatrists, psychologists, social workers, counselors, ministers, or nurses. They also note the fact that these practitioners maintain membership in well-established professional associations having a distinct identity (not in marriage and family therapy organizations). Furthermore, members of these associations clearly identify marriage and family therapy as a professional specialization through division membership within their parent association (e.g., Division 43 Family Psychology within the American Psychological Association; the International Association of Marriage and Family Counselors within the American Counseling Association).

Introducing additional ambiguity into this overall debate is the fact that the AAMFT, although advocating marriage and family therapy as a separate and distinct profession, has prided itself and continues to pride itself on its multidisciplinary membership (Bowers, 1992a). This fact was revealed vividly in a 1988 survey of training directors and clinical members of AAMFT that found that only slightly more than half (51.8%) "believed that marital and family therapy should be treated as a separate discipline" (Keller, Huber, & Hardy, 1988, p. 304). Likewise, most professional journals whose focus is marriage and family therapy, including *Family Process* (the oldest), are interdisciplinary in editorship, authorship, and subscribership.

Bowers (1992a) suggests that the "marketability" of marriage and family therapy is an important element in its evolution as an identifiable profession:

> In the last decade, MFT has become a much more marketable service. As it has gained more acceptance, others, with relatively little history in defining or promulgating standards for the field, have begun to claim it in some way as their own—arguing, in effect, that no independent discipline of MFT exists. How these tensions are resolved, regarding both standards and "ownership" of the field, will be largely determinative of the identity and scope of MFT in the next generation. (p. 18)

Following from this point, it may be that this issue is already being resolved as a "both–and." For example, "freedom of choice" legislation, such as that passed in

Connecticut, mandates specifically marriage and family therapists as being on a par with other mental health providers regarding third-party reimbursement for services (Strong, 1992).

PROFESSIONAL AFFILIATION

One criterion that identifies a profession is that it is self-regulating. Established professions are identified as such because they have developed standards and policies that, to some degree, control entry into the profession, prescribe training standards, and establish procedures and requirements for membership and practice. Professions develop ethical codes that outline standards of service, prescribe members' appropriate relationships to each other and the general public, and identify proper and improper practice. The AAMFT is the organization that highlights marriage and family as a separate and distinct profession. It is described along with three associations that recognize and promote marriage and family therapy as a professional specialization: the American Family Therapy Association (AFTA), Division 43 Family Psychology of the American Psychological Association, and the International Association of Marriage and Family Counselors (IAMFC) of the American Counseling Association.

American Association for Marriage and Family Therapy

The AAMFT had its beginnings in 1942. Originally called the American Association of Marriage Counselors, it was renamed the American Association of Marriage and Family Counselors in 1970 and then in 1979 became the American Association for Marriage and Family Therapy. During most of its existence, the AAMFT has consisted primarily of psychiatrists, social workers, psychologists, and counselors who received degrees in their own specific discipline and then sought master's or doctoral training in marriage and family therapy (W. C. Nichols, 1992). As marriage and family therapy came to be promoted as a separate and distinct profession and relevant training programs at universities were established, an increasing number of members began to receive terminal degrees specifically in marriage and family therapy (Kosinski, 1982).

From its inception, the AAMFT has been active in promoting rigorous standards for gaining and maintaining professional affiliation. Clinical membership calls for the completion of a master's or doctoral degree from a regionally accredited educational institution, or an equivalent course of study. This has been interpreted to mean the completion of a course of study substantially equivalent to the courses described here (AAMFT, 1990):

- *Marital and Family Studies* (three courses minimum). Family development and family interaction patterns across the life cycle of the individual as well as the family.

- *Marital and Family Therapy* (three courses minimum). Family therapy methodology; family assessment; treatment and intervention methods; overview of major clinical theories of marital and family therapy.
- *Human Development* (three courses minimum). Human development, personality theory, human sexuality, psychopathology; behavior-pathology.
- *Professional Studies* (one course minimum). Professional socialization and the role of the professional organization; legal responsibilities and liabilities; independent practice and interprofessional cooperation; ethics; family law.
- *Research* (one course minimum). Research design; methods, statistics, research in marital and family studies and therapy.
- *Clinical Practicum* (1 year, 300 hours). Fifteen hours per week, approximately 8 to 10 hours in face-to-face contact with individuals, couples, and families for the purpose of assessment, diagnosis, and treatment.

This course of study can be completed with or after obtaining a master's or doctoral degree. Individuals who have completed a graduate degree from a program accredited by the Commission on Accreditation for Marriage and Family Therapy Education (COAMFTE) are considered to have completed all educational requirements by virtue of their degree.

Clinical membership also calls for 2 calendar years of supervised professional work experience in marital and family therapy. This experiential requirement is in addition to the supervised clinical practice secured as part of the academic requirements. It requires at least 1,000 hours of direct clinical contact with couples and families and 200 hours of supervision of that work, at least 100 of which shall be in individual supervision. Also, this supervision must be provided by AAMFT-approved supervisors or supervisors acceptable to the AAMFT Membership Committee. Individuals who have completed programs accredited by the COAMFTE may be credited with all clinical contact and supervision completed during their program, provided they have met the aforementioned requirements.

Persons holding a state-issued marriage and family therapy license or certificate recognized by the AAMFT Board of Directors and a graduate degree recognized by their respective state for the licensure or certification are recognized as having met the educational and clinical experience qualifications for clinical membership.

Finally, written endorsement by two Clinical Members of the AAMFT attesting to suitable qualities of personal maturity and integrity for the conduct of marriage and family therapy, are further necessary to complete the basic clinical membership requirements. The AAMFT also maintains associate, student, and affiliate membership categories with lesser requirements than for individuals pursuing clinical membership.

Concurrent with a focus on maintaining high standards for membership, the AAMFT has emphasized the importance of quality training and supervision opportunities in marriage and family therapy. To this end, the AAMFT Board of Directors established standards for marriage and family therapy supervision in 1971.

The Commission on Supervision (now the Supervision Committee), established in 1983, regulates requirements for approved supervisor designation within the AAMFT. The approved supervisor is one who has received advanced recognition for clinical skills, special training, and experience in the supervision of prospective marriage and family therapists, and who meets the highest standards of clinical education and practice. Approved supervisors are recognized as competent to provide supervision to students and potential members of the AAMFT as they seek to fulfill their Clinical Member requirements.

Three tracks are available to gain an approved supervisor designation, each with specific requirements (American Association for Marriage and Family Therapy, Supervision Committee, 1999). Depending on their qualifications, individuals may select the following:

- *The Standard Track* is for marriage and family therapists with limited or no experience as a supervisor.
- *The COAMFTE-Accredited Doctorate Track* is for those who are currently enrolled in doctoral programs accredited by the AAMFT COAMFTE.
- *The Advanced Track* is for individuals with extensive experience in marriage and family therapy, training, and supervision.

The majority of individuals applying for the approved supervisor designation do so under the Standard Track (American Association for Marriage and Family Therapy, 1997). The major requirements for this track include the following criteria that are elaborated on at the AAMFT Web site:

http://www.aamft.org/about/asrequire.htm

- Accumulated 2,000 hours of post–master's marriage and family therapy experience
- Earned a qualifying graduate degree in a mental health discipline from a regionally accredited institution
- Have Clinical Membership in AAMFT or demonstrate equivalency
- Provided at least 180 hours of marriage and family therapy supervision over a minimum period of 18 months and a maximum of 2 years
- Received at least 36 hours of supervision from an AAMFT-Approved Supervisor within 18 months to 2 years
- Completed a one-semester graduate course in marriage and family therapy supervision (at least 30 contact hours) or the equivalent
- Provided at least 3,000 hours of post–master's marriage and family therapy over a minimum of 3 years by the time of application for the Approved Supervisor designation

In addition to the Supervision Committee regulating approved supervisors, the AAMFT sponsors the COAMFTE. The commission serves under a broad mandate from the AAMFT Board of Directors to set standards for and accredit graduate and postdegree clinical training programs in marriage and family therapy. The following represent some of the primary ways in which the commission accomplishes this purpose (Commission on Accreditation for Marriage and Family Therapy Education, 1997):

- Establishes criteria and standards for accreditation
- Provides guidance to programs, preparing self-study reports for candidacy, accreditation, or for renewal of accreditation
- Appoints site visit teams, schedules and conducts visits, as well as considers and evaluates the report of visiting teams
- Arranges for review and appeal when a program believes it has cause to challenge its accreditation status
- Accredits training programs in marriage and family therapy
- Maintains contact with programs relative to their accreditation status, and takes note of substantive changes in programs that might affect accreditation
- Conducts special inquiries into unusual or critical conditions that may develop in an accredited program
- Endeavors to stimulate and promote continued improvement of educational programs

In 1978, the COAMFTE gained official recognition as an accrediting agency for graduate degree and postdegree clinical training programs in marriage and family therapy by the U.S. Office of Education, Department of Health, Education, and Welfare. Since that time, the U.S. Department of Education has continued its recognition of the Commission (Commission on Accreditation for Marriage and Family Therapy Education, 1997).

The COAMFTE's accrediting role is uncommon among bodies recognized by the Department of Education in that it accredits not only university-based degree-granting programs but also "free-standing" postdegree training centers (Shalett & Everett, 1981). These postdegree programs have a unique roll in offering an alternative entry into the marriage and family profession. Ordinarily, the master's degree program is recognized as the entry level into the profession by providing broad theoretical knowledge, basic applied skills, and professional attitudes. The doctoral degree is viewed as offering mastery of further comprehensive theory, advanced supervised practice, basic skills and practice in research, and potential experience in teaching and supervision. The postdegree programs have traditionally offered intensive supervised practice with ongoing didactic seminars for individuals who have already attained allied clinical degrees and are seeking specialized training in marriage and family therapy. As of June 2000, 53 master's degree programs, 17 doctoral degree programs, and 19 postdegree clinical training institutes had been awarded accreditation or were candidates for accreditation by the COAMFTE. These programs are listed in Table 9–1. For the latest update on program accreditation, consult the AAMFT Web site:

http://www.aamft.org/resources/coamfte.htm

Table 9–1 COAMFTE Accredited and Candidacy Status Programs

ALABAMA
Auburn University (M.S.)
Connie Salts, Ph.D.
Human Development and Family Studies
School of Human Sciences
203 Spidle Hall
Auburn, AL 36849
Phone: (334) 844-4478
Fax: (334) 844-1924
E-mail: csalts@humsci.auburn.edu
Next Review Date: 01/01/06

ARKANSAS
Harding University (M.S.-Candidacy)
Lewis L. Moore, Ph.D.
Department of Marriage and Family
  Therapy
College of Bible and Religion
Box 2262
Searcy, AR 72149-0001
Phone: (501) 279-4347
Fax: (501) 279-4042
Next Review Date: 07/01/00

CALIFORNIA
Fuller Theological Seminary (M.S.)
Judith Balswick, Ed.D.
Division of Marriage and Family
Graduate School of Psychology
180 North Oakland Avenue
Pasadena, CA 91182
Phone: (626) 584-5330
Fax: (626) 792-7259
Next Review Date: 07/01/04

Loma Linda University (M.S.)
Mary Moline, Ph.D.
Marriage and Family Therapy Program
Department of Counseling and Family
  Sciences
Loma Linda, CA 92350
Phone: (909) 824-4547
Next Review Date: 01/01/04

University of San Diego (M.A.)
Joellen Patterson, Ph.D.
Marriage, Family and Child Counseling
  Program
School of Education
Alcala Park
San Diego, CA 92110
Phone: (619) 260-4538
Fax: (619) 260-6835
E-mail: joellen@acusd.edu
Next Review Date: 07/01/04

University of Southern California (Ph.D.)
Constance Ahrons, Ph.D.
Department of Sociology
College of Letters, Arts and Sciences
Los Angeles, CA 90089-0032
Phone: (213) 743-2137
Fax: (213) 740-3535
E-mail: ahrons@mizar.usc.edu
Next Review Date: 01/01/01

Southern California Counseling Center
  (Post-Graduate)
Nancy T. Steiny, M.A., M.F.T.
5615 West Pico Boulevard
Los Angeles, CA 90019
Phone: (213) 937-1344
Fax: (213) 937-3487
Next Review Date: 01/01/04

United States International University
  (M.A. and Psy.D.-Candidacy)
Scott Woolley, Ph.D.
Marriage and Family Therapy Program
Department of Psychology and Family
  Studies
College of Arts and Sciences
San Diego, CA 92131
Phone: (858) 635-4772
Fax: (858) 635-4585
E-mail: swoolley@usiu.edu
Next Review Date: 01/01/03 (M.A.);
  01/01/03 (Psy.D.)

Table 9–1 *continued*

COLORADO
Colorado State University (M.S.)
Toni Zimmerman, Ph.D.
Marriage and Family Therapy Program
Department of Human Development
  and Family Studies
College of Applied Human Sciences
Fort Collins, CO 80523
Phone: (970) 491-6922
Fax: (970) 491-7975
E-mail: zimmerman@cahs.colostate.edu
Next Review Date: 01/01/06

Family Therapy Training Center of Colorado,
  Inc. (Post-Graduate-Candidacy)
Steve Litt, L.C.S.W., A.C.S.W.
7200 East Hampden Avenue
Suite 301
Denver, CO 80224
Phone: (303) 756-3340
Fax: (303) 758-6140
E-mail: swlitt@aol.com
Next Review Date: 07/01/00

CONNECTICUT
Central Connecticut State University
  (M.S.)
Ralph S. Cohen, Ph.D.
Marriage and Family Therapy Program
Department of Health and Human Service
  Professions
School of Education and Professional Studies
1615 Stanley Street
New Britain, CT 06050-4010
Phone: (860) 832-2122
Fax: (860) 832-2109
E-mail: cohenr@ccsua.ctstateu.edu
Next Review Date: 01/01/03

University of Connecticut (M.A. and Ph.D.)
Robert G. Ryder, Ph.D.
School of Family Studies
U-58, 348 Mansfield Road
Storrs, CT 06269
Phone: (860) 486-4721
Fax: (860) 486-3452
Next Review Date: 07/01/00 (M.A.);
  07/01/03 (Ph.D.)

Fairfield University (M.A.)
Rona Preli, Ph.D.
Graduate School of Education and
  Allied Professions
Marriage and Family Therapy Program
North Benson Road
Fairfield, CT 06430
Phone: (203) 254-4000, x2475
Fax: (203) 254-4119
E-mail: rpreli@fair1.fairfield.edu
Next Review Date: 07/01/00

Saint Joseph College (M.A.)
Catherine K. Kikoski, Ed.D.
Marriage and Family Therapy Program
1678 Asylum Avenue
West Hartford, CT 06117
Phone: (860) 231-5324
Fax: (860) 233-5695
E-mail: ckikoski@mercy.sjc.edu
Next Review Date: 07/01/05

Southern Connecticut State University
  (M.S.)
Barbara Lynch, M.S.
Marriage and Family Therapy Program
501 Crescent Street
New Haven, CT 06515
Phone: (203) 392-6415
Fax: (203) 392-6441
E-mail: familyclinic@scsu.ctstateu.edu
Next Review Date: 07/01/03

FLORIDA
Florida State University (Ph.D.)
Mary Hicks, Ph.D.
Interdivisional Program in Marriage and
  the Family
Department of Family and Child
  Sciences
College of Human Sciences
Sandels 103
Call Street
Tallahassee, FL 32306-4097
Phone: (850) 644-1588
Fax: (850) 644-4804
E-mail: mhicks@mailer.fsu.edu
Next Review Date: 01/01/05

Gainesville Family Institute (Post-Graduate)
Andres Nazario, Jr., Ph.D.
Center for Couples and Family
    Development
CCFD Training Program
1031 N.W. 6th Street, Suite C-2
Gainesville, FL 32601
Phone: (352) 376-5543
Fax: (352) 376-2042
E-mail: ccfdngfi@afn.org
Next Review Date: 01/01/04

Nova Southeastern University (M.S.)
Margo Weiss, Ph.D.
Department of Family Therapy
School of Social and Systemic Studies
3301 College Avenue
Fort Lauderdale, FL 33314
Phone: (954) 262-3000
Fax: (954) 262-3968
E-mail: margo@nsu.acast.nova.edu
Next Review Date: 07/01/02

GEORGIA
University of Georgia (Ph.D.)
Jerry Gale, Ph.D.
Marriage and Family Therapy Program
Department of Child and Family
    Development
College of Family and Consumer Sciences
Dawson Hall
Athens, GA 30602
Phone: (706) 542-8435
Fax: (706) 542-4862
E-mail: jgale@hestia.fcs.uga.edu
Next Review Date: 07/01/03

Mercer University (M.F.T.-Candidacy)
Lee Bowen, Ph.D.
Marriage and Family Therapy Program
Department of Psychiatry and Behavioral
    Sciences
School of Medicine
1508 College St.
Macon, GA 31207-0001
Phone: (912) 752-4098
Fax: (912) 752-5337
Next Review Date: 01/01/03

ILLINOIS
Advocate-Family Care Network
    (Post-Graduate)
Christopher J. Higgins, Psy.D.
Marriage and Family Therapy Training
    Program
4440 West 95th Street
Oak Lawn, IL 60453
Phone: (708) 346-5169
Fax: (708) 499-5062
Next Review Date: 01/01/03

Family Institute at Northwestern University
    (Post-Graduate)
Linda Rubinowitz, Ph.D.
618 Library Place
Evanston, IL 60201
Phone: (847) 733-4300, x610
Fax: (847) 733-0390
E-mail: lrubin@nwu.edu
Next Review Date: 01/01/06

Northern Illinois University (M.S.)
Brent Atkinson, Ph.D.
Department of Human and Family
    Resources
209 Wirtz Hall
Dekalb, IL 60115
Phone: (815) 753-6349
Fax: (815) 753-1321
E-mail: bja@niu.edu
Next Review Date: 01/01/03

INDIANA
Christian Theological Seminary (M.A.)
Brian Grant, Ph.D.
Marriage and Family Therapy Program
1000 West 42nd Street
Indianapolis, IN 46208
Phone: (317) 924-5205
Fax: (317) 931-2393
E-mail: bgrant@cts.edu
Next Review Date: 07/01/05

Table 9–1 *continued*

Indiana State University (M.S.)
Reece Cheney, Ph.D.
Marriage and Family Therapy Program
Department of Counseling
Se 1511
Terre Haute, IN 47809
Phone: (812) 237-2868
Fax: (812) 237-4348
E-mail: egchane@befac.indstate.edu
Next Review Date: 01/01/01

Purdue University (Ph.D.)
Fred Piercy, Ph.D.
Marriage and Family Therapy Program
Department of Child Development and
   Family Studies
School of Consumer and Family
   Sciences
1269 Fowler House
West Lafayette, IN 47907
Phone: (765) 494-2950
Fax: (765) 494-0543
E-mail: piercy@purdue.edu
Next Review Date: 01/01/01

Purdue University-Calumet (M.S.)
Joseph L. Wetchler, Ph.D.
Marriage and Family Therapy
   Program
Department of Behavioral Sciences
Hammond, IN 46323-2094
Phone: (219) 989-2319
Fax: (219) 989-2777
Next Review Date: 01/01/05

IOWA
Iowa State University (Ph.D.)
Harvey Joaning, Ph.D.
Marriage and Family Therapy Program
College of Family and Consumer
   Sciences
Department of Human Development and
   Family Studies
101 Child Development Building
Ames, IA 50011-1120
Phone: (515) 294-5215
E-mail: joaning@iastate.edu
Next Review Date: 07/01/00

KANSAS
Friends University (M.S.)
Daniel R. Lord, Ph.D.
Marriage and Family Therapy Program
2100 University
Wichita, KS 67213
Phone: (316) 295-5617
Fax: (316) 262-1998
E-mail: dlord@friends.edu
Next Review Date: 01/01/05

Kansas State University (M.S. and Ph.D.)
Mark White, Ph.D.
Marriage and Family Therapy Program
School of Family Studies and Human
   Services
Justin Hall
Manhattan, KS 66506
Phone: (785) 532-1487
Fax: (785) 532-5505
Next Review Date: 01/01/03 (M.S.);
   01/03/03 (Ph.D.)

KENTUCKY
University of Kentucky (M.S.)
Gregory Brock, Ph.D.
Marriage and Family Therapy
Program
Department of Family Studies
315 Funkhouser Building
Lexington, KY 40506-0054
Phone: (606) 257-7750
Fax: (606) 257-4095
E-mail: gwbrock@pop.uky.edu
Next Review Date: 01/01/01

University of Louisville (MSSW-
   Candidacy and Post-Graduate)
Suzanne Midori Hanna, Ph.D.
Family Therapy Program
Kent School of Social Work
Gardiner Hall, Room 304
Louisville, KY 40292
Phone: (502) 852-8793
Fax: (502) 852-4598
E-mail: sohann01@homer.louisville.edu
Next Review Date: 01/03/03 (M.S.S.W.);
   01/01/05 (P.D.I.)

Louisville Presbyterian Theological Seminary (M.A.)
Loren L. Townsend, Ph.D.
Marriage and Family Therapy Program
1044 Alta Vista Road
Louisville, KY 40205
Phone: (502) 895-3411
Fax: (502) 895-1096
E-mail: ltownsend@lpts.edu
Next Review Date: 07/01/04

LOUISIANA

Northeast Louisiana University (M.A.)
Janie Long, Ph.D.
Marriage and Family Therapy Program
Department of Educational Leadership and
    Counseling
306 Strauss Hall
Monroe, LA 71209-0280
Phone: (318) 343-7031
E-mail: jlong@spock.nlu.edu
Next Review Date: 01/01/04

MARYLAND

University of Maryland (M.S.)
Ned L. Gaylin, Ph.D.
Department of Family and Community Development
College of Health and Human Performance
Marie Mount Hall, Room 120 4D
College Park, MD 20742
Phone: (301) 405-3672
Fax: (301) 314-9161
E-mail: ng3@umail.umd.edu
Next Review Date: 07/01/00

MASSACHUSETTS

University of Massachusetts at Boston (M.Ed.)
Maryanna Domokos Cheng Ham, Ed.D.
Counseling Program, Marriage and Family
    Therapy Track
Department of Counseling and School Psychology
Graduate College of Education
100 Morrissey Blvd.
Boston, MA 02125-3393
Phone: (617) 287-7602
Fax: (617) 287-7664
E-mail: ham@umbsky.cc.umb.edu
Next Review Date: 07/01/03

MICHIGAN

Michigan State University (M.A.
    and Ph.D.)
Marsha Carolan, Ph.D.
Department of Family and Child
    Ecology
107 Human Ecology
East Lansing, MI 48824-1030
Phone: (517) 432-2271
Fax: (517) 432-2953
E-mail: carolan@pilot.msu.edu
*Next Review Date: 01/01/02 (M.A.);
    01/01/02 (Ph.D.)*

MINNESOTA

University of Minnesota (Ph.D.)
William J. Doherty, Ph.D.
Marriage and Family Therapy Program
Department of Family Social Science
College of Human Ecology
290 McNeal Hall, 1985 Buford Ave.
St. Paul, MN 55108
Phone: (612) 625-1900
E-mail: bdoherty@che2.che.umn.edu
Next Review Date: 01/01/03

MISSISSIPPI

Reformed Theological Seminary (M.A.)
James B. Hurley, Ph.D.
Marriage and Family Therapy Program
5422 Clinton Boulevard
Jackson, MS 39209-3099
Phone: (601) 922-9108
Fax: (601) 922-1153
Next Review Date: 01/01/03

University of Southern Mississippi (M.S.)
Patricia Sims, Ph.D.
Marriage and Family Therapy Program
School of Family and Consumer
    Sciences
College of Health and Human Sciences
Southern Station Box 5035
Hattiesburg, MS 39406-5035
Phone: (601) 266-4679
Fax: (601) 266-4680
E-mail: psims7456@aol.com
Next Review Date: 07/01/04

Table 9–1 *continued*

MISSOURI

Provident Counseling, Inc.
  (Post-Graduate)
Doris Diamond, M.S.W.
Family Therapy Institute
9109 Watson Rd.
St. Louis, MO 63126
Phone: (314) 371-6500
Fax: (314) 371-6508
E-mail: ddiamond@providentc.org
Next Review Date: 07/01/04

NEBRASKA

University of Nebraska-Lincoln (M.S.)
Richard Bischoff, Ph.D.
Marriage and Family Therapy
  Program
Department of Family and Consumer
  Sciences
College of Home Economics
110 Ruth Leverton Hall
Lincoln, NE 68583-0801
Phone: (402) 472-5801
Fax: (402) 472-9170
E-mail: fmcs145@unlvm.unl.edu
Next Review Date: 01/01/05

NEW HAMPSHIRE

Antioch New England Graduate School
  (M.A.)
David Watts, Ed.D.
Marriage and Family
  Therapy Program
Department of Applied Psychology
40 Avon Street
Keene, NH 03431
Phone: (603) 357-3122, x254
Fax: (603) 357-0718
E-mail: dwatts@antiochne.edu
Next Review Date: 01/01/05

University of New Hampshire
  (M.S.)
Barbara Frankel, Ph.D.
Department of Family Studies
School of Health and
  Human Services
Pettee Hall, Room 202
Durham, NH 03824
Phone: (603) 862-2134
Next Review Date: 07/01/05

NEW JERSEY

Seton Hall University (Ed.S. and M.S.-
  Candidacy)
Robert Massey, Ph.D.
Department of Professional Psychology and
  Family Therapy
College of Education and Human
  Services
400 South Orange Ave.
South Orange, NJ 07079
Phone: (973) 761-9450
Fax: (973) 761-7642
E-mail: masseyro@shu.edu
Next Review Date: 07/01/02

NEW YORK

Blanton-Peale Graduate Institute
  (Post-Graduate)
B. John Hagodom, Ph.D.
Institutes of Religion and Health, Inc.
3 West 29th Street
New York, NY 10001
Phone: (212) 725-7850, x120
Fax: (212) 689-3212
Next Review Date: 01/01/03

University of Rochester Medical Center
  (Post-Graduate)
Dave Seaburn, M.S.
Postgraduate Family Therapy
  Training Program
Division of Family Programs
Department of Psychiatry
300 Crittendon Blvd.
Rochester, NY 14642
Phone: (716) 275-2532
Fax: (716) 271-7706
E-mail: dsbn@db1.cc.rochester.edu
Next Review Date: 07/01/03

Syracuse University (M.A. and Ph.D.)
Linda Stone Fish, Ph.D.
Marriage and Family Therapy Program
College of Human Development
008 Slocum Hall
Syracuse, NY 13244-1250
Phone: (315) 443-3023
Fax: (315) 443-4062
E-mail: flstone@mailbox.syr.edu
Next Review Date: 07/01/01 (M.S.);
  07/01/01 (Ph.D.)

NORTH CAROLINA

Appalachian State University (M.A.)
Jon Winek, Ph.D.
Marriage and Family Therapy Program
Department of Human Development
  and Psychological Counseling
Boone, NC 28608
Phone: (828) 262-2055
E-mail: winekjl@conrad.appstate.edu
Next Review Date: 07/01/05

East Carolina University (M.S.)
David A. Dosser, Jr., Ph.D.
Marriage and Family Therapy Program
Department of Child Development and
  Family Relations
School of Human Environmental Sciences
Greenville, NC 27858-4353
Phone: (252) 328-6908
Fax: (252) 328-4276
E-mail: dosserd@mail.ecu.edu
Next Review Date: 01/01/04

NORTH DAKOTA

North Dakota State University
  (M.S.-Candidacy)
Jean Soderquist, Ph.D.
Marriage and Family Therapy Program
College of Human Development and
  Education
P.O. Box 5057
Fargo, ND 58105-5057
Phone: (701) 231-7335
Fax: (701) 231-9645
E-mail: jsoderqu@plains.nodak.edu
Next Review Date: 07/01/02

OHIO

Ohio State University (Ph.D.-Candidacy)
Julie Serovich, Ph.D.
Marriage and Family Therapy Program
Department of Family Relations and
  Human Development
College of Human Ecology
1787 Neil Avenue
Columbus, OH 43210
Phone: (614) 292-5685
Fax: (614) 292-7536
E-mail: serovich.1
  @postbox.acs.ohio-state.edu
Next Review Date: 01/01/02

OKLAHOMA

Oklahoma State University (M.S.)
Charles C. Hendrix, Ph.D.
Marriage and Family Therapy Program
Department of Family Relations and Child
  Development
242 Home Economics West
Stillwater, OK 74078-0337
Phone: (405) 744-5057
Fax: (405) 744-7113
E-mail: charlie@vm1.ucc.okstate.edu
Next Review Date: 01/01/03

OREGON

University of Oregon (M.A.-Candidacy)
Anna Hultquist, Ph.D.
Center for Family Therapy
973 Hilgard Street
Eugene, OR 97401
Phone: (541) 684-7244/7246
Fax: (541) 343-9159
Next Review Date: 07/01/03

PENNSYLVANIA

MCP Hahnemann (M.F.T.)
Marlene F. Watson, Ph.D.
Graduate Programs in Couple and Family
  Therapy
Bellet Building
1505 Race Street, 10th Floor
Philadelphia, PA 19102-1192
Phone: (215) 762-6933
Fax: (215) 762-6933
Next Review Date: 07/01/00

Family Institute of Philadelphia
  (Post-Graduate)
Gorge Colapinto, Lic.
1527 Brandywine Street
Philadelphia, PA 19130-4002
Phone: (215) 567-1396
Fax: (215) 567-3763
Next Review Date: 01/01/06

Penn Council for Relationships (Post-Graduate)
Kenneth Covelman, Ph.D.
4025 Chestnut Street
Philadelphia, PA 19104
Phone: (215) 382-6680
Fax: (215) 386-1743
Next Review Date: 01/01/01

Table 9–1 *continued*

Philadelphia Child and Family
  Guidance Training Center
  (Post-Graduate)
Marion Lindblad-Goldberg, Ph.D.
Part-Time Intensive Program
P.O. Box 4092
Philadelphia, PA 19118-8092
Phone: (215) 242-0949
E-mail: marionlg@idt.net
Next Review Date: 07/01/05

RHODE ISLAND
University of Rhode Island (M.S.)
Peter E. Maynard, Ph.D.
Marriage and Family
  Therapy Program
Human Development and
  Family Studies
Transition Center
Lower College Road
Kingston, RI 02881
Phone: (401) 874-2440
Fax: (401) 874-4020
E-mail: peterm@uriacc.uri.edu
Next Review Date: 01/01/01

SOUTH CAROLINA
WestGate Training and
  Consultation Network
  (Post-Graduate)
James N. Rentz, D.Min.
167 Alabama Street
Spartansburg, SC 29302
Phone: (864) 583-1010
Fax: (864) 583-6361
E-mail: jrentz@feleplex.net
Next Review Date: 01/01/03

SOUTH DAKOTA
North American Baptist Seminary
  (M.A.-Candidacy)
Don Donaldson, D. Min.
Family Systems Program
1525 S. Grange Ave.
Sioux Falls, SD 57105-1599
Phone: (605) 335-9079
Fax: (605) 335-9090
Next Review Date: 07/01/02

TENNESSEE
East Tennessee State University
  (M.A.-Candidacy)
Brent Morrow, Ph.D.
Marriage and Family Therapy
P.O. Box 70734
Johnson City, TN 37614-0734
Phone: (915) 674-3778
Fax: (915) 674-3749
Next Review Date: 07/01/03

TEXAS
Abilene Christian University (M.F.T.)
Waymon R. Hinson, Ph.D.
Department of Marriage and Family Therapy
P.O. Box 8444
Abilene, TX 79699
Phone: (915) 674-3778
Fax: (915) 674-3749
E-mail: hinson@bible.acu.edu
Next Review Date: 01/01/05

University of Houston-Clear Lake (M.A.)
Leslie King Mizo, Ph.D.
Behavioral Sciences
2700 Bay Area Boulevard
Houston, TX 77058
Phone: (281) 283-3394
Next Review Date: 07/01/03

Our Lady of the Lake University (M.S.)
Glenn Gardner, Ph.D.
Marriage and Family Therapy Program
School of Education and Clinical Studies
411 S.W. 24th Street
San Antonio, TX 78285
Phone: (210) 434-6711
Fax: (210) 436-0824
E-mail: gardg@lake.ollusa.edu
Next Review Date: 07/01/01

St. Mary's University (M.A. and Ph.D.)
Dan Ratliff, Ph.D.
Department of Counseling and Human
  Services
Family Life Center
One Camino Santa Maria
San Antonio, TX 78228-8359
Phone: (210) 436-3226
E-mail: chsdan@stmarytx.edu
Next Review Date: 07/01/05 (M.A.);
  07/01/05 (Ph.D.)

Texas Tech University (Ph.D.)
Karen S. Wampler, Ph.D.
Marriage and Family Therapy Program
Department of Human Development and
    Family Studies
College of Human Sciences
P.O. Box 41162
Lubbock, TX 79409-1162
Phone: (806) 742-3000
Fax: (806) 742-0285
E-mail: kwampler@hs.ttu.edu
Next Review Date: 01/01/03

UTAH

Brigham Young University
    (M.S. & Ph.D.)
Jeffrey Larson, Ph.D.
Department of Family Sciences
Marriage and Family Therapy
274 TLRB
Provo, UT 84602
Phone: (801) 378-3888
Fax: (801) 378-5782
E-mail: larsonj@tlrb.byu.edu
Next Review Date: 01/01/04 (M.S.);
    01/01/04 (Ph.D.)

Utah State University (M.S.)
Thorana Nelson, Ph.D.
Marriage and Family Therapy Program
Department of Family and Human
    Development
Logan, UT 84322-2905
Phone: (435) 753-5791
Fax: (435) 753-0371
E-mail: tnelson@cc.usu.edu
Next Review Date: 07/01/02

VIRGINIA

Virginia Polytechnic Institute and State
    University-Falls Church (M.S.)
Sandra M. Stith, Ph.D.
Department of Human Development
Northern Virginia Graduate Center
7054 Haycock Road, Room 202-F
Falls Church, VA 22043-2311
Phone: (703) 538-8462
Fax: (703) 538-8465
E-mail: sstith@vt.edu
Next Review Date: 01/01/01

Virginia Polytechnic Institute and State
    University-Blacksburg (Ph.D.)
Howard Protinsky, Ph.D.
Department of Human Development
Marriage and Family Therapy
Blacksburg, VA 24061-0515
Phone: (540) 231-7201
Fax: (540) 231-7209
E-mail: hprotins@vt.edu
Next Review Date: 07/01/03

WASHINGTON

Pacific Lutheran University (M.A.)
Charles York, Ph.D.
Department of Marriage and Family Therapy
Division of Social Sciences
Tacoma, WA 98447
Phone: (253) 535-7599
E-mail: yorkcp@plu.edu
Next Review Date: 01/01/06

Presbyterian Counseling Service
    (Post-Graduate)
William K. Collins, Ph.D.
Marriage and Family Therapy Training
    Program
564 N.E. Ravenna Boulevard
Seattle, WA 98115
Phone: (206) 527-2266
Fax: (206) 527-1009
E-mail: mfttcenter@aol.com
Next Review Date: 07/01/01

Seattle Pacific University (M.S.-Candidacy)
Donald MacDonald, Ph.D.
Marriage and Family Therapy Program
3307 Third Avenue West
Seattle, WA 98119-1997
Phone: (206) 281-2629
Fax: (206) 281-2695
Next Review Date: 07/01/02

WISCONSIN

Family Service of Milwaukee
    (Post-Graduate)
Ann Starr, M.S.
Family Therapy Training Institute
P.O. Box 080440
Milwaukee, WI 53208-0440
Phone: (414) 342-4560
Fax: (414) 342-5326
Next Review Date: 01/01/06

Table 9–1 *continued*

University of Wisconsin-Stout (M.S.)
Charles Barnard, Ed.D.
Marriage and Family Therapy Program
School of Education and Human Services
College of Human Development
Department of Psychology
222 Vocational Rehabilitation Building
Menomonie, WI 54751
Phone: (715) 232-2404
E-mail: barnardc@uwstout.edu
Next Review Date: 01/01/03

CANADA
ALBERTA
Calgary Regional Health Authority
    (Post-Graduate)
Maureen Leahey, R.N., Ph.D.
Family Therapy Training Program
Institute of Psychotherapy
First Floor, Colonel Belcher Hospital
1213 4th Street, S.W.
Calgary, Alberta, Canada T2R 0X7
Phone: (403) 541-2104
Fax: (403) 541-2141
E-mail: maureen.leahey@crha-health.ab.ca
Next Review Date: 01/01/05

MANITOBA
Interfaith Marriage and Family Institute
    (M.M.F.T.)
Richard N. Dearing, Th.D.
University of Winnipeg
Family Studies Program in the Faculty of
    Theology
515 Portage Ave.
Winnipeg, Manitoba, Canada R3B 2E9
Phone: (204) 786-9251
E-mail: dearing-r@s-h.uwinnipeg.ca
Next Review Date: 01/01/06

ONTARIO
University of Guelph (M.S.)
Anna Dienhart, Ph.D.
Department of Family Relations and
    Applied Nutrition
Marriage and Family Therapy Centre
Guelph, Ontario, Canada N1G 2W1
Phone: (519) 824-4120, x 3975
Fax: (519) 766-0691
Next Review Date: 07/01/05

Interfaith Pastoral Counseling Centre
    (Post-Graduate)
John Schneider, Ph.D.
151 Frederick Street
Kitchener, Ontario, Canada N2H 2M2
Phone: (519) 743-6781
Fax: (519) 743-0610
E-mail: ipccjch@ionline.net
Next Review Date: 07/01/03

QUEBEC
Argyle Institute of Human Relations
    (Post-Graduate)
Maria Alejos, M.A.
Marriage and Family Therapy Program
4115 Sherbrooke Street W., 5th Floor
Montreal, Quebec, Canada H3Z 1K9
Phone: (514) 932-3254
Fax: (514) 243-6722
E-mail: argyle@total.net
Next Review Date: 01/01/03

Sir Mortimer B. Davis-Jewish General
    Hospital (Post-Graduate)
Liliane Spector, Ph.D.
Couple and Family Therapy Training
    Program
4333 Chemin De La Cote Ste–Catherine
Montreal, Quebec, Canada H3T 1E4
Phone: (514) 340-8210
Fax: (514) 340-7507
Next Review Date: 07/01/01

States and provinces without an accredited MFT program as of June 2000 were
Alaska, Arizona, Delaware, Hawaii, Idaho, Maine, Montana, Nevada, New Mexico,
Vermont, West Virginia, and Wyoming.

Note. From *Directory of MFT Training Programs,* April 3, 2000, http://www.aamft.org/resources/coamfte.htm. Copyright 2000 by AAMFT. All rights reserved. Used with permission of AAMFT. For an updated list of programs, please contact the Commission on Accreditation for Marriage and Family Therapy Education, AAMFT, 1133 15th Street, N.W., Suite 300, Washington, DC 20005-2710; phone (202) 452-0109; fax (202) 223-2329; e-mail coamfte@aamft.org.

Shalett and Everett (1981) assert that the accreditation process provides needed linkages with licensure in the profession. In their view, licensure basically functions to offer the public minimal protection against untrained practitioners; it identifies minimal qualifications for the practitioner but neither ensures competency nor addresses the quality of the individual education and training. Shalett and Everett identify accreditation as the primary way to establish standards for practitioners' educational and training experiences, because licensure is essentially meaningless in the absence of accreditation. The AAMFT has been recognized as the focal point for the marriage and family therapy profession by several states whose licensing boards have incorporated major aspects of AAMFT membership standards and its Commission on Accreditation's program standards into their licensing laws. Further, the AAMFT's methods of giving credentials have provided recognition for practitioners in those states with no licensure, particularly with regard to insurance reimbursement for services.

American Family Therapy Association

The AFTA was founded in 1977 by a small group of mental health professionals who were active during the early years when marriage and family therapy was emerging. Its stated objectives include the following:

1. Advancing family therapy as a science that regards the entire family as the unit of study.
2. Promoting research and professional education in family therapy and allied fields.
3. Making information about family therapy available to practitioners in other fields of knowledge and to the public.
4. Fostering cooperation among those concerned with medical, psychological, social, legal, and other aspects of the family, and those involved in the science and practice of family therapy. (Sauber, L'Abate, & Weeks, 1985, p. 180)

There are five categories of membership in the AFTA: charter, clinical-teacher, research, distinguished, and foreign. Association members represent a wide variety of disciplines. Membership requirements are essentially a terminal professional degree, 5 years of postdegree clinical experience with families, and 5 years of teaching family therapy or performing significant research in the family field. The membership numbers approximately 1,000 family therapy teachers and researchers who meet once a year to share ideas and develop common interests (Kaslow, 1990b). It is a think tank whose annual meeting brings together professionals to address a variety of clinical, research, and teaching topics. In 1981, a joint liaison committee of representatives from the AAMFT and the AFTA was formed to take up the issue of the respective roles of the two organizations within the profession. The AFTA was identified as an academy of advanced professionals interested in the exchange of ideas; the AAMFT retained its recognition as providing credentials to marriage and family therapists (W. C. Nichols, 1992).

Family Psychology (Division 43 of the American Psychological Association)

Family Psychology was established as Division 43 within the American Psychological Association (APA) in 1984. The division emerged in response to the desire of a significant number of psychologists seeking to maintain their professional identity as psychologists while pursuing family therapeutic practices (Kaslow, 1990b). With the forming of the division, a new designation, family psychologist, reconnected these professionals with their original discipline and replaced the hyphenated model of professional identity they had been using: psychologist–family therapist (Liddle, 1987). To a great degree, this reaffiliation had to do with a return to professional values that endorse the role of a scientific base in clinical practice (i.e., the scientist–practitioner model of training and practice in psychology).

To become a division member, one must hold membership in the APA. From the perspective of this group, marriage and family therapy represents one clinical manifestation of family psychology (Liddle, 1992). In 1989, the American Board of Professional Psychology (ABPP) voted to recognize Family Psychology as its seventh specialty, this due to the efforts of Division 43 members. Recognition by ABPP offers family psychologists opportunity to gain advanced certification, that being the "Diplomate in Family Psychology." The major requirements for achieving this designation include (*Specialty Boards: Family*, 1992):

1. A doctoral degree meeting the standards of the APA for doctoral training
2. A minimum of 1,500 hours of supervised training in an organized psychological service setting, completed in no more than 2 years
3. Three graduate courses or their equivalent, two graduate clinical practicum courses or their equivalent, and continuing education and supervision, all in family psychology
4. A minimum of 5 years postdoctoral work, 3 years of which must have been supervised
5. Licensure as a psychologist in the state where one practices

Once a candidate has met these requirements, he or she must complete a work sample. The work sample is offered to demonstrate proficiency in one's primary professional activities as a family psychologist. A 3- to 4-hour oral examination using the work sample as a springboard is then conducted to assess evaluation and intervention skills, ability to articulate a theoretical position, scientific/professional knowledge, ethics, and knowledge of current professional issues. A live consultation with a family or couple is a further component of the oral examination. Further information about this credential can be found on the Division 43 Web site:

http://www.apa.org/divisions/div43

International Association of Marriage and Family Counselors

The IAMFC initially began as an interest group within the American Association for Counseling and Development of 143 members in 1986. This early group was made up of professionals with varied academic backgrounds who maintained interest in and involvement with issues facing couples and families. In 1990, the IAMFC became a division of the American Association for Counseling and Development (now American Counseling Association). As of June 1999, there were over 5,000 members (http://www.iamfc.org/).

The current IAMFC goals and purposes include (*A Brief History of IAMFC*, 1992):

> Promote ethical practices in marriage and family counseling/therapy; encourage research in marriage and family counseling/therapy; share knowledge and emphasize adherence to the highest quality training of marriage and family counselors/therapists; provide a forum for dialogue on relevant issues related to marriage and family counseling/therapy; examine ways to intervene in systems; help couples and families cope more successfully with life challenges; and use counseling knowledge and systemic methods to ameliorate the problems confronting marriages and families. (p. 6)

To become an IAMFC member, one may join directly or join as a part of being a member of American Counseling Association (ACA). The IAMFC has promoted training standards in marriage and family counseling/therapy through the American Counseling Association sponsored Council for Accreditation of Counseling and Related Programs (CACREP). These standards have been used in certifying educational programs under CACREP. "The philosophical stance taken by CACREP and ACA is that marriage and family counseling graduates must have a foundation in basic counseling skills, in conjunction with or prior to training in marriage and family therapy" (R. L. Smith, Stevens-Smith, Carlson, & Frame, 1996, p. 328). Therefore, while COAMFTE has a minimum of 45 semester hours for an accredited masters program, the CACREP-accredited marital and family therapy program requires a minimum of 60 semester hours broken down as follows:

Human Growth and Development (one-course minimum)
Social and Cultural Foundations (one-course minimum)
Helping Relationships (two-course minimum)
Groups (one-course minimum)
Lifestyle and Career Development (one-course minimum)
Appraisal/Assessment (one-course minimum)
Research and Evaluation (one-course minimum)
Professional Orientation/Ethics (one-course minimum)
Theoretical Foundations of Marital and Family Counseling/Therapy (two-course minimum)

Techniques and Treatment in Marital and Family Counseling/Therapy (two-course minimum)

Supervised Practicum and Internship (three-course minimum)

Human Sexuality (one-course minimum)

Substance Abuse Treatment (one-course minimum)

The IAMFC also has established credentialing in marriage and family counseling/therapy through the National Academy of Certified Family Therapists (NACFT), an affiliate of the IAMFC. "According to the NACFT, family therapy certification purports to: (a) promote accountability and visibility and help recognize the practice of family therapy, (b) identify family therapists who have met standards to the public and to professional peers, (c) advocate among groups and agencies actively involved in managed care, (d) encourage the continuing professional growth and development of individuals practicing in marriage and family counseling and therapy, and (e) ensure a national standard" (R. L. Smith et al., 1996, p. 330).

STATE LICENSURE AND MARRIAGE AND FAMILY THERAPY

Established professions are self-regulating, and through self-regulation, gain public acceptance and respectability. Professions are also regulated, however, through legal processes assigning licensure as a symbol of competence to practice the profession. Statute law in all states controls the practice of medical and legal professionals. Since the 1970s, the licensing of psychologists, clinical social workers, counselors, and marriage and family therapists has aroused intense professional interest. While licensure has become synonymous with professionalism, there is no evidence, at least in the professional research literature, that licensure ensures quality services (R. L. Smith et al., 1996). Nevertheless, as J. W. Davis (1981) stated:

> Licensure . . . seems to furnish an objective positive personal identification ("I am a member of a legally recognized, and therefore valuable, group in our society"). There is reflected public agreement that a licensed person must possess unusual, scarce skills to qualify for licensure. The status by association with institutions wielding the power of social control—that is, to other licensed professionals and to government itself—cannot be overlooked. (p. 84)

Licensure is a statutory process of an agency of government, usually of a state, which legally prescribes the qualifications of those who engage in a given occupation or profession and usually limits the use of a particular title or the practice of the profession (R. L. Smith et al., 1996). Unlicensed practitioners in most states with licensing laws are subject to legal penalties should they misrepresent themselves. Thus, licensure can restrict entry into the profession, and those denied entry who persist in their activities can be prosecuted (J. W. Davis, 1981).

Fretz and Mills (1980) identify five major premises supporting licensure efforts:

1. Licensure is designed to protect the public by establishing minimum standards of service. Fretz and Mills (1980) contend that consumers would be harmed by the absence of such standards; incompetent practitioners would have the potential to cause long-term, negative consequences. This position is further developed by B. N. Phillips (1982):

   For all that can be said about legal constraints on practice, one thing is most important. Their purpose is to promote the public's welfare by improving and maintaining the quality of training and practice, maximizing benefits-to-cost service delivery outcomes, and protecting the public from gross incompetence. (p. 924)

2. Licensure is designed to protect the public from ignorance about mental health services. Fretz and Mills (1980) base this assumption on the belief that consumers in need of mental health services typically do not know how to choose an appropriate practitioner or how to judge the quality of services rendered.

3. Licensure increases the likelihood that practitioners will be more competent and their services better distributed and thus more available.

4. Licensure upgrades a profession. Fretz and Mills propose that a licensed profession will have more practitioners committed to improving and maintaining the highest standards of excellence.

5. Licensing allows a profession to define for itself what it will and will not do. Accordingly, a profession is assumed to be more independent, because other professions or the courts cannot specify its functions.

Corey, Corey, and Callanan (1998) concur with this last point, in particular noting the general perception that licensure enhances a profession and is a sign of maturity.

State licensure can contribute to safeguarding consumers' welfare as well as promoting professional identity and enhancement. It is not, however, without its critics. Gill (1982), for example, questions how licensure leads to more informed consumers. He points to the general public's ignorance of differences among *licensed* mental health professionals, such as psychologists, social workers, and counselors. Rinas and Clyne-Jackson (1988) point to the increase of malpractice suits and the increase in mental health licenses as evidence that licensure does not guarantee consumer welfare. They go so far as to suggest that quackery may actually increase as licensure restricts access to practice.

J. W. Davis (1981) maintains that licensing is designed to create and preserve a "union shop" that works more as a monopoly than as a protection for the public from misrepresentation and incompetence. Bertram (1983) asserts more self-serving interests are inherent in licensure, stating: "Let us be clear, this is not an issue of competence, ethics, or morality. What we are dealing with is turf" (p. 7). Corey et al. (1998) likewise decry the potential of licensure for promoting professional jealousy and competition, stating that "the process of licensing often contributes to professional specializations' pitting themselves against one another" (p. 279).

Given these caveats, it seems, however, that licensure has become a fixture within marriage and family therapy practice. As of June 2000, state legislation creating licensure specifically for marriage and family therapy had been enacted in 42 states with active plans to introduce such legislation present in other states.

LICENSURE REQUIREMENTS FOR MARRIAGE AND FAMILY THERAPISTS

The initial wave of legislation that allowed the licensing of marriage and family therapists was passed during the 1960s. California was the first state, passing its law in 1963. Michigan followed in 1966, and New Jersey in 1968. Utah passed its law in 1973, Nevada in 1976, and Georgia in 1976. Georgia's licensure law was "sunsetted" out of existence, however; a new law was enacted in 1984 (Bowers, 1992b). Throughout the 1980s and into the 1990s, the number of states that have licensing laws regulating marriage and family therapy has increased significantly. As of June 2000, the following states had laws defining licensure requirements for marriage and family therapists:

Alabama	Kentucky	Oklahoma
Alaska	Maine	Oregon
Arizona	Maryland	Pennsylvania
Arkansas	Massachusetts	Rhode Island
California	Michigan	South Carolina
Colorado	Minnesota	South Dakota
Connecticut	Mississippi	Tennessee
Florida	Missouri	Texas
Georgia	Nebraska	Utah
Hawaii	Nevada	Vermont
Illinois	New Hampshire	Virginia
Indiana	New Jersey	Washington
Iowa	New Mexico	Wisconsin
Kansas	North Carolina	Wyoming

Significant diversity, however, exists among much of this enacted legislation. Sporakowski (1982) referred to many of the licensure laws regulating marriage and family therapy as a "hodgepodge," given the variety of assumptions and definitions on which they appear to have been based. Corey, Corey, and Callanan (1984) noted several of the partial definitions that have existed in state licensure laws:

Marriage and family counseling is that service performed with individuals, couples, or groups wherein interpersonal relationships between spouses or members of a family are examined for the purpose of achieving more adequate, satisfying, and productive marriage and family adjustments. (California)

Marriage and family counseling also includes premarital counseling, predivorce and postdivorce counseling, and family counseling. It consists of the application of principles, methods and techniques of counseling and psychotherapeutic techniques for the purpose of resolving psychological conflict, modifying perception and behavior, altering old attitudes and establishing new ones in the area of marriage and family life. (Georgia)

Marriage and family counseling consists of the application of established principles of learning, motivation, perception, thinking, emotional, marital and sexual relationships and adjustments by persons trained in psychology, social work, psychiatry, or marital counseling. (Nevada) (pp. 165–166)

Not only definitions but also essential terminology differ by jurisdiction. Not all of the states with licensure regulating marriage and family therapy refer to *therapy–therapist*. Sporakowski (1982) suggests that this appears to be as much a result of a states rights' attitude in legislatures as an attempt by states to meet the individual needs of their citizens. He further asserts other states' lack of legislation is directly related to the issue of the emergence of marriage and family therapy as a distinct profession. Support from the various other major mental health professions has fluctuated. In some states, "omnibus" legislation has been enacted where marriage and family therapists are licensed along with social workers, mental health counselors, school psychologists, art therapists, and/or other mental health professions within the same law. In other states, major mental health professions have been resistant to the anticipated intrusion into what they perceive as their service domains. In these latter states, legislation licensing marriage and family therapists has either been opposed or attempts have been made to regulate marriage and family therapy directly or indirectly through another profession's licensure law (Bowers, 1992b).

Sporakowski (1982) proposed three primary issues for marriage and family therapists to be knowledgeable about relative to state licensure: (a) what and who are covered, (b) required qualifications, and (c) the licensure process. In an attempt to provide a focus for uniformity among state marriage and family licensure laws, the AAMFT drafted a model regulatory code in 1979 and has subsequently revised it several times. Given the diversity existing among various states' laws, excerpts from this model act, *The Model Marriage and Family Therapy Licensure Act*, are used to highlight major points within each of these three issues.

Licensure Coverage

Most licensure legislation negatively defines the boundaries of practice by identifying prohibitions and exemptions. For example, *The Model Marriage and Family Therapy Licensure Act* (American Association for Marriage and Family

Therapy, 1992a) identifies the following "Prohibited Acts" and "Exemptions" in sections 4 and 5, respectively:

Prohibited Acts. Except as specifically provided elsewhere in this Act, commencing on January 1, 19____ , no person who is not licensed under this act shall:

    a.   advertise the performance of marriage and family therapy or counseling service by him or her; or

    b.   use a title or description such as "marital or marriage therapist, counselor, advisor or consultant," "marital or marriage and family therapist, counselor advisor, or consultant," or any other name, style, or description denoting that the person is a marriage and family therapist; or

    c.   practice marriage and family therapy.

Exemptions.

    A.   A person shall be exempt from the requirements of this Act:

        1.   If the person is practicing marriage and family therapy as part of his duties as an employee of:

            a.   a recognized academic institution, or a federal, state, county, or local governmental institution or agency while performing those duties for which she or he was employed by such an institution, agency, or facility;

            b.   an organization which is nonprofit and which is determined by the Board to meet community needs while performing those duties for which he or she was employed by such an agency; or

        2.   If the person is a marriage and family therapy intern or person preparing for the practice of marriage and family therapy under qualified supervision in a training institution or facility or supervisory arrangement recognized and approved by the Board, provided she or he is designated by such titles as "marriage and family therapy intern," "marriage therapy intern," "family therapy intern," or others, clearly indicating such training status; or

        3.   If the person has been issued a temporary permit by the Board to engage in the activity for which licensure is required.

    B.   Nothing in this Act shall be construed to prevent qualified members of other professional groups as defined by the Board, including but not necessarily limited to clinical social workers, psychiatric nurses, psychologists, physicians, or members of the clergy, from doing or advertising that they perform work of a marriage and family therapy nature consistent with the accepted standards of their respective professions. Provided, however, no such persons shall use the title or description stating or implying that they are marriage and family therapists or marriage and family counselors or that they are licensed as marriage and family therapists or marriage and family counselors. (pp. 2–3)

Similar prohibitions and exemptions exist in most states' licensure laws. One particular point of contention in this regard, however, has related to other licensed mental health professionals claiming to practice marriage and family therapy. For example, California is specific in this regard; individuals practicing within the guidelines of another professional license have typically been exempted as long as they do not claim to practice as a marriage and family therapist. This has generally been interpreted to mean that a licensed psychologist, psychiatrist, or social worker could treat marital or family problems but not advertise as a marriage and family therapist (Sporakowski, 1982).

Qualifications

Those states regulating marriage and family therapy all require that the prospective licensee possess a minimum of a master's degree in marriage and family therapy, social work, pastoral counseling, or relevant qualifications in behavioral sciences such as psychology or sociology. Some states have gone beyond that minimum. New Jersey has accepted only one master's degree, social work, or a doctorate in an appropriate field; Michigan has required a doctorate in a relevant field unless the master's degree is specifically in social work, marriage, or pastoral counseling.

In addition to these academic qualifications, states differ in their accompanying experience requirements. Qualifications have varied from 1 year of postgraduate experience in marriage and family counseling (Nevada) to 5 years of full-time counseling experience, at least 2 of which must have been in marriage counseling (New Jersey). Most states require that the majority of clinical experience be gained under supervision.

The Model Marriage and Family Therapy Licensure Act (American Association for Marriage and Family Therapy, 1992a) identifies the following education and experience requirements in section 11:

1. Educational requirements: a Master's degree or a Doctoral degree in marriage and family therapy from a recognized educational institution, or a graduate degree in an allied field from a recognized educational institution and graduate level coursework which is equivalent to a Master's degree in marriage and family therapy, as determined by the Board.
2. Experience requirements: successful completion of two calendar years of work experience in marriage and family therapy under qualified supervision following receipt of a qualifying degree. (p. 6)

An important concern relating to point 2 above is the definition of "qualified supervision." Not anyone can provide the necessary supervision to a potential licensee; only "an individual who has been recognized by the Board as an approved supervisor" (p. 2). Thus, it is incumbent on a potential licensee to early on ascertain that his or her supervision will be with such an approved supervisor.

The Licensure Process

State laws typically require prospective licensees to file a formal application, supplying letters of recommendation, giving proof of their academic credentials, and documenting hours of supervised experience. Many also request a written or oral examination or both. *The Model Marriage and Family Therapy Licensure Act* (American Association for Marriage and Family Therapy, 1992a), for example, specifies that applicants for licensure pass a written or oral examination that includes "questions in such theoretical and applied fields as the Board deems most suitable to test an applicant's knowledge and competence to engage in the practice of marriage and family therapy" (p. 6).

After successful completion of all requirements, the license is awarded. Maintenance of the license normally depends on paying renewal fees and obtaining a requisite number of Continuing Education Units before renewal. Florida, for example, has required that 30 hours of continuing education credit be earned during each biennial renewal period. Continuing Education Units must be relevant to the profession for which license renewal is sought and approved by the state regulatory body governing professional license renewal (Psychological Services Act, 1983).

A license may be suspended or revoked for a variety of reasons that are typically defined within the legislation creating the license. Frequent violations cited include fraud or deceit practiced on the regulatory board, conviction of a crime, abuse of chemical substances, and unethical behavior. Identifying and reporting these violations is viewed as the responsibility of licensed individuals as well as the general public. Usually, a "friendly remonstrance" is seen as sufficient unless violations are repeated or blatant and involve criminal acts (Sporakowski, 1982). In such cases, legal action is taken. Violation of the licensing law itself normally results in a misdemeanor action with possible fines and incarceration. Of course, associated criminal violations could garner more serious legal action and consequences.

In summary, the presence of and specific requirements for licensure as a marriage and family therapist vary from state to state. In seeking a license, prospective licensees should contact the appropriate state professional regulatory agency for information about licensure laws and application requirements.

RESEARCH: A MEANS OF PROMOTING PROFESSIONAL IDENTITY

Liddle (1991a) describes research in marriage and family therapy as a topic influencing "how we see ourselves and how others view us" (p. 327). Cavell and Snyder (1991) draw on the analogy of safeguards imposed by the U.S. Food and Drug Administration before authorizing use of a new drug by licensed physicians in asserting the importance of research for promoting the professional identity of marriage and family therapy:

> Clear demonstration of the drug's efficacy is required, under carefully controlled conditions, with delineation of potential hazards or unwanted effects, before conclusions may be drawn regarding the generalizability of treatment effectiveness for specific symptoms across divergent patient populations. How many of us would give our *informed consent* to some pharmacologic intervention based on an intensive case-study of the drug's efficacy with one patient (or one group of patients) under one unique set of conditions? Yet this is precisely the situation in which we often place clients . . . typically without providing (or even possessing) documentation regarding generalizability of treatment effects. (p. 170)

Despite a history of more than 50 years, marriage and family therapy has been characterized by some as still being in an early stage of conceptual development (Bednar, Burlingame, & Masters, 1988; Liddle, Gurman, Pinsof, & Roberto, 1990; Liddle, 1991b). Bednar et al. (1988) are particularly critical in this regard. They point to the imprecise definition of family therapy's basic concepts in comparison to other forms of psychotherapy. Further, they cite the idiosyncratic development of most family therapy models as contributing to a lack of standardization within the field, thus inhibiting basic accountability efforts. Sprenkle and Moon (1996) go further and state that "the field remains vulnerable because of its lack of attention to developing a solid foundation of research on the process and outcomes of family therapy" (p. 3). Werry (1989), in an article entitled, "Family Therapy—Professional Endeavor or Successful Religion?" characterized family therapy as "a rather sad sack relying for its status on assertion, self-congratulation, guruism and denigration of alternatives" (p. 380).

However, M. P. Nichols and Schwartz (2001), in reviewing the contemporary context of research in marriage and family therapy, argue that despite a lack of specificity within the field, sufficient research studies support the overall effectiveness of systems-oriented marriage and family therapy. Their summary of major reviews of marriage and family therapy research (e.g., Dewitt, 1987; Gurman & Kniskern, 1978; Jacobson & Bussod, 1983; Pinsof & Wynne, 1995) concludes that (a) systems-oriented family therapy is based on concepts, assumptions, and procedures that differ from traditional forms of psychotherapy; (b) family therapy is a useful treatment for a variety of problems; (c) family therapy is at least as effective as other forms of psychotherapy; and (d) further research directed at the process of family therapy and the mechanisms through which change occurs is needed.

Liddle (1992) proposes 10 key considerations for strengthening the research–clinical practice connection in marriage and family therapy, and in doing so, enhancing the professional identity of marriage and family therapy within the mental health community and to the public in general. These include the following:

1. Clearer guidelines incorporating and translating content from both basic and applied research into clinical work need to be developed.
2. Research findings need to better inform clinicians in particular population-, age-, and problem-specific situations (i.e., individual case circumstances).
3. The results of current research efforts need to be critically examined and alternatives generated as applicable; this, instead of engaging in extremist debates that serve primarily political and ideological masters rather than enhancing the knowledge base.
4. Traditional research methods are applicable to family therapy studies in appreciating context and interaction (i.e., systemic processes) and need to be maintained and used; this, even though some maintain that there is insufficient consistency between systemic theories and traditional research frameworks.

5. Productive, mutual influencing between the clinical practice and research domains need to become a priority of supervisors and teachers in marriage and family therapy training programs.

6. Additional models that effectively demonstrate the research–practice and theory interconnection, as well as the benefits that can generate from such interaction, need to be promoted.

7. Additional vehicles are needed to demonstrate how the research and practice divide can be decreased. For example, the *Clinician's Research Digest,* a publication of the APA, provides detailed abstracts of research reports with a notable focus suggesting how findings can affect practice.

8. Marriage and family therapists need to identify a research–training–practice framework to serve as a clear orienting force for itself, somewhat akin to the scientist–practitioner model within psychology.

9. Each individual marriage and family therapist needs to strive to be multi-dimensional in his or her personal practice model so as to more readily incorporate new information and adopt new processes, especially as they relate to case conceptualization decision making.

10. Marriage and family therapy needs to actively promote an attitude and values supportively connecting the research and practice realms.

Liddle (1992) quotes C. M. Anderson (1986) in summarizing the importance of research for promoting the professional identity of marriage and family therapy:

> As a field, we *must* address the issue of what constitutes acceptable evidence of efficacy and how we go about obtaining it. It is absolutely vital that the field of family therapy develop a respect for research, knowledge of basic research methods, and the requirements of scientific inquiry. Without this knowledge and respect, the field of family therapy will not continue to develop and will not receive the support it requires from academic institutions, governmental policies or funding agencies. This does not mean that we all must *do* research, nor that we need to use empirical methods that do not reflect systems thinking. It does mean, however, that we all must be able to evaluate ourselves and our colleagues, using strict research criteria, or we will be no different from psychoanalysts whose work has become increasingly discounted rather than accepted. In the world of increased emphasis on cost effectiveness and decreased resources, unless we can offer proof of efficacy, acceptable to the scientific community, we will eventually cease to exist. (p. 353)

PRAGMATIC ISSUES AND PROFESSIONAL IDENTITY

Marriage and family therapists' training prepares them to acquire an adequate repertoire of intervention strategies. They can select and tailor treatment plans for their clients. Although at times these treatment tasks require attending to significant roadblocks, the competently trained clinician is ready to do so. Many marriage and family therapists' training, however, tends to provide them with a limited awareness of the array of choices they have when they make nonclinical professional decisions. Some of the more pragmatic professional identity issues facing marriage and family therapists include public relations (particularly advertising), professional growth through continuing education, and the importance of maintaining intraprofessional communications.

Professional Advertising

Almost all companies and individuals who provide a product or service to the public advertise. Traditionally, however, most professions have severely restricted their members with regard to advertising. The prevalent conception has been that professionals are devoted to public service rather than making money. Advertising, it was felt, would change that image and undermine public confidence. Yet because advertising is the standard means by which people find out about available services and products, such restrictions tended to prevent average citizens from having equal access to professional help (Bayles, 1981).

In 1977 the Supreme Court declared that professional organizations' "ban on advertising" was restraint of trade. The practice of medicine, dentistry, accounting, psychology, and marriage and family therapy is considered a business as well as a profession and is, therefore, subject to the same regulation as other businesses (Bruce, 1990). In an effort to come to terms with these new realities toward professional advertising, the AAMFT initially developed its *Standards on Public Information and Advertising* (American Association for Marriage and Family Therapy, 1982). The 1985 and subsequent revisions of the *AAMFT Code of Ethics* have incorporated a specific principle addressing "Advertising." Principle 8 Advertising (American Association for Marriage and Family Therapy, 2001) is offered in Figure 9–2.

In 1988, the AAMFT retained the George Alban Company of San Jose, California, to coordinate all orders for the AAMFT trademark (name and logo) and trademark (name only) in telephone directories (i.e., the *Yellow Pages*) in the United States and Canada. This arrangement was continued until 1998 and ensured that only authorized clinical members of the association advertised under the AAMFT name and logo and in a manner consistent with its ethical principles. It also gave all eligible members of the association equal access to participate in advertising at a cost no more than that typically charged by representatives of local directories. In 1998 a new AAMFT Clinical Member logo, shown in Figure 9–3, was issued along with guidelines for its use (American Association for Marriage and Family Therapy, 1998b). The new clinical logo program replaced the George Alban program and allowed clinical members of AAMFT more flexibility.

With regard to newspaper or similar media advertising, two popular formats for mental health services are the announcement advertisement and the public service message (Kissel, 1983). Figures 9–4 and 9–5 illustrate an announcement advertisement and public service message, respectively.

8. Advertising

Marriage and family therapists engage in appropriate informational activities, including those that enable the public, referral sources, or others to choose professional services on an informed basis.

8.1 Marriage and family therapists accurately represent their competencies, education, training, and experience relevant to their practice of marriage and family therapy.

8.2 Marriage and family therapists ensure that advertisements and publications in any media (such as directories, announcements, business cards, newspapers, radio, television, Internet, and facsimiles) convey information that is necessary for the public to make an appropriate selection of professional services. Information could include: (a) office information, such as name, address, telephone number, credit card acceptability, fees, languages spoken, and office hours; (b) qualifying clinical degree (see subprinciple 8.5); (c) other earned degrees (see subprinciple 8.5) and state or provincial licensures and/or certifications; (d) AAMFT clinical member status; and (e) description of practice.

8.3 Marriage and family therapists do not use names that could mislead the public concerning the identity, responsibility, source, and status of those practicing under that name, and do not hold themselves out as being partners or associates of a firm if they are not.

8.4 Marriage and family therapists do not use any professional identification (such as a business card, office sign, letterhead, Internet, or telephone or association directory listing) if it includes a statement or claim that is false, fraudulent, misleading, or deceptive.

8.5 In representing their educational qualifications, marriage and family therapists list and claim as evidence only those earned degrees: (a) from institutions accredited by regional accreditation sources recognized by the United States Department of Education, (b) from institutions recognized by states or provinces that license or certify marriage and family therapists, or (c) from equivalent foreign institutions.

8.6 Marriage and family therapists correct, wherever possible, false, misleading, or inaccurate information and representations made by others concerning the therapist's qualifications, services, or products.

8.7 Marriage and family therapists make certain that the qualifications of their employees or supervisees are represented in a manner that is not false, misleading, or deceptive.

8.8 Marriage and family therapists do not represent themselves as providing specialized service unless they have the appropriate education, training, or supervised experience.

Figure 9–2 Principle 8. Advertising

Note. From *AAMFT Code of Ethics.* AAMFT can make further revision at any time, as the Association deems necessary.

Reprinted from the AAMFT Code of Ethics, Copyright 2001, American Association for Marriage and Family Therapy. Reprinted with permission.

Figure 9–3 Logos of the American Association of Marriage and Family Therapy: corporate logos (left and center) and member logo (right)

Note. From AAMFT Code of Ethics, Copyright 1998, American Association for Marriage and Family Therapy. Reprinted with permission.

Jane Krandell, Ph.D.

Announces the opening of her office for the practice of marriage and family therapy. I am particularly interested in providing consultation and treatment services to couples and families where substance abuse is a concern.

Saturday and evening hours. 1st Avenue, Ocala, Florida 32217, 369-4390.

Figure 9–4 An Announcement Advertisement

Note. From *Private Practice for the Mental Health Clinician* (unpaged), by S. Kissel, 1983, Gaithersburg, MD: Aspen Publishers. Copyright 1983 by Aspen Publishers. Adapted by permission.

Continuing Education

The continuing education of professionals in all fields has, in recent years, become a matter of great and pragmatic concern. There was a time when the basic information employed in practicing a profession, whether medicine, law, theology, or the like, was relatively stable and could be mastered by a student in the course of a reasonable training period. The application of this knowledge was then largely a matter of professional skill. Changes in professions were gradual and relatively easily incorporated by practicing professionals during their careers.

One of the most impressive developments during the last century has been the dramatic increase in knowledge. Scientific and technological developments make it virtually impossible for a professional to rely on initial training in a field for any significant part of a career (Walker, 1981). As Vitulano and Copeland (1980) observe with regard to the health care professions in particular:

First, the knowledge base for these professions is increasing at an astonishing rate. . . . One must continue to learn or suffer from professional obsolescence. Second, the

---

Views On Family Health

by Jane Krandell, Ph.D.

FACTS ABOUT CHILDREN'S EMOTIONAL PROBLEMS

Emotional problems, unlike certain physical ailments, may take years to develop to the point where symptoms cause concern and worry to the individual. The symptoms are indicators of too-heavy burdens, stresses, and conflicts. What are some of these signs for children? Mental health experts agree that the following are *possible* danger signals:

- Prolonged periods of unhappiness without apparent cause.
- Refusal to accept school or parental authority.
- Persistent avoidance of school.
- Excessive fears which are upsetting and interfere with normal functioning.
- Poor achievement in school subjects.
- Returning to activities associated with infancy, such as frequent (and not occasional) bedwetting, soiling, head-banging, thumb sucking, and little ability to tolerate frustration.

If too many of these signals are present, a consultation with your family physician, clergy person, school counselor, or a mental health expert such as a marriage and family therapist may be helpful.

A public service message with the aim of promoting more satisfying family home environments from the office of Jane Krandell, Ph.D., Marriage and Family Therapist, 1st Avenue, Ocala, Florida 32217.

Phone: 369-4390.

Figure 9–5   A Public Service Message

Note. From *Private Practice for the Mental Health Clinician* (unpaged), by S. Kissel, 1983, Gaithersburg, MD: Aspen Publishers. Copyright 1983 by Aspen Publishers. Adapted by permission.

enormous ethical responsibilities of our practice demand the highest standards. Licensure or certification solely at the beginning of one's career merely identifies a minimum standard for professional practice, not the ideal toward which one should strive. Third, lifetime education should constitute an important goal of the training and practice of the health professions. Fourth, a proactive commitment to the maintenance of competency over time would help maintain public confidence in the profession. (p. 891)

Students graduating from most professional programs must immediately begin a program of continuing education and development to have any chance of survival in their chosen field. Should they fail to do this, by the end of 3 years (in most professions), their functioning would be substandard; by the end of 5 years, that functioning would be seriously compromised; by the end of 10 years, they would, no doubt, be totally incompetent (Walker, 1981). Continuing education is even a necessity in the field of professional ethics. "No amount of initial training will replace the need for ongoing training and review of . . . codes of ethics because codes are regularly revised" (K. Jordan & Stevens, 1999, p. 174).

Professional organizations have responded to this potential dilemma by sponsoring and supporting continuing education efforts. They have further posited this pragmatic issue as an ethical responsibility as well, placing it within their ethical codes. The *AAMFT Code of Ethics* (American Association for Marriage and Family Therapy, 2001), for example, states in principle 3.1: "Marriage and family therapists pursue knowledge of new developments and maintain competence in marriage and family therapy through education, training, or supervised experience."

To assist members in keeping abreast of new developments, professional organizations such as the AAMFT, Division 43 of the APA (Family Psychology), and the IAMFC all sponsor regularly published newsletters and journals. These include *The Family Therapy News* and *Journal of Marital and Family Therapy* by the AAMFT; *The Family Psychologist* and *Journal of Family Psychology* by Division 43 of the APA (Family Psychology), and the *IAMFC Newsletter* and *The Family Journal: Counseling and Therapy for Couples and Families* by the IAMFC. A number of other well-established journals and newsletters (e.g., *Family Process, American Journal of Family Therapy, Family Therapist Networker*) devoted to marriage and family therapy offer articles and news of important developments in the field as well.

The aforementioned professional organizations also sponsor state, regional, and national conferences (Division 43 Family Psychology and the IAMFC, primarily within their parent associations) as well as training workshops, publication of monographs and books, and the production of videotapes. Furthermore, they encourage their members to engage in continuing education opportunities sponsored by other professionally recognized groups that are relevant to marriage and family therapy. These all are part of a necessary and ongoing process of continuing education and professional development to encourage competent, high-quality provision of services.

As noted previously, the primary professional organizations of marriage and family therapy practitioners support the concept of continuing education. All, however, promote professional continuing education as a voluntary process. Typically, only marriage and family therapists who are state licensed are required to complete certain continuing education activities to renew and thus maintain their licenses. The concept of mandatory continuing education (MCE) for licensed mental health professionals has its detractors who question whether it is necessary, let alone whether it can be structured in a manner that will actually improve the quality of services being offered. Corey, Corey, and Callanan (1998), for example, cautioned that although MCE can require physical attendance, it cannot ensure intellectual or emotional involvement. The knowledge that is absorbed and integrated into practice may be much less than a certificate of attendance indicates.

L. E. Phillips (1987), in considering all health and allied health professionals together, reported that 70% of professionals in states with MCE approve of the requirement, and more approve of it after its implementation than before. Vande-Creek, Knapp, and Brace (1990) argued convincingly for mandatory continuing education. Based on a thorough review of the literature in this area, they proposed several specific factors that appear to promote optimal MCE:

- Practitioners should be able to fulfill requirements through a variety of activities so as to take account of the diversity of interests and professional responsibilities.
- All continuing education activities should include a method for objectively showing that learning has occurred (e.g., pre- and posttests of knowledge, audio or video demonstration of skills, copies of client records—appropriately disguised—to demonstrate new learning).
- Continuing education should emphasize enhancing existing skills as well as new knowledge.

In summary, VandeCreek et al. (1990) concluded that, essentially, MCE needs to connect continuing education activities to professional practice if it is to be pragmatically purposeful. One primary means of doing so—emanating from their previously noted proposals for promoting optimal MCE—is to require licensees to document specifically how their completed continuing education activities are supposed to improve their performance of identifiable professional services. Whether mandatory or voluntary, these conclusions seem wise counsel for all marriage and family therapists to consider in enhancing their professional development.

Intraprofessional Communications

Mental health professionals are part of the upper strata of the social structure of U.S. society. Their status is partly due to their being among the best-educated persons in society; however, it is also due to their assumption of responsibility for the public welfare inherent to the profession. The AAMFT, for example, has stated this position clearly in its promotional materials: In a broader sense, the AAMFT is concerned not simply with the profession of marriage and family therapy but also with people—the needs and problems they face in relationships, whether they are now married, have been married, or may somehow be affected by marriage in our society. AAMFT is also concerned with the institution of marriage itself—its strengths and weaknesses, its changing patterns, its role in the lives of all people. AAMFT firmly believes that this most important and intimate of human relations demands increased understanding, research, and education at all levels, and that the professional marriage and family therapist must take the lead to ensure that these needs are met (American Association for Marriage and Family Therapy, 2000).

A major facet of this responsibility for the public good includes the preservation and enhancement of one's professional position as well as the profession itself (Bayles, 1981). This also, however, entails an understanding of the even more immediate and pragmatic need to maintain one's "personal–professional wellness." Professional burnout is a phenomenon that has been the topic of numerous publications and has received tremendous attention at professional conferences and continuing education endeavors. *Burnout* is a state of physical, emotional, and mental exhaustion frequently associated with intense involvement with people over long periods. Burnout is particularly critical for professionals working in the mental health field. With so much emphasis on giving to others, there is often not enough focus on giving to oneself (Corey et al., 1998). Regular intraprofessional communications are one major means of preventing or remediating burnout, and they fulfill other professional duties as well.

On a wider level, state/regional, and national professional organizations provide support, facilitate development, bring together colleagues with similar interests, offer opportunities for active participation in leadership roles, disseminate information, and generally provide a regular forum for intraprofessional communications. Both at the state/regional and national levels, opportunities for intraprofessional communications are available for active participation in relevant professional association affairs and through contact via professional journals, newsletters, and meetings. The major professional affiliations for marriage and family practitioners were identified earlier in this chapter.

On a narrower, more local level, regular intraprofessional communications with colleagues is similarly critical for maintaining personal–professional wellness and preventing burnout. For one to truly be in "private practice" is to destine oneself to become a victim of burnout. "Independent practice" has been suggested as a healthier alternative—active networking with colleagues, referral sources, and cooperating and functioning as a team member within the community system (L. R. Peterson, 1992). It is an essential means of keeping oneself fresh and excited as a marriage and family therapist.

SUMMARY AND CONCLUSIONS

During the past five decades, marriage and family therapy has developed from an interdisciplinary and nondistinct foundation of ideas to the recognized status of a profession. The theory, research, practice, and organization of marriage and family therapy have undergone a dramatic evolution that has increasingly delineated it as a separate entity—a peer within the major mental health disciplines. Many individuals who originally studied traditional professions have pursued further training and now identify themselves distinctly as marriage and family therapists. Many others, although they still maintain their original professional identities, clearly specify marriage and family as their area of professional specialization.

With this evolution there has been an equally astonishing increase in those who have taken membership not only in that organization that highlights marriage and family as a separate and distinct profession, the American Association for Marriage and Family Therapy (AAMFT), but also in those associations that recognize and promote marriage and family therapy as a professional specialization: the American Family Therapy Association (AFTA), Division 43 Family Psychology of the American Psychological Association (APA), and the International Association of Marriage and Family Counselors (IAMFC) of the American Counseling Association (ACA).

With this rise in professional association membership has come an equally impressive rise in the legislative recognition of marriage and family therapy through the enactment of licensing laws. Therapists can no longer practice whatever they wish under the guise of an unregulated profession. Accountability is now firmly an active part of marriage and family therapy practice. As of June 2000, state legislation creating licensure specifically for marriage and family therapy had been enacted in 42 states with active plans to introduce such legislation present in other states.

Maintenance of professional credibility is a multidimensional process involving active participation in one's professional development as well as actions to enhance the status and support base of the profession through research, appropriate public relations, continuing education, and intraprofessional communications. These are not separate processes; rather, they are an interrelated series of activities that foster professional identity as a marriage and family therapist.

Chapter 10 provides further opportunities to consider specific situations and questions arising from identifying oneself professionally as a marriage and family therapist.

Professional Issues

Chapters 8 and 9 presented two predominant professional issues for the practice of marriage and family therapy: the implications of valuing for the professional practice of marriage and family therapy and the professional identity of marriage and family therapists. As the professional practice of marriage and family therapy has grown from a radical new approach to an established force within mainstream mental health, many questions and thus challenges have naturally arisen. In its early development, marriage and family therapy was vulnerable to demands that it prove itself (W. C. Nichols, 1992). In seeking to do so, defensive claims purporting the essence of marriage and family therapy theory and practice, systemic epistemology, to be a panacea for all ills were advanced. Responding to these questions and challenges has led to the position that early systemic epistemology must be evolving, open to continuing discovery, if it is to maintain its positive impact. The process of *valuing* was described as a means by which new, common systems containing elements of multiple subsystems as well as the unique properties arising from their interaction can be negotiated. Such negotiation allows marriage and family therapists to maintain the importance of an epistemology that recognizes the benefits of understanding the shapes and patterns of interaction while simultaneously augmenting and deepening that understanding.

Although the roots of marriage and family therapy can be traced to Freud, the profession did not receive formal recognition until the 1970s. In this decade, the American Association of Marriage Counselors changed its name first to the American Association of Marriage and Family Counselors, and later to the American Association for Marriage and Family Therapy (AAMFT). The 1970s also saw the advent of state licensing laws regulating the profession's practice. When compared with some longer-standing professions such as medicine and law, marriage and family therapy is in its adolescence.

Adolescence is a time of many questions that evoke comparisons between what was, what is, and what may be. This chapter raises questions designed to provide answers to pragmatic inquiries about the application of valuing in the practice of marriage and family therapy as well as to contribute to a more concise and "comfortable" professional identity.

QUESTION 1
Evolving Epistemology in Actual Practice

As a marriage and family therapist, I recognize the importance of conceptualizing clients' issues as residing in systems. I also recognize the importance of incorporating the place of the individual in the system. How can I best put this evolving epistemology into actual practice and work with individuals in sessions as well as with the larger family system?

RESPONSE

Experienced marriage and family therapists' employment of a systemic epistemology is not reflected by who is in the room but, rather, by how many persons are involved in the therapist's thinking about the problem. Historically, the work of marriage and family therapists has encompassed a wide variation of ideas about who should actually be seen in sessions. Although it is generally accepted that family therapy is the treatment of choice for marital or family dysfunction, many therapists use individual sessions as a part of ongoing family efforts (M. P. Nichols, 1987a, 1987b).

Berman (1982) suggested several ways that individual sessions can be incorporated within a systemic framework: first, as a part of the diagnostic/planning process and then as a part of ongoing treatment.

Diagnosis/Planning

Alliance Issues
Conjoint or family sessions allow a clear focus on the system but may make it difficult for the therapist to gain the confidence of individual members. Having more than two persons in the room permits a reduction in therapist–individual relationship intensity. Individual sessions can serve to intensify therapist–individual client relatedness that many believe deepens clients' commitment to the therapy. Brock and Barnard (1999), for example, offered an illustration of enhancing the therapeutic engagement of a minimally committed family member in this manner.

History Taking

Marital partners and family members can profit from learning or reviewing each other's history, often adding considerably to it. However, histories taken one-to-one may be quite different from histories taken when a marital partner or family member is present. A client may omit crucial information because of guilt or embarrassment. In individual sessions, the recall process is often facilitated when a client does not have to worry about whether a spouse, parent, or child is recording potentially shameful incidents for future reference. On a more pragmatic level, individual sessions to do family-of-origin work are ideal when regularly scheduled conjoint or family sessions are difficult to coordinate (Brock & Barnard, 1999).

Assessing a Client's Manner of Acting Apart From the System

Systems can significantly contribute to a channeling of their members' behaviors. Rigid systems can often promote highly polarized interactions among members when assembled together. A startling therapeutic event is the change that frequently occurs in persons apart from their family. Direct knowledge of clients' alternative behavioral repertoires is an invaluable therapeutic awareness. Individual sessions can foster this awareness.

Ventilation/Rehearsal

Many clients enter therapy so furiously angry that they are unable to express anything else. To help these clients rehearse more effective ways of relating, it is frequently beneficial to allow some time for ventilating feelings without spouses or other family members present. The therapist can then suggest alternative ways for the client to act. Likewise, if a client is massively afraid of confronting a spouse or family member alone at home, it may help to first practice adaptive responses without feeling the pressure of the other present. Individual sessions can facilitate this type of constructive skill building (Falloon, 1991).

Secrets

Many clients have significant difficulty directly sharing certain past or present feelings and beliefs with marital partners and family members. Such "secrets" can seriously hinder therapy efforts. Individual sessions can provide a context wherein disclosure of relevant secrets is facilitated. Therapists who are aware of relevant, though unshared, marital or family information may find themselves in the difficult position of how to use it. In essence, they may find themselves in a coalition with a family member (Brendel & Nelson, 1999). No easy solutions are available in such situations; potential directions depend on the particular information and context. Thus, family therapists need to have strategies for handling secrets before they are revealed—for example, helping the client sort out how the secret could be revealed to those who have a need to know. Regardless, a therapist who is not privy to this kind of information may spend months doing unprofitable therapy while a marital partner is carrying on an affair, for example, or planning to pursue a divorce.

Individual Sessions During Ongoing Therapy

Individual Issues

One or more members of a marital or family system may be so involved in their own internal conflicts, transition issues, or irrational belief systems that efforts directed at altering their behavior consumes an inordinate amount of time during sessions. Although the system in some way helps to generate or support individual concerns, it may be more efficient and ultimately more effective to spend one or more individual sessions in a concerted effort to diminish that individual's internal conflicts so that work on couple or family goals can proceed with less conflict. Certain developmental times during the family life cycle are particularly appropriate in this regard, for example, an offspring entering young adulthood where individuation–separation issues and inner–outer conflict are pronounced (C. A. Carter, 1987; B. A. Carter & McGoldrick, 1999).

Missing Puzzle Pieces

Occasionally, information may be deliberately withheld or simply not shared early in therapy. Individual sessions offer an opportunity for enhanced awareness. For example: A family had been participating in weekly therapy sessions for almost 4 months with no apparent progress toward agreed-on goals. The therapist requested a second set of individual interviews. During her individual session, the eldest daughter revealed that she had become pregnant shortly after therapy began and has been unable to tell her parents and brother.

Sexual Dysfunction

Certain issues of a more intimate nature often lend themselves particularly well to individual sessions. Sexual difficulties, for example, can frequently be more comfortably addressed in a brief series of individual sessions with a same-sexed therapist, well-trained in human sexuality. Although most sexual education with marital partners should be undertaken with both present, it is often more productive to pursue some educational efforts in private.

Strategic and Structural Maneuvers

Individual sessions are a valuable means of unbalancing. The therapist can use them to give clients private tasks and the like and thereby reduce overinvolvement or reorder alliances. Berman (1982) cautions, however, that before seeing marital partners or family members alone, therapists should discuss the proposed sessions with all members of the system together. Members of the system should be made aware that they may experience some concern or mistrust regarding what was shared outside their presence. The rationale for individual sessions should be explained as well as any confidentiality (or lack of confidentiality) to be in effect. Although using individual sessions in the diagnostic/planning process is more a matter of clinical preference, movement to individual sessions during ongoing therapy can be a choice significantly facilitated by several common indicators: (a) therapy has not been progressing for some period of time; (b) the therapist senses that a hidden agenda is blocking therapy efforts; and (c) a client requests private time (this last indicator calls for careful clinical judgment to balance the possibility of manipulation, i.e., creating an unbalanced alliance versus trust in a client's sense of what is necessary).

QUESTION 2
Marriage and Family Therapy Interventions With Other Systems

My understanding of systemic understandings has so far emphasized the roles, relationships, rules, and balance of forces operating within marital and family systems. As a marriage and family therapist, I am recognized for my work with couples and families. How might my marital and family understandings and interventions be applied in working with other systems?

RESPONSE

Marriage and family therapy from a systemic perspective is not a method but, rather, a viewpoint. It is a clinical orientation applicable to the problems of all systems, not just marital and family systems. For example, a systemic perspective has been extended quite naturally to the school context by a number of practitioners (Colapinto, 1988; Fine & Holt, 1983; Hinkle & Wells, 1995). An individual school is a part of a larger school system, with a hierarchy of faculty, staff, and administrative roles and relationships. Within an individual school, each classroom has likewise a subsystem characterized by the same roles, relationships, rules, and balances of forces operating within couple and family systems.

The following points and case illustration adapted from Fine (1985) provide an overview of what the application of a systemic perspective within a school setting can mean for marriage and family therapists serving as consultants.

1. There is no standard operating procedure for a systemic perspective. The perspective is just that—a perspective—a mental frame of reference for viewing function and dysfunction.

2. A systemic perspective views behavior contextually and in interaction terms: What happens when a student does . . .? What precedes undesirable behaviors? How does the host system contribute to generating and escalating these behaviors? Understanding characteristic sequences of undesirable events presents the means for disrupting them and enacting desirable options.

3. A systemic perspective is concerned with the "fit" of students within the system, for example, the classroom. Do the present instructional components of the classroom match or clash with a student's learning style and developmental readiness to engage in certain learning and socialization experiences? These understandings offer the opportunity for modifying classroom variables such as seating, pace, and content of instruction; number and complexity of assignments; nature of teacher–student interactions; specific teacher control techniques; and more.

4. The systemic perspective recognizes that standard operating procedures in a situation may be exacerbating a problem and, in fact, may have defined the problem. Relevant examples include the use of certain labels that represent static views of students and teachers that, in turn, establish an expectation that influences interactions.

5. A systemic perspective is cognizant that systems overlap and thus can influence each other and that systems seek stability and may resist change as a result of homeostatic forces attempting to exert control. Because students live in multiple systems, one system might seek to influence the other to assume a particular stance. For example, parents who regularly complain to a teacher that their child refuses to listen can project this expectation into the school situation where that behavior may not be a predominant concern. Should the teacher come to accept this view of the student, the two systems become destructively aligned.

Another illustration further clarifies the applicability of a systemic perspective within a school setting:

John was a physically large, mildly retarded 14-year-old who had just completed a year of training in a residential rehabilitation facility because of a history of emotional acting out. Shortly after John enrolled in a primarily self-contained classroom in public school, his teacher became very concerned. In refusing to do a number of tasks he found frustrating, John had pounded his desk and glared menacingly at the teacher. Given John's institutional background and sheer bulk, his teacher feared being attacked.

The consultant, a marriage and family therapist who worked regularly with the schools, was called on for assistance. A review of John's background revealed no instances of physical acting out. It was decided to interpret John's actions to his teacher and other school personnel in a manner that would reduce their anxiety and offer a functional way of working with John's disruptive outbursts. His aggressive stance was defined as "the way he's learned to act to keep away persons who might make frustrating demands of him." In essence, John's emotional outbursts were reframed as poor coping strategies.

Meeting with the teacher and other involved school personnel for several sessions (some of which included John), the consultant assured all that John had never displayed any instances of physical aggression except some minor "normal" scuffles with peers that had occurred more than 4 years previously. The consultant sought enactments among all present to reinforce the reframing of John's behavior as "faulty social learnings." Within this reframing, efforts and successes at teaching more adaptive interaction skills to John were punctuated. Simple diagramming was employed to show how behaviors and reactions were related and to illustrate what was occurring among John, the teacher, and other classmates and school personnel. John, in interaction with his teacher, received training as to how to more adaptively verbalize his frustration to the teacher. The teacher was trained to facilitate and reinforce the new behavior.

In summary, the consultant framed the situation in a way that changed the perception of the problem's severity and identified more adaptive roles for John, the teacher, and other school personnel. In effect, the consultant identified society as the "persecutor," John as the "victim," and the school as the "rescuer." This facilitated movement toward a positive "let's help each other" relationship between John and the school, with the society where John had previously learned his poor coping strategies as the "villain." This way of systemically triangulating relationships represented a constructive shift from the school's initial view as being victimized by both society and John.

Although this response has addressed marriage and family therapy understandings and interventions within the school milieu, similar successes have been evidenced in other settings. One particularly exciting cutting-edge setting in recent years has been marriage and family therapy within the world of business (Cole, 1992).

QUESTION 3
Values Transactions

I recognize that as a marriage and family therapist I need to acknowledge the therapeutic influence of my values on a couple or family and attend to the transactions over values between us. However, I find it difficult at times to ascertain when I should actively seek significant change in a couple's or family's values. Are there guidelines to consider in identifying such situations?

RESPONSE

Negotiations over values are held at different levels of abstraction. They range, for example, from "marital partners should love each other" (general principle) to "this marital partner should love her mate" (particular implication) to "in these circumstances, this marital partner should demonstrate love for her mate in this particular manner" (operational application). The more abstract the value level, the more likely there is agreement between therapist and couple or family. Agreement is also more likely to occur if the therapist and couple or family share similar personal, socioeconomic, racial, cultural, and religious backgrounds. The closer interactions move to operational applications of a value or the greater the background differences between therapist and couple or family, the greater the probability of different values.

The model of therapy, the characteristics of clients, and the professional and personal styles of therapists all influence the degree and level of involvement a therapist has in addressing a couple's or family's values. As a general rule, Aponte (1985) recommends that "the therapist should attempt to exercise no more influence over the family's values than is required adequately to address the family's problems" (p. 335). In expounding this basic premise, Aponte differentiates between structure, function, and values. He identifies these three as formative constructs in a social system, a social system being an aggregate of people who join in patterned *structures* to carry out a *function* or complex of functions in accord with a framework of standards of *values*. Aponte further describes four situations (with case examples) wherein a change in a family's values will be essential to therapeutic change.

VALUES CONFLICTS AS A SOURCE OF DYSFUNCTION

When a conflict between members of a family or between a family and its community is a significant force in the dysfunction being addressed in therapy, a change in values will be essential to therapeutic change. Examples include marital dysfunction when partners are in conflict because they come from different racial, religious, ethnic, or socioeconomic backgrounds, or when a minority family has problems living in a community where there is discrimination against the minority.

Conflicting values may simply serve as superficial issues obscuring deeper emotional issues. Family members may present a values conflict as their principal concern to avoid confronting emotional forces embedded in a structural conflict. For example, an adolescent and parent may present a conflict over values about dress style, but the more significant struggle may really derive from tension over the growing emotional distance, a developmental outgrowth of an adolescent's increasing separation from the family. But although emotional issues may represent the primary source of the family problem, the values conflict, although secondary, may sufficiently influence the predominant problem to demand the therapist's attention.

Incompatible Values, Functions, and Structures

A change in values is an issue when a family's values are incompatible with the function the family intends to carry out or the structures through which it is to operate. This lack of fit between the values of the family and its functions or structures most commonly emerges from evolutionary changes in the family or its social circumstances. For example, in a family where the parents cannot interact intimately within their marital dyad, an overriding value may be placed on centering family interactions around the children. As the children mature and move away from home, however, this priority no longer serves as an adequate standard by which to organize the parents' relationship to each other. When a family's social context changes, parents may continue to guide their children by standards appropriate to the old culture but not appropriate for the new situation. For instance, in moving from a culture where higher education is encouraged to where it is discouraged, not only will there be incompatibility between the family and surrounding society but also between the parents and children, should the children have previously developed aspirations for advanced educational opportunities.

Underdeveloped Values

A change in family values is relevant to therapy efforts if a family or its members have not developed the values needed to guide the evolution of structures necessary to deal with functional issues. An underorganized family not only lacks structure but also lacks a well-elaborated, cohesive, and flexible framework of values. The development of a value framework influences how well organized the structure of a family's relationships will be. A family that has primitive, inconsistent, conflicting, or rigid values will find it difficult to effectively establish functional relationships among its members.

Disagreement Over the Therapeutic Process

Value change represents a further issue in the therapeutic process. A family and therapist struggle to seek agreement on the values framework for addressing the family's dysfunction.

> A therapist sought supervision in a case in which a couple with two children were working to face the husband's ongoing affair with another woman. The therapy had consisted primarily of technical assistance being offered with regard to the couple's decision-making process and was stalled. The therapist was unable to incorporate the family's underlying emotional issues into this framework. The therapist lacked a framework of values to define and direct his approach for working with the couple's emotional struggle. An exploration of the therapist's own family revealed a father who had carried on a long-term affair with his wife's knowledge while the therapist was a child. The therapist had been made part of the family's conspiracy of silence by sharing a number of recreational outings with the father and his woman friend and being cautioned to keep them quiet. Further, in the therapist's current life, problems over relationships were occasioned by the infidelities of a lover and consequent inability to establish an enduring, exclusive committed relationship with anyone. The therapist was unable to decide what fidelity could be expected in a love relationship or marriage. The therapist (as well as the couple) had no personal reference point from which to organize the confusion of the couple being treated about their respective expectations of marital fidelity. Moreover, the therapist, who had not adequately

dealt with personally relevant childhood conflicts, did not even think to consider the effect of the client-father's infidelity on the couple's young children. Without a values framework forged out of a resolution of personal life experiences, the therapist was approaching the family's dilemma without a means to guide interventions. The therapist obviously needed a clear set of values before he could guide the couple in efforts to resolve their conflict.

QUESTION 4
Addressing Ambivalence

As a marriage and family therapist seeking to act responsibly in clarifying my own values and assisting clients to do similarly, I am frequently confronted by ambivalence in myself and my clients. I recognize that at best, such ambivalence is nonproductive and at worst, promotes the disintegration and destruction of relationships. How might I address this ambivalence?

RESPONSE

Marital and family therapists often hear the following types of statements from clients: "I know I don't want a divorce, but I still can't get motivated enough to do what is needed to make the marriage better" or "We know our sex life is not great and want to make it better, but we can't seem to get together no matter how hard we try." Therapists might be making similar statements to themselves as well: "I know that this couple needs to discontinue their extramarital affairs if they are going to significantly improve their marital relationship, but I'm not sure it's my place to put my personal value on them." These statements reflect an ambivalence that keeps the speaker stuck midway between two points, simultaneously attracted toward and pushing away from each point.

Bergin (1991) asserts that values collaboration is critical to successful therapy outcomes. He stated the following in this regard:

> During treatment, therapists must make important decisions about how to enhance clients' functioning. . . . At these decision points, therapist, client, and concerned others should collaborate in arriving at the goals toward which change is directed. (p. 396)

For values collaboration to take place as proposed by Bergin, marriage and family therapists need to be able to provide both themselves and their clients a framework that can be used for probing the bases for their actions. Without such a framework, continued ambivalence will tend to sap available energy and prevent any commitment or concerted movement toward more adaptive options. Further, in interactions between therapists and clients, or within marital or family systems, decision making tends to shift to nonambivalent members, forcing ambivalent members to take reactive and defensive positions. In effect, ambivalent members abdicate decision-making powers and become bystanders or victims instead of active participants.

Accepting the basic concept that actions reflect values—that at any given time, people are doing what is aligned with their most cherished beliefs—calls for a framework based on values analysis. Hof and Dwyer (1982) offer such a framework and suggest that persons can perceive (or can be helped to perceive) what is most important to them and how that can affect what they actually do. This analysis of "behavior as being a consequence of values" is presented by Hof and Dwyer as having five conditions that must be fulfilled if persons are to engage in certain actions:

1. *People must have some minimal perception of self-confidence.* Although the level or intensity of confidence can significantly vary, there still must be some minimal confidence, or fear of failure will lead to avoidance of action or predestined attempts to fail. For example, the marriage and family therapist who desires to confront a couple regarding the effects of extramarital affairs must believe that such a confrontation will ultimately result in the couple's greater commitment to their relationship and consequently lead to greater satisfaction. Further, the therapist must have the self-discipline to follow through and further assist the couple to fully examine the confronted issue.

2. *People must perceive some values fulfillment, at least as potentially available.* Rarely is attention directed at any action unless there is the belief it could potentially deliver values fulfillment. The therapist must have some sense of the importance of personal values that would find fulfillment through the couple's enhanced marital interaction.

3. *People must perceive a reasonable probability that values fulfillment will be delivered.* The perception of some relevant, substantial values is not enough by itself. Again, following the example, the therapist must perceive that confronting the couple's extramarital affairs will, very likely, deliver values fulfillment to the therapist.

4. *People's perception of the costs to be paid by engaging in the behavior—values fulfillment to be given up—must be acceptable relative to the perception and probability of alternative values fulfillment.* A behavior with a high cost in terms of value fulfillment means that a person would lose a great deal of fulfillment by engaging in the proposed behavior. On the other end of the cost continuum are behaviors that have a low cost, in that a person would lose very little, if any, fulfillment when engaging in this behavior.

5. *People's perceptions of the risks to other values involved in the behavior must be acceptable relative to their perceptions and probability of alternative values fulfillment.* Not only are there perceptions of costs in all behavior changes, but there are also perceptions of risks. For example,

a risk is believed to have a probability of less than 1 of occurring. It is therefore less definite and is only a possible consequence of engaging in the proposed behavior. The therapist may have only a vague sense that something unknown may go astray or may worry about the possibility of the couple's rejection, premature termination from therapy, and the like.

To the extent that it can be seen as a function of values fulfillment, behavior constitutes the following equation:

Behavior = confidence + value fulfillment $\times$ probability of value fulfillment $-$ cost + risk

People can therefore be thought of as in a process of continual calculation, often of a subconscious nature. With regard to a proposed behavior change, if the equation results in a negative or neutral conclusion, no change will take place; if it is positive, the behavior change will occur. Current behavior is always the product of a positive result. Any change in behavior requires a change in the amount or intensity of one or more of the five conditions until the end result of the calculation is pushed onto the positive side. In the end, if there is no change in behavior, current behavior is perceived to better serve values fulfillment.

Hof and Dwyer (1982) further offer a listing of areas for exploration and intervention for each of the five conditions. This listing and then an example illustrating the framework's use with a couple in therapy follow:

1. Confidence
    a. Gathering more facts and information
    b. "Testing the water," successive approximation to build confidence
    c. Asking others to assess competence
    d. Sharing with others for self-reinforcement and obtaining reinforcement from others
    e. Practice and rehearsal
2. Conception of values fulfillment
    a. Inventorying values to determine which might be positively affected by a behavior change
    b. Interviewing others about their values fulfillment
3. Probability of values fulfillment
    a. Trying out aspects of the new behavior likely to offer the most immediate values fulfillment
    b. Trying out the new behavior in contexts most likely to be supportive to values fulfillment
    c. Providing self-reward at preset milestones
    d. Seeking information on the success rate of others who have engaged in the new behavior
4. Perception of cost
    a. Careful planning to assess and reduce costs
    b. Experimenting to assess and reduce costs
    c. Placing an upper limit on costs that would be incurred before quitting
    d. Realizing the option of backing out is always available

5. Perception of risks
   a. Planning and taking appropriate precautions to reduce risks
   b. Sharing risks whenever possible
   c. Learning from experience; experimenting to reduce risks
   d. Assessing the worst that could happen and what that might mean to overall values fulfillment

ILLUSTRATION

A couple with two children entered therapy with the intention of ending their marital relationship. It was soon evident that although the physical relationship change could be made rather easily, some factors were causing ambivalence, thereby inhibiting the decision-making process and blocking action. The values analysis construction was presented to the couple emphasizing the relevance of the five conditions, each of which was then considered separately.

1. Does the couple have the self-confidence regarding the task confronting them? Answer: Yes. Both partners were intelligent, self-responsible individuals. Both had achieved individual career success and were professionally well-established. Clearly, both had had to make significant decisions and act on them in their professional lives. They recognized as well that they would survive physically and emotionally if divorced and agreed that joint custody of the children would actually allow them to be even more effective parents. The question remained then: If they have the self-confidence needed to change, what is preventing them from changing?

2. Does the couple perceive values fulfillment in the proposed change? Again, the answer is yes. Exploration of their original marital "contract" indicated an early need by the wife to be taken care of by her husband as her family of origin had done. This dependency stance had since become aversive to her. She perceived divorce as enabling her to pursue and more fully achieve the personal fulfillment the independence in her career had provided her. The husband had brought forth needs to be "the head of the household" from his family of origin and sought to maintain a situation wherein these needs could continue to find satisfaction. His wife's desire for greater personal independence blocked his need. Divorce with potential remarriage to a partner more able to satisfy this need represented a clear values fulfillment. The question remained then: If they see values fulfillment, why do they not actively pursue change?

3. Does the couple believe they will find values fulfillment, that positive benefits would accrue to them if they made a decision and acted on it? When pressed regarding the quality of their lives apart from each other, both maintained the belief that they would develop the quality of life and find values fulfillment more easily if they ended their marriage. Both were finding such

fulfillment only in professional endeavors at present because of their contrasting personal needs. Freedom to pursue more accommodating personal relationships would allow increased personal values fulfillment. The question again, then: If they believe that they will achieve values fulfillment by changing their situation, why do they not act to change it?

4. Does the couple perceive the cost of enacting the behavior change, and do the perceived benefits sufficiently outweigh the costs to move them toward the stated values fulfillment? Again, yes. Perceived costs (what would actually be given up in terms of values fulfillment if the behavior change is undertaken) included selling their current residence and having to move, some reduced income, loss of extended in-law family contacts, and guilt for creating a broken home for their children. These costs were perceived as being inevitable and were therefore direct costs of pursuing a divorce. Each of these costs was examined in-depth; for example, their guilt resulted from a clear breach of values that "children need both parents present." They did, however, present an understanding that these values were changing and needed to be balanced by the negative effects of remaining unhappy and frequently frustrated with their marriage on the children. The guilt was framed as appropriate, but not as necessarily crippling or debilitating. The question still remained: If they perceive the costs of the behavior change, and the cost/benefit ratio is in favor of the perceived benefits, what is preventing change from occurring?

5. Does the couple perceive the risks of engaging in the desired behavior change, and do the benefits sufficiently outweigh the risks to enable them to move toward actively pursuing the behavior change? Once more, a clear yes. Risks (values fulfillment that might be blocked, but with a perceived probability of less than 1) were noted as possible loss of children if either decided to seek single custody and loss of what little satisfaction they had in their marriage if other relationships were unable to produce greater satisfaction. The loss of the children was unlikely because both agreed on joint custody. Because their present satisfaction in their marriage was so low, it was not a very powerful deterrent to action. The question remained, however: If they perceive the risks of engaging in the behavior change and the risk/benefit ratio is in favor of the perceived benefits, why is no change actively being pursued?

The values analysis as undertaken and completed indicated that barriers to movement were not sufficient to deter the couple from taking the desired action. Yet ambivalence still prevailed. The therapist considered the possibility or probability that, although the five conditions were satisfied on an intellectual level in the here and now, perhaps one or more of them were not satisfied at a subconscious level. A review of the process with the couple again proved that this was the case. Condition 4 represented a long-time and strongly held value about family life. Both partners had long ago learned and continually had been other- and self-reinforced in the belief that "children need two parents." At the subconscious level, only two options were being considered with regard to parenting: immediate presence as equaling love and caring, and nonimmediate presence through divorce as equaling rejection.

Identifying these beliefs and the early learning experiences that led to their formation did not result in instantaneous resolution of the couple's ambivalence. It did, however, lead to an agreement to seek resolution in this area through therapy efforts that ultimately led to satisfaction of this fourth condition and the originally desired behavior change—divorce.

QUESTION 5
Professional Advertising

I am moving from my position in a publicly funded agency to pursue an independent practice as a marriage and family therapist. I know that in the past advertising by the professions was frowned on but today is acceptable with conditions. I recognize the importance of advertising in building and maintaining my practice and am concerned about proceeding appropriately. Are there issues relative to advertising my practice that I should be particularly aware of?

RESPONSE

As was discussed and illustrated in Chapter 9, the AAMFT's *Code of Ethics* (American Association for Marriage and Family Therapy, 2001), Principle 8 Advertising, provides guidelines for advertising. These guidelines specify what AAMFT members should and should not do. The following simplified checklist incorporates major aspects of Principle 8 (Ridgewood Financial Institute, Inc., 1984):

- *Only facts, not opinions, should be stated.* Facts represented should obviously be truthful, but also, their accurate meanings should be easily understood by the average layperson.
- *Past performance results should be avoided.* It is almost impossible through advertising media to adequately explain all the relevant and important variables.
- *There should be no guarantees about the outcomes of therapy.* Even the best of therapeutic services are ultimately uncertain, and thus explicit or implicit guarantees cannot be assured.
- *Be cautious about appeals based on fear.* The use of brash or extravagant statements in seeking business could mislead and potentially harm laypersons, particularly those who are emotionally vulnerable.

- *Fee information demands special care.* It is very difficult to adequately provide complete and accurate enough information through advertising sources to avoid misleading, if not deceiving, an uninformed layperson. If a set fee is advertised for a special service, it obviously should be strictly adhered to.
- *Do not use misleading names, titles, or practice descriptors.* Any information that could give an erroneous impression about identity, responsibilities, status, or improperly imply a link to any group should be scrupulously avoided.

To offer further response to Question 5, the following two relevant cases incorporate an analysis using Principle 8 of the *AAMFT Code of Ethics* (American Association for Marriage and Family Therapy, 2001):

> A marriage and family therapist joining a private partnership relocated from another state. The local licensing regulations required an endorsement of the therapist's out-of-state license by the state's Department of Professional Regulation. The therapist allowed the partner to place an advertisement in the telephone book and send out announcements indicating licensure as a marriage and family therapist before completion of the endorsement process.

Both the therapist and partner violated ethical principles in this case. The therapist's approval of the premature telephone book advertisement and announcements represented a direct violation of Principles 8.1, 8.4, 8.6, and 8.7. The therapist not only sanctioned an inaccurate representation of present licensure status but also made no attempt to correct the inaccurate information being disseminated by the partner when the partner presented intentions to do so. The partner's actions represented a particularly flagrant violation of Principle 8.7 in knowingly misrepresenting the qualifications of the therapist. Impatience preempted professionally ethical practice in this instance.

> An announcement was mailed out by two partners in independent practice. The brochure described the types of services available, including marriage and family therapy and educational diagnostic services. No information indicating any distinction between the partners was included, although only one had training and licensure as a marriage and family therapist. The other, a school psychologist, had training and relevant licensure in educational diagnosis.

The brochure in this case violated Principles 8.1, 8.2, and 8.4, because it misled the public in implying the marriage and family therapist was qualified to offer educational diagnostic services and the school psychologist was competent to offer marriage and family therapy services. Principle 8.6 was similarly violated; when informed of the misleading implication, the marriage and family therapist continued to use the brochure, justifying this action by a promise to correct the implications when the present stockpile of brochures had been disseminated and new ones could be printed.

QUESTION 6
Practice Interruptions

I recently established an independent practice as a marriage and family therapist and suddenly found myself having to undergo an operation followed by a 3-week hospital recovery stay. This significant interruption in my practice caught me completely off-guard. Are there any suggested professional guidelines for handling such unexpected circumstances?

RESPONSE

Any absence, even one created by responding to another client's emergency, may appear to some clients as insufficient professional "caring" or, at the extreme, abandonment. No one can control all aspects of their life; emergencies and unanticipated circumstances inevitably arise. Marriage and family therapists, as professional mental health providers, should plan for these exigencies. As professionals, marriage and family therapists also should recognize the importance of maintaining personal wellness as well as enhancing professional development and plan for expected interruptions in providing therapeutic services such as vacations and travel to continuing education activities.

Bennett, Bryant, VandenBos, and Greenwood (1990) recommended strategies to prepare for therapeutic interruptions, both emergencies and longer-term absences.

Planning for Emergencies

1. Arrange for another marriage and family therapist to stand in (as appropriate) during emergency situations.
2. Be sure that a substitute is fully qualified both in training and awareness of the special needs of clients he or she may be called on to see to deliver the necessary services.
3. Fully inform clients about how emergencies are handled as part of their orientation to therapy. Obtain clients' written consent to provide information to anyone who might serve as a substitute therapist in an emergency. This consent is best gained at the onset of therapy in the form of a general release covering emergencies.
4. Discuss with clients the potential for emergencies in their lives as well as in the therapist's. Agree on provisions for emergencies that clients may experience (e.g., what number/whom to telephone).
5. Periodically provide a reminder (e.g., verbal, or printed on an appointment card) of emergency policy.

Planning for Longer-Term Absences

1. Arrange for coverage by another marriage and family therapist who is experienced in areas pertinent to the needs of clients he or she may see. Adequately orient this therapist to these cases.
2. Prepare clients before prolonged absences. Within reason, explain the absence and identify how long it will likely last.
3. Explain to clients the procedures they should follow during the absence.
4. On returning, meet with the substitute therapist and fully address any contacts he or she had with clients.
5. Address any relevant matters having occurred with the substitute therapist with clients immediately on reinitiating sessions with them.

Some reasons for emergencies and absences can be positive ones for the marriage and family therapist (e.g., childbirth, vacation, etc.). No matter how positive for the therapist, however, the consequence can be a painful and upsetting experience for clients, one that manifests itself either before, in the case of planned absences, or on returning from emergencies or longer-term planned absences. For other clients, if the emergency or absence is the result of a positive life event, the experience can be uplifting and potentially enhance the therapeutic process. For those clients who are upset, be prepared for their unhappiness and work to encourage discussion of the issue in a constructive context within therapy (Bennett et al., 1990).

QUESTION 7
Business-Oriented Details

Since entering independent practice as a marriage and family therapist, I have become attuned to the ongoing attention needed to business-oriented details. A major example and area of concern in this regard has been clients who have fallen behind in their payments of fees and/or who have terminated therapy and failed to pay for those services already rendered. The typical business often resolves such situations by either absorbing the losses, by taking action against the debtor through a collection agency, or using other legal alternatives such as obtaining an attorney to attempt collection or bring suit. But should I as a marriage and family therapist, a professional person with whom clients have entered a complex confidential relationship, consider myself a "typical creditor" who possesses these options for action?

RESPONSE

Obviously, the professional practice of marriage and family therapy requires that attention be given to business-oriented details if the therapist is to survive financially. However, because of the professional nature of the "business," extraordinary ethical and legal considerations must be considered, particularly with regard to employing external services to collect delinquent accounts.

Ethically, the question is whether the referral of a delinquent account to a collection service constitutes a breach of confidentiality. The *AAMFT Code of Ethics* (American Association for Marriage and Family Therapy, 2001) states the following regarding confidentiality:

> Marriage and family therapists have unique confidentiality concerns because the client in a therapeutic relationship may be more than one person. Therapists respect and guard confidences of each individual client.

Specifically, the problem is whether the referral of a client's name to a collection service may be interpreted as a confidence. One could readily dispute the contention that disclosing a client's name (and other relevant information such as address and phone number) constitutes a betrayal of confidences conveyed in the clinical relationship. There has traditionally been, however, a consensus that clients have control over who knows that they have sought therapy (Pressman, 1979). Thus, clients' names could just as readily be viewed as a protected confidence of the therapeutic relationship. There is presently no clear general principle addressing referrals to collection agencies.

Still within the *AAMFT Code of Ethics* (American Association for Marriage and Family, 2001), using a collection agency may be clearly ethical if the therapist, before the initiation of therapy, provides the client with full knowledge of the financial conditions of the therapeutic relationship. The client can then decide from the outset whether to enter therapy under these conditions.

Informed consent of clients at the beginning of therapy would therefore seem to settle any possible ethical concerns. If a client had not been properly informed of pertinent financial conditions, a warning that an account may be released (e.g., after the therapy had begun and a debt was incurred) would be a paper tiger and, if acted on, an ethical violation. In other words, warning clients that they had better pay their bills or else a collection service will be brought in would be unethical if the therapist lacked consent to release the relevant information from the outset of therapy.

Although some of the possible ethical ramifications of employing an external collection service may be arguable, much clearer consequences for marriage and family therapists are evident in considering potential legal vulnerability. A legal complaint against a marriage and family therapist may result from a fee dispute. If harassment by collection agencies retained by a marriage and family therapist occurs, the legal situation may become especially troublesome. Bennett et al. (1990) state that use of a collection agency increases the risk of malpractice litigation, particularly if clients fail to pay for services they felt were unsatisfactory, unhelpful, or incompetent.

Clients terminate therapy and leave unpaid bills for numerous reasons. Some clients may be financially overextended and place greater priority on the payment of other accounts. Others may view the therapy efforts as not having been helpful, thus negating their financial obligation. Such clients may view the use of a collection service as harassment even when they gave their informed consent at the onset of therapy, and attempts to obtain payment from such clients may result in their bringing suit against the therapist. The therapist may be falsely accused of a variety of charges, some of which, such as sexual impropriety or abuse, may result in a difficult legal defense. Legal expert Cohen (1979) explicitly suggests, "One thing doctors should never do, however, is routinely turn accounts over to collection agencies. Collection agencies can be coarse in their treatment of patients, and they might push patients thinking about litigation into actually contacting an attorney" (p. 273). Again, Bennett et al. (1990) affirmed Cohen's admonition and suggest attempting to negotiate a payment plan or some such strategy and using a collection agency only as a last resort.

The release of information by marriage and family therapists to a collection service is quite different from the release of material to facilitate a third-party payment. In the case of third-party payments, clients are usually aware of the information to be released, because most will bring claim forms to the therapist or will have to sign forms so that reimbursement can be directed to the therapist. In most cases, clients encourage such a release of information to defray personal financial costs.

The ultimate pragmatic argument may be that a marriage and family therapist has as much right as any other businessperson to take action against debtors. Such an argument notes that clients enter an implied contract at the outset of therapy; services have a price, and clients are obligated to pay for services rendered. Taken alone, this argument is undeniably true, yet it may only hold true in settings other than therapy.

Faustman (1982) recommended that the best means of avoiding the potential ethical and legal problems created by resorting to collection services is to use billing strategies that prevent delinquent payments. He proposed requiring payment at the time of the visit, a practice common among other professionals (e.g., physicians, dentists). The acceptance of credit cards also provides immediate payment. Credit card receipts can be filled out so the confidential nature of clients' therapeutic status is ensured (e.g., listing therapy as "services rendered" and avoiding information relating to the practice of marriage and family therapy). Using extended payment plans in cases of financial hardship offers another avenue.

In summary, although external collection services constitute one source of debt collection, potential legal risks should be considered and extreme caution taken in pursuing financial action against clients, particularly those who might have conveyed dissatisfaction regarding the quality or nature of therapy. When such action is taken, clients should have been properly informed at the start of therapy that external collection services are employed by the therapist when necessary and subsequently offered their informed consent to continue in therapy given this caveat.

QUESTION 8
Independent Practice in a Rural Area

I am presently employed in an urban community mental health center and am considering moving to a small community that has no marriage and family therapist in residence. My training and experiences have been in more urban settings. What can I expect in developing an independent practice in a small town?

RESPONSE

Information about independent mental health providers in small communities is scarce. The majority of potentially relevant professional literature has focused on practitioners employed by community mental health centers in rural areas. Many issues regarding the independent practice of marriage and family therapy in small communities do, however, bear a strong resemblance to those raised by rural community mental health workers, and a review of the professional literature in this area may prove fruitful.

Sobel (1984) raises a number of professional issues considered relevant to small-town practice from the viewpoint of a psychologist. These same issues are applicable to a marriage and family therapist seeking a similar situation and are summarized in the following paragraphs.

Generalist vs. Specialist

Urban-based practices allow marriage and family therapists to specialize, because other therapists are available to deliver a full complement of services to the population. Small-town practice does not permit specialization. For example, consider a therapist who specializes in marital therapy practicing in a community that sees adolescent drug abuse as its major mental health problem. Although the marriage and family therapist may perceive adolescent drug abuse to be primarily precipitated by dysfunctional marital relationships of parents, centering a practice on marital therapy would probably fail because the community's defined need is not being met. However, were the therapist to initially establish a practice to work with adolescent drug abuse and demonstrate success to the community, the therapist's credibility would increase, and he or she could bring greater attention to marital dyads and develop a more direct demand for such services.

Community. Agencies and Organizations

Involvement with community agencies and organizations is important for any independent practitioner, particularly from the standpoint of generating and maintaining referral sources. In a small town setting, a marriage and family therapist will need to pursue an extraordinary involvement. Although one does not usually perceive independent practitioners as taking a major role in community education, the therapist in a smaller community must. Residents need to be educated about the identification of relevant problems and the availability of treatment resources. Thus, involvements with religious, professional, and social organizations become a regular part of the therapist's practice, though it is usually on a pro bono basis. Work within the schools is a particularly valuable service and source of referrals.

Professional Impact on Personal Privacy

The marriage and family therapist in a small town will likely live in the community. Thus, unlike in a larger urban setting, some personal privacy is lost. The expectations of neighbors as well as other community people may call for the therapist to maintain a "professional image" at all times, lest credibility and practice suffer. Sensitivity to the community's standards is critical.

Funding Dilemmas

Small towns are likely to have fewer funding resources than urban communities. The financial resources of residents themselves and the general community revenues that often serve as a source of fees for marriage and family therapists in independent practice will be more limited. Innovative therapeutic practice (e.g., multiple family therapy) as well as innovative business practice (e.g., bartering) may be called for.

Professional Isolation

Independent practice can lead to professional isolation. The isolation of the marriage and family therapist is likely to be much greater in a small community than in urban areas. Peer consultation is not readily available. The therapist must rely on personal resources to keep abreast of new developments as well as creatively consider innovative interventions. Potentially the most frustrating isolation issue may be the lack of a full complement of mental health services within the community. The therapist may often be confronted with the decision of whether to refuse treatment or to deliver a service that is not the treatment of choice.

Continuing Professional Development

Closely tied to the issue of professional isolation is the increased need for continuing education. Needing to assume more of a generalist role calls for working with a wide diversity of presenting problems. To be successful, the therapist needs an eclectic orientation to provide the widest breadth of services possible. Thus, continuing education is critical.

Given the paucity of library resources and limited access to conferences, lectures, and seminars, a multifaceted program is recommended. Subscriptions to relevant professional journals and the regular purchase of appropriate books constitute necessary business expenses. The Internet, especially e-mail, and distance learning courses might be used, too. Attendance at workshops, seminars, and professional meetings must be worked into a schedule even if significant travel is required. Therapists within a reasonable distance of each other, such as a 2- to 3-hour drive, might arrange monthly or bimonthly meetings to discuss professional issues and topics to maintain and enhance clinical skills.

QUESTION 9
Being a "Public" Marriage and Family Therapist

As my practice has expanded and my expertise within the community become more well-known, I have received an increasing number of invitations to be interviewed for the newspaper, appear as a guest on radio, and speak at local gatherings. I feel that I have represented myself as a professional marriage and family therapist well. I question, however, knowing what I now know, how well-prepared a novice therapist might be in such situations.

RESPONSE

The importance of being well-prepared if one is to assume the role of a "public" marriage and family therapist has been strongly asserted within the professional literature. Harkaway (1989), for example, proposes that "Therapists should think twice before they decide to feed the talk-show lion" (p. 3). Yet, she further noted that if experienced therapists do not professionally present marriage and family therapy to the public, the task will be left to less experienced novices, likely ill-suited to the task.

Bennett et al. (1990) offer a list of suggestions for being a "public" psychologist. Adaptations of these suggestions are offered here for being a "public" marriage and family therapist.

1. All "advice" should be scientifically valid.
2. Be especially sensitive to the possibility that information provided to consumers may be misunderstood or misused. Do not assume that the audience will either understand or take the time to understand what is being said.

3. Avoid offering advice or information in any area where your training or experience are insufficient.

4. Clearly state the limitations of any information provided.

5. Always prepare carefully for live presentations. Recognize that nervousness, the pressures of a radically different environment, the presence of an audience, and other factors can contribute to confusion and possible misstatements. Become familiar with the presentation, interview, or broadcast setting in advance, if at all possible.

6. During live presentations, especially those involving questions and answers, take time to think before speaking. Avoid becoming emotional when faced with conflict or issues felt strongly about.

7. Avoid representing theory as fact or beliefs held by some marriage and family therapists as being held by the profession as a whole. Be objective with regard to controversial topics. If not, provide the names of colleagues who can speak to the other side of the issue.

8. Be fully aware of what is being said as well as *how* it is being said. Define terms and use lay language to enhance audience understanding.

9. If documents or films are being produced from the presentation, be clear on editing policies and the opportunity to participate in that process.

10. Be especially sensitive to the limitations of evaluating and providing appropriate diagnoses to consumers by radio, television, telephone, or newspaper articles and books. Always consider the implications of any instructions or advice offered without adequate rehearsal and follow-up.

11. Screen callers and media participants to protect those who should not have such exposure. Develop and maintain referral procedures to qualified professionals.

In summary, those desiring to assume the role of "public" marriage and family therapist should carefully determine the purpose of any media presentation they are invited to make, when and how it will be presented, and the kind of audience that will be addressed. Learn about the sponsor of the presentation, and never accept any invitation unless the sponsor's reliability and respectability can be ensured. Finally, no matter the pressure exerted or possibility of favorable exposure, marriage and family therapists should only agree to address or speak about issues for which they are well qualified and prepared (Bennett et al. 1990).

QUESTION 10
Optimally Serving Oneself and One's Clients

I am presently employed as a marriage and family therapist in a large community mental health center where my caseload consists of an array of physically in-need, as well as emotionally distressed, families. The paperwork alone feels overwhelming most of the time. I'm beginning to question whether I can ever work hard enough to keep offering optimal professional services and yet still take care of myself and my own family responsibilities.

RESPONSE

Several points are relevant to consider in serving oneself as well as one's clients optimally as a marriage and family therapist. First and foremost, it is critical to recognize that the more clients one serves, the greater the potential for stress. Family-oriented service providers, such as marriage and family therapists, comparatively, have a very high likelihood of experiencing excessive job stress. Second, it is important to consider one's initial motivation for becoming a marriage and family therapist. Individuals enter the mental health professions for a variety of reasons, some of which are healthier than others (Gladding, 2000). The marriage and family therapist who enters the profession to help others primarily because of unresolved issues in his or her own family of origin, or the therapist who has an excessive need to be needed, are likely candidates to become overinvolved with client families to the neglect of themselves and their own families.

Guy (1987) points out that the work of being a therapist has the potential for both positive and negative impact on one's family life. On the positive side, marriage and family therapists can become more aware of the importance of their spouses and families in helping them experience meaning and fulfillment in life. They may even take more time to interact with family members because of their increased awareness of the value these persons play in their lives.

On the negative side, marriage and family therapists can feel they are all used up after a day at the office and not have the time or interest to interact meaningfully with their own family members. Consequently, they may retreat into themselves and separate from those who could emotionally and physically nourish them.

Finding a balance between work and personal/family life is critical if marriage and family therapists are to maintain optimal functioning personally and professionally. "Poor counselor self-care is associated with the potential for ethical breaches, reduced self-monitoring, emotional vulnerability, and impaired judgment (Frame, 1999, p. 110). Thus, the advice of Brock and Barnard (1992) is most apt here:

> Therapists engaged in family-based treatment, particularly those who work with families in acute distress, are well advised to continually attend to their own needs to prevent acute distress. (p. 176)

Ways for marriage and family therapists to achieve a balance between their personal/family and professional life are available, including the following:

1. *Have a lifestyle that accurately reflects personal and professional values.* All too often, some marriage and family therapists profess values

they do not live by. For instance, they may advise families to spend more together time while they themselves live at the office instead of blocking out reasonable time periods for personal/family interactions.

2. *Teach and supervise other therapists.* One way of serving oneself and the profession is to teach and supervise other therapists. Through teaching and supervising other therapists, understanding and empathy for oneself and one's own circumstances are increased (Kottler, 1990).

3. *Confront the source(s) of stress.* The source may be anything from one's supervisor to one's caseload. The important point is to investigate the roots of the stressor, not just any manifest symptoms. In such a scenario, marriage and family therapists can look to change the system through environmental structuring or different personal interactions. The critical factor is for the therapist to gain greater power over his or her circumstances and not continue feeling victimized or helpless (Kottler, 1990).

4. *Look for humor.* Although the events that marriage and family therapists face daily are not funny, and are often very serious, there is humor to be found sometime during almost every day. The healing power of small doses of humor can diminish stress considerably (Pittman, 1995).

There are many ways to promote and maintain optimal personal/family and professional well-being, just as there are many ways that contribute to its deterioration. Marriage and family therapists, regardless of their work setting, must be active in pursuit of wellness. Surrounding oneself with a healthy balance of personal/family and professional activities and actively employing coping strategies to deal with stressful events are keys to enjoying one's work and family. As with therapy efforts, it is essential to recognize that mental, physical, family, and professional health are all processes that require continuous monitoring and, at times, modifications.

References

A Brief History of IAMFC. (1992). *IAMFC Newsletter*, p. 6.

Abelson, R., & Nielson, K. (1967). History of ethics. In P. Edwards (Ed.), *The encyclopedia of philosophy* (Vol. 3). New York: Macmillan.

Abroms, G. M. (1978). The place of values in psychotherapy. *Journal of Marriage and Family Counseling, 4,* 3–17.

Allen, J., & Curran, J. (1988). Prevention of AIDS and HIV infection: Needs and priorities for epidemiologic research. *American Journal of Public Health, 78,* 381–386.

Alsager v. District Court of Polk County, Iowa, 406 F. Supp. 10. (1975).

American Association for Marriage and Family Therapy. (1982). *Standards on public information and advertising.* Washington, DC: Author.

American Association for Marriage and Family Therapy. (1990). *AAMFT membership requirements.* Washington, DC: Author.

American Association for Marriage and Family Therapy. (1992a). *The model marriage and family therapy licensure act.* Washington, DC: Author.

American Association for Marriage and Family Therapy. (1992b). *Procedures for handling ethical matters.* Washington, DC: Author.

American Association for Marriage and Family Therapy. (1997). *Approved supervisor designation: Standards and responsibilities.* Washington, DC: Author.

American Association for Marriage and Family Therapy. (1998a, August/September). Guidelines for use of the new AAMFT clinical member logo. *Family Therapy News, 29,* 18–20.

American Association for Marriage and Family Therapy. (1998b).

American Association for Marriage and Family Therapy. (1999, April/May). Therapy by E-mail. *Family Therapy News, 29,* 3.

American Association for Marriage and Family Therapy. (2000). *AAMFT overview.* Available: http://www.aamft.org/about/aamft.htm

American Association for Marriage and Family Therapy. (2001). *AAMFT code of ethics.* Washington, DC: Author. Available: http://www.aamft.org/about/ethic.htm

American Association for Marriage and Family Therapy, Supervision Committee. (1999). *Introduction to the approved supervisor designation.* Available: http://www.aamft.org/about/asrequire.htm

American Counseling Association. (1995). *Code of ethics and standards of practice.* Alexandria, VA: Author.

American Psychiatric Association. (1980). *Diagnostic and statistical manual of mental disorders* (3rd ed.). Washington, DC: Author.

American Psychiatric Association. (1987). *Diagnostic and statistical manual of mental disorders* (Rev. 3rd ed.). Washington, DC: Author.

American Psychiatric Association. (1994). *Diagnostic and statistical manual of mental disorders* (4th ed.). Washington, DC: Author.

American Psychological Association. (1981). *Ethical standards of psychologist* (Rev. ed.). Washington, DC: Author.

American Psychological Association. (1987). *Casebook on ethical principles of psychologists.* Washington, DC: Author.

American Psychological Association. (1992). *Ethical principles of psychologists and code of conduct.* Washington, DC: Author.

Anderson, B. S., & Hopkins, B. R. (1996). *The counselor and the law* (4th ed.). Alexandria, VA: American Counseling Association.

Anderson, C. M. (1986). The all-too-short trip from positive to negative connotation. *Journal of Marital and Family Therapy, 12*, 351–354.

Anderson, C. M., Reiss, D. J., & Hogarty, G. E. (1986). *Schizophrenia and the family.* New York: Guilford.

Andolfi, M., Angelo, C., Menghi, P., & Nicolo-Corigliano, M. (1983). *Beyond the family mask. Therapeutic change in rigid family systems.* New York: Brunner/Mazel.

Aponte, H. J. (1985). The negotiation of values in therapy. *Family Process, 24*, 323–338.

Appelbaum, P. S., Lidz, C. W., & Meisel, A. (1987). *Informed consent: Legal theory and clinical practice.* New York: Oxford University Press.

Appleson, G. (1982). More patients suing their psychiatrists. *American Bar Association Journal, 68*, 1353–1354.

Application of Striegel, 92 Misc.2d 113, 399 N.Y.S.2d 584 (1977).

Ard, B. N., & Ard, C. (Eds.). (1976). *Handbook of marriage counseling* (2nd ed.). Palo Alto, CA: Science and Behavior Books.

Arthur, G. L., & Swanson, C. D. (1993). *Confidentiality and privileged communication.* Alexandria, VA: American Counseling Association.

Atwood, J. D. (1992). The historical aspects of marriage and family therapy. In J. D. Atwood (Ed.), *Family therapy* (pp. 5–28). Chicago: Nelson-Hall.

Atwood v. Atwood, 550 S.W.2d 465 (Ky. 1976).

Baehr v. Lewis, 852 P2d 44 (Haw. 1993), *remanded sub.nom.* Baehr v Miike, No. 91-1394, 1996 L 694235 (Haw. Cir. Ct. Dec. 3, 1996) *order aff'd,* 950 P.2d 1234 (1997).

Bagarozzi, G. A., & Giddings, C. W. (1983). Conjugal violence: A critical review of current research and clinical practices. *American Journal of Family Therapy, 11*, 3–12.

Baier, K. (1958). *The moral point of view.* Ithaca, NY: Cornell University.

Barry, V. C. (1982). *Moral aspects of health care.* Pacific Grove, CA: Brooks/Cole.

Bateson, G. (1977). The birth of a matrix or double bind and epistemology. In M. Berger (Ed.), *Beyond the double bind.* New York: Brunner/Mazel.

Bateson, G. (1979). *Mind and nature: A necessary unity.* New York: Bantam.

Bayles, M. D. (1981). *Professional ethics.* Belmont, CA: Wadsworth.

Beauchamp, T. L., & Childress, J. F. (1994). *Principles of biomedical ethics* (4th ed). New York: Oxford University Press.

Beck, J., & Baxter, P. (1998). The violent patient. In L. E. Lifson & R. I. Simon (Eds.), *The mental health practitioner and the law* (pp. 153–165). Cambridge, MA: Harvard University Press.

Becker, R. F. (1997). *Scientific evidence and expert testimony handbook: A guide for lawyers, criminal investigators and forensic specialists.* Springfield, IL: Charles C. Thomas.

Becvar, D. S., Becvar, R. J., & Bender, A. E. (1982). First let us do no harm. *Journal of Marital and Family Therapy, 8*, 385–392.

Bednar, R. L., Burlingame, G. M., & Masters, K. S. (1988). Systems of family treatment: Substance or semantics? *Annual Review of Psychology, 39*, 401–434.

Behnke, S. H., & Saks, E. R. (1998). Therapeutic jurisprudence: Informed consent as a clinical indication for the chronically suicidal patient with borderline personality disorder. *Loyola of Los Angeles Law Review, 31*, 945–982.

Belcher, D. I., & Pomeroy, L. O. (1998). For richer, for poorer: Strategies for premarital agreements. *Probate and Property, 12*, 54–59.

Bellotti v. Baird (II), 443 U.S. 622 (1979).

Bennett, B. E., Bryant, B. K., VandenBos, G. R., & Greenwood, A. (1990). *Professional liability and risk management.* Washington, DC: American Psychological Association.

Bergantino, L. A. (1978). A theory of imperfection. *Counselor Education and Supervision, 17,* 286–292.

Bergin, A. E. (1985). Proposed values for guiding and evaluating counseling and psychotherapy. *Counseling and Values, 29,* 99–115.

Bergin, A. E. (1991). Values and religious issues in psychotherapy and mental health. *American Psychologist, 46,* 394–403.

Berman, E. M. (1982). The individual interview as a treatment technique in conjoint therapy. *American Journal of Family Therapy, 10,* 27–37.

Berner, M. (1998). Informed consent. In L. E. Lifson & R. I. Simon (Eds.), *The mental health practitioner and the law* (pp. 23–43). Cambridge, MA: Harvard University Press.

Bernstein, B. E. (1982). Ignorance of the law is no excuse. In J. C. Hansen & L. L'Abate (Eds.), *Values, ethics, legalities and the family therapist* (pp. 87–102). Rockville, MD: Aspen.

Berry v. Moensch, 8 Utah 2d 191, 331 P2d 814 (1958).

Bersoff, D. N. (1995). *Ethical conflicts in psychology.* Washington, DC: American Psychological Association.

Bersoff, D., & Jain, M. (1980). A practical guide to privileged communication for psychologists. In G. Cooke (Ed.), *The role of the forensic psychologist.* Springfield, IL: Charles C. Thomas.

Bertram, B. (1983). A threat to licensure. *American Mental Health Counselors Association News, 6*(6), 1, 7.

Besharov, D. J. (1982). Representing abused and neglected children: When protecting children means seeking the dismissal of court proceedings. *Journal of Family Law, 20,* 217–239.

Betancourt, M. (1997). *What to do when love turns violent: a practical resource for women in abusive relationships.* New York: HarperCollins.

Bieluch v. Bieluch, 462 A2d 1060 (Conn. 1983).

Bird, G., & Sporakowski, M. J. (1992). *Taking sides: Clashing views on controversial issues in family and personal relationships.* Guilford, CT: Dushkin.

Bittner, S., Bialek, E., Nathiel, S., Ringwald, J., & Tupper, M. (1999). An alternative to managed care: A "guild" model for the independent practice of psychotherapy. *Journal of Marital and Family Therapy, 25,* 99–111.

Black, D. W., Yates, W. R., & Andreasen, N. C. (1988). Schizophrenia, schizophreniform disorder, and delusional (paranoid) disorders. In J. A. Talbott, R. E. Hales, & S. C. Yudofsky (Eds.), *The American psychiatric press textbook of psychiatry.* Washington, DC: American Psychiatric Press.

Black, M., & Joffe, W. A. (1978). A lawyer/therapist team approach to divorce. *Conciliation Courts Review, 16,* 1–5.

Black's Law Dictionary (4th ed.). (1968). St. Paul, MN: West.

Blades, J. (1984, March). Mediation: An old art revitalized. *Mediation Quarterly,* pp. 146–193.

Blasi, A. (1980). Bridging moral cognition and moral action: A critical review of the literature. *Psychological Bulletin, 88,* 1–42.

Bograd, M. (1984). Family systems approaches to wife battering: A feminist critique. *American Journal of Orthopsychiatry, 54,* 558–568.

Bograd, M. (1986). Holding the line: Confronting the abusive partner. *The Family Therapy Networker, 10*(4), 44–47.

Bograd, M., & Mederos, F. (1999). Battering and couple therapy: Universal screening and selection of treatment modality. *Journal of Marital and Family Therapy, 25,* 291–312.

Bonnington, S. B., Crawford, R. L., Curtis, T., & Watts, R. (1996). Family ethics: Managed care limits on third-party payment. *Family Journal: Counseling and Therapy for Couples and Families, 4,* 239–241.

Bonnington, S. B., McGrath, P., & Martinek, S. A. (1996). The fax of the matter: The electronic transfer of confidential material. *Family Journal: Counseling and Therapy for Couples and Families, 4,* 155–156.

Borys, D. S. (1988). *Dual relationships between therapist and client: A national survey of clinicians' attitudes and practices.* Unpublished doctoral dissertation, University of California, Los Angeles.

Boszormenyi-Nagy, I. (1974). Ethical and practical implications of intergenerational family therapy. *Psychotherapy and Psychosomatics, 24,* 261–268.

Boszormenyi-Nagy, I., & Spark, G. (1973). *Invisible loyalties.* Hagerstown, MD: Harper & Row.

Boszormenyi-Nagy, I., & Ulrich, D. N. (1981). Contextual family therapy. In A. S. Gurman & D. P. Kniskern (Eds.), *Handbook of family therapy.* New York: Brunner/Mazel.

Boughner, S. R., & Logan, J. P. (1999). Robert H. Woody: Legal issues in couple and family counseling. *The Family Journal: Counseling and Therapy for Couples and Families, 7,* 302–310.

Bourne, P. G. (1982). Ethical problems of therapists in government and industry. In M. Rosenbaum (Ed.), *Ethics and values in psychotherapy: A guidebook* (pp. 385–402). New York: Free Press.

Bowen, M. (1978). *Family therapy in clinical practice.* New York: Jason Aronson.

Bowers, M. (1992a). Politics, power, and prestige: The emergence of the profession. *Family Therapy News, 23*(5), 5, 18.

Bowers, M. (1992b). Regulating the profession. *AAMFT 1992 leadership conference proceedings.* Washington, DC: American Association for Marriage and Family Therapy.

Braaten, E. E., Otto, S., & Handelsman, M. M. (1993). What do people want to know about psychotherapy? *Psychotherapy, 30,* 565–570.

Brady v. Hopper, 570 F.Supp. 1333 (D. Colo. 1983); aff'd, 751 F.2d 329 (10th Cir. 1984).

Brandt, R. (1959). *Ethical theory.* Upper Saddle River, NJ: Prentice Hall.

Bray, J. H., Shepherd, J. N., & Hays, J. R. (1985). Legal and ethical issues in informed consent to psychotherapy. *American Journal of Family Therapy, 13,* 50–60.

Brendel, J. M., & Nelson, K. W. (1999). The stream of family secrets: Navigating the islands of confidentiality and triangulation involving family therapists. *Family Journal: Counseling and Therapy for Couples and Families, 7,* 112–117.

Broadhurst, D. D. (1979). *The educator's role in the prevention and treatment of child abuse and neglect.* Washington, DC: National Center on Child Abuse and Neglect, U. S. Department of Health, Education and Welfare.

Brock, G. W. (1998). *Ethics casebook.* Washington, DC: American Association for Marriage and Family Therapy.

Brock, G. W., & Barnard, C. P. (1999). *Procedures in marriage and family therapy* (3rd ed.). Upper Saddle River, NJ: Prentice Hall.

Brodsky, S. L., & Robey, A. (1972). On becoming an expert witness: Issues of orientation and effectiveness. *Professional Psychology, 3,* 173–176.

Bromberg, W. (1979). *The uses of psychiatry and the law.* Westport, CT: Quorum.

Brown, H. I. (1977). *Perception, theory and commitment.* Chicago: University of Chicago.

Bruce, D. K. (1990). Ethicism, advertising, and restraint of trade. *The Family Psychologist, 6*(2), 23.

Budman, S. (1989, August). *Training experienced clinicians to do brief treatment—silk purses into sow's ears.* Paper presented at the 97th Annual Convention of the American Psychological Association, New Orleans, LA.

Budman, S. H., & Gurman, A. S. (1988). *Theory and practice of brief therapy.* New York: Guilford.

Bureau of National Affairs, Inc. (1976). *Uniform parentage act.* Washington, DC: Author.

Bureau of National Affairs, Inc. (1982). *Uniform marriage and divorce act.* Washington, DC: Author.

Bureau of National Affairs, Inc. (1984). *Uniform premarital agreement act.* Washington, DC: Author.

Burgum, F., & Anderson, S. (1975). *The counselor and the law.* Washington, DC: American Personnel and Guidance Association.

Caban v. Mohammed, 441 U.S. 380 (1979).

Cambien, J. (1989). Reality in psychotherapy. *Journal of Family Psychology, 3,* 29–38.

Canfield, B., & Locke, D. W. (1991, Summer). Are we addressing the right problem? *IAMFC Newsletter,* pp. 1, 4.

Canterbury v. Spence, 464 F.2d 772 (D.C. Cir 1972).

Carl, D., & Jurkovic, G. J. (1983). Agency triangles: Problems in agency–family relationships. *Family Process, 22,* 441–451.

Carter, B. (1986). Success in family therapy. *Family Therapy Networker, 10(4)*, 16–22.

Carter, B. A., & McGoldrick, M. (Eds.). (1999). *The expanded family life cycle* (3rd ed.). Needham Heights, MA: Allyn & Bacon.

Carter, C. A. (1987). Some indications for combining individual and family therapy. *American Journal of Family Therapy, 15,* 99–110.

Case Notes. (1985–1986). *Journal of Family Law, 24,* 552–558.

Castro, K., Lifson, A., White, C., Bush, T., Chamberland, M., Lekatsas, A., & Jaffe, H. (1988). Investigations of AIDS patients with no previously identified risk factors. *Journal of the American Medical Association, 262,* 1338–1342.

Caudill, O. B., Jr. (1999, June/July). The technology trap. *Family Therapy News, 30,* 20, 22.

Cavell, T. A., & Snyder, D. K. (1991). Iconoclasm versus innovation: Building a science of family therapy. *Journal of Marital and Family Therapy, 17,* 167–171.

Centers for Disease Control. (1989). First 100,000 cases of acquired immunodeficiency syndrome—United States. *Journal of the American Medical Association, 262,* 1453, 1456.

Centers for Disease Control. (1999). *Division of HIV/AIDS Prevention: Basic statistics—cumulative cases.* Washington, DC: Author. Available: http://www.cdc.gov/ hiv/stats/cumulati.htm

Chaffin v. Chaffin, 239 Or. 374, 397 P.2d 771 (1964).

Chemerinsky, E. (1979). Defining the "best interests": Constitutional protections in involuntary adoptions. *Journal of Family Law, 18,* 79–113.

Christie, G. C., Meeks, J. E., Pryor, E. S., & Sanders, J. (1997). *Cases and materials on the law of torts* (3rd ed.). St. Paul, MN: West.

Claim of Gerkin, 106 Misc.2d 643, 434 N.Y.S.2d 607 (1980).

Clark, H. H., Jr. (1968). *The law of domestic relations.* St. Paul, MN: West.

Clark, H. H., Jr. (1974). *Cases and problems on domestic relations.* St. Paul, MN: West.

Cleary, E. W. (Ed.). (1972). *McCormick's handbook of law evidence* (2nd ed.). St: Paul, MN: West.

COAMFTE Accredited and Candidacy Status Programs. (1992). *AAMFT Accreditation News, 2*(1), program listing.

Cobbs v. Grant. 8 Cal., 3d 229, 502 P.2d 1 (1972).

Cohen, R. J. (1979). *Malpractice: A guide for mental health professionals.* New York: Free Press.

Cohen, R. J., & Mariano, W. E. (1982). *Legal guidebook in mental health.* New York: The Free Press.

Colapinto, J. (1988). Avoiding a common pitfall in compulsory school referrals. *Journal of Marital and Family Therapy, 14,* 89–96.

Cole, P. M. (1992). Family systems business: A merger at last. *Family Therapy News, 23*(2), 29.

Combrinck-Graham, L. (1986). Coercion and therapy. *The Family Therapy Networker, 10*(4), 69.

Commission on Accreditation for Marriage and Family Therapy Education. (1997). *Manual on accreditation.* Washington, DC: Author. Available: http://www.aamft.org/ about/accred.htm

Condoms for prevention of sexually transmitted diseases. (1988). *Journal of the American Medical Association, 259,* 1925–1927.

120 Cong. Rec. 27, 36533 (1974).

120 Cong. Rec. 31, 41381 (1974).

Connell, M. J. (1981). Property division and alimony awards: A survey of statutory limitations on judicial discretion. *Fordham Law Review, 50,* 415–449.

Coogler, O. J. (1978). *Structured mediation in divorce settlement.* Lexington, MA: Heath.

Corey, G., Corey, M. S., & Callanan, P. (1984). *Issues and ethics in the helping professions* (2nd ed.). Pacific Grove, CA: Brooks/Cole.

Corey, G., Corey, M. S., & Callanan, P. (1993). *Issues and ethics in the helping professions* (4th ed.). Pacific Grove, CA: Brooks/Cole.

Corey, G., Corey, M. S., & Callanan, P. (1998). *Issues and ethics in the helping professions* (5th ed.). Pacific Grove, CA: Brooks/Cole.

Cormier, L. S., & Bernard, J. M. (1982). Ethical and legal responsibilities of clinical supervisors. *Personnel and Guidance Journal, 60,* 486–490.

Cottone, R. R. (1988). Epistemological and ontological issues in counseling: Implications of social systems theory. *Counseling Psychology Quarterly, 1,* 357–365.

Cottone, R. R. (1991). Counselor roles according to two counseling world views. *Journal of Counseling and Development, 69,* 398–401.

Cottone, R. R., & Greenwell, R. J. (1992). Beyond linearity and circularity: Deconstructing social systems theory. *Journal of Marital and Family Therapy, 18,* 167–177.

Cottone, R. R., & Tarvydas, V. M. (1998). *Ethical and professional issues in counseling.* Upper Saddle River, NJ: Prentice Hall.

Coyne, J. C., & Anderson, B. J. (1989). The "psychosomatic family" reconsidered II: Recalling a defective model and looking ahead. *Journal of Marital and Family Therapy, 15,* 139–148.

Cruchfield, C. F. (1981). Nonmarital relationships and their impact on the institution of marriage and the traditional family structure. *Journal of Family Law, 19,* 247–261.

Cummings, N. (1985, August). *Therapist–patient sex: Search for a solution to a systems problem.* Symposium presented at the annual meeting of the American Psychological Association, Los Angeles.

Darom, D. (1988). Freedom and commitment: Values and issues in humanistic education. *Journal of Humanistic Education and Development, 26,* 98–108.

Daubner, E. V., & Daubner, E. S. (1970). Ethics and counseling decisions. *Personnel and Guidance Journal, 48,* 433–442.

Davis, J. W. (1981). Counselor licensure: Overkill? *Personnel and Guidance Journal, 60,* 83–85.

Davis, L. (1991). *Allies in healing.* New York: Harper Perennial.

Davis v. Lhim, 430 Mich. 326 (1988).

Dawidoff, D. J. (1973). *The malpractice of psychiatrists.* Springfield, IL: Charles C. Thomas.

Day, D. (1977). Termination of parental rights statutes and void for vagueness doctrine: A successful attack on the parens patriae rationale. *Journal of Family Law, 16,* 213.

Defense of Marriage Act, Pub. L. No. 104-199, 110 Stat. 2419; codified at 1 U.S.C. §7, 28 U.S.C. §1738c (1996).

DeKraai, M. B., & Sales, B. D. (1982). Privileged communications of psychologists. *Professional Psychology, 13,* 372–388.

Delaware Rules of Evidence, 503 (1981).

DelCampo, R. L., & Anderson, A. S. (1992). Court-ordered family mediation: A brief overview. *Topics in Family Psychology and Counseling, 1*(2), 72–77.

Dell, P. (1982). Beyond homeostasis: Toward a concept of coherence. *Family Process, 21,* 21–41.

Dell, P. (1983). From pathology to ethics. *The Family Therapy Networker 7*(6), 29–31, 64.

Denkowski, K. M., & Denkowski, G. C. (1982). Client–counselor confidentiality: An update of rationale, legal status, and implications. *Personnel and Guidance Journal, 60,* 371–375.

Denton, W. H. (1989). DSM-III-R and the family therapist: Ethical considerations. *Journal of Marital and Family Therapy, 15,* 367–377.

Denton, W. H. (1990). A family systems analysis of DSM-III-R. *Journal of Marital and Family Therapy, 16,* 113–125.

Denton, W. H. (1996). Problems encountered in reconciling individual and relational diagnoses. In F. W. Kaslow (Ed.), *Handbook of relational diagnosis and dysfunctional family patterns* (pp. 35–45). New York: John Wiley & Sons.

Denton, W. H., Patterson, J. E., & Van Meir, E. S. (1997). Use of the DSM in marriage and family therapy programs: Current practices and attitudes. *Journal of Marital and Family Therapy, 23,* 81–86.

DePauw, M. E. (1986). Avoiding ethical violations: A timeline perspective for individual counseling. *Journal of Counseling and Development, 64,* 303–305.

De Shazer, S. (1999). *Patterns of brief family therapy: An ecosystem approach.* New York: Guilford.

Deutsch, M. (1973). *The resolution of conflict.* New Haven, CT: Yale University.

Dewitt, K. N. (1987). The effectiveness of family therapy: A review of outcome research. *Archives of General Psychiatry, 35,* 549–561.

Dincin, J., Selleck, V., & Streicker, S. (1978). Restructuring parental attitudes: Working with parents of the adult mentally ill. *Schizophrenia Bulletin, 4,* 597–608.

Doe v. Bolton. Rehearing denied, 410 U.S. 959 (1973).

Doherty, W. J. (1992). Values and ethics in family therapy. In M. T. Burke & J. G. Miranti (Eds.), *Ethical and spiritual values in counseling* (pp. 75–80). Alexandria, VA: Association for Religious and Values Issues in Counseling.

Dooley, J. A. (1977). Malpractice: Professional liability and the law. *Professional Psychology, 9,* 467–477.

Douthwaite, G. (1979). *Unmarried couples and the law.* Indianapolis: Smith.

Duncan, D. M., & Watts, R. E. (1999). Counseling and the internet. In P. Stevens (Ed.), *Ethical casebook for the practice of marriage and family counseling* (pp. 159–170). Alexandria, VA: American Counseling Association.

Eady v. Alter, 380 N.Y.S. 2d 737 (New York, 1976).

Efran, J., & Lukens, M. (1985). The world according to Humberto Maturana. *The Family Therapy Networker 9*(3), 22–28, 72–75.

Eisikovits, Z. C., Edleson, J. L., Guttmann, E., & Sela-Amit, M. (1991). Cognitive styles and socialized attitudes of men who batter: Where should we intervene? *Family Relations, 40,* 72–77.

Elias, M. (1988, August 15). Many lie about AIDS risk. *USA Today,* p. D-1.

Engelberg, S. L. (1985). General counsel's report: Ethics committee's procedures outlined. *Family Therapy News, 16*(2), 16.

Erickson, G. D. (1988). Against the grain: Decentering family therapy. *Journal of Marital and Family Therapy, 14,* 225–236.

Erickson, S. H. (1998). Counseling a couple with AIDS. *Family Journal: Counseling and Therapy for Couples and Families, 6,* 223–225.

Eskridge, W. N., Jr. (1993). A history of same-sex marriage. *Virginia Law Review, 79,* 1419–1514.

Ethics Committee of the American Psychological Association. (1988). Trends in ethics cases, common pitfalls, and published resources. *American Psychologist, 43,* 564–572.

Evans, J. (1983). The treatment specialist: An emerging role for counselors within the criminal court system. *Personnel and Guidance Journal, 61,* 349–351.

Everstine, L., Everstine, D. S., Heymann, G. M., True, R. H, Frey, D. H., Johnson, H. G., & Seiden, R. H. (1980). Privacy and confidentiality in psychotherapy. *American Psychologist, 9,* 828–840.

Falloon, I. R. H. (1991). Behavioral family therapy. In A. S. Gurman & D. P. Kniskern (Eds.), *Handbook of family therapy: Volume II* (pp. 65–133). New York: Brunner/Mazel.

Family Educational Rights and Privacy Act of 1974, 20 U.S.C.A. §1232g.

Family Rights and Privacy Act, 20 U.S.C.A. §1232g (West, 1997).

Faustman, W. O. (1982). Legal and ethical issues in debt collection strategies of professional psychologists. *Professional Psychology, 13,* 208–214.

Felstiner, W. L., & Williams, L. A. (1978). Mediation as an alternative to criminal prosecution. *Law and Human Behavior, 2,* 223–244.

Fenell, D. L., & Hovestadt, A. J. (1986). Family therapy as a profession or professional specialty: Implications for training. *Journal of Psychotherapy and the Family, 1,* 25–40.

Ferraro, K. J., & Johnson, J. M. (1983). How women experience battering: The process of victimization. *Social Problems, 30,* 325–339.

Fieldsteel, N. D. (1982). Ethical issues in family therapy. In M. Rosenbaum (Ed.), *Ethics and values in psychotherapy: A guidebook* (pp. 258–268). New York: Free Press.

Final Regulations: Family Educational Rights and Privacy Act. (1976). *Federal Register, 41,* 24670–24675.

Fine, M. J. (1985). Intervention from a systems-ecological perspective. *Professional Psychology: Research and Practice, 16,* 262–270.

Fine, M. J., & Holt, P. (1983). Intervening with school problems: A family systems perspective. *Psychology in the Schools, 20,* 59–66.

Fischer, L., & Sorenson, G. P. (1985). *School law for counselors, psychologists, and social workers.* New York: Longman.

Fish, V. (1990). Introducing causality and power into family therapy theory: A correction to the systemic paradigm. *Journal of Marital and Family Therapy, 16,* 21–37.

Fisher, L., Anderson, A., & Jones, J. E. (1981). Types of paradoxical interventions and indications/contraindications for use in clinical practice. *Family Process, 20,* 25–35.

Fisher, M. A. (1991). *Ethical issues in clinical practice under Virginia law: A clinical psychology handbook.* Charlottesville, VA: Author.

Flax, M. (1977). *Couples therapy in battering relationships.* Paper presented at Colorado Women's College Conference of Battered Women, Denver.

Folberg, J. (1984). Custody overview. In J. Folberg (Ed.), *Joint custody and shared parenting* (pp. 3–10). Washington, DC: Bureau of National Affairs, Inc.

Folberg, J., & Graham, M. (1979). Joint custody of children following divorce. *University of California, Davis Law Review, 12,* 523–581.

Fong, M. L., & Sherrard, P. A. D. (1990). Ethical dilemmas in marketing counseling services. In B. Herlihy & L. B. Golden, *Ethical standards casebook* (pp. 127–136). Alexandria, VA: American Association for Counseling and Development.

Foos, J. A., Ottens, A. J., & Hill, L. K. (1991). Managed mental health: A primer for counselors. *Journal of Counseling and Development, 69,* 332–336.

Foster, H. H. (1976). An overview of confidentiality and privilege. *Journal of Psychiatry and the Law, 4,* 393–401.

Foster, H. H. (1978). Informed consent of mental patients. In W. E. Barton & C. J. Sanborn (Eds.), *Law and the mental health professions: Friction at the interface.* New York: International Universities.

Foster, N. J., & Kelly, J. B. (1996). Divorce mediation: Who should be certified? *University of San Francisco Law Review, 30,* 665–680.

Fowers, B. J., & Wenger, A. (1997). Are trustworthiness and fairness enough? Contextual family therapy and the good family. *Journal of Marital and Family Therapy, 23,* 153–169.

Frame, M. W. (1997). The ethics of counseling via the internet. *Family Journal: Counseling and Therapy for Couples and Families, 5,* 328–330.

Frame, M. W. (1999). The impaired counselor. In P. Stevens (Ed.), *Ethical casebook for the practice of marriage and family counseling* (pp. 103–112). Alexandria, VA: American Counseling Association.

Framo, J. L. (1981). The integration of marital therapy with sessions with family of origin. In A. Gurman & D. Kniskern (Eds.), *Handbook of family therapy* (pp. 133–158). New York: Brunner/Mazel.

Fraser, J. S. (1984). Paradox and orthodox: Folie a'deux. *Journal of Marital and Family Therapy, 10,* 361–372.

Freed, D. J., & Foster, H. H. (1981). Divorce in the fifty states: An overview. *Family Law Quarterly, 14,* 229–284.

Freeny, M. (1995). Do the walls have ears? *Family Therapy Networker, 19* (5), 36–39, 41, 43, 65.

Fretz, B. R., & Mills, D. H. (1980). *Licensing and certification of psychologists and counselors.* San Francisco: Jossey-Bass.

Fricke v. Fricke, 42 N.W. 2d 500 (Wis. 1950).

Friedman, D., & Kaslow, N. (1986). The development of professional identity in psychotherapists: Six stages in the supervision process. In F. W. Kaslow (Ed.), *Supervision and training models, dilemmas and challenges* (pp. 29–50). New York: Haworth.

Friedman, S. E. (1992). *The law of parent–child relationships: A handbook.* Chicago: American Bar Association.

Fulero, S. M. (1988). Tarasoff: 10 years later. *Professional Psychology: Research and Practice, 19,* 184–190.

Gangel-Jacob, P. (1997, August). Without lawyers, mediation sacrifices justice. *Trial, 33,* 45–50.

Gardner, R. (1989). *Family evaluation in child custody mediation, arbitration and litigation.* Cresskill, NJ: Creative Therapeutics.

Geller, J. A., & Wasserstrom, J. (1984). Conjoint therapy for the treatment of domestic violence. In A. R. Roberts (Ed.), *Battered women and their families: Intervention strategies and treatment programs.* New York: Springer.

Gelles, R. J., & Maynard, P. E. (1987). A structural family systems approach to intervention in cases of domestic violence. *Family Relations, 36,* 270–275.

Giblin, P., & Chan, J. (1995). A feminist perspective. *Family Journal: Counseling and Therapy for Couples and Families, 3,* 234–238.

Gill, S. J. (1982). Professional disclosure and consumer protection in counseling. *Personnel and Guidance Journal, 60,* 443–446.

Gillespie v. Gillespie, 631 S.W. 2d 592 (Tex. App. 1982).

Gladding, S. T. (1998a). *Counseling as an art: The creative arts in counseling* (2nd ed.). Alexandria, VA: American Counseling Association.

Gladding, S. T. (1998b). *Family therapy: History, theory, and practice* (2nd ed.). Upper Saddle River, NJ: Prentice Hall.

Gladding, S. T. (2000). *Counseling: A comprehensive profession* (4th ed.). Upper Saddle River, NJ: Prentice Hall.

Gladding, S. T. (2001). *The counseling dictionary: Concise definitions of frequently used terms.* Upper Saddle River, NJ: Prentice Hall.

Glaser, B., & Kirschenbaum, H. (1980). Using values clarification in counseling settings. *Personnel and Guidance Journal, 58,* 569–574.

Glendon, M. A. (1976). Marriage and the state: The washing away of marriage. *Virginia Law Review, 62,* 663–720.

Glendon, M. A. (1980). Modern marriage law and its underlying assumptions: The new marriage and the new property. *Family Law Quarterly, 13,* 441–460.

Glosoff, H. L. (1997). Multiple relationships in private practice. In B. Herlihy & G. Corey (Eds.), *Boundary issues in counseling* (pp. 114–120). Alexandria, VA: American Counseling Association.

Golden, L., & Schmidt, S. J. (1998). Unethical practice as perceived by mental health professionals: The next generation. *Counseling and Values, 42,* 166–170.

Gomez v. Perez, 409 U.S. 535 (1973).

Goodyear, R. K., Crego, C. A., & Johnston, M. W. (1992). Ethical issues in the supervision of student research: A study of critical incidents. *Professional Psychology Research and Practice, 23,* 203–210.

Gould, J. W. (1998). *Conducting scientifically crafted child custody evaluations.* Thousand Oaks, CA: Sage.

Graham, D., Rawlings, E., & Rimini, N. (1988). Survivors of terror: Battered women, hostages and the Stockholm syndrome. In K. Yllo & M. Bograd (Eds.), *Female perspectives on wife abuse* (pp. 217–233). Newbury Park, CA: Sage.

Gray, L. A., & Harding, A. I. (1988). Confidentiality limits with clients who have the AIDS virus. *Journal of Counseling and Development, 66,* 219–223.

Green, S. L., & Hansen, J. C. (1989). Ethical dilemmas faced by family therapists. *Journal of Marital and Family Therapy, 15,* 149–158.

Gross, S. J. (1977). Professional disclosure: An alternative to licensure. *Personnel and Guidance Journal, 55,* 586–588.

Grosslight v. Superior Court of Los Angeles County, 72 Cal. App. 3d 502, 140 Cal. Rptr. 278 (1977).

Grumet, B. R. (1988). The standard of care: Legal considerations in protocols and standing orders. *HMO, 2,* 20–23.

Grunebaum, H. (1984). Comments on Terkelsen's "Schizophrenia and the family: II. Adverse effects of family therapy." *Family Process, 23,* 421–428.

Guernsey, T. F. (1981). The psychotherapist–patient privilege in child placement: A relevancy analysis. *Villanova Law Review, 26,* 955–966.

Guggenheim, P. D. (1979, March). The juvenile offender. *Bulletin, Area 11, American Psychiatric Association.*

Guillette, W. (1979). Is psychotherapy insurable? *National Association of Private Psychiatric Hospitals Journal, 9,* 30–32.

Gulliver, P. H. (1979). *Disputes and negotiations: A cross-cultural perspective.* New York: Academic Press.

Gumper, L. L., & Sprenkle, D. H. (1981). Privileged communication in therapy: Special problems for the family and couples therapist. *Family Process, 20,* 11–23.

Gurman, A. S. (1978). Contemporary marital therapies: A critique and comparative analysis of psychoanalytic, behavioral and systems theory approaches. In T. J. Paolino & B. S. McCrady (Eds.), *Marriage and marital therapy: Psychoanalytic, behavioral, and systems theory perspectives* (pp. 445–566). New York: Brunner/Mazel.

Gurman, A. S., & Kniskern, D. P. (1978). Deterioration in marital and family therapy: Empirical, clinical and conceptual issues. *Family Process, 17,* 3–20.

Gurman, A. S., & Kniskern, D. P. (1981). Family therapy outcome research. Knowns and unknowns. In A. S. Gurman & D. P. Kniskern (Eds.), *Handbook of family therapy* (pp. 742–776). New York: Brunner/Mazel.

Gurman, A. S., & Kniskern, D. P. (1991). *Handbook of family therapy: Volume II.* New York: Brunner/Mazel.

Guy, J. D. (1987). *The personal life of the psychotherapist.* New York: Wiley.

H. L. v. Matheson, 450 U.S. 398 (1981).

Haas, L. J., & Cummings, N. A. (1991). Managed outpatient mental health plans: Clinical, ethical, and practical guidelines for participation.

Professional Psychology: Research and Practice, 22, 45–51.

Haas, L. J., & Malouf, J. L. (1995). *Keeping up the good work: A practitioner's guide to mental health ethics* (2nd ed.). Sarasota, FL: Professional Resource Exchange.

Hagan, M. A. (1997). *Whores of the court: The fraud of psychiatric testimony and the rape of American justice.* New York: Regan Books.

Hahman v. Hahman, 628 P.2d 984 (Ariz. App. 1981).

Hahn, R. A., & Kleist, D. M. (2000). Divorce mediation: Research and implications for family and couples counseling. *Family Journal: Counseling and Therapy for Couples and Families, 8,* 165–171.

Haley, J. (1971). *Changing families: A family therapy reader.* New York: Grune & Stratton.

Haley, J. (1976). *Problem-solving therapy: New strategies for effective family therapy.* San Francisco: Jossey-Bass.

Haley, J. (1984). Marriage or family therapy. *The American Journal of Family Therapy, 12*(2), 3–14.

Haley, J. (1987). The disappearance of the individual. *The Family Therapy Networker, 11*(2), 39–40.

Halleck, S. L. (1976). Another response to "Homosexuality: The ethical challenge. *Journal of Consulting and Clinical Psychology, 44,* 167–170.

Hammond, J. M. (1981). Children, divorce, and you. *Learning, 9,* 83–84, 88–89.

Handel, W. W., & Sherwyn, B. A. (1982). Surrogate parenting. *Trial, 18,* 57–60, 77.

Handler, J. F. (1990). *Law and the search for community.* Philadelphia: University of Pennsylvania Press.

Hardy, K. V., & Laszloffy, T. A. (1992). Training racially sensitive family therapists: Context, content, and contact. *Families in Society, 73,* 364–370.

Hare-Mustin, R. T. (1980). Family therapy may be dangerous for your health. *Professional Psychology, 11,* 935–938.

Hare-Mustin, R. T., Marecek, J., Kaplan, A. G., & Liss-Levinson, N. (1979). Rights of clients, responsibilities of therapists. *American Psychologist, 34,* 3–16.

Harkaway, J. (1989). Circus maximus. *The Family Therapy Networker, 13*(2), 3, 42–46, 78–79.

Harp, B. S., Jr. (1982). Post judgement proceedings. In *Program materials for seminars on family law practice.* Athens, GA: Institute of Continuing Legal Education in Georgia.

Harrar, W. R., VandeCreek, L., & Knapp, S. (1990). Ethical and legal aspects of clinical supervision. *Professional Psychology: Research and Practice, 21,* 37–41.

Harvard Law Review. (1985). Developments in privileged communications. *Harvard Law Review, 98,* 1450–1605.

Haynes, J. (1978). Divorce mediation: A new role. *Journal of Social Work, 23,* 5–9.

Haynes, J. (1981). *Divorce mediation: A practical guide for therapists and counselors.* New York: Springer.

Hedlund v. Superior Court, 34 Cal. 3d 695, 669 p. 2d 41 (1983).

Held, B. S. (1990). What's in a name? Some confusions and concerns about constructivism. *Journal of Marital and Family Therapy, 16,* 179–186.

Hendrick, S. S. (1988). Counselor self-disclosure. *Journal of Counseling and Development, 66,* 419–424.

Hendrickson, R. M. (1982). Counselor liability: Does the risk require insurance coverage? *Personnel and Guidance Journal, 61,* 205–207.

Hendrickson, R. M., & Mangum, R. S. (1978). *Governing board and administrator liability.* (ERIC Higher Education Research Report No. 9)

Hennessey, E. F. (1980). Explosion in family law litigation: Challenges and opportunities for the bar. *Family Law Quarterly, 14,* 187–201.

Henry, M. (1994). Legal implications of *in vitro* fertilization with donor eggs: A research guide. *Legal Reference Services Quarterly, 13* (2), 5–34.

Heppner, M. (1978). Counseling the battered wife: Myths, facts and decisions. *Personnel and Guidance Journal, 56,* 522–525.

Herlihy, B., & Corey, G. (1992). *Dual relationships in counseling.* Alexandria, VA: American Counseling Association.

Herlihy, B., & Corey, G. (1996). *ACA ethical standards casebook* (5th ed.). Alexandria, VA: American Counseling Association.

Herrington, B. S. (1979). Privilege denied in joint therapy. *Psychiatric News, 14*(1) 1, 9.

Hines, P. M., & Hare-Mustin, R. T. (1978). Ethical concerns in family therapy. *Professional Psychology, 9,* 165–171.

Hinkle, J. S., & Wells, M. (1995). *Family counseling in the schools.* Greensboro, NC: ERIC/CASS.

Hirschfeld, R. M. A., & Goodwin, F. K. (1988). Mood disorders. In J. A. Talbott, R. E. Hales, & S. C. Yudofsky (Eds.), *The American psychiatric press textbook of psychiatry.* Washington, DC: American Psychiatric Press.

Hof, L., & Dwyer, C. E. (1982). Overcoming ambivalence through the use of values analysis. *The American Journal of Family Therapy, 10*(1), 17–26.

Hoffmann, L. (1981). *Foundations of family therapy.* New York: Basic.

Hoffman, L., & Long, L. (1969). A systems dilemma. *Family Process, 8,* 21 1–234.

Hopkins, B. R., & Anderson, B. S. (1990). *The counselor and the law.* Alexandria, VA: American Counseling Association.

Huber, C. H. (1995). Counselor responsibility within managed mental health care. *Family Journal: Counseling and Therapy for Couples and Families, 3,* 42–44.

Huber, C. H. (1996). Facilitating disclosure of HIV-positive status to family members. *Family Journal: Counseling and Therapy for Couples and Families, 4,* 53–55.

Hulnick, H. R. (1977). Counselor: Know thyself. *Counselor Education and Supervision, 17,* 69–72.

Hundert, E. M. (1987). A model for ethical problem solving in medicine, with practical applications. *American Journal of Psychiatry, 144,* 839–846.

Hunter, N. D. (1991). Marriage, law, and gender: A feminist inquiry. *Law and Sexuality, 1,* 9–22.

Huntley, D. K., & Konetsky, C. D. (1992). Healthy families with adolescents. *Topics in Family Psychology and Counseling, 1*(1), 62–71.

Huston, K. (1984). Ethical decisions in treating battered women. *Professional Psychology: Research and Practice, 15,* 822–832.

In re Adams, 174 Ill. App. 3d 595, 528 N.E. 2d 1075 (1988) rev'd and remanded, 133 Ill. 2d 437, 551 N.E. 2d 635 (1990).

In re Carrafa, 77 Cal. App. 3d 788, 143 Cal. Rptr. 848 (1978).

In re Fred J., 89 Cal. App. 3d 168, 152 Cal. Rptr. 327 (1979).

In re Marriage of Gove, 572 P.2d 458 (Ariz. App. 1977).

In re Marriage of Kovash, 858 P.2d 351 (Mont. 1993).

In re Marriage of Winegard, 278 N.W.2d 505 (Iowa, 1979).

In Roger B., 84 Ill. 2d 323, 418 N.E.2d 751 (1981).

International Association of Marriage and Family Counselors (IAMFC). (1993). Ethical code for the International Association of Marriage and Family Counselors. *Family Journal: Counseling and Therapy for Couples and Families, 1,* 73–77.

Jablonski v. United States, 712 F.2d 391 (9th Cir. 1983).

Jacobson, N. S., & Bussod, N. (1983). Marital and family therapy. In M. Herson, A. E. Kazdin, & A. S. Bellack (Eds.), *The clinical psychology handbook.* New York: Pergamon.

Jacobson, N. S., & Margolin, G. (1979). *Marital therapy: Strategies based on social learning and behavior exchange principles.* New York: Brunner/Mazel.

Janeway, E. (1980). *Powers of the weak.* New York: Knopf.

Jantsch E. (1980). *The self-organizing universe: Scientific and human implications of the emerging paradigm of evolution.* New York: Pergamon.

Johnson, T. R. (1965). Medical malpractice—Doctrines of *res ipsa loquitur* and informed consent. *University of Colorado Law Review, 37,* 182–195.

Jones, K. D. (1999). Ethics in publication. *Counseling and Values, 43,* 99–105.

Jones, W. T., Sontag, F., Beckner, M. O., & Fogelin, R. J. (Eds.). (1977). *Approaches to ethics* (3rd ed.). New York: McGraw-Hill.

Jordan, A. E., & Meara, N. M. (1990). Ethics and the professional practice of psychologists: The role of virtues and principles. *Professional Psychology: Research and Practice, 21,* 107–114.

Jordan, K., & Stevens, P. (1999). Revising the ethics code of the IAMFC—A training exercise for counseling psychology and counselor education students. *Family Journal: Counseling and Therapy for Couples and Families, 7,* 170–175.

Jory, B., Anderson, D., & Greer, C. (1997). Intimate justice: Confronting issues of accountability, respect, and freedom in treatment for abuse and violence. *Journal of Marital and Family Therapy, 23,* 399–419.

Kain, C. D. (1988). To breach or not to breach: Is that the question? A response to Gray and Harding. *Journal of Counseling and Development, 66,* 224–225.

Kaplan, D. (1999). Models of ethical decision making in marriage and family counseling. In P. Stevens (Ed.), *Ethical casebook for the practice of marriage and family counseling* (pp. 3–16). Alexandria, VA: American Counseling Association.

Kaplan, D., & Culkin, M. (1995). Family ethics: Lessons learned. *Family Journal: Counseling and Therapy for Couples and Families, 3,* 335–338.

Kaplan, H., Sager, C., & Schiavi, R. (1986). Editorial: Preventing the spread of AIDS. *Journal of Sex and Marital Therapy, 12,* 159–164.

Karpel, M. A. (1980). Family secrets: I. Conceptual and ethical issues in the relational context: II. Ethical and practical considerations in therapeutic management. *Family Process, 19,* 295–306.

Karpel, M. A., & Strauss, E. S. (1983). *Family evaluation.* New York: Gardner.

Kaslow, F. W. (1990a). Children who sue parents: A new form of family homicide. *Journal of Marital and Family Therapy, 16,* 151–163.

Kaslow, F. W. (1990b). *Voices in family psychology.* Newbury Park, CA: Sage.

Kass, A. (1990). *Mediation* (VHS recording). Albuquerque, NM: Second Judicial District.

Katz, J. (1977). Informed consent—A fairy tale? Law's vision. *University of Pittsburgh Law Review, 39,* 137–174.

Katz, S. N. (1981). *Child snatching: The legal response to the abduction of children.* Chicago: American Bar Association.

Kausch, O., & Resnick, P. J. (1998). The assessment of violence in the workplace and its legal ramifications. In F. Flach (Ed.), *Malpractice risk management in psychiatry* (pp. 332–246). New York: Hatherleigh.

Kavanaugh, P. B. (1989, March–April). People v. Cavaiani: Cavaiani wins. *Michigan Psychologist,* p. 8.

Kazen, B. A. (1977). *When father wants custody: A lawyer's view.* Austin: State Bar of Texas.

Keary, A. O. (1985). Criminal law and procedure. In N. T. Sidney (Ed.), *Law and ethics: A guide for the health professional* (pp. 63–102). New York: Human Sciences.

Kegeles, T., Catania, J., & Coates, T. (1988). Intentions to communicate positive HIV antibodies status to sex partners [Letter to the Editor]. *Journal of the American Medical Association, 259,* 216–217.

Keim, J. (2000). Strategic family therapy: The Washington school. In A. M. Horne (Ed.), *Family counseling and therapy* (3rd ed., pp. 170–207). Itasca, IL: F. E. Peacock.

Keller, J. F., Huber, J. R., & Hardy, K. V. (1988). Accreditation: What constitutes appropriate marriage and family therapy education? *Journal of Marital and Family Therapy, 14,* 297–305.

Kelly, G. (1955). *The psychology of personal constructs.* New York: Norton.

Kemp, A. (1998). *Abuse in the family.* Pacific Grove, CA: Brooks/Cole.

Kempin, F. (1982). *Historical introduction to Anglo-American law* (2nd ed.). St. Paul, MN: West.

Kennedy, C. (1973). The psychotherapists' privilege. *Washburn Law Review, 12,* 297–315.

Kessler, S. (1978). *Creative conflict resolution: Mediation.* Atlanta: National Institute for Professional Training.

Kidder, R. M. (1995). *How good people make tough choices.* New York: Fireside.

Kimberly, J. A., Serovich, J. M., & Greene, K. (1995). Disclosure of HIV-positive status: Five women's stories. *Family Relations, 44,* 316–322.

Kissel, S. (1983). *Private practice for the mental health clinician.* Rockville, MD: Aspen.

Kitchener, K. S. (1984a). Ethics in counseling psychology: Distinctions and directions. *Counseling Psychologist, 12,* 15–18.

Kitchener, K. S. (1984b). Intuition, critical evaluation, and ethical principles: The foundation for ethical decisions in counseling psychology. *Counseling Psychologist, 12,* 43–55.

Kitchener, K. S. (1985). Ethical principles and ethical decisions in student affairs. In H. J. Canon & R. D. Brown (Eds.), *Applied ethics: Tools for practitioners.* San Francisco: Jossey-Bass.

Kitchener, K. S. (1986). Teaching applied ethics in counselor education: An integration of psychological processes and philosophical analysis. *Journal of Counseling and Development, 64,* 306–310.

Kitchener, K. S. (1988). Dual role relationships: What makes them so problematic. *Journal of Counseling and Development, 67,* 217–221.

Kitchener, K. S. (1992). Posttherapy relationships: Ever or never? In B. Herlihy & G. Corey (Eds.), *Dual relationships in counseling* (pp. 145–148). Alexandria, VA: American Association for Counseling and Development.

Kitchener, K. S., & Harding, S. S. (1990). Dual role relationships. In B. Herlihy & L. B. Golden (Eds.), *AACD Ethical standards casebook* (4th ed., pp. 146–154). Alexandria, VA: American Counseling Association.

Kluckhohn, F., & Strodtbeck, F. L. (1961). *Variations in value orientation.* Evanston, IL: Row, Peterson.

Knapp, S., & VandeCreek, L. (1982). Tarasoff: Five years later. *Professional Psychology, 13,* 511–516.

Knapp, S., & VandeCreek, L. (1985). Psychotherapy and privileged communications in child custody cases. *Professional Psychology: Research and Practice, 16,* 398–407.

Knapp, S., & VandeCreek, L. (1987). *Privileged communications in the mental health professions.* New York: Van Nostrand Reinhold.

Knapp, S., & VandeCreek, L. (1990). Application of the duty to protect HIV-positive patients. *Professional Psychology: Research and Practice, 21,* 161–166.

Knapp, S., VandeCreek, L., & Zirkel, P. A. (1985). Legal research techniques: What the psychologist needs to know. *Professional Psychology: Research and Practice, 16,* 363–372.

Knudson-Martin, C. (1997). The politics of gender in family therapy. *Journal of Marital and Family Therapy, 23,* 421–437.

Koocher, G. P., & Keith-Spiegel, P. (1998). *Ethics in psychology: Professional standards and cases* (2nd ed.). New York: Oxford University Press.

Kosinski, F. A. (1982). Standards, accreditation, and licensure in marriage and family therapy. *Personnel and Guidance Journal, 60,* 350–352.

Kottler, J. A. (1990). *On being a therapist.* San Francisco: Jossey-Bass.

Kovacs, K. E. (1995). Recognizing gay and lesbian families: Marriage and parental rights. *Law and Sexuality, 5,* 513–539.

Kral, R., & Hines, M. (1999). A survey on developmental stages in achieving a competent sense of self as a family therapist. *The Family Journal, 7,* 102–111.

Kramer, D. T. (1994). *Legal rights of children* (2nd ed.). New York: McGraw-Hill.

Krause, H. D. (1977). *Family law in a nutshell.* St. Paul, MN: West.

Krause, H. D. (1982). Child support enforcement: Legislative tasks for the early 1980's. *Family Law Quarterly, 15,* 349–370.

Kristensen v. Kristensen, 406 So. 2d 1210 (Fla. 5th DCA 1981).

Krugman, S. (1986). Challenging tradition: Sometimes violence is a way of life. *The Family Therapy Networker, 10*(4), 41–43.

Kurilla, V. (1998). Multicultural counseling perspectives: Culture specificity and implications in family therapy. *Family Counseling: Counseling and Therapy for Couples and Families, 6,* 207–211.

L'Abate, L. (1982). Introduction. In J. C. Hansen & L. L'Abate (Eds.), *Values, ethics, legalities and the family therapist* (pp. xv–xvi). Rockville, MD: Aspen.

Lamb, D. H., Clark, C., Drumheller, P., Frizzell, K., & Surrey, L. (1989). Applying Tarasoff to AIDS-related psychotherapy issues. *Professional Psychology: Research and Practice, 20,* 37–43.

Lane, P. J., & Spruill, J. (1980). To tell or not to tell: The psychotherapist's dilemma. *Psychotherapy: Theory, Research, and Practice, 17,* 202–209.

Langsley, D. C., & Kaplan, D. M. (1968). *The treatment of families in crisis.* New York: Grune & Stratton.

Larson v. Larson, 24 Ill. App.2d 467, 192 N.E.2d 594 (1963).

Lavori, N. (1976). *Living together, married or single: Your legal rights.* New York: Harper & Row.

Lebow, J. (1992). Systemically evaluating custody disputes. *Family Therapy News, 23*(2), 15.

Leedy v. Hartnett, 510 F.Supp. 1125 (M.D. Penn. 1981).

Lehr v. Robertson, 463 U.S. 248 (1983).

Leslie, L. A., & Clossick, M. L. (1996). Sexism in family therapy: Does training in gender make a difference? *Journal of Marital and Family Therapy, 22*, 253–265.

Liddle, H. A. (1987). Family psychology: The journal, the field. *Journal of Family Psychology, 1*, 5–22.

Liddle, H. A. (1991a). Empirical values and the culture of family therapy. *Journal of Marital and Family Therapy, 17*, 327–348.

Liddle, H. A. (1991b). Training and supervision in family therapy: A comprehensive and critical analysis. In A. S. Gurman & D. P. Kniskern (Eds.), *Handbook of family therapy: Volume II* (pp. 638–697). New York: Brunner/Mazel.

Liddle, H. A. (1992). Family psychology: Progress and prospects of a maturing discipline. *Journal of Family Psychology, 5*, 249–263.

Liddle, H. A., Gurman, A. S., Pinsof, W. M., & Roberto, L. G. (1990, October). *What's wrong with family therapy?* Symposium conducted at the annual meeting of the American Association of Marriage and Family Therapy, Washington, DC.

Lifson, L. E., & Simon, R. I. (Eds.). (1998). *The mental health practitioner and the law.* Cambridge, MA: Harvard University Press.

Loving v. Virginia, 388 U.S. 1 (1967).

Mabe, A. R., & Rollin, S. A. (1986). The role of a code of ethical standards in counseling. *Journal of Counseling and Development, 64*, 294–297.

MacDonald, J. M. (1969). *Psychiatry and the criminal* (2nd ed.). Springfield, IL: Charles C. Thomas.

Mace, D. R. (1976). Marital intimacy and the deadly love-anger cycle. *Journal of Marriage and Family Counseling, 2*, 131–137.

Madanes, C. (1980). Protection, paradox, and pretending. *Family Process, 19*, 73–85.

Madanes, C. (1983). Strategic therapy of schizophrenia. In W. R. McFarlane (Ed.), *Family therapy in schizophrenia*. New York: Guilford.

Madonna, J. M. (1986). A treatment of a case of marital abuse. *American Journal of Family Therapy, 14*, 235–246.

Malcolm, J. C. (1988). *Treatment choices and informed consent*. Springfield, IL: Charles C. Thomas.

Mappes, D. C., Robb, G. P., & Engels, D. W. (1985). Conflicts between ethics and the law in counseling and psychotherapy. *Journal of Counseling and Development, 64*, 246–252.

Margolin, G. (1982). Ethical and legal considerations in marriage and family therapy. *American Psychologist, 7*, 788–801.

Marlow, L. (1985). Divorce mediation: Therapists in the legal world. *The American Journal of Family Therapy, 13*, 3–10.

Marvin v. Marvin, 18 Cal. 3d 660, 134 Cal. Rptr.815, 557 P.2d 106 (1976).

Maslow, A. H. (1959). *New knowledge in human values*. New York: Harper & Row.

Massachusetts General Laws, ch. 119, §63 (West Supp. 1980).

Massachusetts General Laws Annotated, ch. 233 §20B (e) (West Supp. 1980).

Mathias, B. (1986). Lifting the shade on family violence. *The Family Therapy Networker, 10*(4), 20–29.

Matter of Atkins, 316 NW. 2d 477 (Mich. App. 1982).

Maturana, H. R. (1978). Biology of language: Epistemology of reality. In G. A. Miller & E. Lenneberg (Eds.), *Psychology and biology of language and thought*. New York: Academic.

May, K. M. (1998). A feminist and multicultural perspective in family therapy. *Family Journal: Counseling and Therapy for Couples and Families, 6*, 123–124.

McCarty v. McCarty, 101 S. Ct. 2728 (1981).

McG Mullen, R., & Carroll, M. (1983). The battered-woman syndrome: Contributing factors and remedial interventions. *American Mental Health Counselors Association Journal, 5*, 31–38.

McGoldrick, M., Giordano, J., Pearce, J. K., & Giordano, J. (1996). *Ethnicity and family therapy* (2nd ed.). New York: Guilford.

McGrath, P., Browning, F., Martinek, S., Beck, E., & Culkin, M. (Eds.). (1995). Family ethics: Dual relationships. *Family Journal: Counseling and Therapy for Couples and Families, 3*, 142–144.

McGuire, J. M., & Borowy, T. D. (1978). Confidentiality and the Buckley-Pell amendment: Ethical and legal considerations for counselors. *Personnel and Guidance Journal, 56*, 554–557.

McIntosh, D. M., & Cartaya, C. Y. (1992). Pychotherapist as clairvoyant: Failing to predict and warn. *Defense Counsel Journal, 59*, 569–573.

McIntosh v. Milano, 403 A.2d 500 (N.J. 1979).

McKenzie, D. J. (1978). The setting up of a family court counseling system in Australia. *Conciliation Courts Review, 16*, 23–30.

McLaughlin, B. (1999). Planned Parenthood of the Blue Ridge v. Camblos: Further impediment to a minor's right to abortion. *Thomas Jefferson Law Review, 21*, 147–164.

Melito, R. (1988). Combining individual psychodynamics with structural family therapy. *Journal of Marital and Family Therapy, 14*, 29–43.

Melton, G. B. (1988). Ethical and legal issues in AIDS-related practice. *American Psychologist, 43*, 941–947.

Meyer, R., & Smith, S. (1977). A crisis in group therapy. *American Psychologist, 32*, 638–643.

Meyerstein, I., & Todd, J. C. (1980). On the witness stand: The family therapist and expert testimony. *The American Journal of Family Therapy, 8*(4), 43–51.

Mills, T. (1985). The assault on the self: Stages in coping with battering husbands. *Qualitative Sociology, 8*, 103–123.

Milne, A. (1978). Custody of children in a divorce process. A family self-determination model. *Conciliation Courts Review, 16*, 1–10.

Minuchin, S. (1974). *Families and family therapy.* Cambridge, MA: Harvard University.

Minuchin S., & Fishman, H. C. (1981). *Family therapy techniques.* Cambridge, MA: Harvard University.

Mnookin, R. (1973). Foster care in whose best interest? *Harvard Educational Review, 43*, 599–638.

Mnookin, R. H., & Weisberg, D. K. (1995). *Child, family and state: Problems and materials on children and the law.* Boston: Little, Brown.

Morreim, E. H. (1988). Cost containment: Challenging fidelity and justice. *Hastings Center Report, 18*, 20–25.

Morrison, J. K., Layton, B., & Newman, J. (1982). Ethical conflict in clinical decision making: A challenge for family therapists. In J. C. Hansen & L. L'Abate (Eds), *Values, ethics, legalities and the family therapist* (pp. 75–86). Rockville, MD: Aspen.

Mowrer, O. H. (Ed.). (1967). *Morality and mental health.* Chicago: Rand McNally.

Mulvey, E. P., Reppucci, N. D., & Weithorn, L. A. (1984). Mental health, law, and children. In N. D. Reppucci, L. A. Weithorn, E. P. Mulvey, & J. Monahan (Eds.), *Children, mental health, and the law* (pp. 15–24). Beverly Hills: Sage.

Napier, A. Y., & Whitaker, C. (1978). *The family crucible.* New York: Harper & Row.

Nathanson v. Kline. 186 Kan. 393, 350 P.2d 1093 (1960) affirmed on rehearing, 187 Kan. 186, 354 P.2d 1093 (1960).

National Association of Social Workers. (1996). *Code of ethics* (rev. ed.). Silver Springs, MD: Author.

Navin, S., Beamish, P., & Johanson, G. (1995). Ethical practices of field-based mental health counselor supervisors. *Journal of Mental Health Counseling, 17*, 243–253.

Negligence §1. (2000). *American Jurisprudence 2d, 57A*, 63.

Nelson, L. J., Clark, H. W., Goldman, R. L., & Schore, J. E. (1989). Taking the train to a world of strangers: Health care marketing and ethics. *Hastings Center Report, 19*, 36–43.

Neukrug, E., Lovell, C., & Parker, R. J. (1996). Employing ethical codes and decision-making models: A developmental process. *Counseling and Values, 40*, 98–106.

Newman, R., & Bricklin, P. M. (1991). Parameters of managed mental health care: Legal, ethical, and professional guidelines. *Professional Psychology: Research and Practice, 22*, 26–35.

Newman v. Newman, 653 P.2d 728 (Colo Sup. Ct. 1982).

New Mexico Center for Dispute Resolution. (1990). *Parent–child mediation training manual.* Albuquerque, NM: Parent–Child Mediation Training Institute.

New Mexico ex. rel. Human Services Department v. Levario, 649 P.2d 510 (N.M. Ct. App. 1982).

Nichols, M. P. (1987a). The individual in the system. *The Family Therapy Networker, 11*(2), 33–38, 85.

Nichols, M. P. (1987b). *The self in system: Expanding the limits of family therapy.* New York: Brunner/Mazel.

Nichols, M. P., & Schwartz, R. C. (2001). *Family therapy: Concepts and methods* (5th ed.). Boston: Allyn & Bacon.

Nichols, W. C. (1986). Understanding family violence: An orientation for family therapists. *Contemporary Family Therapy, 8,* 188–201.

Nichols, W. C. (1992). *The AAMFT: Fifty years of marital and family therapy.* Washington: American Association for Marriage and Family Therapy.

Norcross, J. C., Alford, B. A., & DeMichele, J. T. (1992). The future of psychotherapy: Delta data and concluding observations. *Psychotherapy, 29,* 150.

Nozick, R. (1968). Moral complications and moral structure. *Natural Law Forum, 13,* 1–50.

Okun, B. F., & Rappaport, L. J. (1980). *Working with families: An introduction to family therapy.* North Scituate, MA: Duxbury.

Olson, D. H., Russell, C. S., & Sprenkle, D. H. (1980). Marital and family therapy: A decade review. *Journal of Marriage and the Family, 42,* 973–993.

Oppenheim, C. L. (1968). Valid consent to medical treatment: Need the patient know? *Duquesne Law Review, 4,* 450–577.

Orlando, F. A. (1978). Conciliation programs: Their effect on marriage and family life. *Florida Bar Journal, 52,* 218–221.

Orton, G. L. (1997). *Strategies for counseling with children and their parents.* Pacific Grove, CA: Brooks/Cole.

Osborne v. Osborne, 428 N.E. 2d 810 (Mass. 1981).

O'Shea, M., & Jessee, E. (1982). Ethical, value, and professional conflicts in systems therapy. In J. C. Hansen & L. L'Abate (Eds.), *Values, ethics, legalities and the family therapist* (pp. 1–22). Rockville, MD: Aspen.

Packer, P. (1988, October 3). Let's put a stop to the "insurance diagnosis." *Medical Economics,* 19–28.

Painter, S., & Dutton, D. (1985). Patterns of emotional bonding in battered women: Traumatic bonding. *International Journal of Women's Studies, 8,* 363–375.

Papp, P. (1984). The creative leap. *The Family Therapy Networker, 8*(5), 20–29.

Parniawski v. Parniawski, 359 A.2d 719 (Conn. 1976).

Patten, C., Barnett, T., & Houlihan, D. (1991). Ethics in marital and family therapy: A review of the literature. *Professional Psychology: Research and Practice, 22,* 171–175.

Pearson, B., & Piazza, N. (1997). Classification of dual relationships in the helping professions. *Counselor Education and Supervision, 37,* 89–99.

Pearson, J., & Thoennes, H. (1982). Mediation and divorce: The benefits outweigh the costs. *Family Advocate, 4*(3), 25–32.

Peck v. Counseling Service of Addison County, Inc., 499 A. 2d 422 (Vt. 1985).

Pederson, P. (1996). The importance of both similarities and differences in multicultural counseling: Reaction to C. H. Patterson. *Journal of Counseling and Development, 74,* 236–237.

Pell, E. R. (1979). A theory of imperfection: An imperfect theory? *Counselor Education and Supervision, 19,* 54–59.

People v. Cohen, 98 Misc.2d 874, 414 N.Y.S.2d 642 (1977).

Perry v. Fiumano, 403 N.Y.S.2d 382 (1978).

Peterson, K. S. (1999, June 29). Criticism, new ideas pull marital therapists asunder. *USA Today,* D1–D2.

Peterson, L. R. (1992). Practice pointers. *Family Therapy News, 23*(2), 21.

Petrashek v. Petrashek, 232 Neb. 212, 440 N.W. 2d 220 (1989).

Pfeiffer, S., & Tittler, B. (1983). Utilizing the multidisciplinary team to facilitate a school–family systems orientation. *School Psychology Review, 12,* 168–173.

Phillips, B. N. (1982). Regulation and control in psychology: Implications for certification and licensure. *American Psychologist, 37,* 919–936.

Phillips, L. E. (1987). Thoughts on improving mandatory continuing education. *Lifelong Learning Forum, 4,* 1–2.

Physicians, surgeons, and other healers §99. (2000). *American Jurisprudence 2d, 61,* 241–242.

Piercy, F. P., & Sprenkle, D. H. (1983). Ethical, legal and professional issues in family therapy: A graduate level course. *Journal of Marital and Family Therapy, 9,* 393–401.

Pinsof, W. M., & Wynne, L. C. (Eds.). (1995). The effectiveness of marital and family therapy [Special issue]. *Journal of Marital and Family Therapy, 21.*

Pittman, F. (1985). Gender myths. *Family Therapy Networker, 9*(6), 24–33.

Pittman, F. (1995). Turning tragedy into comedy. *Family Therapy Networker, 19*(6), 36–40.

Planned Parenthood Association v. Ashcroft, 462 U.S. 476, 103 S.Ct. 2517, 76 L.Ed. 2d 733 (1983).

Planned Parenthood of Central Missouri v. Danforth, 428 U.S. 52 (1976).

Planned Parenthood of the Blue Ridge v. Camblos, 155 F3d 352 (4th Cir. 1998).

Polikoff, N. C. (1993). We will get what we ask for: Why legalizing gay and lesbian marriage will not "dismantle the legal structure of gender in every marriage." *Virginia Law Review, 79,* 1535–1550.

Pope, K. S., & Vasquez, M. J. T. (1999). *Ethics in psychotherapy and counseling: A practical guide for psychologists* (2nd ed.). San Francisco: Jossey-Bass.

Posner v. Posner, 233 So.2d 381 (Fla. 1979).

Pressman, R. M. (1979). *Private practice: A guide for the independent mental health practitioner.* New York: Gardner.

Prosser, W. (1971). *Handbook of the law of torts.* St. Paul, MN: West.

Prosser, W. L., Wade, J. W., & Schwartz, V. E. (1988). *Cases and materials on torts* (8th ed.). Westbury, NY: The Foundation Press.

Psychological Services Act, Florida Statutes, Chapter 490 (1983).

Purtilo, R., & Sorrel, J. (1986). The ethical dilemmas of a rural physician. *Hastings Center Report, 16,* 24–28.

Reed, J. M. (1985). The origin and functions of American law. In N. T. Sidney (Ed.), *Law and ethics: A guide for the health professional* (pp. 1–10). New York: Human Sciences Press.

Reen v. Reen, 8 Fam. L. Rep. 2193 (Mass. 1981).

Remley, T. P. (1990). Counseling records: Legal and ethical issues. In B. Herlihy & L. B. Golden (Eds.), *Ethical standards casebook* (pp. 162–169). Alexandria, VA: American Counseling Association.

Remley, T. P. (1991). *Preparing for court appearances.* Alexandria, VA: American Association for Counseling and Development.

Remley, T. P., Jr., & Herlihy, B. (2001). *Ethical, legal, and professional issues in counseling.* Upper Saddle River, NJ: Prentice Hall.

Reppucci, N. D., Weithorn, L. A., Mulvey, E. P., & Monahan, J. (Eds.). (1984). *Children, mental health and the law.* Beverly Hills: Sage Publications.

Rest, J. R. (1982, February). A psychologist looks at the teaching of ethics. *Hastings Center Report,* pp. 29–36.

Rest, J. R. (1983). Morality. In J. Flavell & E. Markman (Eds.), *Cognitive development* (Vol. 4). New York: Wiley.

Rice, M. E., & Harris, G. T. (1995). Psychopathy, schizophrenia, alcohol abuse, and violent recidivism. *International Journal of Law and Psychiatry, 18,* 333–342.

Richardson, L. M., & Austad, C. S. (1991). Realities of mental health practice in managed-care settings. *Professional Psychology: Research and Practice, 22,* 52–59.

Richman, J. (1979). Family therapy of attempted suicide. *Family Process, 18,* 131–142.

Ridgewood Financial Institute, Inc. (1984). *Psychotherapy finances: Guide to private practice.* Ho-Ho-Kus, NJ: Author.

Riley, P., Hartwell, S., Sargent, G., & Patterson, J. E. (1997). Beyond law and ethics: An interdisciplinary course in family law and family therapy. *Journal of Marital and Family Therapy, 23,* 461–476.

Rinas, J., & Clyne-Jackson, T. (1988). *Professional conduct and legal concerns in mental health practice.* Norwalk, CT: Appleton & Lange.

Roberts, A. R. (1996). *Helping battered women: new perspectives and remedies.* New York: Oxford University Press.

Roe v. Wade, 410 U.S. 113 (1973).

Rohrbaugh, M., Tennen, H., Press, S., & White, L. (1981). Compliance, defiance, and therapeutic paradox: Guidelines for strategic use of paradoxical interventions. *American Journal of Orthopsychiatry, 5,* 454–467.

Rokeach, M. (1968). A theory of organization and change within value-attitude systems. *Journal of Social Issues, 24,* 13–33.

Rokeach, M. (1973). *The nature of human values.* New York: Macmillan.

Roller v. Roller, 37 Wash. 242, 79 P. 788 (1905).

Rosen, C. E. (1977). Why clients relinquish their right to privacy under sign-away pressures. *Professional Psychology, 8,* 17–24.

Rosenberg, M. S., & Hunt, R. D. (1984). Child maltreatment: Legal and mental health issues. In N. D. Reppucci, L. A. Weithorn, E. P. Mulvey, & J. Monahan (Eds.), *Children, mental health, and the law* (pp. 79–102). Beverly Hills: Sage.

Ruback, R. B. (1982). Issues in family law: Implications for therapists. In J. C. Hansen & L. L'Abate (Eds.), *Values, ethics, legalities and the family therapist* (pp. 103–124). Rockville, MD: Aspen.

Ruback, R. B. (1984). Family law. In R. H. Woody & Associates (Eds.), *The law and the practice of human services* (pp. 113–154). San Francisco: Jossey-Bass.

Ryder, R., & Hepworth, J. (1990). AAMFT ethical code: "Dual relationships." *Journal of Marital and Family Therapy, 16,* 127–132.

Sack, S. M. (1987). *The complete legal guide to marriage, divorce, custody, & living together.* New York: McGraw-Hill.

Salgo v. Leland Stanford, Jr., University Board of Trustees. 154 Cal. App. 2d 560, 317 P.2d 170 (1957).

Samantha Baskin v. Peter Baskin, No. 77368, Fairfax City. Ct., VA (1988).

Satir, V. (1972). *Peoplemaking.* Palo Alto, CA: Science and Behavior Books.

Sauber, S. R., L'Abate, L., & Weeks, G. R. (1985). *Family therapy: Basic concepts and terms.* Rockville, MD: Aspen.

Sauerkof v. City of New York, 438 N.Y.S 2d 982 (Sup Ct. 1981).

Saunders, D. (1984). Helping husbands who batter. *Social Casework, 65,* 347–353.

Saunders, D. (1988). Other "truths" about domestic violence: A reply to McNeely and Robinson-Simpson. *Social Work, 33,* 179–183.

Sayette, M. A., & Mayne, T. J. (1990). Survey of current clinical and research trends in clinical psychology. *American Psychologist, 45,* 1263–1266.

Scalise, J. J. (2000). The ethical practice of marriage and family therapy. In A. M. Horne (Ed.), *Family counseling and therapy* (pp. 565–596). Itasca, IL: F. E. Peacock.

Schlossberger, E., & Hecker, L. (1996). HIV and family therapists' duty to warn: A legal and ethical analysis. *Journal of Marital and Family Therapy, 22,* 27–40.

Schoyer, N. L. (1980). Divorce and the pre-school child. *Childhood Education, 57,* 2–7.

Schultz, B. (1982). *Legal liability in psychotherapy.* San Francisco: Jossey-Bass.

Schwartz, R. (1987). Our multiple selves. *The Family Therapy Networker, 11*(2), 24–31, 80–83.

Schwartz, S. H. (1977). Normative influences on altruism. In L. Berkowitz (Ed.), *Advances in experimental social psychology* (Vol. 10). New York: Academic.

Schwitzgebel, R. K. (1975). A contractual model for the protection of the rights of institutionalized mental patients. *American Psychologist, 30,* 815–820.

Schwitzgebel, R. K. (1976). Treatment contracts and ethical self-determination. *Clinical Psychologist, 29*(3), 5–7.

Schwitzgebel, R. L., & Schwitzgebel, R. K. (1980). *Law and psychological practice.* New York: Wiley.

Scott, E. (1984). Adolescents' reproductive rights: Abortion, contraception, and sterilization. In N. D. Reppucci, L. A. Weithorn, E. P. Mulvey, & J. Monahan (Eds.), *Children, mental health, and the law* (pp. 125–150). Beverly Hills: Sage.

Searight, H. R., & Openlander, P. (1984). Systemic therapy: A new brief intervention model. *Personnel and Guidance Journal, 62,* 387–391.

Selvini-Palazzoli, N., Boscolo, L., Cecchin, G., & Prata, G. (1978). *Paradox and counterparadox.* New York: Jason Aronson.

Selvini-Palazzoli, N., Boscolo, L., Cecchin, G., & Prata, G. (1980). The problem of the referring person. *Journal of Marriage and Family Therapy, 6,* 3–10.

Serovich, J. M., & Mosack, K. E. (2000). Training issues for supervisors of marriage and family therapists working with persons living with HIV. *Journal of Marital and Family Therapy, 26,* 103–111.

Seymour, W. R. (1982). Counselor/therapist values and therapeutic style. In J. C. Hansen & L. L'

Abate (Eds.), *Values, ethics, legalities and the family therapist* (pp. 41–60). Rockville, MD: Aspen.

Shah, S. (1969). Privileged communications, confidentiality, and privacy. *Professional Psychology, 1,* 56–69.

Shah, S. (1970). Privileged communications, confidentiality, and privacy: Privileged communications. *Professional Psychology, 1,* 159–164.

Shalett, J. S., & Everett, C. A. (1981). Accreditation in family therapy education: Its history and role. *The American Journal of Family Therapy, 9*(4), 82–84.

Shapiro, R. (1984). Therapy with violent families. In S. Saunders, A. M. Anderson, C. A. Hart, & G. M. Rubenstein (Eds.), *Violent individuals and families: A handbook for practitioners.* Springfield, IL: Charles C. Thomas.

Shapiro, R. (1986). Passing the buck: Too often family therapists steer clear of violent cases. *The Family Therapy Networker, 10*(4), 48, 64–66.

Shea, T. E. (1985). Finding the law: Legal research and citation. In N. T. Sidney (Ed.), *Law and ethics: A guide for the health professional* (pp. 411–424). New York: Human Sciences.

Shipman v. Division of Social Services, 442 A. 2d 101 (Del. Fam. Ct. 1981).

Shrybman, J., & Halpern, W. I. (1979, March). *The mental health clinician's day in court.* Workshop presented at the Rochester Mental Health Center, Rochester, NY.

Shulte, J. M. (1990). The morality of influencing in counseling. *Counseling and Values, 34,* 103–118.

Sidley, N. T. (Ed.). (1985). *Law and ethics: A guide for the health professional.* New York: Human Sciences.

Sidley, N. T., & Petrila, J. P. (1985). On being involved personally in a lawsuit, as a plaintiff, expert witness, or defendant. In N. T. Sidley (Ed.), *Law and ethics: A guide for the health professional* (pp. 351–378). New York: Human Sciences.

Siegel, M. (1979). Privacy, ethics, and confidentiality. *Professional Psychology, 10,* 249–258.

Silber, D. E. (1976). Ethical relativity and professional psychology. *Clinical Psychologist, 29,* 3–5.

Silva, A., Leong, G., & Weinstock, R. (1989). An HIV-infected psychiatric patient: Some clinicolegal dilemmas. *Bulletin of the American Academy of Psychiatry and Law, 17,* 33–43.

Simola, S. K., Parker, K. C. H., & Froese, A. P. (1999). Relational V-code conditions in a child and adolescent population do warrant treatment. *Journal of Marital and Family Therapy, 25,* 225–236.

Simon, R. (1997). Fearsome foursome: An interview with the women's project. *Family Therapy Networker, 21*(6), 58–68.

Sims v. Sims, 243 Ga. 276, 253 S.E. 2d 763 (1979).

Slovenko, R. (1973). *Psychiatry and law.* Boston: Little, Brown.

Slovenko, R. (1978). Psychotherapy and informed consent: A search in judicial regulation. In W. E. Barton & C. J. Sanborn (Eds.), *Law and the mental health professions: Friction at the interface.* New York: International Universities.

Slovenko, R. (1980). Legal issues in psychotherapy supervision. In A. K. Hess (Ed.), *Psychotherapy supervision.* New York: Wiley.

Sluzki, C. E. (1978). Marital therapy from a systems theory perspective. In T. J. Paolino, Jr., & B. S. McCrady (Eds.), *Marriage and marital therapy: Psychoanalytic, behavioral and systems theory perspectives* (pp. 366–394). New York: Brunner/Mazel.

Smith, R. L., Stevens-Smith, P., Carlson, J., & Frame, M. W. (1996). Marriage and family therapy: Critique of accreditation, certification, and licensure. *Family Journal: Counseling and Therapy for Couples and Families, 4,* 327–336.

Smith, T. S., McGuire, J. M., Abbott, D. W., & Blau, B. I. (1991). Clinical ethical decision making: An investigation of the rationales used to justify doing less than one believes one should. *Professional Psychology: Research and Practice, 22,* 235–239.

Sneyd, R. (2000, April 26). Gay civil unions bill awaits Vermont governor's pen. *The Times-Picayune, 94,* A-10.

Snider, P. D. (1985). The duty to warn: A potential issue of litigation for the counseling supervisor. *Counselor Education and Supervision, 25,* 66–73.

Sobel, S. B. (1984). Independent practice in child and adolescent psychotherapy in small communities: Personal, professional, and ethical issues. *Psychotherapy, 21*, 110–117.

Sosna v. Iowa, 419 U.S. 393 (1975).

Specialty Boards: Family. (1992). *The Diplomate, 12*(1), 14–15.

Sperry, L. (1989). Contemporary approaches to brief psychotherapy: A comparative analysis. *Individual Psychology: The Journal of Adlerian Theory, Research, and Practice, 45*, 3–25.

Sporakowski, M. J. (1982). The regulation of marital and family therapy. In J. C. Hansen & L. L'Abate (Eds.), *Values, ethics, legalities and the family therapist* (pp. 125–143). Rockville, MD: Aspen.

Sprenkle, D. H., & Moon, S. M. (1996). Toward pluralism in family therapy research. In D. H. Sprenkle & S. M. Moon (Eds.), *Research methods in family therapy* (pp. 3–19). New York: Guilford.

Stack, C. R. (1993). Should children be allowed to sue their parents? *Human Rights, 20* (2), 2.

Stadler, H. A. (1986). To counsel or not to counsel: The ethical dilemma of dual relationships. *Journal of Counseling and Human Service Professionals, 1*, 134–140.

Stadler, H. A. (1990). Confidentiality. In B. Herlihy & L. B. Golden (Eds.), *AACD ethical standards casebook* (4th ed., pp. 177–187). Alexandria, VA: American Association for Counseling and Development.

Stanley v. Illinois, 406 U.S. 645 (1972).

Stanton, M. D. (1981). Strategic approaches to family therapy. In A. S. Gurman & D. P. Kniskern (Eds.), *Handbook of family therapy* (pp. 361–402). New York: Brunner/Mazel.

State ex rel. Hickox v. Hickox, 410 N.Y.S 2d 81 (1978).

State v. Driscoll, 193 N.W. ed 851 (Wisconsin, 1972) 50 ALR 3d 544 (1973).

State v. Vickers, 633 P 2d 315 (Ariz. 1981).

Stensrud, R., & Stensrud, K. (1981). Counseling may be hazardous to your health: How we teach people to feel powerless. *Personnel and Guidance Journal, 59*, 300–304.

Stevens, P. (Ed.). (1999). *Ethical casebook for the practice of marriage and family counseling*. Alexandria, VA: American Counseling Association.

Stevens-Smith, P. (1997a). A case of individual rights versus the common good: "Right versus right." *Family Journal: Counseling and Therapy for Couples and Families, 5*, 250–252.

Stevens-Smith, P. (1997b). Of cyberspace, managed care, and family counseling: Entering the 21st century. *Family Journal: Counseling and Therapy for Couples and Families, 5*, 53–55.

Stevens-Smith, P., & Hughes, M. M. (1993). *Legal issues in marriage and family counseling*. Alexandria, VA: American Counseling Association.

Strickman, L. P. (1982). Marriage, divorce and the Constitution. *Family Law Quarterly, 15*, 259–348.

Strong, L. D. (1992). Freedom of choice legislation passes in Connecticut. *Family Therapy News, 23*(4), 1, 25.

Strupp, H. H., Hadley, S. W., & Gomes-Schwartz, B. (1977). *Psychotherapy for better or worse: The problem of negative effects*. New York: Jason Aronson.

Stuart, R. B. (1980). *Helping couples change: A social learning approach to marital therapy*. New York: Guilford.

Stude, E. W., & McKelvey, J. (1979). Ethics and the law: Friend or foe? *Personnel and Guidance Journal, 57*, 453–456.

Swanson, J. L. (1979). Counseling directory and consumer's guide: Implementing professional disclosure and consumer protection. *Personnel and Guidance Journal, 58*, 190–193.

Swanson, J. W. (1993). Alcohol abuse, mental disorder, and violent behavior. *Alcohol Health and Research World, 2*, 123–132.

Symonds, A. (1979). Violence against woman: The myth of masochism. *American Journal of Psychotherapy, 33*, 161–173.

Taggart, M. (1982). Linear versus systemic values. Implications for family therapy. In J. C. Hansen & L. L'Abate (Eds.), *Values, ethics, legalities and the family therapist* (pp. 23–40). Rockville, MD: Aspen.

Taggart, M. (1989). Epistemological equality as the fulfillment of family therapy. In M. McGoldrick,

C. Anderson, & F. Walsh (Eds.), *Women in families: A framework for family therapy.* New York: Norton.

Tarasoff v. Regents of the University of California, 13 Cal. 3d 177, 529 P.2d 553 (1974), vacated, 17 Cal. 3d 425, 551 P2d 334 (1976).

Teismann, M. W. (1980). Convening strategies in family therapy. *Family Process, 19,* 393–400.

Terkelsen, K. G. (1983). Schizophrenia and the family: II. Adverse effects of family therapy. *Family Process, 22,* 191–200.

Terkelsen, K. G. (1984). Response by Kenneth G. Terkelsen, M. D. *Family Process, 23,* 425–428.

Thomas, A. J. (1998). Ethical mandates for multicultural sensitivity for family counseling. *Family Journal: Counseling and Therapy for Couples and Families, 6,* 49–51.

Thompson, R. A., Tinsley, B. R., Scalora, M. J., & Parke, R. D. (1989). Grandparents' visitation rights: Legalizing the ties that bind. *American Psychologist, 44,* 1217–1222.

Thompson v. County of Alameda, 167-Cal. Rptr. 70 (1980).

Thompson v. Thompson, 484 U.S. 174 (1988).

Thompson-Schneider, D. (1997). The arc of history: Or, the resurrection of feminism's sameness/difference dichotomy in the gay and lesbian marriage debate. *Law and Sexuality, 7,* 1–30.

Torres, A., Forest, J., & Eisman, S. (1980). Telling parents. Clinic policies and adolescents' use of family planning and abortion services. *Family Planning Perspectives, 11,* 284–292.

Toulmin, S. (1950). *An examination of the place of reason in ethics.* Cambridge, England: Cambridge University.

Trimble v. Gordon, 430 U.S. 762 (1977).

Tymchuk, A. J., Drapkin, R., Major-Kingsley, S., Ackerman, A. B., Coffman, E. W., & Baum, M. S. (1982). Ethical decision making and psychologists' attitudes and training in ethics. *Professional Psychology, 13,* 412–421.

U.S. Advisory Board on Child Abuse and Neglect. (1990). *Child abuse and neglect: Critical first steps in response to a national emergency* (No. 017-092-00104-5). Washington, DC: U.S. Government Printing Office.

U.S. Bureau of the Census. (1981). *Statistical abstract of the United States.* Washington, DC: Government Printing Office.

Van Hoose, W. H. (1980). Ethics and counseling. *Counseling and Human Development, 13*(1), 1–12.

Van Hoose, W. H., & Kottler, J. A. (1985). *Ethical and legal issues in counseling and psychotherapy* (2nd ed.). San Francisco: Jossey-Bass.

Vance, G. A. (1995). Rock-a-bye lawsuit: Can a baby sue the hand that rocked the cradle? *The John Marshall Law Review, 28,* 429–469.

VandeCreek, L., Knapp, S., & Brace, K. (1990). Mandatory continuing education for licensed psychologists: Its rationale and current implementation. *Professional Psychology: Research and Practice, 21,* 135–140.

VanZandt, C. E. (1990). Professionalism: A matter of personal initiative. *Journal of Counseling and Development, 68,* 243–245.

Vasquez, M. J. T. (1991). Sexual intimacies with clients after termination: Should a prohibition be explicit? *Ethics and Behavior, 1,* 45–61.

Vitiello, M. (1999). How imperial is the Supreme Court? An analysis of Supreme Court abortion doctrine and popular will. *University of San Francisco Law Review, 34,* 49–98.

Vitulano, L. A., & Copeland, B. A. (1980). Trends in continuing education and competency demonstration. *Professional Psychology, 11,* 891–897.

von Weizsacker, E., & von Weizsacker, C. (1974). *Offene systeme I: Beitrage zur zeitstruktur von information, entropie and evolution.* Stuttgart, West Germany: Klett.

Vroom, P. (1983). The anomalous profession: Bumpy going in the divorce mediation movement. *The Family Therapy Networker, 7*(3), 38–42.

Wachtel, E. F. (1979). Learning family therapy: The dilemmas of an individual therapist. *Journal of Contemporary Psychotherapy, 10,* 122–135.

Wald, M. S. (1975). State intervention on behalf of "neglected" children: A search for realistic standards. *Stanford Law Review, 27,* 985–1040.

Wald, M. S. (1976). State intervention on behalf of "neglected" children: Standards for removal of children from their homes, monitoring the status of children in foster care, and termination of parental rights. *Stanford Law Review, 28,* 625–706.

Wald, M. S. (1982). State intervention on behalf of endangered children: A proposed legal response. *Child Abuse and Neglect, 6*, 3–45.

Walker, C. E. (1981). Continuing professional development. In C. E. Walker (Ed.), *Clinical practice of psychology.* New York: Pergamon.

Walker, L. (1979). *The battered woman.* New York: Harper Colophon.

Walker, L. (1981). Battered women: Sex roles and clinical issues. *Professional Psychology, 12*, 81–90.

Walker, L. (1984). *The battered woman syndrome.* New York: Springer.

Walter, M. I., & Handelsman, M. M. (1996). *Informed consent for mental health interactional patterns, pathologies and paradoxes.* New York: Norton.

Walters, M., Carter, B., Papp, P., & Silverstein, O. (1988). *The invisible web: Gender patterns in family relationships.* New York: Guilford.

Waltz, J. R., & Scheuneman, T. W. (1969). Informed consent to therapy. *Northwestern University Law Review, 64*, 628–650.

Watts, A. (1961). *Psychotherapy east and west.* New York: Random House.

Watts, R. E. (1999). Confidentiality and the duty to report: A case study. *Family Journal: Counseling and Therapy for Couples and Families, 7*, 64–66.

Watzlawick, F., Beavin, J. H., & Jackson, D. D. (1967). Pragmatics of human communications: A study of counseling: Effects of information specificity on clients' ratings of counselors. *Journal of Mental Health Counseling, 18*, 253–262.

Watzlawick, P., Weakland, J. H., & Fish, R. (1974). *Change: Principles of problem formation and problem resolution.* New York: Norton.

Weber v. Aetna Casualty & Surety Co., 406 U.S. 164 (1972).

Webster v. Reproductive Health Services, 109 S. Ct. 3040 (1989).

Weidman, A. (1986). Family therapy with violent couples. *Social Casework, 67*, 211–218.

Weikel, W. J., & Hughes, P. R. (1993). *The counselor as an expert witness.* Alexandria, VA: American Counseling Association.

Weinrach, S. G. (1989). Guidelines for clients of private practitioners: Committing the structure to print. *Journal of Counseling and Development, 67*, 299–300.

Weiss, R. S. (1979). Issues in the adjudication of custody when parents separate. In G. Levinger & O. C. Moles (Eds.), *Divorce and separation.* New York: Basic.

Welfel, E. R. (1998). *Ethics in counseling and psychotherapy.* Pacific Grove, CA: Brooks/Cole.

Welfel, E. R., & Lipsitz, N. E. (1984). The ethical behavior of professional psychologists. *Counseling Psychologist, 12*(3), 31–43.

Wentzel, L., & Ross, M. A. (1983). Psychological and social ramifications of battering: Observations leading to a counseling methodology for victims of domestic violence. *Personnel and Guidance Journal, 61*, 423–428.

Werry, J. S. (1989). Family therapy: Professional endeavor or successful religion? *Journal of Family Therapy, 11*, 377–382.

Weyrauch, W. O., & Katz, S. N. (1983). *American family law in transition.* Washington, DC: Bureau of National Affairs, Inc.

Widiger, T. A., & Rorer, L. G. (1984). The responsible psychotherapist. *American Psychologist, 39*, 503–515.

Wilcoxon, S. A., & Fenell, D. (1983). Engaging the non-attending spouse in marital therapy through the use of therapist-initiated written communication. *Journal of Marital and Family Therapy, 9*, 199–203.

Wilcoxon, S. A., & Puleo, S. G. (1992). Professional development needs of mental health counselors: Results of a national survey. *Journal of Mental Health Counseling, 14*, 185–187.

Willbach, D. (1989). Ethics and family therapy: The case management of family violence. *Journal of Marital and Family Therapy, 15*, 43–52.

Williams, C. (1999). Ethical considerations in multicultural family counseling. In P. Stevens (Ed.), *Ethical casebook for the practice of marriage and family counseling* (pp. 124–132). Alexandria, VA: American Counseling Association.

Williams, R. M. (1968). Values. In E. Sills (Ed.), *International encyclopedia of the social sciences* (pp. 1–38). New York: Macmillan.

Wilson, G. F. (1985). Ethical and legal aspects of peer review. In J. M. Hamilton (Ed.), *Psychiatric peer review: Prelude and promise.* Washington, DC: American Psychiatric Press.

Winborn, B. B. (1977). Honest labeling and other procedures for the protection of consumers of counseling. *Personnel and Guidance Journal, 56,* 206–209.

Winkle, C. W., Piercy, F. P., & Hovestadt, A. J. (1981). A curriculum for graduate-level marriage and family therapy education. *Journal of Marital and Family Therapy, 7,* 201–210.

Wisconsin Statutes Annotated, 905.04 (1981–1982 Supp.).

Witmer, J. M. (1978). Professional disclosure in licensure. *Counselor Education and Supervision, 18,* 71–73.

Witnesses §190 (1976). *American Jurisprudence, 2d.*

Wohlman, B., & Stricker, G. (1983). *Handbook of family and marital therapy.* New York: Plenum Press.

Wolf-Smith, J. H., & LaRossa, R. (1992). After he hits her. *Family Relations, 41,* 324–329.

Woody, R. H. (1988). *Fifty ways to avoid malpractice.* Sarasota, FL: Professional Resource Exchange.

Woody, R. H., & Associates. (1984). *The law and the practice of human services.* San Francisco: Jossey-Bass.

Woody, R. H., & Mitchell, R. E. (1984). Understanding the legal system and legal research. In R. H. Woody & Associates (Eds.), *The law and the practice of human services* (pp. 1–38). San Francisco: Jossey-Bass.

Wylie, M. S. (1989). Looking for fence posts. *Family Therapy Networker, 13*(2), 22–33.

Wylie, M. S. (1995). Diagnosing for dollars? *Family Therapy Networker, 19*(3), 23–26, 28–33, 65–69.

Yaron v. Yaron, 372 N.Y.S.2d 518 (1975).

Zablocki v. Redhail, 434 U.S. 374 (1978).

Zajonc, R. B. (1980). Feeling and thinking: Preferences need no inferences. *American Psychologist, 35,* 151–175.

Zibert, J., Engels, D. W., Kern, C. W., & Durodoye, B. A. (1998). Ethical knowledge of counselors. *Counseling and Values, 43,* 34–48.

Zimet, C. N. (1989). The mental health care revolution: Will psychology survive? *American Psychologist, 44,* 703–708.

Ziskin, J. (1995). *Coping with psychiatric and psychological testimony, Vols. I, II, & III* (5th ed.). Los Angeles, CA: Law and Psychology Press.

Name Index

Abbott, D. W., 11
Abelson, R., 11
Abroms, G. M., 62
Allen, J., 64
Anderson, A., 55, 56
Anderson, A. S., 144, 145, 146
Anderson, B. J., 72
Anderson, B. S., 6, 155, 160, 178, 197
Anderson, C. M., 280
Anderson, D., 76
Anderson, S., 211
Andolfi, M., 242
Andreasen, N. C., 75
Angelo, C., 242
Aponte, H. J., 232, 241, 296
Appelbaum, P. S., 207
Appleson, G., 161
Ard, B. N., 252
Ard, C., 252
Arthur, G. L., 199, 200
Atwood, J. D., 252
Austad, C. S., 81, 83

Bagarozzi, G. A., 79
Baier, K., 11
Barnard, C. P., 290, 291, 314
Barnett, T., 12, 48

Barry, V. C., 3
Bateson, G., 234, 236–237
Baxter, P., 130
Bayles, M. D., 281, 286
Beamish, P., 223
Beauchamp, T. L., 13–14, 15, 70, 83
Beavin, J. H., 49
Beck, E., 68
Beck, J., 130
Becker, R. F., 152
Beckner, M. O., 4
Becvar, D. S., 235
Becvar, R. J., 235
Bednar, R. L., 279
Behnke, S. H., 207
Belcher, D. I., 169, 216
Bender, A. E., 235
Bennett, B. E., 161, 162, 197, 303–306, 308, 312, 313
Bergantino, L. A., 233
Bergin, A. E., 231, 298
Berman, E. M., 290, 292
Bernard, J. M., 223, 224
Berner, M., 207
Bernstein, B. E., 119, 165, 168–169
Bersoff, D., 22, 90

Bertram, B., 273
Besharov, D. J., 181
Betancourt, M., 14
Bialek, E., 226
Bird, G., 245
Bittner, S., 226
Black, D. W., 75
Black, M., 145
Blackmun, Harry, 178
Blades, J., 144
Blasi, A., 11
Blau, B. I., 11
Bograd, M., 76, 78, 79, 238
Bonnington, S. B., 83, 84, 226
Borowy, T. D., 213
Borys, D. S., 69
Boscolo, L., 56
Boszormenyi-Nagy, I., 54, 76, 246, 248
Boughner, S. R., 198
Bourne, P. G., 61
Bowen, M., 57, 58, 59, 245
Bowers, M., 254, 274, 275
Braaten, E. E., 156, 207
Brace, K., 286
Brandt, R., 3
Bray, J. H., 20, 38, 207
Brendel, J. M., 291

Subject Index